Russian Foreign Policy
Since 1990

Russian Foreign Policy Since 1990

EDITED BY

Peter Shearman

UNIVERSITY OF MELBOURNE

p.86

Westview Press

BOULDER • SAN FRANCISCO • OXFORD

Published in 1995 in the United States of America by Westview Press, Inc., 5500 Central Avenue, Boulder, Colorado 80301-2877, and in the United Kingdom by Westview Press, 12 Hid's Copse Road, Cumnor Hill, Oxford OX2 9JJ

Library of Congress Cataloging-in-Publication Data
Russian foreign policy since 1990 / edited by Peter Shearman.
    p.   cm.
  Includes bibliographical references and index.
  ISBN 0-8133-8778-7—ISBN 0-8133-2633-8 (pbk.)
  1. Russia (Federation)—Foreign relations.   I. Shearman, Peter,
1950–   .
DK510.764.R87   1995
327.47—dc20   94-42983
                                                                                              CIP

Printed and bound in the United States of America

The paper used in this publication meets the requirements
of the American National Standard for Permanence of Paper
for Printed Library Materials Z39.48-1984.

10   9   8   7   6   5   4   3   2   1

To my mother and father,
Elsie and Norman Shearman

Contents

Preface   ix

List of Acronyms   xi

1   Soviet Foreign Policy, 1917–1991, *Peter Shearman*   1

2   Russian Foreign Policy Decision-making, *Neil Malcolm*   23

3   Russian Relations with the "Near Abroad,"
    Wynne Russell   53

4   Russian Policy Toward Central and Eastern Europe,
    Mike Bowker   71

5   Russian Policy Toward Western Europe: The German Axis,
    Peter Shearman   93

6   Russian Policy Toward the United States,
    Peter Shearman   111

7   Russian Policy Toward Japan, *Robert F. Miller*   135

8   Russian Policy Toward China, *Eugene Bazhanov*   159

9   Russian Policy Toward the Two Koreas, *Yoke T. Soh*   181

10 Russian Policy Toward Vietnam, *Carlyle A. Thayer*   201

11 Russian Policy Toward India: A Relationship on Hold,
    Ramesh Thakur   225

12 Russian Policy Toward Latin America and Cuba,
    Yuri Pavlov   247

13   Russian Policy Toward Central Asia and the
     Middle East, *Amin Saikal*   267

14   Russia's New Agenda in Sub–Saharan Africa,   283
     Robert G. Patman

About the Book   303
About the Editor and Contributors   305
Index   307

Preface

This book is the product of a conference that did not take place. Due to both a lack of funds and difficulties in getting all contributors to Melbourne at the same time, a planned conference on Russian foreign policy had to be cancelled. It was nevertheless considered worthwhile pursuing the original idea—to produce a book that would provide a comprehensive coverage of Russia's foreign relations with the most important countries and regions of the world. It is important to chronicle and assess these early, formative years in Russia's foreign relations following the disintegration of the Soviet Union, both to better understand the dynamics of policy making and to be better able to predict likely future developments. The purpose of this volume is to improve Western understanding of the sources, objectives, and impact of contemporary Russian foreign policy.

I would like to acknowledge here the hard work put in by Craig Lonsdale, professional officer of the Department of Political Science at the University of Melbourne. He gave technical help at many stages and put the book into camera-ready form. I also thank Nikki Muldoon for her library assistance—and apologize for putting her to work when she was supposed to be on her summer vacation from Ireland. But she did volunteer! Thanks also to Remy Davison and Tony Phillips of Melbourne University for help in editing. Ita Shearman, as always, has been a great support. I would like to thank my sons, Peter and Michael, for providing me with pleasurable distractions that always reminded me what life was *really* all about. And thank you to Rebecca Ritke of Westview Press for her encouraging e-mail messages and useful and constructive suggestions.

Peter Shearman
Melbourne

Acronyms

ANC	African National Congress
APR	Asia-Pacific Region
ARB	Africa Research Bulletin
ASEAN	Association of South-East Asian Nations
CANF	Cuban-American Foundation
CIS	Commonwealth of Independent States
CMEA	Council for Mutual Economic Assistance
CODESA	Convention for a Democratic South Africa
CPSU	Communist Party of the Soviet Union
CSCE	Conference on Security and Cooperation in Europe
EBRD	European Bank for Reconstruction and Development
EC	European Community
ECU	European Currency Unit
EPLF	Eritrean People's Liberation Front
EU	European Union
FBIS	Foreign Broadcast Information Service
FRELIMO	Mozambique Liberation Front
FSU	Former Soviet Union
GATT	General Agreement on Tariffs and Trade
GCC	Gulf Cooperation Council
IAEA	International Atomic Energy Agency
IAF	Indian Air Force
ICBM	Intercontinental Ballistic Missile
IFPC	Interdepartmental Foreign Policy Commission
INF	Intermediate Nuclear Forces
KAL	Korean Air Lines
KOTRA	Korean Trade Promotion Corporation
LDP	Liberal Democratic Party (Japan)
LDPR	Liberal Democratic Party of Russia
MFA	Ministry of Foreign Affairs
MFN	Most Favored Nation
MIC	Military Industrial Complex

MOD	Ministry of Defense
MPLA	Movement for the Popular Liberation of Angola
MTCR	Missile Technology Control Regime
NACC	North Atlantic Cooperation Council
NATO	North Atlantic Treaty Organization
NEP	New Economic Policy
NPT	Non-Proliferation Treaty
NWFZ	Nuclear Weapon Free Zone
OAS	Organization of American States
PFP	Partnership for Peace
PLO	Palestine Liberation Organization
PRC	People's Republic of China
RFE/RL	Radio Free Europe/Radio Liberty
RIA	Russia Information Agency
RPF	Russian Pacific Fleet
SACP	South African Communist Party
SALT	Strategic Arms Limitation Talks
SIGINT	Signals Intelligence
START	Strategic Arms Reduction Talks
SVR	(Russian) Foreign Intelligence Service
UAE	United Arab Emirates
UN	United Nations
UNITA	National Union for the Total Independence of Angola
USSR	Union of Soviet Socialist Republics
WEU	West European Union

1

Soviet Foreign Policy, 1917–1991

Peter Shearman

Introduction

It has become common to talk of the turbulence in world politics that marks our time.[1] With the end of the Cold War and the spectacular demise of communism in the late twentieth century, old certainties have given way to confusion as the world crosses the threshold of a new era. The world as we knew it is being remade in front of our very eyes. It is difficult enough trying to make sense of transformative dynamics in global politics as they take place all around us—seeking to understand, as it were, moving targets on their way to unknown destinations. It is doubly difficult when we have lost confidence in the theories and approaches that dominated academic studies on international relations and Soviet and communist politics during the Cold War period. Realism as a political theory failed to predict the end of great-power rivalry, the unilateral Soviet withdrawal from its sphere of influence, and the rise of nationalism. Kremlinology and Sovietology gave no indications of the imminent collapse of the neo-Stalinist communist system—indeed, most Soviet area specialists, right up to the end, were confidently predicting the continuing territorial integrity and stability of the Soviet state.

Russia is being reborn into this uncertain world of complex and shifting forces for change, and as the last of the great empires to disintegrate at this juncture in human affairs, Russia is clearly particularly susceptible to these transformative dynamics—indeed, globalizing trends were in part responsible for the collapse of the Soviet Union. It is not just the time at which the Russian empire collapsed that distinguishes it from most other former empires but the fact that the Russian-Soviet state itself was significantly undermined by the loss of the former constituent republics of the Union. Russia is searching for a new identity, seeking to formulate a new constitutional framework, and developing new general approaches and specific policies toward different countries and regions of the world even as that world itself is changing.

We may not know exactly where the world is heading, but we are in a better position now, with the end of the Cold War and the collapse of the USSR, to assess whence it came to reach its present condition. The main dynamics of global politics between the ends of World War Two and the Cold War were linked to the bipolar strategic competition between the so-called superpowers, the United States and the Soviet Union. Russia, as the core of the former Soviet Union, was therefore a central actor in the bipolar system, and if we wish to have a complete picture of the Cold War we need to have an understanding of the motives, goals, and processes of Soviet foreign policy during this period. This chapter presents the background of Russia's role in the world up to the collapse of the Soviet Union in December 1991, providing a historical context for the other chapters in this volume, which focus primarily on the contemporary period.

Clearly one cannot cover everything of significance when looking at history, but history by any definition has to be summarized and hence will always be incomplete. The historical background of Soviet foreign policy that now follows must be selective in the events and issues it covers, but its selection is designed to be illustrative of the important patterns that helped to shape the present.

Defining Foreign Policy

It would be helpful to define "foreign policy" before proceeding further. The concept has two elements: *foreign*, i.e., something outside the boundaries of the state, and *policy*, a plan of action devised within the state to achieve certain objectives. Thus we could say that foreign policy is a plan of action drawn up by the state's representatives to obtain favored outcomes in other territories. Foreign policy can be seen as a domestic process for developing a program of action directed beyond the territorial and juridical borders of the state. We can separate the two elements and state that the *process* of policy-making relates to domestic politics and that the *consequences* of this process relate to international politics. Realist theory views states as unitary rational actors that provide the theory's analytical focus, with politics at the domestic level of no consequence for an understanding of the way states behave at the international level. Ideological differences for realists are irrelevant for an understanding of international relations, for each and every state's foreign behavior is determined by the structural properties of anarchy in the international system.[2]

There is, however, a fundamental problem in making such a simple distinction between domestic and international politics.[3] Although when he first became president of the United States, George Bush was criticized for lacking any concept or clear vision in foreign affairs (the "vision thing," as he called it), he ultimately failed to get reelected to a second term of office due to a perception among the voters that he focused too much on foreign policy and too little on domestic affairs. Clinton won the election in part due to American voters desire that their president concentrate on the problems in the U.S. economy and *not* on foreign policy. Domestic politics at the mass level, not simply government officials representing a personified state, became an important factor in debates over foreign policy during the election campaign. Bill Clinton was elected as president to deal with the domestic economic agenda, yet it soon became evident that this could not be separated from larger, external, international politics concerning trade, subsidies, tariffs, GATT, etc. Complex interdependencies are said to prevent nation-states from delinking domestic politics from international politics. Foreign policy is affected by influences from both the domestic and international environments, and often the two overlap. It will be useful to utilize these levels of analysis in assessing the history of Soviet foreign policy.

The International Level

War and Revolution

The obvious reference point when discussing the external environment on the eve of the Bolshevik coup in Russia is the First World War. Without the Great War of 1914–1918 it is questionable whether the tsarist Russian empire would have given way to the Soviet communist empire. Indeed, as Richard Pipes notes, having occurred in the turmoil of the most destructive war in history, the Russian Revolution was considered by contemporaries ". . . as an episode in that war rather than as an event in its own right."[4] When the Bolsheviks seized power in October 1917 more than fifteen million men had been mobilized for war; almost half of them had been killed or wounded or were missing in action. The war cost the Romanovs their throne, cut short the life of the provisional government, and facilitated the Bolshevik victory.

The overall Bolshevik project in 1917 was an *internationalist* one, hence the initial revolutionary government's agenda was dominated by external concerns. This is not to say that the salient issues required an emphasis on foreign policy as traditionally conceived, for in Lenin's theory of imperialism *classes* are the most important actors and no distinction is made between domestic and international politics. The sources of international conflict had *economic* determinants emanating from the internal contradictions of monopoly capitalism. Lenin saw the

War of 1914–1918 as an imperialist war and the revolution in Russia in 1917, undertaken in the name of the international proletariat, as the breaking of the weakest link in the wider imperial chain. The Revolution was undertaken not in the name of the Russian people but in the name of the workers of the world, who, stimulated by the revolutionary spark in Russia, would unite in a larger class war against the bourgeoisie. The Bolsheviks were relying upon *external* events—socialist revolutions in the more developed capitalist states of Europe—to ensure the success of their *domestic* agenda.

However, it soon became evident to the leaders of the Revolution that they faced external conditions that undermined their original theoretical assumptions. For workers in belligerent countries did not, as predicted, turn their guns on their indigenous bourgeoisie but rather kept them trained on the workers of other nation-states. People were willing to die for their nation and state, but not for their class. It is common to note that Leon Trotsky, the first communist in charge of foreign affairs, said on taking office that all he needed to do was to issue a few decrees and close up shop. How wrong he was. The international political system determined the specific options and structured the general dynamics of Russian foreign policy as it moved from its tsarist to its Soviet eras. In the absence of revolution in the West and because of the generally hostile reaction to the Bolshevik Revolution (many Western states sent limited contingents to fight against the Red Army during the civil war), it was necessary to concentrate energies on constructing a new Soviet state from the ruins of the old Russian empire.

Peace and State Consolidation

Most historical accounts of Russia's foreign policy have chronicled a ceaseless and sustained territorial expansionism based upon an inherent logic emanating from geographical insecurity.[5] It is often stressed that because of a lack of natural boundaries from the time of Kievan Rus' in the tenth century Russian leaders have consistently felt the need to expand frontiers in all directions out from the heartland. It has been estimated that from the middle of the sixteenth through the end of the seventeenth century "Russia conquered territory the size of the modern Netherlands every year for 150 years running."[6] Thus, one explanation for the general expansionist dynamics of later Russian foreign policy focuses upon the external geopolitical momentum established early on. Following an early period of state consolidation involving a temporary forced retreat at Brest-Litovsk, this momentum continued into the Soviet period. The first major foreign policy decision of the new revolutionary government in 1918 was a reaction to outside circumstances. Lenin was forced to accept conditions for peace set by the Central Powers at Brest-

Litovsk, which resulted in Russia losing a large proportion of its territory and population. Although for Lenin the revolution in Russia was not a domestic event but part of an international revolution (". . . in one country it is impossible to accomplish such work as a socialist revolution"[7]), the international system determined that Russia had to look inward. As Alvin Rubinstein put it, "The Brest-Litovsk crisis served as a crucible from which emerged the outlines of a foreign policy."[8]

Russia needed to develop the necessary industrial infrastructure to be able to strengthen its capacity to defend itself against any external aggression. The diplomatic shop was not shut; on the contrary, the Soviet Foreign Ministry began to engage actively in the pursuit of Soviet national interests utilizing traditional (i.e., Western, "bourgeois") means of diplomacy. It should be noted that there was a duality (some would say double-dealing[9]) in foreign policy with the establishment of the Comintern in 1918, a body whose role was to coordinate the activities of communist parties to further the world revolutionary movement. However, by 1921 domestic economic reform, with the introduction of the New Economic Policy (NEP), necessitated a *peredyshka*, a "breathing space," in relations with the capitalist states. Rather than advocating class warfare and international revolution, Soviet leaders were calling for peaceful coexistence and for foreign investments in the Russian economy. Although external factors forced the Bolsheviks to seek an accommodation with the West, Soviet Marxist ideology continued to predict and, at least in ideological tracts, to encourage socialist revolution in the advanced capitalist states. Nevertheless, in the conduct of foreign policy in the early Soviet years Lenin has come to be seen more as a realist, responding pragmatically to external events, than as an adventurous revisionist seeking to undermine the interstate system of international relations.

The Bolsheviks as inheritors of the tsarist Russian empire were faced with the problem, or the "question," as it has come to be known, of nationalities. Russia's socialist revolutionaries had referred to this empire as the "prison of nations," as, following centuries of Russian expansionism, numerous nationalities were constantly incorporated into an ever larger tsarist state. Their Marxist beliefs led socialists to anticipate that nationalist sentiments and identities, in the absence of capitalist exploitation, would naturally give way to a collective identity based upon class solidarity. Circumstances did not fit the theory, and the eventual result was the formation of a federal political system of fifteen Union republics, each one based upon the majority national grouping that gave the republic its title (i.e., the "titular nationality"). As Zbigniew Brzezinski has put it, the Soviet Union became the ". . . political expression of Russian nationalism."[10] With complete state control over all means of socialization, the predominantely Russian leadership in Moscow sought to Russify and Sovietize the various ethnic communities in order to create a loyal citizenry of the new Soviet state. Ultimately, of course, this too failed.

From Class Interests to National Interests

Not long after the Revolution of 1917 the Bolsheviks, due to external factors, were forced to strengthen the state that their theoretical assumptions had predicted would wither away. At the same time, they had to forge that state on a federal basis that acknowledged the importance and diversity of national identities. Marxist-Leninist international class theory proved to be of little value in predicting these outcomes; perhaps a state-centric realist theory of international relations offers a more convincing interpretation. For a realist, anarchy in the international system (i.e., the absence of a hierarchical institutional structure of international governance) creates a security dilemma for all states that then requires them to develop strategies to defend their "national interests" as opposed to "class interests." This in turn requires both a defensive capability to deter potential aggressors and also, where necessary, participation in shifting security alliances to maintain a balance of power. Classical realist theory has three basic assumptions: (1) states are the most important actors, i.e., territorial entities organized around the idea of the nation; (2) states, personified as it were, act rationally, i.e., they choose the most rational alternative from a number of possibilities to enhance the national interest of the state; (3) the state's national interest is defined in terms of power: it is the perennial lack of complete security (i.e., the constant possibility of external aggression) that determines this search for power.

Contemporary realist theory as developed by Kenneth Waltz focuses more upon the *structure* of the international system. This structure is said to have two elements that are constant and one that is variable. The two constants are (1) the system is anarchy, rather than hierarchy, and (2) similarly functioning units (i.e., nation-states). The variable element of the structure is the distribution of power capabilities among these similarly functioning units.[11] The behavior of these units is determined not by their domestic political, ideological, or economic properties but by structural anarchy at the international systemic level. Waltz makes an analogy with economic markets, where the behavior of individual firms is not determined by their specific attributes so much as by the structural properties of the market. Hence, just as economic outcomes change when the structure of markets shifts from, say, duopoly to oligopoly to perfect competition, depending upon concentration or diffusion of capabilities across the system, so too will international political outcomes change depending upon whether we have one power (a unipolar system), two powers (a bipolar system), or many powers (a multipolar system) dominating.

Like the actions of other revolutionary states before and after their revolutions, Russia's foreign behavior in the 1920s was determined to a great degree by the structure of international anarchy. The uncertain multipolarity that characterized the international system after World War I forced Russia to search for alliances with other states rather than to pursue the nebulous ideological conception of an "international working class alliance." The Soviet Union's diplomatic initiatives began to pay off in 1921 with the conclusion of a trade agreement with the United Kingdom. The following year the Soviet Union's first international treaty was signed with Germany at Rapallo. As was Moscow's intent the treaty effectively precluded an alliance among the main Western powers that was aimed against the USSR. German-Soviet cooperation stemming from this treaty even included the secret exchange of military officials and information. Lenin was adept at employing classical methods of exploiting conflicts among other powers to ensure the survival of the state. Lenin recognized that due to the prevailing balance of power, Germany, following the Versailles peace, had no option but to form an alliance with Russia: "The German bourgeois Government madly hates the Bolsheviks, but the interests of its international position impel it toward peace with Soviet Russia against its own wish."[12]

Stalin, Machiavelli, and the German Question

After Lenin's death in 1924, even though Stalin had terminated Lenin's NEP, he continued to conduct a foreign policy that was designed to secure and strengthen the Soviet state rather than to foster world revolution. In the 1930s Russia was faced with potential threats, as it had been so many times before in its history, from both its western and eastern borders, with the rise of Hitler in Europe and a threatening Japan in the Far East. In their history of Soviet foreign policy Joseph L. Nogee and Robert H. Donaldson note that during this period, "as the USSR once used Germany to balance Britain and France, so the democracies were now courted to counter the German threat."[13] In 1933 the United States finally recognized the USSR and resumed trade relations, in 1934 Moscow joined the League of Nations, and in 1935 the Soviet Union signed treaties of alliance with France and Czechoslovakia. Soviet Russia sought alliances with Western powers, urging them to unite under the umbrella of the League of Nations to institute the principles of collective security against the threat of fascism. The USSR was the only state among the main powers to send forces to fight against Franco's army in the Spanish civil war. In 1938 while Neville Chamberlain was appeasing Hitler at Munich, the Soviet Union was the only country advocating armed assistance for the Czechs.

Finally, the Nazi-Soviet pact of 1939 was a last attempt, in classical balance-of-power terms, to stave off Soviet participation in what appeared to be an inevitable European war until such a time as the other antagonists had weakened themselves, thus facilitating an advantageous position for the Soviet Union.

It may be the case that the pact did not work out exactly that way, but the important thing to note here is the international systemic determinants (i.e., the *external* determinants) of Soviet foreign policy as the USSR sought to maintain a balance of power most favorable for its own national security. In his memoirs former Soviet leader Nikita Khrushchev refers to the Soviet pact with Germany as being designed to turn the German army away from Russia and direct it at the West.[14] The non-aggression pact with Germany in 1939, in addition to turning German arms away from the USSR and buying time to build up Soviet military capabilities, provided territorial gains: as part of a secret protocol attached to the pact the Soviet Union was to annex the three Baltic states (Latvia, Lithuania, and Estonia) and Rumanian Bessarabia—all previously provinces of tsarist Russia—and parts of Poland. The secret protocol was a crude but classic balance-of-power agreement to delimit set spheres of influence. Referring to this protocol, John G. Stoessinger states that "Marxism-Leninism was sacrificed on the altar of Machiavelli," and Alvin Z. Rubinstein notes in similar vein: "Machiavelli, not Marx, inspired Stalin's foreign policy."[15] Khrushchev is clear about the geo-strategic imperative behind the agreement with Hitler's Germany: "The access we gained to the Baltic Sea significantly improved our strategic situation. By reaching the shores of the Baltic, we deprived the western powers of a foothold that they might use against us . . . for establishing a front against the USSR."[16] In a speech to the Soviet Parliament justifying his signature on the pact with Germany, Soviet Foreign Minister Vyacheslav Molotov made the simple point that "the art of politics in the sphere of foreign relations does not consist in increasing the number of enemies for one's country."[17]

The friendship with Germany was recognized as temporary, but the breathing space proved to be much shorter than had been anticipated by Stalin, who overestimated the strength of France, Poland, and the United Kingdom and underestimated the power of the German war machine, misreading, or failing to consider, intelligence reports of a possible German attack. German troops invaded the Soviet Union on June 22, 1941. Now the Soviet Union's security required the friendship of the Western powers, first Britain and then the United States. At enormous cost to life and property the Soviet Union emerged from the war on the winning side with increased territory and a much wider sphere of influence, which incorporated the whole of Eastern Europe, including the eastern half of a divided, defeated Germany. The war in the USSR was named the "Great Patriotic War," it was fought in the name of the "Motherland," and the Russian Orthodox Church was rehabilitated in the struggle against the German invaders. Stalin himself invoked the names of figures from Russian history whom the Bolsheviks had previously seen as part of a past to be decried: "Let the manly images of our great ancestors—Alexander Nevsky, Dimitry Donskoy, Kuzma Minin, Dimitry Pozharsky, Alexander Suvorov, and Mikhail Kutuzov—inspire you in this war!"[18] The war was fought not in the name of the proletariat but in defense of the Russian-Soviet nation; not for Marx as representing the international working class but for Moscow as representing the center of the Soviet nation-state. Soviet foreign policy during its formative period can be seen, then, as being determined by the necessity to engage in shifting alliances in order to ensure the territorial integrity and security of the state in the face of an anarchic international setting.

The Onset of the Cold War

Why did the alliance that defeated Germany (and Japan in the East) so quickly break down after 1945, resulting in a Cold War among the former allies? At the level of the international setting the argument would focus upon that one element in structural realist theory that is variable: the distribution of power capabilities among the major states. In the absence of a legitimate hierarchical structure of binding laws to guide and enforce rule-bound behavior, states operate in a self-help system of anarchy in which the security dilemma, based upon worst-case scenarios of others' possible intentions, determines threat perceptions. These perceptions of threat then produce foreign policy orientations. Given the changes in the overall distribution of power capabilities that emerged after the war, it was inevitable, to continue this realist line of reasoning, that the USSR and the USA would perceive one another, when calculating the relative power of other countries, as potential threats. The world had moved from a complex multipolar structure to one distinguished by a bipolar balance of power. Germany, France, and Britain had been terminally weakened in the power stakes as a result of the war, and now only two states could pose a realistic threat to each other: the United States and the Soviet Union. In other words, it was where they were positioned in the structural condition of anarchy that determined U.S.-Soviet rivalry and hence the onset of the Cold War. Irrespective of competing ideologies, individual leaders, or domestic decision-making processes, realism posits that both states sought to maximize their power in pursuit of national security in the face of the security dilemma.

Spheres of Influence

Security for the Soviet leadership after the war was conceived in traditional terms as requiring the preservation of state sovereignty and political and economic viability. With a devastated economy to rebuild, the USSR's priority was to reconstruct the industrial infrastructure to ensure the viability and integrity of the state. The "iron curtain" dividing Europe simply reflected the shift in the military balance of power after 1945 based upon a bipolar structure.

For the Soviet Union, continuing the centuries-old strategic logic of Russian imperialism, it was necessary to keep control over Eastern Europe principally for perceived national security objectives, as a buffer zone against possible future attempts at military invasion from the major powers in the West. After the war Stalin was happy to agree to mutual "spheres of influence" with Britain and the United States, as he had been with Germany before the war. In talks in Moscow in October 1944 British Prime Minister Winston Churchill and Stalin casually agreed on respective spheres of influence in the Balkans in terms of percentages for each side in each country (e.g., in Bulgaria Russia would have 80 percent predominance to Britain's 20 percent, while in Greece these percentages would be reversed).[19] In April of the following year Stalin wrote to President Harry Truman expressing his concern at U.S. reluctance to recognize Poland as part of the Soviet sphere of influence, stating that "Poland is to the security of the Soviet Union what Belgium and Greece are to the security of Great Britain" and that "Poland borders on the Soviet Union, which cannot be said about Great Britain or the USA . . . . I do not know whether a genuinely representative government has been established in Greece, or whether the Belgian government is a genuinely democratic one . . . . I cannot understand why in discussing Poland no attempt is made to consider the interests of the Soviet Union in terms of security as well." Stalin made it plain that ". . . the Soviet Government cannot agree to the existence in Poland of a Government hostile to it."[20]

A significant feature of strategic bipolarity was the development of nuclear weapons. When the United States demonstrated the awesome nature of the atomic bomb in Japan in 1945, this signalled for the USSR the urgent need to itself successfully test such a weapon, which eventually took place in 1949. From that time on a nuclear arms "race" developed between the United States and the Soviet Union that gained its own technological momentum and that would become both a further provocation fuelling the Cold War competition and yet also a stimulus for finding a way of managing the conflict.

Soviet tanks ensured that Poland, and the other states in Eastern Europe, remained tightly in the Soviet embrace. The Stalinist model of political economy was also imposed on these states, designed initially both to benefit the Soviet economy and as a further means to ensure compliance to Moscow's wishes. This policy would later have a negative impact on the USSR itself when Stalinism eventually collapsed in Eastern Europe in 1989–1990, for this collapse had a demonstration effect on the titular nationalities of the republics of the Soviet Union. The Cold War began in Europe and rival military alliance systems were established (the North Atlantic Treaty Organization and the Warsaw Treaty Organization), largely as a framework to manage the German problem in the unarticulated mutual interests of both sides, for neither wanted to see a resurgence of German power that could again threaten the status quo. But as the Soviet Union rebuilt its industrial and military capacity, the Cold War took on global proportions until the template of the East-West strategic competition was placed upon almost all areas of tension, whether in Korea, the Middle East, Southern Africa, or Central America.[21]

Detente

For realists this global competition for power and influence between the "superpowers" was simply the logical affirmation of the way states have traditionally behaved. Soviet foreign policy took on global dimensions due to the bipolar structure of the international system, which determined a struggle for power and influence with the United States. Although the system was essentially bipolar, this did not prevent shifting alliances outside the core of the system or prevent some states from maintaining a nonaligned status. China, for example, was, after the Communist Revolution, briefly allied with the USSR, but it later split off from the Soviet bloc to move much closer to the United States in the 1970s and 1980s, despite differences in ideology. This is offered by realists as further evidence that domestic political, economic, and societal factors are not important apart from when they determine the power attributes of the state. China and Russia, it is pointed out, have been traditional foes in a regional struggle for power and influence in Asia, and the antagonism that developed in the 1960s was simply a reflection of this age-old rivalry that enabled the United States to "play the China card."

The most intense period of the Soviet Union's relationship with the United States was between 1946 and 1962 as both sides muddled through a series of crises before any rules and norms had been developed to manage their competition. After the Cuban missile crisis of 1962, attempts were made to find a framework for managing relations in such a way as to avoid a direct military confrontation.[22] The distribution of capabilities across the system (the variable element in Waltz's theory) was by the 1960s beginning to change; tight bipolarity was giving way to what John Spanier has termed "bipolycentrism"—that is, a looser bipolarism with centrifugal tendencies, which more recently has resulted in what some see as a return to a complex multipolarity.[23] Germany in Europe and Japan in Asia had become major economic powers, and in successive waves of decolonization large numbers of new states were being formed, making it increasingly more difficult for the superpowers to dominate global politics. Indeed, the tightness of bipolarity was slackened and its level of tensions reduced as a result of initiatives independent of Moscow or Washington.

The seeds of East-West detente of the 1970s, for example, are to be found in West German Chancellor Willy Brandt's Ostpolitik, a strategic program of fostering "change through rapprochement" and reconciliation with East Germany.[24] At this time China was taking a more active and independent stance among the superpowers, holding negotiations with both Japan and the United States. The Soviet Union, careful to maintain political control over its client states in Eastern Europe, was forced to react to these changing shifts in polarity and actively engaged in detente.[25]

The Demise of Detente

East-West tensions, however, were to rise again in the late 1970s, largely due to regional conflicts in the periphery of the international system. In its strategic competition with the United States the USSR tried to legitimate its support for the Sandinistas in Nicaragua, the MPLA in Angola, and the radical Arab states in the Middle East as defensive policies aimed against neo-imperialism. The nail in the coffin of detente was the Soviet invasion of Afghanistan in 1979, justified in classical geostrategic terms as a defensive action designed to ensure national security on the southern periphery of the state.[26]

Realism as the dominant theory that has been used to explain international relations during the Cold War period becomes increasingly less convincing as we move into the 1980s. Realism holds that radical structural changes usually occur after warfare and certainly did not predict the events that unfolded in the late 1980s when the Soviet Union for all intents and purposes conceded defeat in the Cold War. The Soviet Union withdrew from Afghanistan, gave up Eastern Europe, and finally allowed the state to dissolve in 1991.[27] These are events difficult to understand from a realist standpoint. At the least it would be necessary to reevaluate definitions of power to give more prominence to non-military sources. In military terms the Soviet Union was still a superpower in 1991—indeed, Russia can still be seen as such today.

Yet in attempting to salvage realism, theorists might simply argue that the USSR overstretched its economic capacity in an attempt to keep up with the United States in the military and strategic realm and that President Ronald Reagan's 1983 development of a Strategic Defense Initiative ("Star Wars") finally forced the pace and bankrupted the Soviet economy. Like previous colonial powers, the Soviet Union had overstretched itself and could no longer afford the burden of maintaining its empire. The Soviet Union may not have lost a hot war, but the Cold War had inflicted some real defeats nevertheless. Reviewing Soviet foreign policy when he came to power in the mid-1980s, Gorbachev was faced with failures and dilemmas all around: a crisis of legitimacy in communist power in Poland; an apparently unwinnable war in Afghanistan; tensions with an economically dynamic China; unprofitable investments in Cuba, the Horn of Africa, Southern Africa, the Middle East, Southeast Asia, and Central America; tensions with Western Europe over the deployment of INF missiles; stagnation in East European economies requiring Soviet subsidies at a time of declining domestic growth; a collapse of detente and external restrictions on Soviet foreign trade; and a resurgent America challenging Moscow in every corner of the globe under the Reagan Doctrine.

New Thinking

It should not be forgotten (yet it has rarely been noted) that in this global East-West struggle for power the odds were extremely uneven. It was essentially the Soviet Union against the rest of the most powerful states in the world: the United States and all the other permanent members of the United Nations Security Council (United Kingdom, France, China), plus all other major powers among the capitalist states without a single exception, most significantly among this list, of course, West Germany and Japan. It may have been the world's largest country in terms of territory, but this provided little in the way of security, as much of the USSR bordered potentially hostile states (e.g., China) or regions of instability (e.g., Southwest Asia). Those states in Eastern Europe that served as a buffer against the West were in an *involuntary* alliance with Moscow, and in the event of hostilities with NATO the Soviet Union could not have been certain of the loyalty of all Warsaw Treaty members. Gorbachev's new thinking in foreign policy reflected these realities and was designed to preserve the USSR's status as a superpower.[28] Central to the 1986–1990 Five Year Plan was a radical shift of capital investments to the high-technology sector, tightly linked to the military industrial complex. This plan was designed in part to keep pace with the United States in weapons technology, hence to retain the USSR's military superpower status. But it was also designed to restructure the Soviet economy to make it more competitive in the global market, thereby transforming the USSR into a *complete* superpower. The logic of foreign policy then was still power politics, and the determinants, in such a reading, were still external, structural ones. But in the final analysis Gorbachev's program failed because it unleashed *domestic* forces that he could not ultimately control. In other words, the West won the Cold War, and with changes in the distribution of power capabilities, we are likely to see shifting patterns in the balance of power.

Yet surely, even if a realist account of the history of Soviet foreign policy is useful for understanding some of the underlying dynamics at the international level, it cannot tell the whole story. Other theories of Soviet foreign policy have stressed the role of Marxist-Leninist ideology as a critical factor, still others have focussed upon individual leaders and power struggles. Any theory that ignores Stalin and the struggles for power in the Kremlin in the 1930s or Gorbachev and the struggle for power in the 1980s must surely be incomplete. To gain a comprehensive picture of Soviet foreign policy, we need to look inside the nation-state, to the internal determinants of policy.

The Domestic Setting

Foreign policy decision-making in the Soviet Union was highly centralized, controlled, and coordinated by the CPSU Politburo. The old Supreme Soviet did not really legislate but simply ratified decisions already made by the party. Party control of the ministries was maintained by overlapping membership: where important ministers also served on the higher councils of the party. For example, it became the rule from the 1970s, when foreign policy issues were central to Brezhnev's authority building, that the ministers of foreign affairs and defense and the chairman of the KGB would sit on the Politburo. Other institutions dealing with foreign issues included non-ministerial, purely party organs, such as the International Department of the Central Committee (whose chief was also a candidate member of the Politburo). Organizational disputes arose between the various institutions inasmuch as conflict is endemic to any bureaucratic setting over such issues as budgets, policies, and personnel. Particularly in the Brezhnev era, bureaucratic competition was seen by a number of observers to be a major variable in the process of reaching foreign policy decisions. Even if, to a degree, this could be described as a form of pluralism, as some Western academics asserted, it was one of a particularly exclusive and restricted kind. There were no free, democratic elections, free media, competing parties, or any channels for mass political participation. Any bureaucratic politics that did take place did so largely in secret and needed to be expressed in ideological terms, and although one could clearly be creative in utilizing Marxism-Leninism, there were boundaries that could not be overstepped.

Ideology

National security, however defined, is dependent upon economic viability. It was evident to the Soviet leadership in the 1970s that Khrushchev's boast that the USSR would surpass the United States in productive capacity by the 1980s would not be realized. Capitalism had continued to demonstrate its comparative superiority to the Stalinist command economy in the development of modern technologies, and while the Soviet Union was a military superpower in terms of economic penetration of the global economy, it had failed to make an impact. It was a unidimensional power (or, as one writer put it, an "incomplete superpower"[29]), and as such, due to the dominance of realist thinking in both academies and ministries, its stability as a major power in the international system was exaggerated. International relations theorists, military and security establishments, secretaries of state, presidents and prime ministers, overprivileged the Soviet Union in international relations and exaggerated its power and stability and were hence unable to foresee its final collapse.

Yet there was perhaps logic to this, for the Soviet Union was born from a revolution whose objective was to overthrow international capitalism in the name of the proletariat. In this sense Lenin and the Bolsheviks posed a greater problem to the West than would have a traditional military challenge to the international status quo. Soviet Russia threatened the very essence of American identity, predicting and prescribing on the basis of a scientific ideology the overthrow of the democratic liberal state. Having failed to stimulate revolution in the mature capitalist democracies after 1917, Soviet ideology, with some slight variations, continued to perceive the world in bipolar terms based upon two competing socio-economic systems up to the Gorbachev period.

There has been no consensus in writings on Soviet foreign policy as to the relative weight Marxist-Leninist ideology had on decision-making.[30] George F. Kennan, recalling his views in 1946, states: "In no way did the Soviet Union appear to me, at that moment, as a military threat . . . . What I did think I saw . . . was what I might call an ideological-political threat."[31] Yet Rubinstein argues that "just as a belief in Christianity has rarely affected the foreign policy decisions made by Christian rulers, so, too, a belief in Marxism-Leninism has rarely led Soviet leaders to act in a manner contrary to their perceptions of what is necessary and good for the 'national interest' of the Soviet Union."[32] Certainly ideology, as noted above, did not prevent Lenin from agreeing to Brest-Litovsk or Stalin from making a pact with Hitler or Khrushchev from breaking with China or Brezhnev from signing friendship treaties with countries whose governments repressed local communists, such as Egypt and Iraq. Clearly, in each of these cases, considerations of national interest were paramount and were not ideological priorities.

But we cannot dismiss ideology as having had no impact on Soviet foreign policy. It can be argued that Soviet perceptions of what was in the national interest were actually linked to ideological considerations. Lenin's thesis about the inherent incompatibility of capitalism and socialism was proven correct, for the bipolar competition reflected more than a classical strategic balance-of-power struggle—it was also a struggle between two competing views of how society should be organized. Marxist-Leninist ideology provided the legitimizing rationale for one-party communist rule, without which the system, as we more recently witnessed, would collapse. Marxist-Leninist ideology was also the glue that held the internal and external empires together and facilitated Russian hegemony. Again, as we would later see, take away the belief system and the empires collapse. The communist leadership in Moscow knew this better than anyone and could not therefore afford to let up in the ideological struggle with the West. Detente, too, was defined in ideological terms—as a more peaceful means of waging the class struggle.

While the USSR concluded treaties with Third World states that were *not* communist, not only was its overall global strategy justified in anti-imperialist terms but specific foreign policies were devised on the basis of ideology. For example, the concept of "socialist orientation" was elaborated as a developmental model (based on the Soviet system) for close Third World allies. This resulted in vast resources being wasted in countries such as Angola and Ethiopia. Cuba and Vietnam, due to their rapid progress in the construction of communism, became beneficiaries of staggering amounts of Soviet aid and trade credits and military hardware.[33]

Leadership and Ideology

In the former Soviet Union, disputes over ideology were often at the center of internal power struggles, especially given the absence of any formal institutionalized mechanisms for leadership succession. Some of these disputes had at their core issues of foreign policy. Debates over these issues were not articulated in traditional Western-type discourse of competing conceptions of what is in the national interest, but in ideological terms. From the internal debate over the Brest-Litovsk Treaty through the debates over detente in the 1970s to Gorbachev's reformism in the 1980s, the implications for world socialism, the world revolutionary movement, and the world correlation of forces in the fight against imperialism were salient issues. Stalin's advocacy of "socialism in one country" was part of his power struggle against Trotsky, who called for permanent international revolution. Leadership in the USSR was personalized, and in order to build authority and power individuals needed to formulate programs identified with themselves that would appeal to a winning coalition in the Politburo and Central Committee of the CPSU. Detente became the main policy program associated with Brezhnev's bid for power, and the discourses of the factions that both supported it and opposed it were conducted in ideological terms. In the early 1970s members of the Politburo were expressing critical views of any economic opening to the capitalist West, and it was a number of years before Brezhnev succeeded in gaining a stable winning majority, and then only after convincing party ideologues that engagement with the West would not threaten socialism at home.[34]

Clearly, engagement with the West had to be limited (to trade relations and political relations at the elite level), for it was feared, correctly as it turned out, that any mass contact with the capitalist world would undermine Marxism-Leninism and the legitimacy of the communist system in Eastern Europe. Foreign policy toward the West therefore had a fundamental ideological component that restricted the extent of contact. This was true of Gorbachev too, who in his first years in power neither proposed nor envisaged a complete normalization of relations with "imperialism." His detente policy was still articulated in the language of the competition between two opposing socio-economic systems. Struggle with the West was the *raison d'être* of the Soviet system, a necessary cement for the ideological structure legitimating communist rule. It was also the central plank for ensuring Moscow's control over the non-Russian republics of the USSR and the rationale of the Brezhnev doctrine pertaining to Eastern Europe.

Interdependency and Interpenetration

It is perhaps at this point that we should consider the question of increased interdependency, a concept that was developed in the 1970s to describe changing agendas and competencies in international relations and the linkages between foreign and domestic policies. One impetus for Brezhnev's policy of detente was to gain access to Western technology, in part to stave off the need for reform at home. Economic interactions increased substantially between East and West during the detente period, but still, as a percentage of overall Soviet trade, that with the capitalist countries remained very small. It is incorrect to refer to economic interdependence to describe the relationship that developed between the USSR and the USA, the two most important states in the international system of the 1970s. Interdependence implies *mutual dependency*, and neither side was really dependent upon the other for critical products. This was demonstrated most clearly when the United States imposed a grain embargo on the Soviet Union in response to its invasion of Afghanistan. Moscow simply found alternative suppliers. Where there do exist mutual economic dependencies, as between Japan and the United States, then there would appear to be more potential for conflict.

Perhaps a better term to describe the process that did impact in the USSR and the Eastern bloc during this period is *interpenetration*. Here I refer to the penetration into the USSR of knowledge and ideas, as well as consumer products. It was not so much economic interdependency that undermined the competency of the Soviet party leaders but a challenge to their legitimacy from increasing numbers of ordinary citizens who were gaining knowledge of the outside world. It was not NATO tanks that penetrated the iron curtain but the Voice of America and the BBC World Service, not U2-spy planes that had any impact on Soviet society but U2 rock bands. And it was not army officers in military uniform on the opposite side of the Berlin Wall but young tourists in Levi jeans on the streets of Moscow who had a greater effect in undermining communist party legitimacy.

Party leaders in Moscow had made a compact with the people, enshrined in the Soviet constitution, for a continuous raising of the standard of living. By the early 1980s this was becoming more difficult to fulfill, and the people knew it. Gorbachev admitted it and attempted to do something about it. Perestroika was designed in its initial stages to stimulate the economy in order for the Soviet Union to reach world levels of production by the year 2000 (Gorbachev was still working according to standard five-year plans). The Soviet command economy, though, had failed to keep pace with the global development of science and technology, being easily surpassed by many much smaller Third World states in penetrating the world marketplace.

Conclusion

For a realist, radical systemic change can come only with war, hence it is often claimed that realism is of no use in explaining the collapse of the Soviet Union and the end of the Cold War. It is most common also to state that the Soviet Union imploded due to a failure in the economy. The critique of realism is only partly fair, and the economic explanation for the USSR's demise is not the whole of the matter. The Cold War *was a war*: it was a war of ideas, of opposing, competing systems—according to Fred Halliday, it was an "inter-systemic war."[35] As with all wars, there are winners and losers, and in this case the Soviet Union was the loser. The economic explanation cannot suffice, for other states have suffered much worse economic crises and, albeit with difficulty and threats to stability, have pulled through. Why should economic crises threaten the territorial integrity of the state from within? The Soviet economy was in a mess, but not such that it would have been prevented from muddling along for many more years. Unemployment was still practically non-existent, and most people had roofs over their heads and food on the table.

The Soviet Union collapsed *because it lost the Cold War*. Its identity and legitimacy were linked to a competition with the West. Yet by the 1980s it had become clear to the party leadership that it could not keep up in the competition. This, then, was the dilemma: how to justify communist party rule and control over the Russian-Soviet empire without the architecture of the bipolar Cold War confrontation. China could engage in economic reform without risking serious political fallout and political system change because its legitimacy was not based upon this inter-systemic conflict. The nature of Soviet society was also radically different from that of China: Tiananmen was an expression of the relatively limited interpenetration of Chinese society. Peasant soldiers from the countryside were brought in to put down protests by students, many of whom had studied in Western universities. In the Soviet Union, in contrast, society had been more highly penetrated, and not only intellectuals but also many other groups recognized the futility of the Cold War competition. Francis Fukuyama refers to a proto-civil society existing beneath the surface of seeming Soviet stability, and he states that "the most fundamental failure of totalitarianism was its failure to control thought."[36]

The Russian-Soviet empire collapsed so quickly because the belief system that glued it together and legitimated it collapsed. And the belief system collapsed because, unlike Christianity, where salvation is to be found in another world, Marxism-Leninism offered salvation, although not in the here and now, at least in the here and not-too-distant future.[37]

That is to say that Soviet citizens were promised the good life on earth, but with the interpenetration of society and the development of glasnost, this promise was unmasked for the fraud that it was, thereby creating a crisis in ideology. The Soviet Union, bereft of its Leninist cement, gave way to centrifugal forces as the nations it comprised demanded statehood. The Russian Parliament and the Russian president took advantage of these forces and by December 1991, four months after the failed coup against Gorbachev, Russia gained independence from the Soviet "center," resulting in the demise of the Union. What Russia has made of its independence in terms of its global identity and foreign policy is the subject of the remaining chapters in this book.

Notes

1. For an attempt to reconceptualize international politics after the Cold War utilizing the concept of turbulence, see James N. Rosenau, *Turbulence in World Politics: A Theory of Change and Continuity*, New York, Harvester/Wheatsheaf, 1990.

2. The classical realist paradigm was outlined in Hans Morgenthau, *Politics Among Nations*, 4th edn., New York, Knopf, 1967.

3. J. David Singer made a distinction between levels of analysis: "The Level of Analysis Problem in International Relations," in Klaus Knorr and Sidney Verba (eds), *The International System: Theoretical Essays*, Princeton University Press, 1961, pp. 77–92. For recent debates stemming from this question, see Martin Hollis and Steve Smith, *Explaining and Understanding International Relations*, Cambridge University Press, 1990, A. Wendt's review of this book in the *Review of International Studies*, vol. 17, no. 4, 1991, pp. 383–92, and the subsequent correspondence between Wendt and Hollis and Smith in the *Review of International Studies*, vols. 17, no. 4, 1991, and 18, no. 2, 1992.

4. Richard Pipes, *The Russian Revolution, 1889–1919*, London, Collins Harvill, 1990, p. 607.

5. See M. T. Florinsky, *Russia: A History and Interpretation*, London, 1953.

6. Richard Pipes, "Detente: Moscow's View," in Erik P. Hoffmann and Frederic Fleron (eds), *The Conduct of Soviet Foreign Policy*, New York, Aldine Publishing, 1980, pp. 353–385, p. 358.

7. Quoted in *The Bolsheviks and the October Revolution: Minutes of the Central Committee of the RSDLP (Bolsheviks), August 1917–February 1918*, London, Pluto, 1974, p. 313.

8. Alvin Rubinstein, *Soviet Foreign Policy Since World War II*, 4th edn., New York, HarperCollins, 1992, p. 25.

9. For example, see Robert F. Miller, *Soviet Foreign Policy Today*, Sydney, Allen and Unwin, 1991, chapter 3, pp. 43–61.

10. Zbigniew Brzezinski, "The Soviet Union: Her Aims, Problems, and Challenges to the West," in Robbin F. Laird and Erik P. Hoffmann (eds), *Soviet Foreign Policy in a Changing World*, Berlin, Walter de Gruyter, 1986, pp. 3–15, p. 4.

11. Kenneth Waltz, *Theory of International Politics*, New York, Random House, 1979.

12. Quoted in Lionel Kochan, *The Making of Modern Russia*, Harmondsworth, Penguin, 1963, p. 301.

13. Joseph L. Nogee and Robert H. Donaldson, *Soviet Foreign Policy Since World War II*, 2nd ed., New York, Pergamon, 1984, p. 12.

14. *Khrushchev Remembers: The Glasnost Tapes*, with a foreword by Strobe Talbott, translated and edited by Jerrold L. Schecter with Vyacheslav V. Luchkov, Boston, Little, Brown, 1990, p. 51.

15. John G. Stoessinger, *The Might of Nations: World Politics in Our Time*, 10th edn., New York, McGraw-Hill, 1993, p. 44. Rubinstein, *Soviet Foreign Policy*, p. 35.

16. *Khrushchev Remembers: The Glasnost Tapes*, p. 51.

17. Quoted in Rubinstein, *Soviet Foreign Policy*, p. 43.

18. Quoted in Isaac Deutscher, *Stalin: A Political Biography*, Harmondsworth, Penguin, 1966, p. 458.

19. Deutscher, *Stalin*, p. 502. It is often overlooked that Churchill, when he referred to Soviet Russia in a famous phrase as a "riddle wrapped in a mystery inside an enigma," went on to say that perhaps there was a key for understanding Russian policy: "That key is Russian national interest," BBC Radio, October 1, 1939.

20. *Stalin's Correspondence with Roosevelt and Truman 1941–1945*, New York, Capricorn Books, 1965, p. 220.

21. On Soviet foreign policy in the Third World, see Margot Light (ed), *Troubled Friendships: Moscow's Third World Ventures*, London, British Academic Press/Royal Institute of International Affairs, 1993.

22. See on this question Roy Allison and Phil Williams (eds), *Superpower Competition and Crisis Prevention in the Third World*, Cambridge, Cambridge University Press, 1990.

23. John Spanier, *Games Nations Play*, 5th edn., New York, Holt, Rinehart and Winston, 1989, pp. 266–288. For a recent evaluation of the question of polarity see Charles W. Kegley Jr. and Gregory Raymond, *A Multipolar Peace? Great Power Politics in the Twenty-First Century*, New York, St. Martin's Press, 1994.

24. See Michael J. Sodaro, *Moscow, Germany, and the West from Khrushchev to Gorbachev*, Ithaca, Cornell University Press, 1990, p. 167.

25. On the various determinants and aspects of detente see Mike Bowker and Phil Williams, *Superpower Detente: A Reappraisal*, London, Sage/Royal Institute of International Affairs, 1988.

26. On Soviet support for revolutionary forces in the Third World, see Peter Shearman, "Soviet Foreign Policy in Africa and Latin America: A Comparative Case Study," *Millennium: Journal of International Studies*, vol. 15, no. 3, 1986, pp. 339–366, and Bruce D. Porter, *The USSR in Third World Conflicts: Soviet Arms and Diplomacy in Local Wars 1945–1980*, Cambridge, Cambridge University Press, 1984. On the eventual decision to withdraw from Afghanistan, see Amin Saikal and William Maley (eds), *The Soviet Withdrawal from Afghanistan*, Cambridge, Cambridge University Press, 1989.

27. See, for an assessment of Russia's changing relations with Eastern Europe, Alex Pravda, *The End of the Outer Empire: Soviet–East European Relations in Transition, 1985–1990*, London, Sage/Royal Institute of International Affairs, 1992. On the collapse of the "internal empire" and its consequences for foreign policy, see Karen Dawisha and Bruce Parrott, *Russia and the New States of Eurasia: The Politics of Upheaval*, Cambridge, Cambridge University Press, 1994.

28. On Gorbachev's foreign policy, see, for example, Sylvia Woodby, *Gorbachev and the Decline of Ideology in Soviet Foreign Policy*, Boulder, Westview, 1989, Peter Shearman, "Gorbachev and the Third World: An Era of Reform," *Third World Quarterly*, vol. 9, no. 4, 1987, pp. 1083–1117, and Peter Shearman, "New Political Thinking Reassessed," *Review of International Studies*, vol. 19, no. 2, 1993, pp. 139–158.

29. Paul Dibb, *The Soviet Union: The Incomplete Superpower*, London, 1986.

30. For different views on this question then pertaining see the still useful compilation of articles in Erik P. Hoffmann and Frederic J. Fleron (eds), *The Conduct of Soviet Foreign Policy*, Aldine, 1980, Part 3, chapters 7–11, pp. 91–212.

31. George F. Kennan, "Reflections on Containment," in Terry L. Diebel and John Lewis Gaddis (eds), *Containing the Soviet Union*, Washington, D.C., Pergamon-Brasseys, 1988, pp. 15–19, p. 16.

32. Rubinstein, *Soviet Foreign Policy*, p. 18.

33. On policy toward Cuba, see Peter Shearman, *The Soviet Union and Cuba*, London, Routledge and Kegan Paul/Royal Institute of International Affairs, 1987, and Peter Shearman, "The Soviet Union and Cuba: The 'Best' of Friends," in Light (ed), *Troubled Friendships*, pp. 166–190. On Vietnam see Victor Funnell, "The Soviet Union and Vietnam: Bilateral Relations in a Great-Power Triangle," in Light (ed), *Troubled Friendships*, pp. 82–109.

34. On Brezhnev's authority building see George W. Breslauer, *Khrushchev and Brezhnev as Leaders: Building Authority in Soviet Politics*, London, Allen and Unwin, 1982. On the domestic politics of detente see H. Gelman, *The Brezhnev Politburo and the Decline of Detente*, Ithaca, Cornell University Press, 1984.

35. Fred Halliday, "The Cold War as Inter-systemic Conflict: Initial Theses," in Mike Bowker and Robin Brown (eds), *From Cold War to Collapse: Theory and World Politics in the 1980s*, Cambridge University Press, 1993, pp. 21–34.

36. Francis Fukuyama, *The End of History and the Last Man*, London, Penguin, p. 29. Also see his "The Modernizing Imperative: The USSR as an Ordinary Country," *The National Interest*, no. 31, Spring 1993, pp. 10–18.

37. For a similar line of reasoning see Ernest Gellner, "Islam and Marxism: Some Comparisons," *International Affairs*, vol. 67, no. 1, 1991, pp. 1–6.

2

Russian Foreign Policy Decision-making

Neil Malcolm

After two and a half years of Russian statehood, a stable foreign policy–making system had still to emerge in Moscow. The task of this chapter is to give a sense of how things were changing and, if possible, to identify tendencies of development. This can be done by only giving some consideration to the wider social and historical context that is shaping events.

In the period under review Russian society was in turmoil, old values had been discredited, and economic hardships were mounting. Opportunities for participation in politics had expanded, but institutions were shaky and lacked authority. It was difficult to predict whether Russia would follow a path of gradual institutionalization, consensus building, and partnership with the Western powers or slide into political decay, demagogy, and dictatorship, possibly associated with aggressive international behavior.[1] This discussion of the development of foreign policy–making cannot be insulated from these wider questions.

The section that follows is an analysis of the Soviet legacy in foreign policy. In the rest of the chapter I examine the operation of the main foreign policy institutions of post-communist Russia and their interaction with each other, paying particular attention to the influence of the wider political environment. The chapter ends with some tentative conclusions concerning the direction of change.

Foreign Policy–making in the Late Soviet Period

In the 1960s and 1970s Western commentators devoted a good deal of attention to analyzing similarities and differences between the Soviet foreign policy bureaucracy and its counterparts in the West. Franklyn

Holzman and Robert Legvold, for example, listed three important features that distinguished the Soviet policy-making system:

1. It enforced greater *centralization* (concentration of decision-making power).
2. It maintained deeper *differentiation* (role specialization of institutions and individuals).
3. It allowed much less *participation* (access to the decision-making process).[2]

Thus the right to have an overall view about foreign policy issues was in essence restricted to the Politburo—the job of other participants was to provide specialized information and to carry out specialized tasks of implementation. Such compartmentalization fostered a powerful version of bureaucratic parochialism.[3] Information, as a rule, was distributed on a "need-to-know" basis, and opinions were sought only as and when those in power thought appropriate. Of course there were informal channels of access and privileged information sources for a slightly wider elite, and policy could be argued about by specialists in oblique terms; but in general it would have been misleading to talk about a "foreign policy debate" or about an "informed public."

Here as in other areas of policy, the Communist Party was at the core of the process. Decisions were taken by the Politburo or by key groups drawn from its members; the Secretariat acted as the main channel, sifter, and organizer of the information the Politburo needed to make its decisions.[4] Party spokesmen and publications articulated the doctrinal framework of policy. Party officials watched over the implementation of policy, and maintained discipline among those responsible.

As several writers demonstrated, however, it would have been wrong to exaggerate the scope or the effectiveness of party control. The powers of institutions fluctuated. The general secretary, who did not have the advantage of endorsement by popular vote and who was no longer able to use terror against his rivals, had to maneuver and build coalitions among powerful groups in the apparatus. At times of weakness he arguably had to defer to military leaders.[5] The Politburo itself had become a more representative body by the 1970s: the minister of defense, the minister of foreign affairs, and the head of the KGB, for example, seemed to attend virtually ex officio. The Soviet Union was clearly by no means immune to the effects of bureaucratic politics in the foreign policy field. Roles were distributed in an untidy, ad hoc fashion; there were frequent demarcation battles between the party International Department, the military, and the Foreign Ministry; and policy frequently appeared to lack coherence and flexibility.[6]

In the second half of the 1980s Gorbachev succeeded in opening up discussion of foreign policy issues and in breaking down some of the barriers of specialization. The overall effect of the first phase of reforms in this area was to shift the balance of influence somewhat in favor of the Foreign Ministry. The party International Department grew less involved in implementing policy and became more of an information and analysis center. The military monopoly on defense-related data and judgements was eroded.[7]

Yet even in 1991, despite the institutional changes (for example, the downgrading of the Politburo) associated with the setting up of an executive presidency, there were still strong continuities with the past. Gorbachev was able to draw on the authority of a party general secretary of five years standing. The presidential apparatus employed numerous former senior party officials and cooperated with party bodies. The Central Committee departments continued to function. There was still widespread deference to the symbols and values of the Soviet period.

Insofar as central control had been relaxed, moreover, the consequences were not encouraging. What power was lost to the general secretary seemed to flow, as during previous phases of ineffective leadership, to the bureaucracies. In a system that had been held together by strict central control and where debate had been discouraged, there was no underlying agreement on national goals to soften the rivalry between the different agencies. During the winter of 1990–1991 the KGB, the armed forces, and the International Department appeared at times to be forwarding their own foreign policies, jarringly at odds with the new political thinking of Gorbachev and the Foreign Ministry. This led to uncomfortable complications in relations with the West and with the former Soviet-bloc states.[8]

Thus the legacy inherited from the Soviet Union made it particularly difficult to establish effective foreign policy–making in post-communist Russia:

1. The effective operation of the previous ultra-centralized system had depended on the party apparatus. When this vanished at a stroke at the end of August 1991, an enormous overload was placed on the information-processing and political-control capacity of the presidency and the Foreign Ministry.

2. Earlier differentiation of roles, and exclusion from access to policy debate even of senior officials in relevant institutions, meant it would be difficult to build a more collegial, cooperative approach to foreign

even at top level. Blinkered bureaucratic perspectives were likely to dominate.

3. The entire political and administrative system had to be reconstructed in a country where formal institutional hierarchies and predictable procedures in policy-making had never been given a chance to take root and where organizational changes had always tended to be linked to top-level power struggles. The scope for conflict and disorder was very great.

4. The breakup of the Soviet Union created a whole new sphere of foreign relations fraught with the problems generated by deep economic interdependence and contested borders. The specialized knowledge needed to deal with these problems was difficult to find.

5. The new politically active elite had in most cases little experience of foreign policy matters. They were therefore more likely to be willing to support unrealistic and destabilizing policies.

6. Political views were sharply polarized, and foreign policy issues soon began to be used by the opposition in an increasingly bitter struggle for power. There was resentment in army and defense-industrial circles about the material implications for them of the demilitarized foreign policy line preferred by the Foreign Ministry. Old conceptions of Russia's role in the world had been challenged and there was no agreement on what was to replace them. Wounded national feeling was further offended by Foreign Minister Kozyrev's conciliatory approach to the West. The prospects for a broad consensus on international matters emerging looked poor.

Already enough time has passed to provide material for discussion about how the Russians are coping with their unpromising inheritance in foreign policy–making. In the pages that follow I shall focus on how successful or unsuccessful they have been in this field in building the "consensus, community, legitimacy and organization" that Huntington describes as the hallmarks of a developed civic polity.[9]

The Foreign Policy–making Process in Russia

Unlike the other former Soviet republics, Russia has no shortage of foreign policy institutions. Indeed, it can be argued that the field is too crowded. What it lacks, with the passing of the CPSU, is a means of controlling and coordinating them. The office of the president is now at the apex, but it has neither the capacity nor the unity of action of the old Central Committee apparatus.

The change of constitution introduced at the end of 1993 reflected a real shift in the balance of power toward the executive arm. As in other states, there has been a wide gap between legal prescription and everyday practice in foreign policy–making, but it is worth noting some of the constitutional details.

According to the Russian constitution in force at the moment of independence in 1991, it was the prerogative of the parliament to lay down the main lines of foreign policy and the duty of the president and the government to implement it. The current constitution simply states that the president "directs the foreign policy of the Russian Federation" (within the framework set by the constitution and laws of the country) (Art. 86, 80). As before, he has the right to appoint members of the government, proposed by the prime minister (but without any longer having to seek parliamentary approval of his appointments). He forms and presides over the Security Council and conducts international negotiations (Art. 83). For its part, parliament still enjoys the right to ratify and denounce major treaties and international agreements (Art. 106 [g]). Ambassadors are appointed by the president "in consultation with the appropriate committees" of parliament (Art. 83 [m]). In the first constitution the Council of Ministers was supposed to coordinate the work of different agencies of government, whereas in the new one the emphasis is placed on the prime minister, who determines the main policies of the government "in accordance with the Constitution, federal legislation and the decrees of the president" and "organizes its work" (Art. 113).

In reality the role of the Council of Ministers as a body has consistently been negligble, the prime minister has played a subsidiary, albeit increasing role, and the parliament has always had a fairly peripheral part to play on most issues. The presidential apparatus and government ministries have occupied the center of the stage. Formulating the national interest, and drawing up goals and strategies have been the work of government agencies, research institutes, and the mass media, rather than of the legislature. The president and his officials have made the important decisions and have fulfilled the task, with greater or lesser success, of coordinating and harmonizing policy.[10]

Relations among the institutions involved in foreign policy, and the balance of influence among them, have varied markedly over time. The elimination, splitting up, or general disarray of the main bureaucratic rivals in foreign policy–making in the aftermath of the August coup and the Soviet breakup led at first to a period of unprecedented dominance for the Foreign Ministry. All other agencies were supposed to obtain its endorsement of their international activities, and it enjoyed the direct patronage of Yeltsin's state secretary, Gennady Burbulis. By the middle of 1992, however, the Ministries of Defense and Security were regrouping, and, with the assistance of the Supreme Soviet, questioning the Foreign Ministry's role.[11] In May Yeltsin authorized the setting up of a Security Council inside his office. This body was meant to provide a point of access for a wider range of agencies and to prepare presidential decisions on matters of internal and external security, broadly defined, but it did not take on a general coordinating function in foreign relations.[12] In November, after a series of embarrassing failures of coordination, the key position of the Foreign Ministry was again confirmed by presidential decree:

> The Russian Foreign Ministry will be entrusted with the function of coordinating and monitoring work by other Russian ministries, committees and departments to ensure a unified political line by the Russian Federation in relations with foreign states. . . .[13]

However, by the following month Burbulis had lost his position as state secretary, and an Inter-departmental Foreign Policy Commission had been set up inside the Security Council to take on the coordinating function.[14] In general, by the end of 1992 the foreign minister was showing greater deference to other institutions, including his critics in parliament, and policy continued to evolve in a "centrist" direction over the following year. Throughout 1993 and early 1994 relations between the various agencies continued, however, to be dominated by the internal political struggle. I shall look in turn at the activities of the most important of these bodies.[15]

The President's Office

A decree issued in February 1992 made Yeltsin's state secretary, Gennady Burbulis, responsible for "operative leadership of the activity of the Foreign Ministry."[16] Although Burbulis chaired a number of temporary and permanent committees dedicated to particular foreign policy matters, such as the president's planned visit to Japan in June 1992, it became clear that rather than build up his own office, he intended to entrench the position of the Foreign Ministry as a center of expertise and coordination and to bolster the position of his liberal ally Andrei Kozyrev.[17]

More conservative figures such as Yury Petrov (chief of the president's staff until December 1992) and Yury Skokov (secretary of the Security Council and chair of its Foreign Policy Commission until May 1993) were also in a position, however, to influence foreign policy. Petrov was suspected by liberals of obstructing communications between Kozyrev and Yeltsin in the first part of 1992 and (through his chairmanship of the "Higher Certification Commission") of interfering with diplomatic appointments. Skokov was accused by them of playing the game of the Ministries of Defense and Security and of trying to cut the Foreign Ministry out of the policy process.[18]

The setting up of the Security Council failed to justify the worst fears of Kozyrev's supporters, however. It did seem ominous that Burbulis was not included. Members with a "deciding vote" were the chairman (the president), the vice-president, the prime minister (Yegor Gaidar, being only acting prime minister, did not automatically qualify), the deputy chairman of the Supreme Soviet, and the secretary. Members with a "consultative vote" might not necessarily attend all sessions; they included the ministers of defense, security, the interior, foreign affairs, justice, the economy, finance, health, and ecology and the head of the Foreign Intelligence Service (SVR).[19] The Council immediately went on the offensive against the Foreign Ministry over its supposed passivity in relations with the other former Soviet states, recommending the dismissal of Kozyrev and of the deputy minister responsible, Shelov-Kovedyaev, and the setting up of a separate ministry for CIS affairs. Although the latter suggestion was not taken up, Kozyrev was reportedly reprimanded and his deputy was removed from office.[20]

Initially the foreign minister was reluctant to criticize the new institution openly, maintaining that its task in the area of foreign policy was to ensure "horizontal coordination." After Skokov's removal from the post of secretary in the summer of 1993, however, he accused him of having tried to use the Security Council to resurrect party-style controls and to restrict policy in "a suffocating embrace."[21]

Yet in practice the Security Council's involvement in foreign policy was episodic: it discussed only a small selection of issues (the situations in Abkhazia, South Ossetia, and Trans-Dniester; Baltic troop withdrawals; and the visit to Japan).[22] Even formally, the Security Council's role was described as consultative, not decision-making: it was clear that Yeltsin had no intention of permitting the establishment of the "new Politburo" warned against by some. It turned out to be a mainly advisory body sustained by a relatively small staff, and estimates of its role continued to fluctuate.[23]

Skokov's dismissal from the job of Security Council secretary in May 1993 was reportedly precipitated by his failure to demonstrate sufficient solidarity with the president in his confrontation with the parliament in April. During the summer the status of the institution hung in the balance. For Dmitry Riurikov, the president's aide for international affairs and a former diplomat, the greatest problem was not lack of coordination (this already occurred, he claimed, inside the president's office and on a bilateral basis between the agencies concerned). What had to be avoided, in his opinion, was the emergence of over-powerful bodies on the model of the old Communist Party Central Committee departments, separating the president from the government—the Foreign Ministry, he argued in an interview in June 1993, "is precisely called upon to be the head agency in shaping foreign policy." Critics of the Foreign Ministry, in contrast, continued to push for the strengthening of an institution that formalized consultation with other bodies such as the Defense Ministry, the Foreign Intelligence Service, and the Supreme Soviet.[24]

In mid-June, following the disappearance of his post as commander in chief of the combined armed forces of the CIS, General Yevgeny Shaposhnikov was appointed secretary in Skokov's place, but he retired on August 10 amid talk of a wholesale reorganization of the Security Council. In September an influential member of Yeltsin's apparatus, Oleg Lobov, took over as Council secretary.

After the political crisis of autumn 1993, the institution entered a phase of expansion as Yeltsin tightened his personal control of all agencies concerned with national security. The permanent membership was widened and came to include the prime minister; the ministers of the interior, defense, justice, foreign affairs, and civil defense; and of the heads of the nationalities and regional policy state committee, of the foreign intelligence services, and federal counter-intelligence services. By mid-1994 it had expanded further to include the speakers of the two chambers of parliament and the commander in chief of the frontier troops. Its list of interdepartmental joint commissions extended to seven, most concerning "security" only in the very broadest sense. Although its apparatus had become more substantial and it was claimed that the Security Council was capable of generating a well-founded common view on key issues among the major bureaucracies and a shared strategic outlook, its very wide purview meant that it still tended to act in a fire-fighting mode, concentrating attention on the most pressing issue of the moment.[25]

The Inter-departmental Foreign Policy Commission was one of the first to be set up, on December 16, 1992. It was chaired by Yury Skokov and included the ministers of foreign affairs, defense, the interior, security, justice, foreign economic relations; the chief of the general staff; the head of the Foreign Intelligence Service; and others. It was given analytical and forecasting responsibilities and was required to coordinate the work of ministries; maintain communication among the Security Council, the Supreme Soviet, and the government; prepare draft decisions for the president on matters of external security; and examine proposals on military-political issues and foreign economic activity and adjust them to the foreign policy interests of the country.[26]

If the IFPC had been given the resources and the necessary powers, it could have become a real coordinating and controlling center for foreign policy, and by the end of 1992 there was certainly a widespread feeling in Moscow that such a body was required.[27] Yet it appears that it operated largely by setting up ad hoc working parties and task forces; in February 1993 its staff was only ten strong; by June 1993 it had had only one full session, in April, to approve the new "concept" of Russian foreign policy. It is worth noting that both the two men who are known to have occupied the post of chairman of the Security Council IFPC in the first half of 1994 were senior Foreign Ministry officials.[28]

It is arguable that much of the responsibility for the fragmentation of Russia's foreign policy lay with the top level of the executive arm. At first the major source of confusion appeared to be the activities of the vice-president, Alexander Rutskoi. He employed his own group of advisers and advanced a line often jarringly at odds with that of the Foreign Ministry, especially in regard to the former Soviet republics. In early 1992 he attracted attention by making inflammatory remarks about Crimea being part of Russia and implying a partisan, pro-Russian mission for the ostensibly peacekeeping forces in Moldova. He became the most senior spokesman for the opinions of powerful groups in the military, complicating the Foreign Ministry's task at every turn. It was not until after the constitutional crisis of March and April 1993 that Rutskoi was formally disowned by Yeltsin.

More serious in its effects in the long term was the style of action favored by the president himself. It appears that he repeatedly failed to consult with the Foreign Ministry, for example, over the recognition of Macedonia, the suspension of troop withdrawals from the Baltic states in October 1992, and the sanctioning of NATO expansion into Central-Eastern Europe during his visit to Warsaw and Prague in August 1993.[29] In general, Yeltsin seemed rather too ready to go along with diplomatically questionable Defense Ministry initiatives (see below) and to call off international meetings and visits (for example to Tokyo) at the last minute. Most damaging have been the lack of collegiality inside his administration, his method of maneuvering between rival factions, and his refusal to allow a stable framework of institutions and procedures to crystallize.[30]

The flux of organizational and personnel changes in and around the office of the Russian president has been so relentless since December 1991 that it would be difficult to justify a detailed description here. One positive effect of the luxuriant growth of the apparatus is that a variety of viewpoints and ideas have had a chance to make themselves felt, in however arbitrary a way. In particular, Yeltsin has maintained expert consultative groups (of which the most well known by 1994 was the "Presidential Council"[31]) and has appointed a string of "advisers" (in addition to his full-time aides, or "assistants"). Yeltsin's adviser on foreign policy matters after January 1992 was the senior diplomat Yuly Vorontsov. However, Vorontsov seems to have spent most of his time in New York, carrying out his duties as Russian ambassador to the United Nations.[32] As the irate testimony of a number of advisers demonstrates, their status was far from being a guarantee of access to the president.[33] Certain international affairs experts who are members of the Presidential Council are reputed to have had an influence on top-level foreign policy thinking, but not because of their membership in that rather ceremonial body.

There have been constant complaints about petty rivalries and intrigues, incompetence, and corruption in Yeltsin's inner circle.[34] After the inconclusive outcome of the December 1993 elections, the president seemed even less willing to give an energetic lead and to discipline his officials. While the wider effect of the election outcome was to intensify consensual trends in foreign policy (see below) as Yeltsin and Kozyrev redoubled their efforts to find common ground with the political "center," confusion and embarrassment surrounded the details of policy. Negotiations with NATO over the conditions on which Moscow might join its Partnership for Peace were hampered by contradictions between statements from the Foreign Ministry and the Defense Ministry on the one hand and from the president's office on the other. Relations with the Baltic states were set back when Yeltsin issued a document referring to the use of "military bases" in the CIS states "and Latvia" (Russia had recently managed, in sensitive talks, to reach agreement with Riga on continued use of a radar station only). The statement was later described as "a mistake." Andrei Kozyrev was reported as saying that after this episode "both diplomats and the military were left with their mouths hanging open."[35]

Viktor Chernomyrdin, prime minister and a possible successor to Yeltsin, gradually began to assume a more visible role in foreign policy matters. As early as August 1993 he attracted attention by taking up an uncompromising public position on the territorial dispute with Japan, declaring "Russia is not going to cede the Kurile Islands to anyone." In February 1994, *Izvestiia* drew attention to Chernomyrdin's distinctive stance on the conflict in Bosnia-Herzegovina, and in particular his opposition to NATO air strikes against Bosnian Serb forces. The prime minister became particularly closely involved in relations with other former Soviet states. When an acute and potentially dangerous crisis over Crimean separatism from Ukraine blew up in May 1994, negotiations between Kiev and Moscow were led by Chernomyrdin and his Ukrainian counterpart.[36]

The Foreign Ministry

At the beginning of 1992 the Foreign Ministry found itself in an unfamiliar position. Its Soviet predecessor had always occupied a relatively junior position in the foreign policy system: all the papers it produced, for instance, were subject to approval by the KGB, the Ministry of Defense, and the Communist Party Central Committee apparatus. Now, however, the security service had been split up, there was no defense ministry (till May 1992), and the CPSU had been abolished. In Burbulis's strategy the Foreign Ministry was to play a much more central role. "I would not like to talk about a 'monopoly' here," commented one deputy minister, ". . . because the president, of course, has his own advisers and so on, but we are the agency responsible both for working out the general foreign policy line and for planning concrete foreign policy actions."[37]

At the same time the focus and scope of foreign policy were changing: the demands of global competition with the West had receded, and the very complicated task had emerged of managing relations with fourteen other former Soviet states. There was little likelihood of resources being made available from the budget to support any substantial expansion of the Foreign Ministry. Kozyrev acted cautiously, making no serious attempt to turn his apparatus into a "super-ministry" controlling all aspects of foreign policy activity and moving slowly to develop the capacity to deal with the former Soviet "near abroad."

Inevitably the uncoordinated activity of different ministries led to a series of scandals in the foreign policy area. Although he himself was to a large extent responsible for the confusion, Yeltsin castigated Kozyrev for failing to keep things under control:

> As far as everything to do with the course of foreign policy was concerned, the [Soviet] Foreign Ministry cooperated with everyone, but did not let them interfere in matters that were the responsibility of the Foreign Ministry of the former Soviet Union. Now, however, everyone who feels like interfering does so, and all the Russian Foreign Ministry does is to shut itself up in its own diplomatic debates and visits.[38]

As we have seen, matters culminated in November and December 1992 with, first, a reasserting of the ministry's coordinating role, and, second, the formal transferring of this role to the Inter-departmental Foreign Policy Commission of the Security Council. Yet in practice the IFPC has turned out to be less important than was expected, and a good deal of what coordination does take place appears still to be centered in the Foreign Ministry.

In May 1992, Yeltsin announced that the Russian foreign service had "proved unprepared to deal with the CIS countries," and he criticized it yet again in November for failing to produce a "well-thought out, forward-looking policy towards the CIS countries."[39] Deputy Minister Shelov-Kovedyaev's resignation followed in July. Kozyrev succeeded, however, in retaining responsibility for this sphere inside his ministry and, after the initial damaging delay, moved to reallocate the necessary resources.

The slowness with which things changed is explainable in part by the unfavorable circumstances in which the new leadership of the Foreign Ministry had to operate. Most obviously, there was a severe shortage of funds. Thirty-six embassies and consulates were closed between 1991 and the start of 1993. Over 2,000 staff were shed when the old Soviet ministry was absorbed into the Russian one: approximately 3,200 were left by autumn 1992.[40] The older generation was demoralized and antagonized by the new minister's uncompromising pro-Western line, his confident style, and his appointing of a string of younger individuals to the posts of deputy minister and head of department—the average age of ministers and deputy ministers dropped to forty-six in 1992.[41] After a wave of unrest and criticism of their alleged "unprofessionalism" in the first part of 1992, however, Kozyrev and his colleagues appear to have succeeded in establishing their authority, and even some respect, among subordinates.

At first a lot of attention was absorbed by overall organizational changes, which no doubt served both functional and political ends. An extra tier—"department" (*departament*)—was added above the existing "administrations" (*upravlenie*) and "sections" (*otdel*). The Analysis and Forecasting Administration was rejuvenated and strengthened and reported directly to the minister. In 1994 it became part of the ministry's Executive Secretariat. New departments were set up to deal with economic relations, scientific cooperation, and other areas previously outside the ministry's sphere.

A Department for the CIS Countries was established in March 1992, but the decree setting up embassies in the capitals of the "near abroad" was issued only in September, and the whole operation was scantily funded.[42] The department had an Administration for CIS Affairs (multilateral) and an Administration for the Community Countries (for bilateral relations). It experienced enormous problems in attracting staff, especially high-quality staff with specialized knowledge of the countries concerned. Even those other departments that could offer substantial hard-currency salaries had difficulty in retaining talented younger employees. Bilateral relations with CIS states are now handled in the framework of departments that deal with adjacent European or Asian countries (i.e., cutting across the "near abroad/far abroad" boundary so emphasized by centrists and conservatives).[43]

The Foreign Ministry's role in respect to the other former Soviet republics has been complicated by the multidimensionality of relations. Many other agencies are involved, dealing with the dense network of economic, social, and cultural interactions with neighboring states. To improve coordination of intra-CIS relations, the ministry set up and led over a dozen inter-agency "state delegations" at deputy-minister level focussing on particular issues. They met regularly with their counterparts in other former Soviet republics (except in the case of Ukraine). There was also a small number of "conflict delegations" formed jointly by two countries (for example, Russia and Moldova) and a special group was set up for Tajikistan.

During the second half of 1993 and into 1994 as the new, more active policies toward the former Soviet states began to bear fruit, attempts were made to strengthen the framework of multilateral CIS institutions, for example, at the parliamentary level and in the areas of defense and economic cooperation. If this system thrives, the outcome will no doubt be a greater role in CIS affairs for specialized ministries of the Russian Federation and a diminution of Foreign Ministry control, but the future of the CIS and its institutions is still unclear. In January 1994 a new Ministry of Cooperation with the CIS States was established. It is led by Vladimir Mashchits and appears to have responsibility mainly for economic relations (it was initially set up, on the basis of an existing state committee, under the supervision of Economics Minister Alexander Shokhin). In May this ministry set up a body with the task of coordinating Moscow's dealings with CIS consultative organizations. It included representatives of the Central Bank of Russia and directors of a number of large state-owned and private companies.[44]

In the middle of 1992 the Foreign Ministry had faced a dangerous situation. Its policies and its leadership were closely identified with the liberal wing of Russian politics, which was beginning to come under determined attack from the political "center" and from the conservative opposition. Worse, it was struggling to cope with huge new responsibilities in the areas of foreign policy coordination and of relations with the newly independent states; it had neither the experience, the political weight, nor the resources to exercise these responsibilities effectively. Kozyrev's survival in office in 1993 and 1994, and the continuing powers of the ministry in international policy matters, are probably best explained by three main factors. The first is the president's continued support, despite all his public criticisms and disruptive interventions; he was no doubt well aware of the necessity of continuing to present an acceptable face to the West. The second is the disproportionate share of expertise on foreign affairs, especially outside the former Soviet Union, that the ministry has at its disposal. The third is undoubtedly Kozyrev's sensitivity to domestic political pressures and his flexibility in adjusting policy to cater to them. These qualities have been well demonstrated in the ministry's relations with the other main institutions involved in foreign policy.

The Ministry of Defense

The Ministry of Defense of the Russian Federation was formally reestablished in March 1992, with President Yeltsin fulfilling the role of minister. In May he was replaced by General Pavel Grachev. From that moment the ministry appeared to be engaged in a determined struggle to recapture the influential position in foreign policy matters occupied by its Soviet predecessor. Although in the new regime its approval was formally required for any decisions affecting its sphere of competence and its representatives were routinely included in delegations dealing with arms control and defense matters, there was a strong sense that its views were being ignored and that options for the future were being foreclosed. At the end of 1992 the military newspaper *Krasnaia zvezda* complained, "We do not have a procedure for inter-agency consultation prior to the taking of foreign policy decisions. That is *prior to*, and not *after* the decisions have been made."[45]

It was not just changes in the process of foreign policy–making that antagonized the military: the whole course of Moscow's policies over recent years cut against the grain of its training and its view of Russia's place in the world. Most difficult to accept was the breakup of the Soviet Union. Only months after his appointment, General Grachev was already posing as the defender of the 25 million Russians living outside the boundaries of the Russian Federation, declaring himself ready to fight for "the honor and dignity of the Russian population" in any part of the former USSR.[46]

As numerous statements of this kind, made not only by officials but even by uniformed officers, demonstrate, the Russian armed forces have shown little reluctance to comment publicly on foreign policy issues. They have also not been slow to act directly to forward their own foreign policy goals. Disorder and conflict in the former Soviet area, often in zones considered strategically significant or inhabited by large numbers of Russian speakers, have created numerous opportunities. As one British expert concludes, "The scale, intrusiveness and partisan character of Russian military activity in the near abroad has significantly increased the role of the Russian military command in foreign policy decision-making."[47]

Underlying all this was the radical change that had taken place in civil-military relations. Soviet-era controls and supervisory agencies had been eroded, but no authoritative civilian institutions and conventions about the limits on military involvement in political matters had emerged to take their place. At times, as in the spring and autumn of 1993, the armed forces came under pressure to act to resolve the political stalemate between president and parliament. Civilian leaders from Yeltsin to Rutskoi and Zhirinovsky made transparent bids for military support.

Political discipline inside the armed forces was weak. A variety of groups were at work among the officer corps. During 1992 activists in the "Officers' Assemblies" acted in tacit concert with the leaders of expatriate Russian communities and with reactionary opposition groups in Moscow. In general neither the Ministry of Defense nor the president seems to have been willing to exercise much restraint over overzealous or even frankly insubordinate generals in distant trouble spots.

Thus General Lebed, commander of the 14th Army, supposedly sent to Moldova in the summer of 1992 on a peacekeeping mission, outraged Chisinau with his partisan statements about the "fascist" character of the Moldovan government and about his understanding of his task as one of defending the Russian-speaking population of the country. Not only did he stay in post, but he was promoted later in the year.[48] This was the first, and perhaps the most blatant, case of Russia making military interventions elsewhere in the CIS with formal consent from but with scant regard to the preferences of the governments concerned. In 1993 it became clear that resistance to Georgian rule in the rebel province of Abkhazia was being substantially bolstered by help from local Russian commanders.

This kind of behavior at first provoked an understandably strong reaction from the Foreign Ministry: "The party of war, the party of neo-bolshevism, is rearing its head in our country," declared Kozyrev, and he called for a thorough restructuring of the military and the former KGB. "Wholesale transfers of arms are taking place in the Transcaucasus and Moldova," he complained. ". . . Under what agreement is this effected, I would like to ask . . .? Why are the military deciding the most important political issues?"[49] Such protests, however, appeared to have little effect. In early September 1992, for example, the Russian and Lithuanian military authorities reached agreement on a timetable for Russian troop withdrawals. The Foreign Ministry "received the agreement a mere two days before it was to be signed and was physically unable to make the necessary amendments." A few weeks later the Ministry of Defense announced that withdrawals would be suspended in the case of those units for which suitable accommodation was not ready on Russian territory. Then on October 29, Yeltsin signed a directive stopping the withdrawal. Foreign Ministry officials claimed not to have been consulted about this move either.[50] There was friction, too, over the leading part played by the Ministry of Defense in initiating peacekeeping operations in Tajikistan and over its refusal to go along with plans to withdraw troops from the Kurile Islands.

It would be misleading to interpret all this as a straightforward running battle between hawkish soldiers and doveish diplomats to influence foreign policy. For example, a lot of what happened in 1992 was part of a wider struggle in Russian politics to discredit Kozyrev and the other liberals. As the balance shifted in favor of the political "center" and Yeltsin repeatedly deferred to pressures from the military for a more active policy in the CIS, the leadership of the Foreign Ministry evidently decided to take the path of compromise. Toward the end of 1992 Foreign Ministry spokesmen began to use a more conciliatory tone about the military. In May 1993 senior officials from both ministries held a joint meeting to discuss international peacekeeping operations.[51]

During 1993, especially after the announcement of agreement in Moscow on a new Concept of Russian Foreign Policy (see below), it became clear that despite continuing frictions and differences of opinion, the gears of the foreign policy machine were beginning to mesh more smoothly than before. The Foreign Ministry continued to insist on adherence to international law in relations with the other former Soviet republics and to warn against the danger of provoking a nationalist reaction among their leaders; but it had accepted the goal of establishing Russia as the dominant power in the "near abroad," and this meant that its diplomatic activities pushed in the same direction as the more concrete pressures applied directly or indirectly by the Russian military. This was well demonstrated in the months that led up to the consolidation of the CIS at the end of 1993. In some cases, indeed, the appearance of differences between the two agencies may have been illusory, more an effect of the natural division of labor. The armed forces, after all, were given the job of acting on the ground in parts of the world where conflict was becoming endemic and where little short of the application of military might could achieve results; the Foreign Ministry had the task of smoothing the process of establishing Russia's dominance in the CIS while preserving good relations with the West.[52]

Yeltsin's use of the army to crush resistance from the remnants of the Supreme Soviet in October 1993 and the ultranationalist Zhirinovsky's successes in the subsequent elections helped to aggravate further the problem of civilian control of Russia's foreign policy. The leadership's dependence on the military had become even more transparent. It emerged that an alarmingly high proportion of army officers had voted for Zhirinovsky's Liberal-Democratic Party. The new parliament contained many supporters of the muscular line that the military had been following in the former Soviet states. At the same time, internal divisions in the armed forces became more evident as the weakening of civilian authority undermined the authority of the minister of defense over his subordinates.[53]

The Legislature

The Russian legislature has been vocal on foreign policy matters, but its involvement in foreign policy–making has been of a different order than that of the executive agencies just discussed. Like its counterparts in other states, it has been obliged to operate mainly in public with only a small professional staff and with expertise on foreign affairs relatively thinly spread among its members. Deputies' primary interests relate to domestic politics.

Although actions in the Supreme Soviet and subsequently in the Federal Assembly are acknowledged by members of the executive arm to have had tangible effects on policy in particular cases, these bodies' interventions have been sporadic. They have tended to center on a limited number of issues (especially ones perceived to be likely to have a wider resonance with public opinion).[54] The legislature has provided a forum in which disgruntled members of the executive can indirectly express their dissatisfaction with existing policy and mobilize opposition to it. When the political temperature has risen, foreign policy issues have been exploited in order to belabor Yeltsin and to try to displace Kozyrev from the government. In calmer moments the parliament has been used by foreign policy officials as a sounding board of elite opinion.

According to the constitution in force in 1992 and 1993, the legislature ("the supreme organ of state power") had the right to pass resolutions binding on the Foreign Ministry (such a resolution was passed on December 18, 1992, obliging the minister to vote against any UN Security Council decision to undertake an armed intervention in Bosnia-Herzegovina).[55] Its committees for international affairs and foreign economic relations, and for defense and security, could make recommendations that had to be "considered" by relevant government agencies, which were required to deliver a report delivered to parliament within a fixed period.

In the early months of 1992 the leaders of the Supreme Soviet kept a low profile on international issues, describing their role in this area as primarily consultative:

> The foreign policy of the country is determined primarily by the president. We support the foreign policy of our president. However the Supreme

Soviet has the duty of making a significant contribution to the state's foreign policy and of exercising effective democratic control over the activity of those agencies responsible for carrying out that policy, where necessary introducing adjustments, and expressing an opinion about particular diplomatic actions or the absence of such actions.[56]

Yet even then signs of future trouble were beginning to appear. The International Affairs Committee, chaired by Vladimir Lukin, began to develop what was described as a Russian Monroe Doctrine, categorizing the whole former Soviet area as a zone of Russia's vital interests and predominant influence.[57] In February tension between Moscow and Kiev increased when the deputies passed a resolution calling on the executive to take sole control of the disputed Black Sea Fleet and to review the constitutionality of Khrushchev's transfer of Crimea to Ukraine in 1954. Already in April, Yevgeny Ambartsumov, Lukin's successor, was criticizing the Foreign Ministry for neglecting CIS concerns and especially the plight of Russian speakers in Moldova.[58] Subsequently, as relations between the legislature and the executive worsened and as "centrist" and "demo-patriotic" criticism of the liberals and their foreign policies grew, parliament became more assertive. An early triumph was to bring about, with the help of allies in the president's office, the cancellation of Yeltsin's visit to Japan in September.

Ambartsumov reacted sharply to Russia's vote in the United Nations in favor of sanctions against Yugoslavia in June 1992. The government, he said, was kowtowing to Washington and ignoring the national interest.[59] He subsequently launched his own diplomatic initiative, visiting Belgrade in order to try to arrange a meeting between Yeltsin and local leaders. Kozyrev responded by inviting the committee chairman to join him in the Russian delegation to the London Conference on Yugoslavia at the end of August. This turned out to be an astute move. Ambartsumov later spoke approvingly of the Foreign Ministry's conduct during the talks, in particular complementing Deputy Minister Churkin on his professionalism. Russian policy, he declared, had become "more adequate."[60] Indeed, Moscow's line did harden somewhat at the end of the year as the Foreign Ministry resisted proposals for armed intervention in Bosnia-Herzegovina. Ambartsumov laid the credit for this change at the door of the Supreme Soviet.[61]

By the autumn of 1992 the Foreign Ministry had begun to trim its rhetoric and its actions in a fairly consistent and determined way in order to suit the requirements of the political climate in Moscow. Contacts between ministry officials and members of the Foreign Affairs Committee became more frequent. Deputy ministers and department heads more often attended sessions in person and explained their policies to members.[62]

This turn became evident in an overall shift to greater assertiveness and in a slight cooling of relations with the West in Russian foreign policy at the beginning of 1993. At the end of January, after returning from India, President Yeltsin stated, "The recent series of state visits to South Korea, China and now to India are indicative of the fact that we are moving away from the Western emphasis." In February Yeltsin himself proposed the adoption of a Russian Monroe Doctrine covering the former Soviet states.[63] As the year proceeded, the contours of Moscow's new, less conciliatory foreign policy line became clearer in territorial negotiations with Japan, in talks over conflict resolution in the former Yugoslavia, in arms export policy, in the negotiations for a partnership and cooperation agreement with the European Community, in attitudes toward the expansion of NATO to the east, and, most strikingly, in behavior in the former Soviet area.

Despite Ambartsumov's claim that pressure from parliament was responsible for moderating what he called foreign ministry "utopianism," it is clear that no such simple explanation will do. A number of factors were at work:

1. During 1992 a lengthy debate had been going on among foreign policy specialists concerning the nature of the new Russia's "national interests." This helped to build wider agreement on the country's place in the world and the appropriate hierarchy of priorities in its foreign policy, based on a much more "realist" view of international relations than had prevailed during the dominance of new political thinking. The Ministry of Foreign Affairs was by no means isolated from this evolution of thinking.

2. The passage of time played an important part. The initial euphoria about "joining the West" had faded. The international community had accepted that "democratic" Russia had broken with its Soviet past. It was time now to turn to practical matters, in particular to limiting the damage caused by the fragmentation of the USSR. It was also possible to bargain harder with the West.[64]

3. Parallel to these developments, changes were occurring in internal politics. Yeltsin was being forced to seek an accommodation with the political "center" and elements in the military. Both favored a much more active policy in the CIS, that was designed to preserve or recreate as much as possible of the preexisting single economic and strategic space.

Insofar as the parliament created formal channels of contact on such matters, it played an important part, of course. Yet it must be said that in 1992 and 1993 the Supreme Soviet's interventions in foreign policy were highly selective, and it would seem they were motivated above all by a desire to cause embarrassment to the government. Thus the Supreme Soviet focussed almost exclusively on issues such as the "loss" of the Black Sea Fleet and Crimea to Ukraine, the "plight" of Russian speakers outside Russia, the "giving away" of Russian territory to Japan, and the "betrayal" of Russia's Orthodox brother Serbs.

Indeed, as 1993 proceeded, it could be argued that, because of its increasingly bitter rivalry with the executive arm and because of its internal fragmentation and amateurishness, the Russian Supreme Soviet played a more destructive than constructive part. Despite loud warnings from the Foreign Ministry, resolutions were often framed that had a disruptive and inflammatory effect, especially on relations with Ukraine. One of the most damaging was the one passed in July 1993, which declared the Ukrainian port and home of the Black Sea Fleet, Sevastopol, to be "a Russian city."[65]

Such events prompted one eminent Russian international affairs specialist to complain in July 1993, "Russia not only creates opportunities for the external world to exploit its internal political contradictions, but actually suggests that it do just that."[66] Visits by parliamentary delegations to Yugoslavia and Iraq, for example, did not always appear to go with the grain of Foreign Ministry policy. In addition, the process of ratifying treaties was dragged out, committee hearings appeared to be designed to discredit official policy, and overtly hostile institutional innovations were made, such as the setting up of a legislative oversight committee in August 1993 "to study and make a thorough appraisal of the activities of the Russian Federation's Foreign Affairs Ministry."[67]

The overall effect was to introduce elements of uncertainty and to create uneasiness abroad, for example, in regard to Moscow's policy in the former Yugoslavia. In Belgrade in June 1993, for example, Ambartsumov was eloquent about Russia's support for Serbia and, on his return to Moscow, spoke out strongly against any reinforcing of UN economic sanctions, announcing that Russia would use its veto power in the Security Council to block any military intervention against the Bosnian Serb forces. When this position was denied by Deputy Foreign Minister Churkin, Ambartsumov proceeded to push through the Supreme Soviet a resolution that warned that military intervention in Bosnia-Herzegovina could lead to "a continuation of the conflict and possibly a new European war."[68]

As has been noted, the new constitution in force in 1994 enshrines the president's dominance in foreign policy–making, and there has been an overall shift in power toward the executive that guarantees, at least for the time being, that the new Federal Assembly is unlikely to try to exercise what powers it does have in a disruptive way. However the fresh endorsement that the legislature received from the electorate at the end of 1993 and the swing in public opinion away from the Western-oriented reformism, which the elections appeared to demonstrate, gave confidence to critics of Foreign Ministry liberalism. Vladimir Lukin's return from his post as ambassador in Washington to the chairmanship of the International Affairs Committee of the State Duma (the lower house), now as one of the leaders of an important faction of deputies, lent authority to that body's statements on foreign affairs.

In any case neither side seemed willing, in the first half of 1994, to engage in a new trial of strength. The speaker of the Council of the Federation (the upper house) announced that his views on Russian foreign policy coincided "98 per cent" with those of the foreign minister and that his colleagues would give him their full support.[69] Asked by a journalist in April whether the Duma should exploit its treaty-ratifying prerogative to express disapproval of government policy, Lukin responded that such an approach would be altogether unwise and that deputies and officials should work together to develop a single foreign policy:

> A consensus is taking shape . . . , which makes me very happy because foreign policy should be at minimum based on a broad consensus. . . . Why were we able to play a serious role in Yugoslavia? Because of consensus. The Duma, which is an indicator of public opinion, supported the government's line and at the same time strengthened its determination to pursue this particular line. . . .[70]

In 1994 Kozyrev and Yeltsin appeared to intensify their bridge-building with internal critics, even at the cost of a certain cooling of relations with the West and with some of the other former Soviet states.[71] Russia's dominance in the CIS was asserted even more vigorously. Moscow (unsuccessfully) demanded recognition of its special security role in the region as a condition for adhering to NATO's Partnership for Peace and resisted military intervention by NATO in Bosnia-Herzegovina.

The foreign minister now began to attract criticism from the liberals.[72] Yeltsin, too, came under fire for failing to resist pressure from nationalist elements. His decision in May 1994, for example, to postpone long-planned joint U.S.-Russian military exercises in the Urals region was contrary to the preferences of his own minister of defense and was lamented by the chairman of the Duma's Defense Committee as "evidence of the weakness of the Presidency."[73]

Conclusion

In the first part of this chapter I emphasized how difficult the USSR legacy was Russian foreign policy–makers. I pointed in particular to the problems caused by the dismantling of the powerful coordinating and political control system operated by the Communist Party in a situation where there was little respect for institutional rights and regular procedures and where political preferences were becoming sharply polarized. A new state had to be built on new principles, and a framework for considering new policies had to be hammered out before one could even begin to speak of anything resembling a coherent "Russian foreign policy."

The record since 1991 has been mixed. Russia possesses the undoubted asset of a body of highly trained and experienced Foreign Ministry staff. However, if we look at foreign policy–making more widely, the picture is discouraging. Few would claim that impressive advances have been made toward developing a stable and respected legal and institutional order. The distribution of responsibilities and prerogativesamong agencies is still far from clear; decisions are often uncoordinated and ill-prepared and once made may very well be ignored or contradicted. There is still a damaging shortage of Huntington's "legitimacy" and "organization."

There is evidence, in contrast of some progress in building "consensus" and "community" in the circle of those engaged in foreign policy matters. Negotiations between institutions and political groupings have generated movement in the direction of a common view among the relevant elites on the broad lines of foreign policy, and polarization, which was acute in 1991 and 1992, seems to have declined.

The striking thing is that the experience of 1992–1994 has not been worse than it has. For all the destructiveness of the political battles between the Yeltsin administration and its opponents, they do seem to have taught the necessity of reaching for agreements with political rivals and to have fostered practices of negotiation and compromise.

There has also been some institutional development and there have been changes of procedure intended to improve coordination and coherence of policy. Examples are the setting up of the Security Council and its Inter-departmental Foreign Policy Commission, the establishment of the Ministry for Cooperation with the CIS and its coordinating unit, and the growth of a thicker network of interaction between the legislature and the Foreign Ministry.

The community of independent research institutes and foreign policy thinktanks has widened, and efforts have been made to reach a common view on Russian national interests. Here the activity of the Council on

Foreign and Defense Policy has been important insofar as it has tried to represent as wide a spread of moderate liberal and centrist opinion (civilian and military) as possible.[74] It is instructive to compare the council's "Strategy for Russia," published in August 1992, with the Foreign Ministry's "Concept" of Russian Foreign Policy of January 1993 and the version of the "Concept" approved by the Security Council IFPC and the president in April 1993 and to observe the convergence that had taken place, if only at the level of rhetoric.[75] The revised "Strategy for Russia" published by the council in May 1994 expressed an even closer harmony of views.[76]

The importance of such documents should not be exaggerated. Their appearance does not signify that the actors involved have abandoned all their differences and intend to stick faithfully in future to a commonly agreed line. But the willingness to sign them does reflect an acceptance of the need for compromise, and conceivably some degree of a genuine coming together of views among broad sections of the Russian political class. This is by no means a sufficient condition for the building of an effective foreign policy mechanism, but it is a vitally necessary one.

Notes

This chapter is based on research carried out as part of an RIIA project investigating new domestic factors in the foreign policies of Russia, Ukraine, and Kazakhstan and supported by the Fritz Thyssen Stiftung.

1. The concept of "political decay" is taken from S. Huntington, *Political Order in Changing Societies*, Yale, Yale University Press, 1968. Jack Snyder ("Averting Anarchy in the New Europe," *International Security*, vol. 14, no. 4, pp. 5-41) proposed three possible models of development for Russia and the rest of Eastern Europe—civic-democratic, praetorian (Huntington's term in *Political Order in Changing Societies*, pp. 79-80), and democratic corporatist. He compared the Soviet Union in its last years to Wilhelmine Germany, with its truncated democracy and mobilization of heavy-industry workers and managers, the military, the CPSU apparatus, nationalists and ethnic minorities, and suggested a "praetorian" outcome was possible there, entailing protectionism and militarism in foreign policy.

2. F. Holzman, R. Legvold, "The Economics and Politics of East-West Relations," in E. Hoffmann, F. Fleron, eds., *The Conduct of Soviet Foreign Policy*, New York, Aldine, 1980, p. 455.

3. The term was used by Graham Allison in his "Conceptual Models and the Cuban Missile Crisis," *American Political Science Review*, vol. 63, no. 3, 1969, p. 700. Soviet officials called again and again for the overcoming of "departmentalism." For Western views see J. Valenta, *Soviet Intervention in Czechoslovakia, 1968: Anatomy of a Decision*, London, Johns Hopkins University Press, 1979, p. 34; T. Gustafson, *Reform in Soviet Politics: Lessons of Recent Policies on Land and Water*, Cambridge, Cambridge University Press, 1981, pp. 93–4.

4. A. Ulam, "Anatomy of Policymaking," *The Washington Quarterly*, vol. 6, no. 2, 1983, pp. 72–3; J. Hough, *Soviet Leadership in Transition*, Washington, D.C., Brookings Institution, 1980, pp. 109–10; R. Kitrinos, "The CPSU Central Committee's International Department," *Problems of Communism*, vol. 33, no. 5, 1984, pp. 47–65; M. Kramer, "The Role of the CPSU International Department in Soviet Foreign Relations and National Security Policy," *Soviet Studies*, vol. 42, no. 3, 1990, pp. 429–46; J. Hough, "Soviet Policymaking Towards Foreign Communists," *Studies in Comparative Communism*, vol. 15, no. 3, 1982, pp. 166–83. Kitrinos claims a bigger role for the International Department apparatus in preparing Politburo foreign policy decisions than do other authors.

5. G. Breslauer, *Khrushchev and Brezhnev as Leaders*, London, Allen and Unwin, 1982; A. Brown, "The Power of the General Secretary of the CPSU," in T. Rigby, A. Brown, P. Reddaway, eds., *Authority, Power and Policy in the USSR*, London, Macmillan, 1980; H. Gelman, *The Brezhnev Politburo and the Decline of Detente*, London, Cornell University Press, 1983; C. Linden, *Khrushchev and the Soviet Leadership*, London, Johns Hopkins University Press, 1990.

6. For some illustrations see N. Malcolm, "Soviet Decision-making and the Middle East," in P. Shearman, P. Williams, eds., *The Superpowers, Central America and the Middle East*, London, Brassey's, 1988, pp. 90–104.

7. A. Pravda, "The Politics of Foreign Policy," in S. White, A. Pravda, Z. Gitelman, eds., *Developments in Soviet and Post-Soviet Politics*, London, Macmillan, 1992, pp. 259–60; G. Smith, *Soviet Politics: Struggling with Change*, London, Macmillan, 1992, pp. 316–7; Kramer, "The CPSU International Department," pp. 43–48.

8. Jeffrey Checkel cites a report that at this time "relations between two of the primary contestants—the Ministries of Defense and Foreign Affairs—had become so bad that at many high-level meetings representatives of the two institutions would not even address each other." "Russian Foreign Policy: Back to the Future?" *RFE/RL Research Report*, October 16, 1992, p. 22. Similar stories were told about the relationship between Gromyko and Grechko. On the making of policy toward Central-Eastern and South-Eastern Europe at this time, see the chapters by Hannes Adomeit and Alex Pravda in N. Malcolm, ed., *Russia and Europe: An End to Confrontation?*, London, Frances Pinter, 1993. One example of Ministry of Defense assertiveness was the shifting of military equipment east of the Urals to evade the provisions of the CFE disarmament agreement.

9. Huntington, *Political Order in Changing Societies*, p. 1.

10. For much of the material in this and the following sections I am indebted to Yury Fedorov, Moscow State Institute of International Relations (MGIMO). Much of the other material was gathered through interviews with British and Russian officials in London and Moscow during 1992 and 1993. Where there is no indication of a source, data has been taken from one of these interviews.

11. According to *Nezavisimaia gazeta*, July 31, 1992, officials in these two ministries were stating that they "refused to cooperate with the Foreign Ministry under the current Minister," Cited by Suzanne Crow, *The Making of Foreign Policy in Russia under Yeltsin*, Munich, Radio Free Europe/Radio Liberty, 1993, p. 72.

12. The Security Council was explicitly copied from the U.S. model.

13. *Rossiiskaia gazeta*, November 18, 1992. Decree signed on November 3.

14. *Nezavisimaia gazeta*, January 29, 1993; *Rossiiskaia gazeta*, February 3, 1993.

15. For reasons of space, and in some cases for reasons of shortage of data, important agencies in the area of foreign trade and intelligence are not covered, nor is the role of foreign policy research institutes and pressure groups discussed in detail.

16. *Diplomaticheskii vestnik*, no. 6, 1992, p. 16; *Rossiiskaia gazeta*, February 27, 1992.

17. *Rossiiskaia gazeta*, August 24, 1992; S. Semendaev in *Rossiiskaia gazeta*, January 17, 1992. See Checkel, "Russian Foreign Policy: Back to the Future?" pp. 19–20. Burbulis was the central figure in the Presidential Council founded in 1990, in the Presidential Consultative Council, which replaced it in 1991, and in the State Council. When the latter was abolished in May 1992 and Burbulis retired from the position of deputy prime minister, he was appointed "the representative of the president in the legislature, the executive and the judicial organs of power." *Rossiiskie vesti*, May 29, 1992. He remained state secretary to the president until October (*Moskovskie novosti*, no. 51/52, 1992), and he was head of the group of consultants at the president's office until December. *Rossiiskaia gazeta*, December 18, 1992; *Moskovskie novosti*, no. 9, 1993; V. Yasmann, "The Russian Civil Service: Corruption and Reform," *RFE/RL Research Report*, April 16, 1993, p. 19. It was reported in March 1993 that Burbulis was still "sitting in the Kremlin."

18. This section draws on information supplied by Vladimir Orlov (*Moscow News*). See, too, Gleb Yakunin reported by Interfax, December 17, 1992; *Sobesednik*, no. 32, 1992, p. 2; and Kozyrev's view that enemies of reform were "trying to encircle the Russian president" and "dictate policy to him" (both cited by Crow, *The Making of Foreign Policy*, pp. 32–3). Also see V. Orlov in *Moscow News*, 1993, no. 7.

19. By early 1993 the full voting members included Sergei Shakhrai, chairman of the Security Council Commission on the North Caucasus, and Yury Nazarkin, deputy chairman of the Security Council and head of its Department of Strategic Security. After the first deputy chairman of the parliament (Filatov) had been transferred to head Yeltsin's office, it was not clear whether he remained on the Security Council. Meanwhile the parliament passed a resolution stating that its chairman (Khasbulatov) or his nominee should sit on the council. Crow, *The Making of Foreign Policy*, pp. 13–16. For a substantial account of the first months of the Security Council's work, see E. Jones, J. H. Brusstar, "Moscow's Emerging Security Decision-making System: The Role of the Security Council," *Journal of Slavic Military Studies*, vol. 6, no. 3, September 1993, pp. 345–74.

20. *Rossiiskaia gazeta*, August 8, 1992; *Nezavisimaia gazeta*, July 31, 1992; *Nezavisimaia gazeta*, October 15, 1992.

21. NBC Television, "Meet the Press," January 3; *Vek*, May 14–21, 1993. See A. Rahr, "Yeltsin's New Team," *RFE/RL Research Report*, May 28, 1993, p. 19; Crow, *The Making of Foreign Policy*, pp. 33, 37.

22. *Rossiiskie vesti*, August 13, 1992; *Rossiiskaia gazeta*, September 10, 1992.

23. For contrasting liberal views on the threat posed by the Security Council, see the articles previously cited by Vladimir Orlov (and his piece in *Moscow News*,

1993, no. 20) and *Izvestiia*, December 18, 1992. See also *Rossiiskie vesti*, December 19, 1992, p. 1. The initial staff ceiling was 80. Jones, Brusstar, "Moscow's Emerging Security Decision-making System," p. 365.

24. "Yeltsin's Line: Who Shapes It and How?" *Moscow News*, no. 25, 1993, p. 3.

25. *Moscow News*, no. 39, 1993, p. 3; S. Foye, "Russia's Defense Establishment in Disarray," *RFE/RL Research Report*, October 10, 1993, pp. 52–3; V. Yasmann, "Security Services Reorganized," *RFE/RL Research Report*, February 11, 1994, pp. 7–11; "Key Officials in the Russian Federation: Executive Branch," *RFE/RL Research Report*, March 4, 1994; "The Security Council Without a Security Classification," *Moscow News*, no. 23, 1994, p. 2 (an interview with Deputy Secretary Lieutenant-General Valery Manilov). The Joint Commissions were devoted to combatting crime and corruption and to defense security, ecological safety, economic security, information security, scientific and technical questions of the defense industry, and foreign policy.

26. *Nezavisimaia gazeta*, January 29, 1993; *Rossiiskaia gazeta*, February 3, 1993.

27. Crow, *The Making of Foreign Policy*, pp. 71–2, cites a number of views. Interfax, November 26, 1992, quoted a Ministry of Defense official as saying, "The Foreign Ministry is not an agency capable of controlling the international activity of Russian ministries and departments." It also quoted an employee of the Ministry of Foreign Economic Relations: "The Foreign Ministry cannot do its own work, let alone the coordination of international activity for other ministries." On December 18, it reported a Foreign Ministry official saying, "Our ministry lacks the necessary powers to overcome inter-departmental conflicts."

28. Ednan Agaev, head of the Analysis and Forecasting Administration, and First Deputy Minister Anatoly Adamishin. V. Yasmann, "Security Services Reorganized," *RFE/RL Research Report*, February 11, 1994, p. 10; "Andrei Kozyrev's Trojan Horse," *Inside Russia and the CIS*, European Press Agency bulletin, March 1994, p. 1. A. Rahr, "Yeltsin and the New Elections," *RFE/RL Research Report*, August 22, 1993, p. 4, concluded that the Security Council appeared "to have lost its decision-making role in Russian politics."

29. *Gazeta Wyborcza*, August 20, 1993. The dissonance with the Foreign Ministry is examined by J. B. de Weydenthal in "Russia Mends Fences with Poland, the Czech Republic and Slovakia," *RFE/RL Research Report*, September 10, 1993, p. 34.

30. One official interviewed who has observed Russian foreign policy-making at close quarters notes that there is nothing approaching a standard procedure for making decisions: above ministry level there is "complete turmoil."

31. The current membership is given in "Key Officials in the Russian Federation: Executive Branch," *RFE/RL Research Report*, March 4, 1994.

32. *Diplomaticheskii vestnik*, no. 6, 1992, p. 16; *Moscow News*, no. 32, 1992, p. 14; *Rossiiskie vesti*, August 13, 1992. Yeltsin's full-time aide for foreign policy, former middle-ranking diplomat Dimitry Ryurikov, has a relatively small staff.

33. Mikhail Malei, adviser on conversion of military industry, claimed that he tried in vain for three months to see Yeltsin. *Komsomolskaia pravda*, September 17, 1993 ("I don't want to be the adviser of someone I see only on television," he

complained). Malei repeated the comment made to him by Sergei Filatov, head of the president's administration, that as a rule "Yeltsin only receives three people."

34. Former Minister of Justice Nikolai Fedorov made a particularly scathing attack on the "talented imitators and conjurors" and the cynical careerists at work in the president's entourage. See, too, A. Rahr, "Yeltsin and the New Elections," *RFE/RL Research Report*, August 27, 1993; S. Blagovolin, "Who Stands to Gain from the Mess in the Power Structure?" *Moscow News*, no. 15, 1994, p. 5; "The New Kremlinology," *Inside Russia and the CIS* (European Press Agency), March 1994, pp. 7–8.

35. *The New York Times*, April 7, 1994. Cited in A. Rahr, "Russia's Future: With or Without Yeltsin," *RFE/RL Research Report*, April 29, 1994.

36. *Moscow News*, no. 35, 1993, p. 2; *Izvestiia*, February 3, 1994. The policy differences were not so marked as to pose a challenge to Yeltsin and Kozyrev and may even have been orchestrated, as the *Moscow News* commentary suggests, but they did signal a shift in the distribution of roles.

37. *Diplomaticheskii vestnik*, 1992, no. 2/3, p. 44.

38. Radio Mayak, October 27, 1992. Cited in Crow, *The Making of Foreign Policy*, pp. 55–6.

39. *Rossiiskaia gazeta*, May 6, 1992; *Rossiiskaia gazeta*, October 24, 1992.

40. Checkel, "Russian Foreign Policy: Back to the Future?" p. 24. The Soviet Foreign Ministry had 3,746 staff in Moscow in November 1990. "The Foreign Policy and Diplomatic Activity of the USSR," *International Affairs* (Moscow), no. 4, 1991.

41. Four of the seven deputy ministers had postgraduate degrees. Checkel, "Russian Foreign Policy: Back to the Future?" p. 25. The radical journalist from *Novoe vremia*, Galina Sidorova, was put in charge of Kozyrev's Information Service (S. Crow, "Personnel Changes in the Russian Foreign Ministry," *RFE/RL Research Report*, April 17, 1992. *Izvestiia*, April 1, 1992 [evening]) and came to play an important part in the inner circle of the ministry.

42. Checkel, "Russian Foreign Policy: Back to the Future?" p. 24.

43. Checkel, "Russian Foreign Policy: Back to the Future?" p. 24.

44. Interfax, May 19, 1994. Cited in *RFE/RL Daily Report* (Electronic mail edition), May 20, 1994.

45. *Krasnaia zvezda*, December 23, 1992. Before May 1992 the decision-making rights of the Defense Ministry were exercised by the joint CIS command.

46. *Izvestiia*, June 5, 1992; ITAR-TASS (in Russian), June 29, 1992.

47. R. Allison, "Military Factors in the Foreign Policy-making of Russia, Ukraine and Kazakhstan," paper presented to RIIA Study Group, November 1993, p. 57.

48. *Rossiiskaia gazeta*, April 21, 1992; ITAR-TASS (in Russian), June 29, 1992. Cited in Checkel, "Russian Foreign Policy: Back to the Future?" pp. 22–3. See, too, V. Socor, "Russian Forces in Moldova," *RFE/RL Research Report*, August 28, 1992, pp. 41–2. Skokov apparently played an important part in supervising senior appointments and promotions in the Russian armed forces in 1992.

49. *Izvestiia*, June 30 (evening edition). This whole topic is thoroughly

analyzed by Crow in *The Making of Foreign Policy*, pp. 47–57. See, too, Kozyrev reported in *Krasnaia zvezda*, November 26, 1992.

50. Crow, *The Making of Foreign Policy*, pp. 53–4.

51. Kozyrev described the defense minister as "a man of flexible intellect, a man able to listen to interlocutors." Crow, *The Making of Foreign Policy*, p. 56.

52. A. Lynch, "After Empire: Russia and Its Western Neighbors," *RFE/RL Research Report*, March 25, 1994; N. Malcolm, "The New Russian Foreign Policy," *The World Today*, February 1994; A. Adamishin in *Moscow News*, 1994, no. 19, p. 1; S. Crow, "Why Has Russian Foreign Policy Changed?" *RFE/RL Research Report*, May 6, 1994, pp. 1–6.

53. On Russian Television on May 17, 1994 General Lebed declared that he would have refused to accept the order from Grachev to attack the Supreme Soviet in October 1993; that he "never served the president," only the fatherland. Forty-one percent of the 14th Army (in Moldova) were reported to have voted for the LDP. See *RFE/RL Daily Report* (Electronic mail edition), May 18, 1994. On Grachev's relations with Yeltsin and his own subordinates, see S. Foye, "Civilian and Military Leaders in Russia's 'New' Political Arena," *RFE/RL Research Report*, April 15, 1994.

54. V. Savel'ev, R. Huber, "Russian Parliament and Foreign Policy," *International Affairs* (Moscow), no. 3, 1993, pp. 37–8, 43.

55. *Nezavisimaia gazeta*, December 19, 1992. The constitution did not, however, define what should happen if the president were to take up a position contradicting that of the legislature.

56. Ruslan Khasbulatov, chairman of the Supreme Soviet, on February 6, 1992. *Diplomaticheskii vestnik*, no. 6, 1992, p. 32.

57. *Nezavisimaia gazeta*, March 28, 1992.

58. *Nezavisimaia gazeta*, April 10, 1992; N. Melvin, *Forging the New Russian Nation: Russian Foreign Policy and the Russian-speaking Communities of the Former USSR*, London, RIIA Discussion Paper no. 50, 1994. Lukin left to take up the post of ambassador in Washington, but reportedly remained influential with Yeltsin.

59. *Izvestiia*, July 27, 1992; July 29, 1992. This account is based largely on S. Crow, "Ambartsumov's Influence on Russian Foreign Policy," *RFE/RL Research Report*, May 7, 1993, pp. 36–41.

60. *Trud*, September 3, 1992. See too "Parliament and Foreign Ministry: A Rapprochement," *Moscow News*, 1993, no. 9, p. 9.

61. Interfax, January 26, 1993. "Serious positive moves," he said, "have been noticed in the actions of the Russian Foreign Ministry."

62. Savel'ev, Huber, "Russian Parliament and Foreign Policy," p. 38. The authors provide statistics demonstrating an impressively high frequency of appearances by officials.

63. For further references to the idea, see Ambartsumov's August 1992 report to the Supreme Soviet, in *Izvestiia*, August 7, 1992. Yeltsin made his proposals in a speech to the "centrist" Civic Union group, ITAR-TASS, March 1, 1993. Both cited in Crow, "Ambartsumov's Influence on Russian Foreign Policy," p. 40. See also Crow, *The Making of Foreign Policy*, pp. 38–47.

64. N. Malcolm, "The New Russian Foreign Policy,"; S. Crow, "Why Has Russian Foreign Policy Changed?," *RFE/RL Research Report*, May 6, 1994.

65. J. Adams, "Who Will Make Russia's Foreign Policy in 1994?" *RFE/RL Research Report*, February 11, 1994, pp. 36–40; Savel'ev, Huber, "Russian Parliament and Foreign Policy," p. 37.

66. Yury Davydov, in *Moscow News*, no. 31, 1993, p. 4. See, too, N. Gonchar in *Moscow News*, no. 31, 1993, p. 2.

67. Adams, "Who Will Make Russia's Foreign Policy in 1994?" pp. 38–9; Crow, *The Making of Foreign Policy*, pp. 43–5. By this time Ambartsumov was calling on his fellow deputies to moderate their hostility to the government foreign policy line and was finding his own position under threat from the speaker, Khasbulatov.

68. ITAR-TASS, April 28, 1993.

69. See the interview with Vladimir Shumeiko in *Moscow News*, no. 13, 1994, p. 4.

70. Interviewed in *Moscow News*, no. 16, 1994, p. 4.

71. See the argument put by First Deputy Foreign Minister Anatoly Adamishin in *Moscow News*, no. 19, 1994, that the basis for a broad consensus on foreign policy in Moscow had virtually been achieved.

72. See, for example, Anatoly Cherniaev in *Frankfurter Allgemeine Zeitung*, April 14, 1994; Georgi Arbatov in *Nezavisimaia gazeta*, April 14, 1994.

73. The holding of the exercises was also supported by Vladimir Shumeiko, influential speaker of the upper house. *RFE/RL Daily Report* (Electronic mail edition), May 11, 1994.

74. The Council on Foreign and Defense Policy was described in August 1992 as "a non-government organization containing thirty-seven members, including politicians, entrepreneurs, members of the armed forces, diplomats and scholars. One of its main tasks is to collaborate in working out strategic conceptions of the development of the country, especially in the foreign policy and defense spheres." *Nezavisimaia gazeta*, August 19, 1992. Its membership covers a relatively wide section of the political spectrum.

75. *Nezavisimaia gazeta*, August 19, 1992; *Diplomaticheskii vestnik*, January 1993, Special Issue; *Nezavisimaia gazeta*, April 29, 1993; *Moscow News*, no. 20, 1993, p. 9.

76. *Nezavisimaia gazeta*, May 27, 1994.

3

Russian Relations with the "Near Abroad"

Wynne Russell

The term "near abroad" was coined by Russians in 1992 to refer to the fourteen states that once were Russia's fellow republics in the Union of Soviet Socialist Republics. The term was necessitated by the differing attitudes of the former republics toward any continuing institutional association with the USSR. Latvia, Lithuania, Estonia, Georgia, and Azerbaijan have at one time or another refused or renounced membership in the Commonwealth of Independent States (CIS), the loose association that attempts to provide a coordinating mechanism for the territory of the former Union.[1] Eleven of the non-Russian states—Ukraine, Belarus (formerly Belorussia), Moldova (formerly Moldavia), Armenia, Azerbaijan, Georgia, Kazakhstan, Kyrgyzstan (formerly Kirghizia), Uzbekistan, Turkmenistan, and Tajikistan—currently are CIS members, but for how long is not clear. So, tired of always having to use "former" or of trying to linguistically link together CIS and non-CIS members, Russians adopted the phrase "near abroad."

But the phrase also highlights the difficulty experienced by many Russians in accepting the notion of former fellow republics as foreign countries. Some of the republics—in particular Ukraine and Belarus— are viewed by many Russians as not merely former family members but in fact as indivisible from the concept of Russia itself. The presence of significant numbers of ethnic Russians in nearly all of the former republics and the intricacy of economic links on the territory of the former Union make the line between foreign and domestic policy all the more indistinct in the minds of many Russians. Many Russians continue to confidently predict the eventual reintegration of the republics.

Russian relations with the near abroad have followed a tortuous path since the breakup of the USSR in December 1991. Russia's relations with its most powerful new neighbor, Ukraine, have been severely strained from the start by a number of issues, including the division of Soviet military property and the fate of nuclear weapons left on Ukrainian territory after the breakup of the Union. The Russian government has been involved in protracted negotiations with the Baltic states over the status of Russian speakers and Russian soldiers living or stationed in the Baltic region. In Moldova, Tajikistan, and Georgia, troops under Russian control have become involved in local conflicts. Critics of Russian President Boris Yeltsin have accused the Russian government of neglecting the safety of Russians living in the near abroad and of lacking a coherent policy toward the region. The task of this chapter is to outline the major problems in Russian relations with the countries of the near abroad and to examine how domestic political battles, and differing conceptions of Russia's position in the territory of the former Union, have complicated the Russian government's attempts to formulate a coordinated policy toward the near abroad.

Russia Looks to the Commonwealth of Independent States

The abrupt collapse of the Soviet empire left Russian policy-makers with little time to formulate their conceptions of the basic aims of Russian policy toward the countries of the near abroad. While different members of the Russian foreign policy–making community had different objectives and approaches, most Russian decision-makers agreed at the beginning of 1992 that Russian policy should be designed to promote close ties, particularly economic and military, between Russia and the former republics; to secure the transfer to Russia of strategic nuclear elements of the former Soviet arsenal; to inhibit a Yugoslav-style collapse along the periphery of the Russian state, as well as to prevent existing local conflicts in the southern republics from spilling over into Russia; and to protect the rights of Russian speakers and Russian citizens living in the near abroad.

Most Russian leaders assumed that some of these problems could be best addressed through the building of an administrative framework that would to some degree replace the administrative links of the former Union. First, and most importantly, they argued, the fifteen former republics had, at least through 1991, highly integrated economies. For example, decades of Soviet planning had promoted a division of labor that left Russian textile mills dependent on Central Asian cotton and Ukrainian spare parts. The fact that most of the new states were bound together by a single currency, the ruble, provided incentive for, and a head start toward, cooperation on monetary policy as well. Second, they noted, military cooperation, in particular the maintenance of joint armed forces, would permit participating new states to economize on defense measures, as well as preserve an efficient early-warning system, communications network, and air defense network. Coordinating bodies for national forces could assist in formulating coherent policies toward the distribution of Soviet military assets and the redeployment of nuclear weapons.[2] And third, they pointed out, political cooperation would ease the unavoidable diplomatic tasks that accompanied the USSR's breakup—such as working out the assumption of the Soviet Union's international treaty obligations and dealing with problems of citizenship.

Most Russian leaders assumed that the new Russian government had accumulated a stock of goodwill in the non-Russian states that would ease potential conflict. The government shared with most of the other new governments a history of opposition to the Soviet system and to the former Communist Party. In 1990–1991 Yeltsin had supported independence for the Baltic states and self-determination for those republics remaining within a "renewed" Soviet Union and had shown himself ultimately willing to scrap the Union entirely. Bilateral treaties, economic and political, already existed between Russia and most of the other republics. Many Russian policy-makers, as well as ordinary Russians, also held a naive and sentimental perception of the degree of longing felt by other nationalities for continued association.[3]

While arguments for continued association were powerful enough to induce an initial ten of the fourteen non-Russian former republics to band together with Russia in the CIS, most governments and populations nevertheless harbored the fear that Russia would inevitably take the lead in any new institutional arrangement. Russia had immediately emerged as the most economically powerful country in the region, having the greatest military potential and the most political clout in relations with countries both inside and outside the former Union borders.[4] At the most basic level, Russia so dominated the economic scene—particularly since the Russian government controlled the ruble—that no other state could be said to be fully economically independent. The high degree of economic interdependence made smaller states vulnerable to the vagaries of Russian economic policies and foreign trade decisions. By gaining international recognition as the legal continuation of the USSR—a move contested by many of the new governments, particularly that of Ukraine[5]—the Russian government had already gained a significant advantage in the impending battles over the apportionment of the Union's former assets, as well as the right to assume the USSR's nuclear arsenal without violating the conditions of the Nuclear Non-Proliferation Treaty. New governments feared Russian intentions, suspecting that the Russian leadership and population were not in fact resigned to the loss of empire. Ukrainians in particular feared that Russians contemplated a reconstitution, possibly forced, of a Slavic heartland comprising Russia, Ukraine, and Belarus.[6] The Russian foreign policy establishment was well aware of these fears. Yeltsin, Foreign Minister Andrei Kozyrev, and other Russian leaders had repeatedly addressed them in public statements, assuring the world that Russia had no imperialistic or interventionist intentions. The Russian leadership continued to hope, however, that an emphasis on multilateral relations with former Union members would foster the image of equal partners working together for a mutually advantageous future. The preferred vehicle for multilateral relations was the Commonwealth of Independent States (CIS).

The CIS was an amorphous body at the time of its creation in December 1991 and has only gradually acquired functions and a structure. The eleven original member governments established almost immediately regular meetings for heads of state, heads of government, foreign and defense ministers, and heads of legislatures. These meetings, and those of additional functional groupings (intelligence, customs, health care councils), produced a steady flow of agreements on the creation of still more coordinating mechanisms.

Despite the proliferation of pro-cooperation rhetoric that accompanied the foundation of the CIS, cooperation was in fact not forthcoming on many issues. In some cases, the administrators of the new bureaucracies showed a tendency to simply substitute "CIS" for "Soviet." As one commentator noted, the largely Russian CIS military leadership, although more progressive than its predecessors, failed to comprehend that for the non-Russian republics, national sovereignty meant escaping from existing relationships, long dominated by Russia, and establishing independent security policies and national armies.[7] In other cases, prospects for cooperation were hampered by the member governments' unwillingness to diminish their newly won sovereignty in any way. In their haste to set up the Commonwealth, its founders—most of whom were relatively inexperienced—had not taken adequate heed of their immensely disparate interests or of their very different visions of the organization's functions. Russian and Central Asian leaders looked forward to a lasting association; Ukrainian leaders, in particular, looked on the CIS as a civilized transition to complete separation. The implicit expectation of many Russian policy-makers appeared to be that a forthcoming CIS superstructure would suffice to govern Russia's relations with other CIS members by placing bilateral disputes in a multilateral context. Not only was a CIS structure slow in coming, however, but bilateral disputes persisted.

By the second week of January 1992, by which time Ukraine and Russia were already engaged in a diplomatic battle over the fate of the Black Sea naval fleet, it was becoming evident that the Commonwealth was not equipped to mediate in bilateral disputes. The Commonwealth's ineffectiveness in bringing pressure to bear on difficult bilateral issues was due in part to the divergence of interests of its member governments, in part to its lack of procedural guidelines for dealing with crises, and in part to its lack of effective sanctions against governments such as Ukraine, which frequently threatened to take Kiev out of the Commonwealth. Consequently, by spring of 1992 Russian policy-makers were beginning to play down the multilateral approach and to address at the bilateral level two of the most pervasive problems in Russian relations with the near abroad, both of which were linked to a large degree to security concerns—the division of USSR property and the status of Russians in the territory of the former Union.

Property Division

The first pervasive problem, that of property division, arose almost immediately between the two most powerful successor states to the USSR, Russia and Ukraine. Most of the other hard-currency-starved new governments had already accepted the Russian government's offer to assume the Union's foreign debt in return for assumption of the Union's assets.[8] The majority of the new governments also entered 1992 with the intention of participating in a joint CIS military that would make the issue of military property ownership substantially less urgent. Ukraine, however, had the resources—economic power, strategic location, population—to be able to challenge Russia on property claims, as well as a government itching to break out of a pattern of relations molded by centuries of Russian domination.

Unsurprisingly, the most bitter Russo-Ukrainian disputes arose over military assets. Disputes over non-military assets—embassies and foreign exchange reserves being the most contentious—have generated acrimonious debate[9] but almost by definition have lacked the aura of paranoia found in the disputes over military assets, which have been both motivated by, and catalysts for, security fears. At the time of the establishment of the CIS, Russian leaders believed themselves to be largely free of major military threats from the former republics.[10] The Ukrainian government's subsequent claims, however, of entitlement to the majority of the Black Sea naval fleet—which the Russian government and the CIS military had considered a strategic, and therefore shared, resource—raised Russian concerns over an erosion of security along Russia's southwest flank. Russian leaders also had to consider the threat of the Ukrainian government's refusing to surrender its nuclear weapons, with the possibility of the Kazakh and Belarusian governments following suit.

Russians in the "Near Abroad"

The second pervasive problem was that of the status of Russian speakers and Russian citizens living in the near abroad. In 1989, some 73.7 million Soviet citizens lived in national territories of ethnic groups other than theirs.[11] Russians constituted the largest proportion—some 25.3 million Russians (17.4 percent of all Russians) lived outside the Russian republic in 1989. Of these, around 45 percent lived in Ukraine, where they made up 22 percent of the population; 25 percent lived in northern Kazakhstan, a republic in which they made up 41 percent of the population. The remainder were scattered across the former Union, with the lowest concentration in the Caucasus. In addition, ethnic Russian soldiers, deliberately posted to non-Russian republics by the Soviet military, populated strategically significant military bases across the territory of the former Union. Prior to the dissolution of the Union, the Russian republic government had repeatedly expressed its concern for the fate of Russian speakers outside the republic's borders. Yeltsin had indicated his hope that bilateral treaties signed with the other republics in the course of 1990–1991 would provide a legal basis for the protection of Russian minorities; force, he stressed, was not a realistic option.

Russian governmental involvement in securing the welfare of both civilians and military personnel stemmed from a number of concerns.[12] The first was a desire to secure the physical safety of both civilians and military personnel. This desire did not stem from purely humanitarian concerns—the Russian economy could not absorb a huge flow of refugees, or even the abrupt return of large numbers of servicemen, due to a lack of housing and, in the case of civilians, high unemployment.[13] And second, the right of Russians and Russian speakers, and of the Russian military, to remain unmolested in the territory of the former Union was a key emotional issue for those Russians who questioned whether the collapse of the USSR was necessary, avoidable, or reversible. In addition to being concerned about the human rights of Russians in the near abroad, the latter group also expressed fears that a withdrawal of military forces would reduce Russia's ability to intervene in strategically important areas.

The Russian government has been forced to respond to three basic categories of problems—those of Russian-speaking civilians demanding integration into new societies, those of Russian-speaking civilians demanding some level of autonomy from new states, and those of Russian servicemen stationed abroad. Into the first category, that of Russians seeking greater integration, fit the Russian-speaking populations of Estonia and Latvia, which were the only new states that did not grant automatic citizenship to residents on their territory.[14] Both governments imposed a series of requirements for potential citizens who were not residents or who were descendents of residents of the interwar independent republics, including a language competency examination and a minimum period of residence. These tough regulations were inspired in part by demographic fears—Russians made up 33 percent of the population of Latvia in 1989 and 28 percent of the population of Estonia. They also were a response to a vocal minority of ethnic Russians living in the Baltic republics who had formed movements opposing Baltic independence from the USSR during the last years of the Union.

The second group, seeking greater autonomy or independence, included segments of the Russian-speaking populations of Ukraine and Moldova, as well as some groups with ethnic or political ties to minorities in the Russian Federation. These include Ossetians resident in Georgia, who have coethnics in the Russian Federation, and the Abkhaz in Georgia, who have political ties to the Confederation of Caucasian Mountain People, made up primarily of Caucasian minorities whose homelands lie within the Russian Federation. These Russians and non-Russians, fearing discrimination at the hands of new national governments, have attempted to remove themselves from their administrative control by establishing autonomous or independent regions, sometimes requesting incorporation into the Russian Federation in the process. Russians of the Crimean Peninsula in Ukraine—who make up the majority of the population of the peninsula—have argued that their region's transfer from Russian to Ukrainian jurisdiction in 1954 by the USSR legislature was invalid and have repeatedly, if ineffectually, declared autonomy or separation from Ukraine. Russians living to the east of the Dniester River in Moldova went a step further and took up arms in 1991 to carve out an independent Trans-Dniester Republic despite the fact that they only make up 25 percent of the self-styled republic's population.[15] Abkhazians and Ossetians have come under prolonged attack by Georgian forces for attempting to remove their existing autonomous units from Georgian control; these conflicts have made refugees or hostages of several thousand local ethnic Russians.

In all of these cases, the presence in the region of servicemen under Russian command but still stationed at former Soviet military installations has been a complicating factor. These servicemen are largely ethnic Russian; in Ukraine, for example, ethnic Russians made up 44 percent of troops on Ukrainian soil in early 1992, and ethnic Ukrainians made up 40 percent.[16] In the Baltics, these servicemen had been treated with the hostility reserved for occupying forces since the beginning of the Baltic independence drives in 1988–1989, and particularly since the Soviet military crackdown in Lithuania of January 1991. In Moldova and in Georgia, Soviet-Russian troops became involved to a greater or lesser degree in the fighting between Moldovan or Georgian government troops and irregulars from the breakaway regions. In each case, the Yeltsin government stressed initially that Russian troops were ordered to remain neutral. The Moldovan and Georgian governments, however, accused Russian troops of violating these orders, possibly with the complicity of the military leadership in Moscow, and their government troops have engaged Russian positions.[17] The Russian military and political position in both of these cases has been complicated by the presence of Russian mercenaries and of volunteer Russian Cossack and Caucasian fighters.[18]

In the case of Ukraine, the government in Kiev did not demand the withdrawal of Russian forces per se, offering instead to servicemen of any nationality the opportunity to continue in service on Ukrainian soil provided that they accept an oath of loyalty to Ukraine. Nevertheless, the historical association with Russia of the Crimean Peninsula—which is home to the Black Sea Fleet—as well as the peninsula's strategic significance has made the issue of continued Russian basing rights there an emotional as well as a practical one to the Russian military leadership.

Bureaucratic and Conceptual Complications

The process of working out a response to these problems has been greatly complicated by the intense political infighting that has accompanied the formulation of policy toward the near abroad. During the course of 1990–1991, negotiating teams dealing with the other republics drew heavily on legislators, academics, and other governmental figures. By the beginning of 1992, however, the Russian Foreign Ministry technically bore responsibility for the day-to-day work of implementing relations with the near abroad, with responsibility for the course of policy lying nominally with the president. The Foreign Ministry sometimes appeared not to relish its task. For one thing, the ministry was physically unprepared; it started 1992 with only around ten people in the Commonwealth Affairs Department and had trouble finding people who spoke the languages of the former republics. By July 1992, for example, the ministry had opened only one embassy in the CIS, in Kiev, due to financial strains. Poor salaries for diplomats serving in the CIS made good diplomats seek other posts.[19] The ministry's leadership, and the Russian leadership in general, were also intellectually and mentally unprepared for the task of formulating relations with the former republics. Despite Foreign Minister Kozyrev's statements at the beginning of 1992 that the CIS was a top foreign policy priority, he dedicated his immediate attention to explaining the changes that were occurring in the former Union to the rest of the world. Apart from a quick trip to Estonia, his first trip to the near abroad took place in April 1992, after trips to Western

Europe, North America, Africa, the Middle East, and the Far East. Kozyrev probably intended to give multilateral structures time to work, as CIS meetings were occurring regularly during this period.

By the spring of 1992, as bilateral problems continued to pile up, criticism began to mount in Russian governmental circles of the Yeltsin team's handling of CIS relations. Some of these criticisms came, predictably enough, from conservative critics of the Yeltsin government such as Vice President Alexander Rutskoi and from power-hungry politicians such as parliamentary chairman Ruslan Khasbulatov. Others, however, came from ostensible supporters of democratic reforms such as presidential adviser Sergei Stankevich and influential parliamentarian Oleg Rumyantsev. Their common theme was that the Russian government had neglected relations with the near abroad in favor of relations with the West, tailoring policy toward the former Union to suit Western interests (for example, in the area of troop withdrawals) and putting too much faith in multilateral institutions. In particular, the Foreign Ministry was accused of ignoring the rights and needs of Russian speakers and Russian troops abroad.

Kozyrev and the Foreign Ministry were left largely on their own to defend the government's policy. Kozyrev, adhering to the approach championed by Yeltsin in 1990–1991, remained adamant that good Russian government relations with the new states were the only solution, as belligerent actions by the Russian government would lead to Russophobia.[20] Legislators and military figures, however, cited attacks on military personnel in the Baltics and in Transcaucasus, discrimination against Russian populations in the Baltics and Moldova, and increasing attacks on Russian-speaking civilians in the context of military conflicts in Moldova and Georgia as evidence that a tougher policy was necessary. Critics called for a more concrete formulation of Russian foreign policy in which top priority would go to establishing stable relations with the former republics.[21] By late May 1992, the need for a harder line was broadly accepted in Russian policy circles.

The situation was complicated by the proliferation of bureaucratic players in the foreign policy decision-making process; the legislature, the military, the Russian Security Council, and groups outside the formal decision-making process such as the Civic Union and the Council on Foreign Policy became increasingly involved in foreign policy debates and decision-making. In addition to being burdened by the sheer confusion caused by multiple actors, Russian policy formulation began to suffer from competition between organizations as well as between individuals. The lack of standard procedures for the formulation of foreign policy made decision-making particularly vulnerable to such infighting, as did the state of constitutional flux that blurred the lines of responsibility for policy-making. Competition became visible between the conservative, populist legislature and the Yeltsin government, as well as between the military and civilian leaderships. In the case of Moldova, for example, the Supreme Soviet showed itself more sympathetic to the demands of Trans-Dniester Russians than did the Russian government and delayed ratification of bilateral agreements in response to Trans-Dniestrian Russian pressure. Similarly, when in May 1992 Yeltsin suggested publicly that the 14th Army would be withdrawn from Moldova, Defense Minister Grachev—an outspoken champion of the rights of Russian speakers in the near abroad, a group which he believed only the military could effectively protect under current conditions[22]— immediately qualified Yeltsin's statement, saying that the 14th could be withdrawn only after the conflict in the area had been defused and following a bilateral agreement.[23]

Underlying these bureaucratic battles were ideological disputes stemming from the decision by the Russian government, before the breakup of the USSR in December 1991, to not only accept but accelerate the Union's dissolution. At the heart of these problems is the issue of Russian identification with the Soviet empire, an identification for the most part encouraged by the Soviet regime. Many scholars have stressed that Russians in the Soviet Union did not live noticeably better than most of the titular peoples of the minority republics (with the exception of the Central Asians). For example, Alain Besancon wrote in 1986:

> The Russian people has no privileges. It has advantages, certainly, as the surest ally of communism, and party leaders are often drawn from its ranks, even in the national republics . . . . [However,] these advantages are not rights . . . . A Russian who enjoys his privileges as a Communist owes his privileges to his communism, not to his Russianness.[24]

Nevertheless, there can be no question that the Russian people were encouraged by the Soviet regime—most explicitly during World War II and in the late Brezhnev years—to conjoin the concepts of "Russian" and "Soviet." As a consequence, independence for the non-Russian former Soviet republics not only left Russians faced with economic adjustment and hardship but also brought on a crisis of prestige. The coincidence of this loss of domestic clout with a drastic loss of international standing led many Russians to believe that they had witnessed the end of Russia as a great power. The most visible consequence of this abrupt loss of prestige was the increasing prominence, over the course of 1992, of a vocal nationalism displaying a high independent value placed on national autonomy, an intense concern with national status, and a tendency to define very broadly the community of fellow nationals, or "kith and kin."[25] Nationalists of this ilk viewed the fate of Russians in the near abroad as a harbinger of the fate of the 11.8 million Russian-speaking citizens living in the autonomous regions of the Russian Federation and similarly saw the erosion of Russian security in the territory of the former Union as a presage of a collapse of Russian governmental authority within the Federation. Concern over the consequences of the dissolution of the Union was in no way unique to Russian ultranationalists, however. The questions of whether to split the Union and whether the autonomous regions of Russia should have the right to self-determination in fact provoked a split in November 1991, just before the Union collapsed, in the Democratic Russia movement, which played a decisive role in Yeltsin's election to the Russian presidency. Parliamentarian Oleg Rumyantsev was not far from the mark when he complained that by taking a laissez-faire attitude toward Russians in the near abroad, a highly emotional issue for many otherwise moderate Russians, the Russian Foreign Ministry had ceded the label of "patriot" to conservatives[26]—an excellent example of how a government's foreign policy can have domestic consequences, as well as domestic sources.

Kozyrev attempted several times to mount a counter-offensive. In a much-discussed article published in *Izvestiia* in July 1992, he warned that Russians abroad were being used as a pretext for strong-arm threats and that the Russian military in Moldova was becoming an autonomous force.[27] Gradually, however, his opinion was overruled by the changing attitudes of Yeltsin himself.

The General Pattern of Relations

In the midst of these bureaucratic and ideological battles, Yeltsin was for the most part the final arbiter of Russian foreign policy. Throughout 1992 and 1993, Yeltsin both took personal initiative in relations with the near abroad and acted to pull compromises out of the decision-making turmoil. On the personal front, all evidence suggests that Yeltsin considers relations with Ukraine to be a top priority, followed by multilateral relations with the CIS. He has used personal diplomacy to achieve a series of partial solutions to the problem of the division of military property with Ukraine. The initial reaction of the Russian government and legislature to Ukraine's claim to the Black Sea Fleet was to respond in kind. Throughout the first months of 1992, despite the steady, if unspectacular, progress of bilateral negotiations,[28] the two governments publicly traded defiant statements. Conflicting orders provoked chaos in the military; "defections" by ship crews and air divisions received extensive press coverage.[29] In June 1992, Yeltsin and Kravchuk began a string of personal meetings that have produced temporary lulls in the storm. While protracted complications have led to frequent renegotiations, the two sides agreed in April 1994 to divide equally strategic and non-strategic elements of the Fleet, with Ukraine retaining just under 20 percent of the Fleet and selling the remainder of its half to Russia. Yeltsin and Kravchuk also met to tackle the highly charged question of ownership of Soviet nuclear weapons. This question resurfaced after the Ukrainian parliament, citing disputes over the division of the Fleet as evidence that the Russians could not be trusted, dragged its feet through 1992–1993 on the ratification of START-1, the Lisbon Protocol, and the Nuclear Non-Proliferation Treaty (NPT). Yeltsin's offers of security guarantees finally eased Ukrainian ratification of START-1, although not of the NPT, in early 1994.

Yeltsin did not become similarly personally involved in 1992–1993 in bilateral relations with the rest of the near abroad, preferring to maintain a high profile at CIS meetings. (The exception to this rule has been Yeltsin's involvement with Georgian leader Eduard Shevardnadze; the two have held a series of meetings on the situation in Abkhazia.) He nevertheless became steadily more vocal in his support for Russians abroad. In October 1992 he gave the Russian Foreign Ministry a dressing-down in which he accused it of displaying "the imperial syndrome in reverse" in relations with the "near abroad"—of being too shy in speaking about national interests for fear of being accused of "great-power chauvinism." He ordered the ministry to uphold more actively the interests of the Russian speaking population abroad, especially in the Baltics, and said that the world community should be urged to defend of Russian speakers' rights.[30]

Yeltsin's creation, in December 1992, of a Security Council commission on foreign policy was instrumental in bringing some degree of coordination into Russian policy toward the near abroad. While a November 1992 presidential decree gave the Foreign Ministry the responsibility for coordinating Russia's foreign political and economic activity, the ministry was subordinated in its turn to the Foreign Policy Commission for coordination.[31] Kozyrev had accepted from the beginning the need for a coordinated foreign policy, and by the end of 1992 he appeared to have accepted the domestic political imperatives for a policy that took into account conservative concerns; in his report to the Supreme Soviet's international relations committee in January 1993, he indicated that Russia's top foreign policy priorities would be closer CIS integration and the protection of Russians abroad.[32] The ministry also announced in early 1993 its intention to create a special envoy for the protection of rights of Russians living abroad.[33] Kozyrev's new approach won over former opponents such as Ambartsumov, who said in March

1993 that Kozyrev's approach had changed sufficiently to make him retract his calls for Kozyrev's resignation.[34]

One of the indicators of the sea change in the Foreign Ministry was the much-discussed Foreign Ministry Concept of Russian Foreign Policy, in draft since February 1992 at the behest of critics of Yeltsin's and Kozyrev's foreign policy. In effect, the Concept of Russian Foreign Policy was to play the role close to that of Bolshevik ideology in Soviet foreign policy—to offer a generally recognized basis for action enshrining a particular intellectual approach to foreign policy problems.[35] Successive Foreign Ministry drafts were rejected by the legislature over the course of 1992 as being insufficiently strong on the defense of Russians in the near abroad. Finally, a draft drawn up by the Security Council Foreign Policy Commission on the basis of a Foreign Ministry draft was approved by the Security Council in March 1993. The Concept of Russian Foreign Policy lists as Russia's most important foreign policy tasks in the near abroad the curtailment and regulation of armed conflicts around Russia and the guarantee of strict observation in the near abroad of human and minority rights, especially of Russians.[36]

Virtually all Russian leaders now accept the notion that Russia must play a leading role on the territory of the former Union. Yeltsin has publicly called for Russia to act as guarantor of peace and security in the former Union's territory.[37] Yeltsin and other leaders have argued that Russia must be acknowledged by the West as having special interests in the territory of the Union and have suggested to the United Nations that Russian troops be given special peacekeeping responsibilities on the former Union's territory.[38] Kozyrev has pressed for the recognition of the CIS by the United Nations and the Conference on Security and Cooperation in Europe (CSCE) as a "regional" or "international" organization that would have the right to mount peacekeeping operations on the territory of its members without UN or CSCE consultation.[39]

Throughout this process, relations with the near abroad have been influenced by Russian leaders' attitudes toward relations with the West. On the one hand, the Russian government has attempted to use international pressure to secure rights for Russians in the near abroad. Russian leaders have international organizations such as the CSCE and the Council of Europe to put pressure on countries of the near abroad to respect the rights of local Russians. On the other hand, Russian leaders have reacted negatively to Western criticism of Russian policy toward the near abroad and pressure for troop withdrawals from the Baltic states. In January 1994, Kozyrev complained about Western claims of Russian neo-imperialism in the near abroad, saying that such claims were intended to divert attention from the real problem of CIS stability; he said that Russia will not listen to the West's "lessons and lectures."[40]

Presidential National Security Adviser Yury Baturin told Western journalists in February 1994 that although the U.S. treats Russia like a "developing country," Russia has a duty as a great power to protect Russians in the near abroad.[41]

As might be expected, the Russian government has shown an increasing willingness to drive a hard bargain in its relations with the near abroad, sometimes using the presence of Russian military forces as a bargaining chip. In the Baltic states the Russian government has used the timing of the eventual withdrawal of troops as leverage in negotiations to secure basic rights for Russians on Baltic soil. In late October 1992, for instance, Yeltsin formally suspended the withdrawal of troops from the Baltic states pending agreements with the Baltic governments on guarantees of social services and protection for troops still stationed there.[42] In Moldova and Abkhazia, Russian military forces stationed in the region were given the explicit duty of protecting local Russian speakers, and withdrawals of military forces were made dependent on the achievement of a political solution that guarantees local Russian speakers' rights. After the Estonian legislature passed a law in June 1993 requiring Russian speakers to apply for residency permits, the Russian government suspended natural gas deliveries; the Estonian prime minister subsequently suspended the law.

Nevertheless, Russian relations with the near abroad are far from universally confrontational. Relations with Belarus and, for the most part, the states of Central Asia have been largely trouble-free. Troop withdrawals from Lithuania were completed in August 1993 and were completed from Latvia and Estonia in August 1994.[43] A troop withdrawal agreement was also signed with Moldova in October 1994. Problems over the status of ethnic Russians have shown themselves to be resolvable. For example, the Russian government has signed agreements with Ukraine, Belarus, and Lithuania on the rights of expatriate Russians; in each case, the Russian leadership appears, at least for the time being, to be treating the matter as closed.[44] Similarly, the Russian government announced in February 1993 that it was satisfied with Moldovan policies toward Russians; Yeltsin subsequently severed direct links between Moscow and the breakaway Trans-Dniester government.[45] The July 1994 election to the Ukrainian presidency of Leonid Kuchma, who has emphasized the need for close relations with Russia, offers hope that the confrontational rhetoric of Russo-Ukrainian relations will be toned down.

Yeltsin and the Russian government continued to signal interest in better multilateral relations through the first half of 1994, an interest that other CIS member states, including, for the first time Ukraine, increasingly shared. Progress continues toward the codification of an effective economic Union that would reduce or eliminate trade and investment barriers; the CIS has also agreed on the formation of an interstate bank, a vital part of economic integration.[46] Russia and six other states[47] have signed a CIS Charter that spells out a basis for relations (and that is open to additional signatories), and six states have signed a collective security agreement.[48] The Russian government is exploring new approaches to thorny multilateral problems such as the issue of citizenship—the Foreign Ministry is currently attempting to work out principles of dual citizenship with countries of the near abroad.[49]

Conclusion

Russian relations with the countries of the near abroad have been severely complicated by domestic bureaucratic and conceptual conflicts, and a unified, codified policy toward the former Union only began to emerge by the end of 1994. Given the different problems and opportunities that each of the fourteen bilateral relationships afford, a single approach might not in fact have averted many of the bilateral crises of 1992–1993. Nevertheless, the Russian foreign policy decision-making community's increasing clarity in determining and pursuing goals in relations with the near abroad, in particular the clearer approach to the problems of Russians living in the near abroad, is likely to lend a more decisive character to negotiations with the countries of the near abroad. Given the domestic resonance of Russian policy toward the countries of the near abroad, however, it seems reasonable to predict that Russian policy toward these states will remain volatile as long as Russian domestic politics remain volatile. The chances of issues such as the continuing dispute with Ukraine over the Black Sea Fleet, border conflicts with Estonia and Latvia, and disagreements over Russian military basing rights in the near abroad intruding into Russian domestic politics remain high.

An area in which disagreements are likely to grow is that of economics, specifically trade relations. Continuing disputes between Ukraine and Russia over gas and oil delivery levels and payment for deliveries are an ominous example. While all the former republics are increasingly aware of their need to maintain good trade relations, the decline in economic performance is likely to lead to trade shortfalls that could have disastrous effects on neighboring economies; problems of payment are also likely to continue to cause serious frictions.

Notes

1. The Commonwealth of Independent States was created on December 21, 1991, in Alma-Ata, the capital of Kazakhstan. It represented an expansion of a commonwealth of Slavic states composed of Russia, Ukraine, and Belarus,

founded on December 8, 1991, the date of the formal dissolution of the Soviet Union. The three Baltic states (whose independence had been recognized by the Soviet government in August 1991) and Georgia refused membership in the CIS from the start; Azerbaijan withdrew from the CIS in 1992. Since then Georgia has joined and Azerbaijan has rejoined the CIS.

2. See, for example, "Concept of Joint Armed Forces Assessed," *Izvestiia*, December 31, 1991, p. 3, in FBIS-SOV-92-001, January 2, 1992, p. 30.

3. Polls at the end of 1991, for example, showed that 66.2 percent of Russians believed that the USSR would be reborn, voluntarily, in the shape of the CIS. *Rossiiskaia gazeta*, December 26, 1991, p. 1.

4. In keeping with Russian policy-makers' interest in a unified military, the Russian Federation did not declare the formation of an independent Russian military until May 7, 1992, by which time an effective unified CIS military force seemed highly unlikely.

5. See, for example, *RFERL Daily Report*, no. 28, February 11, 1993. Russian leaders, however, point out that Russia was the only republic that did not declare independence from the USSR.

6. See, for example, *RFERL Daily Report* no. 15, January 13, 1992.

7. Stephen Foye, "The CIS Armed Forces," *RFERL Daily Report*, November 24, 1992.

8. Although some are now working out new formulations; the Azerbaijani government, for example, has renegotiated to pay a share of the Union's debt in return for an unfreezing of hard currency accounts in the now-Russian-controlled Vneshekonombank. Interestingly enough, Ukraine has since accepted the debt-for-assets swap. *RIA Novosti*, March 16, 1993.

9. See, for example, *RFERL Daily Report*, no. 29, February 12, 1992, on Ukraine's claims to Soviet assets.

10. The leaders of Ukraine, Belarus, and Kazakhstan, the three states other than Russia with Soviet strategic nuclear missiles stationed on their territory, had declared their intention to give up these weapons; they ultimately agreed in the Lisbon Protocol of May 1992 to transfer all nuclear weapons on their territories to Russia, where a percentage of them would be destroyed according to the provisions of START-1. Ukraine, Azerbaijan, and Moldova had announced in December 1991 their intentions to form independent armies through the resubordination of Soviet general purpose forces materiel stationed on their territories but had agreed that strategic forces should remain under CIS control. Extension of the same principle of transfer of materiel to the other members of the CIS has greatly eased potential disputes with these states over military issues.

11. *Nationalities Papers*, vol. XX, no. 2, Fall 1992, p. 36.

12. The lines between the two categories periodically blur in discussion of officers, many of whom have served lengthy periods in a particular location and have acquired property and sentimental ties to an area.

13. According to the head of the Russian Federal Migration Service, there were already on Russian soil in late 1992 470,000 refugees fleeing violence and 800,000 forced migrants fleeing poverty and discrimination. RIA Novosti, November 28, 1992.

14. All of the new governments of the former Union except those of Estonia and Latvia had granted automatic citizenship to anyone residing on their territory on the day that the citizenship law came into effect; the vast majority of Russian speakers abroad, therefore, were guaranteed rights of citizenship in their country of residence. In addition, the Russian Federation citizenship law gave any Soviet citizen resident in the USSR on September 1, 1991, regardless of ethnicity, the right to take out Russian citizenship within three years, provided that he or she had not assumed another citizenship in the interim.

15. And, in fact, only 35 percent of Moldova's total Russian population.

16. Interfax, January 3, 1992, in FBIS-SOV-92-003, January 6, 1992, p. 17.

17. Moldovan allegations were confirmed during a period of fierce fighting in May 1992, when the commander of the Soviet/Russian 14th Army, stationed in the Trans-Dniester region, admitted that several of his units were disobeying his orders to observe neutrality. Additional reports suggest that military figures in Moscow may have sanctioned the attacks. See *RFERL Daily Report*, no. 97, May 21, 1992; *RFERL Daily Report*, February 4, 1994.

18. RIA Novosti, September 8, 1992; RIA-Novosti, September 9, 1992.

19. *Nezavisimaia gazeta*, July 30, 1992, p. 1, in FBIS-SOV-92-154, August 10, 1992, p. 28.

20. Moscow Radio Rossii Network, April 18, 1992, in FBIS-SOV-92-078-S, April 22, 1992, p. 20.

21. See, for example, Sergei Stankevich's article in *Nezavisimaia gazeta*, March 28, 1992.

22. ITAR-TASS, June 29, 1992, and FBIS-SOV-92-126, June 30, 1992, p. 26.

23. *Izvestiia*, 30 May 30, 1992, p. 7, in FBIS-SOV-92-107, June 3, 1992, p. 18; *RFERL Daily Report*, nos. 102-4, May 29-June 2, 1992; Moscow Russian Television Network (in Russian), June 8, 1992, in FBIS-SOV-92-111, June 9, 1992, p. 9.

24. Alain Besancon, "Nationalism and Bolshevism in the USSR," in Robert Conquest, ed., *The Last Empire*, Stanford, CA., Hoover Institution Press, 1986, pp. 10–11. See also John Dunlop, "Russia: Confronting a Loss of Empire," in Ian Bremmer and Ray Taras, eds. *Nation and Politics in the Soviet Successor States*, Cambridge, Cambridge University Press, 1993.

25. Stanley Hoffmann, *Decline or Renewal?* New York, Viking Press, 1974, pp. 367–368.

26. Interfax, July 20, 1992, in FBIS-SOV-92-140, July 21, 1992, p. 8.

27. *Izvestiia*, July 1, 1992, p. 3, in FBIS-SOV-92-127, July 1, 1992, p. 11.

28. *RFERL Daily Report*, no. 34, February 19, 1992.

29. See, for example, *RFERL Daily Report*, no. 34, February 19, 1992.

30. RIA Novosti, October 27, 1992.

31. *Rossiiskaia gazeta*, December 18, 1992, p. 1, in FBIS-SOV-92-247, December 23, 1992, p. 19.

32. ITAR-TASS, January 26, 1993.

33. RIA-Novosti, January 26, 1993.

34. *RFERL Daily Report*, March 15, 1993.

35. Kozyrev disagreed with the very notion, saying that "no country has an official description of its national interests." *Nezavisimaia gazeta*, April 1, 1992, p. 1.

36. *Rossiiskaia gazeta,* April 29, 1993.

37. ITAR-TASS, March 1, 1993.

38. *RFERL Daily Report,* March 4, 1993.

39. *RFERL Daily Report,* February 24, 1994.

40. *RFERL Daily Report,* January 28, 1994.

41. *RFERL Daily Report,* February 8, 1994.

42. Estonia, for instance, has periodically cut off food supplies to Russian garrisons in retaliation for shortfalls in Russian deliveries of goods. *Baltfax,* January 8, 1992, in FBIS SOV-92-006, Jan 9, 1992, p. 77.

43. *RFERL Daily Report,* February 8, 1994.

44. RIA Novosti, May 19, 1993; RIA Novosti, February 12, 1993.

45. RIA Novosti, February 9, 1993.

46. *RFERL Daily Report,* May 17, 1993.

47. Armenia, Kazakhstan, Kyrgyzstan, Uzbekistan, Tajikistan, and Belarus.

48. Russia, Armenia, Kazakhstan, Kyrgyzstan, Uzbekistan, and Tajikistan. *The Age,* May 17, 1993, p. 9.

49. *RIA Novosti,* January 18 and 26, 1993.

4

Russian Policy Toward Central and Eastern Europe

Mike Bowker

When Mikhail Gorbachev came to power in 1985, Soviet foreign policy was in turmoil. Nowhere, however, was the upheaval so great as in Moscow's relations with Eastern Europe. Throughout the post-war period, the region was clearly the top foreign policy issue for Moscow. The Soviet Union imposed its will on the region after the war and maintained its position by force or the threat of force throughout the post-war period. Yet from 1989, the communist regimes in all East European countries were dismantled without the Soviet Union firing a shot. In 1991, the Soviet-dominated alliance organizations, the Warsaw Pact and Council for Mutual Economic Assistance (CMEA), were both abolished, and Soviet troop withdrawal from Eastern Europe was completed by the summer of 1994.

Under Yeltsin's administration, Eastern Europe became the region of forgotten neighbors as Russia concentrated on relations with the West and the near abroad. Although these priorities never fundamentally changed, Yeltsin made a speech in October 1992 in which he acknowledged the continuing strategic importance of Eastern Europe, implying a more active Russian role in the region.[1] At the same time, Moscow began to adopt a less pro-Western, more nationalist stance in foreign policy generally. Then the strong electoral performance of the ultranationalist Vladimir Zhirinovsky in December 1993 alarmed the world and added to the fears in Eastern Europe of a renewed Russian imperialism.

As a result, the central issue for East Europeans became the future role of Russia in the region. What are the dangers of Moscow attempting to reimpose its dominance over Eastern Europe in a way similar to its tactics in the near abroad? The upheavals witnessed in recent times caution against any rash predictions, and the emergence of Zhirinovsky as a central figure in Russian politics is a greatly worrying feature; but it is argued below that there is little likelihood of Russia attempting to reassert itself in the region by force. To show this, it is necessary first to review the reasons for the Soviet withdrawal from Eastern Europe in 1989.

The Withdrawal

The central debate over withdrawal relates to the extent of Soviet readiness to pull out of Eastern Europe. One view, forcibly expressed by the British journalist Steve Crawshaw, argues that Moscow did not choose to give up its dominance over the region but was forced to do so through mass demonstrations of discontent.[2] Popular discontent with the communist system was obviously a critical factor in the ultimate demise of the communist system in Eastern Europe. However, a series of studies has shown that the radical restructuring of Russian–East European relations was initiated in Moscow with support from reformist leaders in Hungary and Poland.

From the Brezhnev Doctrine to the Sinatra Doctrine

As early as 1986, the core issue of Soviet dominance over Eastern Europe—the Brezhnev Doctrine, or the concept of limited sovereignty—was being critically discussed by the Politburo in Moscow.[3] The decision that force should not be used to defend Soviet interests in Eastern Europe was taken as early as 1987. This crucial decision was transmitted at that time to the party leaders of Eastern Europe.[4]

The more reform-minded states of Eastern Europe, Hungary, and Poland began to respond positively to these Soviet initiatives. In July 1988, Karoly Grosz, having replaced the long-serving Hungarian communist party leader Janos Kadar in May, met with Gorbachev in Moscow. At this remarkable meeting, the Soviet leader agreed in principle both to the introduction of a multiparty system and to the total withdrawal of Soviet troops from Hungary.[5]

The Hungarian party acted on this agreement and began to dismantle the communist system. After Kadar's fall, the Hungarian press became free of state censorship and foreign passports were issued virtually on demand.[6] The leading role of the party was abandoned in February 1989 and multiparty elections were set for the following year. In October 1989, the Hungarian communist party voted to change its name and formally abandon Marxism-Leninism as a guiding principle of the party. As a result, revolution came to Hungary in the most unexpected way possible—through the democratic vote of communist party officials.

The Hungarian revolution occurred peacefully, without mass demonstrations, and to a large extent unnoticed by the world outside. More dramatic events were happening in Poland with the convocation of the roundtable in February 1989 and the formal unbanning of Solidarity in April. Only two months later, in June, multiparty elections were held with Solidarity competing for seats in parliament. The election was rigged to favor the communists. Sixty-five percent of all seats in the lower house were reserved for the party in the hope of ensuring the continuation of communist government. However, the party was humiliated by the election results. It failed to win a single contested constituency for the lower house, and only five communists received the absolute majority required in the reserved seats. The results created a constitutional crisis. Although the party had lost all legitimacy to rule, Solidarity feared that a bid for power would be intolerable for Moscow.[7]

At this point, Gorbachev made a series of important interventions on the side of change and democracy. First, in a well-publicized speech on July 7, to the European Council in Strasbourg, Gorbachev underlined his administration's abandonment of the Brezhnev Doctrine:

> Social and political orders in one or another country changed in the past and may change in the future. But this change is the exclusive affair of that country and is their choice. Any interference in domestic affairs and any attempts to restrict the sovereignty of states, both friends and allies or any others, is impermissible.[8]

The same month, the Warsaw Pact issued a communiqué ruling out the use of force within the alliance.

Then on August 22, Gorbachev, in a telephone conversation with Polish Prime Minister Mieczyslaw Rakowski, declared that the communist party should accept the results of the election and accept a minority position in the coalition government led by Solidarity activist Tadeusz Mazowiecki.[9] Gorbachev's advice was accepted, and the first non-communist coalition government in Eastern Europe since the earliest days of the post-war period came into office in September 1989. This was the most important moment in the post-war history of Eastern Europe, setting a precedent for systemic change throughout the region.

Poland had always been of vital strategic interest to Moscow. The collapse of communism there threatened to undermine the Soviet Union's dominant position in all of Eastern Europe. Nevertheless, Moscow was prepared to risk the total collapse of its European policy by attacking the hard-line regime of Erich Honecker in East Germany. In June 1989, Gorbachev confided to the West German chancellor, Helmut

Kohl, that Honecker's days were numbered.[10] In October, as thousands of East Germans were emigrating through Hungary, Gorbachev's foreign policy spokesman, Gennady Gerasimov, declared formally that the Brezhnev Doctrine was dead. It had been replaced, he said, by the "Sinatra Doctrine"—Eastern Europeans could do it *their* way. After the public relations disaster surrounding the celebrations for the fortieth anniversary of the GDR in October, Gorbachev encouraged moves by the communist party to oust Honecker. When Honecker's fall failed to curb the demonstrations, Gorbachev told Egon Krenz, the new East German leader, to open the state's borders.[11] Thus, the Berlin Wall came down on November 9, 1989.

Gorbachev and the Fall of Communism in Eastern Europe

The end of the Berlin Wall signified not only the end of communism in East Germany but also the end of the post-war international system. The Cold War was over. Why then did the Gorbachev administration take such a radical view regarding its relations with Eastern Europe? The argument that mass protest forced the USSR out is incomplete. A better analysis accepts that Gorbachev prompted reform in Eastern Europe but argues that the process got out of control and the revolutionary outcome of his initiatives was never expected or desired.[12] This is a view also held by many in the former Soviet Union.[13]

It cannot be denied that this analysis contains much truth. In most cases, reforms were enacted by the leaders in order to maintain rather than abolish the communist system. Thus, the June 1989 elections in Poland were devised not to bring the post-war system to a close but to legitimize the continuation of communist government. Even opening the Berlin Wall was perceived as a means of preserving the GDR and not a prelude to "recarving" European borders.[14] It was only when the people of East Germany and other East European countries continued to call for systemic change that the authorities were forced to acquiesce to revolutionary demands. As Gorbachev admitted later, the only alternative was a Tiananmen Square scenario—Soviet tanks on the streets and blood on the pavement.[15]

All this is true, but there remains the danger of underestimating the radical nature of thinking around Gorbachev at the time. The Brezhnev Doctrine had been buried in 1987, long before the people of Leipzig took to the streets. It needs emphasizing too that the Soviet leadership accepted the principle of multiparty elections for Hungary back in 1988 after the fall of Kadar. In the case of Poland, the June 1989 election was rigged in favor of the communists, but it had been agreed that the subsequent nationwide election would be wholly free. Furthermore, it was Moscow that pressed the Polish communist party to accept the judgement of the electorate. As Michael McGwire has written, "The pattern of events in 1987–1988 argues strongly that the Gorbachev leadership deliberately set in motion the process that would lead to the collapse of communist rule throughout Eastern Europe by the end of 1989."[16]

In the avalanche of events in 1989, inevitably Gorbachev became concerned over the eventual outcome of Soviet withdrawal from the region. The implications of a reunified Germany were of particular concern, although this was by no means restricted to Moscow. Both Mrs. Thatcher and President Mitterrand were worried that a bigger, more powerful Germany in the center of Europe could seriously unbalance the power structures on the continent. Nevertheless, for Gorbachev the main surprise and concern resulting from his policy in Eastern Europe related more to the speed of change rather than its nature or scope.[17] Gorbachev's critics in Moscow argued that he had acted with minimal consultation over policy toward Eastern Europe. Yevgeni Primakov, a leading foreign policy adviser to Gorbachev, told Henry Kissinger privately that tearing down the Berlin Wall had all been Gorbachev's idea.[18] In fact, the issue of the Berlin Wall had been firmly on the policy agenda as early as 1986, provoking Honecker to issue a public statement that, as far as he was concerned, the Wall would remain in place for a further fifty or a hundred years.[19]

On the issue of Eastern Europe more generally, there was a surprising level of agreement across the political spectrum on the need for change in Moscow's relationship with its Warsaw Pact allies. Yegor Ligachev, a conservative member of the Soviet communist party elite, acknowledged the need for the USSR's East European allies to have more independence. In April 1987 he said in Budapest, "Each country can act independently. In the past Moscow conducted the orchestra and everyone else listened. This is no longer the case."[20] Shevardnadze has said that he was placed under considerable pressure to use force during the course of 1989, but once the revolutions had taken place it was recognized there was no going back.[21] A secret analysis on the Polish crisis, commissioned by the CPSU Politburo after the non-communist coalition had been formed, argued in favor of seeking to cooperate with the new Polish government.[22] The International Department also produced a document that agreed with the Politburo analysis that there was no question of trying to restore Moscow's former position in the region.[23]

Why, then, was Moscow so willing to embrace the concept of radical change in a region traditionally of such strategic interest to Moscow? Although Gorbachev's policy did represent a radical break from the past, it is also true that it formed part of a process of change in Soviet–East European relations that had been developing since the death of

Stalin. This was reflected in every aspect of the relationship: economic, strategic, and ideological.

The Burden of the Outer Empire

Initially, Stalin had milked the region to rebuild the shattered Soviet economy after the war. However, this unequal relationship soon changed after his death, and by the time Gorbachev came to power in 1985, the position had been reversed. Then it was Moscow that was subsidizing Eastern Europe, largely through the supply of cheap Soviet oil and gas. M. Marrese and J. Vanous, in the most frequently cited work on the subject, estimated that Soviet subsidies amounted to as much as $80 billion in the period 1971–1980.[24] This was very high. Karen Dawisha has estimated it came to as much as 2 percent of Soviet GNP.[25] All these statistics remain little more than informed guesses, but there can be no doubt that Eastern Europe was perceived in Moscow to be a drain on the USSR's faltering economy.

In the past, Moscow had been willing to accept the cost of the "outer empire" because of the region's strategic and ideological importance. As Gorbachev introduced new political thinking, however, neither of these factors looked as relevant for the Soviet Union of the future.

In strategic terms, even before Gorbachev came to power, Eastern Europe had been divided effectively into two tiers. The southern tier had been downgraded in importance and Moscow's influence in those countries correspondingly reduced. Yugoslavia and Albania were both independent, neutral states, outside the Warsaw Pact. Romania was only a semi-detached member of the alliance and followed an increasingly independent foreign policy line under Ceausescu. Sofia and Budapest were Moscow's but no Soviet troops were deployed in Bulgaria; Hungary (which at various times has been placed both in the southern and northern tier) introduced far-reaching economic reform in 1968 that led to it becoming the most liberal state in the Warsaw Pact.

However, in most Western analyses up to 1989, the northern tier, consisting of East Germany, Poland, and Czechoslovakia, retained its vital strategic importance to Moscow.[26] The northern tier was both a defensive buffer against the possibility of Western attack and an offensive bridgehead in case of military action in Western Europe. However, according to Gorbachev's new political thinking, war in Europe was regarded as unlikely in the modern era, since neither the USSR nor the West entertained aggressive intentions. A buffer zone in these circumstances was of greatly reduced value. In the light of new political thinking, a Warsaw Pact commission reported in 1988 that unilateral cuts in Soviet forces, including total withdrawal from Hungary and

Czechoslovakia, could be made without affecting Soviet strategic interests.[27]

For Soviet leaders in the past, Eastern Europe was more than a strategic asset; it was also important for ideological reasons. The "conversion" of Eastern Europe to Marxism-Leninism after the war was evidence of the ideology's dynamism in the modern age. The Soviet Union was no longer an isolated island of communism surrounded by threatening capitalist states. Under Stalinism, socialism in one country had become socialism in one zone.

However, as Gorbachev became more critical of the communist experiment, more willing to embrace aspects of the Western experience, and eager to reintegrate the USSR into the political as well as the economic world community, the ideological nature of states became unimportant in the context of Soviet foreign relations. No longer did Moscow want to keep the West at a distance; instead it wished to draw closer and become a respected member of the world community. In those circumstances, the East European buffer looked an increasingly costly encumbrance to improved relations with the West. As a result, when the Berlin Wall finally fell on November 9, 1989, the pro-Western and reformist press in the Soviet Union welcomed the move as natural and beneficial for the USSR in its relations with the rest of the world.[28]

In sum, although many in the Soviet Union were shocked by the speed and comprehensiveness of the communist collapse in Eastern Europe, withdrawal from the region was part of a process begun in the mid-1980s that had support among most sections of the Soviet elite. This meant that the chances of a reimposition of Soviet dominance was greatly reduced. It was clear too that such was the defeat in 1989 of communism that Moscow's former dominance could be restored only through force.

The Post-Revolutionary Period

Although communism collapsed in Eastern Europe, Russian leaders hoped initially that Moscow would be able to retain influence in the region. This could be achieved through economic or military alliances.

Declining Economic Ties

In spite of Gorbachev's hopes, the CMEA had few supporters in the region. It compared badly with its mirror image in the West, the European Community. The CMEA had singularly failed to integrate the communist economies since its inception in 1947 and had scarcely facilitated multilateral trade. As it had failed as an institution in the communist era, it was unlikely to have any relevance when the East Europeans abandoned the state planning system. The CMEA was formally abolished on June 28, 1991, but it had ceased to have any operative function long before that.

However, the secret document produced by the International Department argued that the end of the CMEA did not mean the end of Soviet influence in the region.[29] On the contrary, it was pointed out that Eastern Europe remained economically highly dependent on the Soviet Union, both as a market for consumer goods, which were often uncompetitive on the world market, and as a source of energy and natural resources. The document reckoned that as much as 80 percent of the region's oil and almost 100 percent of its gas came from the Soviet Union. It was hoped, therefore, to use such dependency to defend Soviet interests in the area—a policy that both Gorbachev and Yeltsin have followed in Moscow's relations with recalcitrant nationalist leaders in the Soviet republics and successor states.

There was evidence that the USSR was attempting a policy of economic blackmail in the case of Czechoslovakia when Moscow threatened to cut oil supplies after Prague condemned Soviet military action in the Baltic republics in January 1991. The Czechs responded by threatening to unilaterally leave the Warsaw Pact.[30] It all came to nothing, as the attempted coup in Lithuania and Latvia fizzled out. In any case, the proposed linkage policy collapsed, since the state of the Soviet economy gave Moscow little in the way of leverage. On the contrary, the USSR, in the new economic circumstances after 1989, soon found itself facing significant trade deficits with its former East European allies.

The International Department had been right, however, in sensing the importance of the USSR to the immediate economic prospects of its former allies. The economies of Eastern Europe suffered when all trade with the Soviet Union was conducted in hard currency from January 1991. This meant an end to cheap Soviet oil and gas, which had been so vital for economic growth in the region. At the same time, the collapse of the Soviet economy meant that trade between the USSR and Eastern Europe was roughly halved in the period 1989–1993.[31] As a result, the years immediately after 1989 were very difficult; Eastern European countries began to restructure their economies and were forced to redirect their trade away from the Soviet Union.

Security Concerns

The CMEA was given up without much of a struggle. The dissolution of the Warsaw Pact was a more painful process. Moscow was greatly worried by the threat of a political vacuum in an area of traditional instability. The fear of renewed encirclement by NATO powers prompted army officers such as General Mikhail Moiseev to argue that Soviet troops should remain in Eastern Europe as long as there were U.S. troops on the continent.[32]

In those states that had security concerns beyond Moscow, a long-term process of withdrawal looked acceptable. Bulgaria perceived Moscow as a protector against the Turks, while many in Poland feared German revanchism. Polish fears were set aside, however, by the multilateral treaty of unification of September 1990 and the bilateral Polish-German treaty of November 14, when the western frontiers of Poland were fully recognized in international law. In contrast, the Hungarians and Czechs always believed the main threat to security and independence came from the East. As long as Soviet troops remained, there was felt to be a danger of the reimposition of Soviet control. In spring 1990, the Soviet authorities bowed to international pressure and agreed to start the process of troop withdrawal.

The issue of the GDR was always likely to present particular problems. This proved to be the case. The central rationale of Soviet post-war policy in Europe had been to prevent the rise of a strong, militarized Germany allied to the West. However, in January 1990, Hans Modrow, then the East German leader, convinced Gorbachev that the German people would accept nothing less than reunification.[33] This view was confirmed in the March elections by the overwhelming victory for Helmut Kohl's political allies, the Christian Democratic alliance.

As the GDR collapsed economically and politically, the Soviet Union was unprepared to defend it as a sovereign state with economic subsidy or military force.[34] Therefore, Russia was forced to compromise. Shevardnadze accepted the idea of rapid economic and monetary union as early as February, but he was less happy at the prospect of NATO membership. However, by the summer Moscow had come around to the view, advocated by most Europeans East and West, that the best way to contain the power of a reunified Germany was through its membership in viable Western institutions. Thus, Soviet ideas of a neutral Germany, or a Germany straddling both NATO and the Warsaw Pact, were dropped. At a momentous meeting with Helmut Kohl in Sevastopol in July, Gorbachev agreed to German political union by October, to the unified state's full membership in NATO, and to the withdrawal of all Soviet troops from the territory of the former GDR by the end of 1994 (later brought forward to August).

In return, Gorbachev won some important concessions. First, he gained commitments on security that were aimed at reassuring Moscow that a reunified Germany posed no military threat to the USSR or Europe. Thus, it was agreed that the unified German army would have a ceiling of 370,000 troops, 100,000 less than the number in the West German army at that time. Furthermore, NATO troops would not be deployed in the zone of the former GDR, and Germany would remain a non-nuclear signatory of the Non-Proliferation Treaty. NATO also formally committed itself in its July Declaration to reduce and restructure its military forces and to redefine its purpose as no longer anti-Soviet. Second, Kohl agreed to provide massive economic aid to the Soviet Union and to act as the Soviet representative in international forums such as the G-7.

Despite these concessions, a reunified Germany in NATO was more than many conservatives could stomach. Shevardnadze faced outraged generals at the 28th CPSU Congress in July 1990. But after fierce debate, Gorbachev and the reformers emerged from the congress victorious. This was important in allowing Moscow to press ahead with its German policy, and the final agreement on a reunified Germany was signed on September 12.

After the July party congress, hard-line forces in the USSR regrouped and began to put pressure on the reformers, provoking concern in Eastern Europe. Their worst fears were realized when the power struggle in Moscow climaxed in the August coup of 1991. There are reasons to believe relations with the West would have worsened had the coup been successful. However, during the coup, international borders remained open and there was no unusual military activity except at Tallinn in Estonia. The emergency committee said little on foreign policy, but what it did say emphasized continuity. Most important, the leader of the committee declared that the withdrawal of Soviet troops from Germany would still be completed on schedule. This emphasizes two points made earlier. There was a reluctant acceptance, even among the hard-liners, of the changes in Eastern Europe. And there was a desire among all sections of the Soviet elite to maintain reasonable relations with the West.

The Post-Soviet Period

When the USSR formally ceased to exist in December 1991, relations between Moscow and Eastern Europe were transformed in a number of ways. Some of these changes were long-term, others proved to be less durable.

Geopolitics, Economics, and Nationalism

First, there was a geopolitical shift. Russia, as a new sovereign state, no longer shared borders with Eastern Europe—except in the case of Kaliningrad, which bordered Poland. Instead, western Soviet successor states such as Belarus, Ukraine, the Baltic states, and Moldova provided a new buffer zone between Russia and Eastern Europe. This was of some comfort to the states of Eastern Europe that no longer had the mighty Soviet Union as a neighbor. But new uncertainties had entered the equation. A political vacuum opened up in Eastern Europe at the same time that economic dislocation, social upheaval, and political instability added to security fears.

Economic problems ran deep in the first few years after the revolutions of 1989, but since then there have been encouraging signs of improvement even in the southern tier of the region. Poland was the first to experience positive growth—2 percent in 1992, and 4 percent in 1993 with inflation down to 12 percent.[35] The former East Germany, after unprecedented levels of investment, reaped the benefit with an 8 percent increase in output in the first quarter of 1994.[36] On the downside, economic reform has usually been accompanied by social problems, including unemployment, growing wage differentials, rising crime, and cuts in welfare provision. Only the Czech Republic has managed to record levels of growth (1 percent in 1993) while keeping both inflation (20 percent) and unemployment (3 percent) at acceptable levels.[37] As a result, political disaffection has continued in much of the region. Unstable coalition governments have bedeviled politics in Poland, and nationalism has created problems in Yugoslavia, Russia, and Hungary.

Three states have split up under nationalist pressure—the USSR and Yugoslavia in 1991 and Czechoslovakia in 1993. Only the Czech Republic has prospered. In Hungary, there are reports of a virulent strain of nationalism emerging. Although Hungary is a relatively homogenous society—90 percent of the population is native Magyar—a large number of Hungarians live abroad: 2 million in Romania, 600,000 in Slovakia, and 400,000 in Vojvodina in the former Yugoslavia. Despite growing concern over the fate of these Hungarians, opinion polls reveal the Hungarian public to be unwilling to risk military intervention in their defense.[38] Growing popular dissatisfaction with the government, however, could provoke further ethnic tensions.

The main fear, of course, is the former Yugoslavia. There is a real danger of the war spilling over its present borders, and if this does happen it could engulf many countries in the region, including Hungary, Bulgaria, Albania, and Russia.

With war in the former Yugoslavia accompanied by the rise of nationalism in Russia, Eastern Europe has become more concerned than ever over security issues. As a result, the leaders of Eastern Europe have tended to look westward in an attempt to fill the uneasy political vacuum in the region.[39] The Visegrad group, including the Czech Republic, Slovakia, Hungary, and Poland, was set up in early 1991 largely to promote membership of Western institutions.

NATO, Russia, and Eastern Europe

In security matters, the problem has been twofold. First, there has been an unwillingness on the part of some Western countries, notably France and Britain, to offer a collective security agreement to the former Warsaw Pact states. Second, Russia has been reluctant to countenance any eastward extension of NATO, which is still perceived by some in Moscow as an anti-Russian military coalition. Some kind of compromise was reached in November 1991 when NATO introduced the NACC (North Atlantic Cooperation Council), whose aim was to act as a consultative body on security issues. The NACC is open to all NATO countries and those of Eastern Europe. The operations of NACC introduced the workings of NATO to East European countries, but its overall role was unclear. Was membership in this council a prelude to full NATO membership and a security guarantee or would the NACC develop into a credible security institution in its own right?

Poland's full membership in NATO looked possible, if only briefly, after Yeltsin's visit to that country in September 1993. In a joint declaration, the Russian president stated that Polish membership in NATO "does not go against the interests of other states, including the interests of Russia."[40] The president's declaration took the Russian Foreign Ministry by surprise, and the defense lobby was deeply suspicious. Yevgeni Primakov, the head of the Russian Foreign Intelligence Service, put forward the military view at a press conference in November: "This expansion would bring the biggest military grouping in the world, with its colossal offensive potential, directly to the borders of Russia. If this happens, the need would arise for a fundamental reappraisal of all defense concepts on our side, a redeployment of armed forces and changes in operational plans." [41]

Recognizing the importance of the military in his standoff with the White House, Yeltsin retracted his earlier agreement with Walesa. In a letter to Western leaders, Yeltsin wrote that NATO membership for East European states was acceptable only if Russia was also a member. To the consternation of Eastern Europe, Yeltsin proposed that Russia and the West should jointly guarantee security for countries in the region. Kozyrev and the Foreign Ministry fell in line, arguing that NATO was ill-suited to deal with the main problems of the region—migration, economic dislocation, and nationalism. The Russian foreign minister suggested that the CSCE (Conference on Security and Cooperation in Europe), a non-military body that included all states in Europe—and most importantly Russia as a full member—was more suited to the future demands of Eastern Europe.[42]

In an attempt to move the process along, President Clinton formulated the Partnership for Peace (PFP), which was formally introduced at the NATO summit in January 1994. The PFP was open to all NACC and CSCE states. The Visegrad group was disappointed because it did not include a collective security guarantee, but NATO committed itself to "consult with any active participant in the Partnership, if that partner perceives a direct threat to its territorial integrity, political independence, or security."[43] Initially, Clinton's initiative was welcomed in Moscow. Kozyrev described the PFP as a step in the right direction. Between February 28 and March 1, 1994, a NATO briefing team went to Moscow to give more details to the Russian leadership on the PFP agreement. All the former Warsaw Pact countries signed up for the partnership, but Russia hesitated, indicating that it would demand a special position in the partnership.

Eastern Europe and the European Union

As full membership in NATO looked unlikely in the short term, the East Europeans turned to the European Union (EU). Being a non-military organization, the EU will always be more acceptable to Moscow. Membership in the EU also means funds for restructuring and close integration into Western Europe. Furthermore, any member of the EU automatically becomes eligible for the West European Union (WEU), seen by some as the future defense arm of the European Union. Although Moscow might well oppose its former allies becoming members of the WEU, the WEU is less threatening than NATO, since it does not include the United States as a member. All the former Warsaw Pact states have become associate members of the EU, with the promise of full membership by the year 2000. Formal applications for full membership were first made by Hungary and Poland in April 1994.

Problems remain, however. Little aid from the EU has actually reached the East in terms of "actual grants."[44] Furthermore, EU tariffs remain in place on the goods Eastern Europe is eager to export, such as agricultural products, coal, steel, and textiles. As a result, a growing trade imbalance between the two parts of Europe has emerged. An EU deficit in trade of $1 billion in 1990 turned into a $5 billion surplus in 1993.[45] In these circumstances, the EU has offered aid for Eastern Europe to rebuild its trade with the former Soviet Union.

As integration into the West has been slower than Eastern Europe had hoped and expected, a number of alliances have been set up among East European states, some of which include West Europe. In addition to the Visegrad group, they include the Central European Initiative (formerly the Pentagonale), the Council of Baltic States, and the Central East

European Free Trade Area. However, these alliances have been of minimal importance, since they are seen either as temporary or as a means of easing the passage to full membership in NATO or the EU. The East has no desire to make any of these alliances appear viable as an alternative to integration into the West, which is perceived to be the only practical way to secure independence and economic prosperity in the long term.

The Threat from Russia

Russian Nationalism

The main threat to these aspirations is believed to come from Russia. The situation in Russia remains highly inflammatory The continuing domestic crisis has led to considerable disillusionment among the Russian people with the Yeltsin administration and the process of reform. Under nationalist pressure, Yeltsin toughened Russian foreign policy after 1992 and adopted a more interventionist stance in the Soviet successor states. The relative success of Vladimir Zhirinovsky in the December 1993 elections sent shock waves around the world. Eastern Europe feared that an imperialist revival in Russia would pose a direct threat to its continued independence. How real is that threat?

Zhirinovsky, undoubtedly, is a Russian imperialist who openly advocates Russian expansionism into Eastern Europe. After December, the possibility of Zhirinovsky winning the presidential election in 1996 could no longer be ruled out: Zhirinovsky's electoral performance was strong, building on the 7.8 percent of the vote that he received in the June 1991 presidential elections. However it is important not to exaggerate his power in the country. His party, the Liberal Democratic Party of Russia (LDPR), which has split since the election, won 23 percent on the party list but performed poorly in the constituencies, gaining only five further seats for a total of sixty-four. The reformist Russia's Choice, led by Gaidar, won most seats in the State Duma, with seventy-eight. Although no party got close to a majority in the 450-seat State Duma, arguably the communists (in alliance with the agrarian party) won the election overall with eighty-seven seats combined.

The poor showing in the constituencies reveals that the LDPR, at the organizational level, is fairly weak. The vote was a personal one for Vladimir Zhirinovsky as leader of the LDPR. Yet even those who voted for Zhirinovsky in the parliamentary elections have indicated in opinion polls that they would not support him in a presidential race.[46] The majority supported Zhirinovsky less because of his policy program than as a general protest against the government.

Nevertheless, it cannot be denied that nationalism is on the upswing in Russia, especially among the young and the military.[47] Parliament has been vociferous in demanding a more nationalist agenda from its executive. In that sense, Zhirinovsky is the tip of an iceberg. If Zhirinovsky fails to capitalize on his current prominence, it is highly likely that another nationalist, such as the more pragmatic Alexander Rutskoi, will emerge as an alternative.

This rise in nationalism has been reflected in Yeltsin's renewed activism in foreign policy. Moscow has acted to bring the CIS countries closer together and to re-emphasize Russia's political dominance over the territory of the former Soviet Union. Of the former Soviet republics, only the Baltic republics remain outside the CIS. Agreements have been signed for Russia to maintain bases in CIS states, and Russian troops guard all the borders of the former Soviet Union save Moldova and the Baltics. From the East European point of view, the Russian army has returned as an uncomfortable neighbor.

However, such moves should not be viewed merely as a prelude to renewed imperialism in Eastern Europe. There are many obvious differences between the near abroad and Eastern Europe. Most important, even at the height of the Cold War, the states of Eastern Europe were recognized in international law as sovereign states. In contrast, the non-Russian CIS states have little history of independence. The close ties and mutual strategic interests remain for the countries of the former Soviet Union. This is less obviously so in the case of the more distant region of Eastern Europe, with only three possible exceptions: Kaliningrad, the Moldova-Romania issue, and the former Yugoslavia. We will take each in turn.

The Kaliningrad Question

Formerly a German city called Konigsberg, Kaliningrad was taken by the Russians during the war. The population of 900,000 is predominantly Russian, although an increasing number of ethnic Germans, estimated at about 20,000, have recently begun to settle there. There are few signs, however, of the ethnic Germans wishing to secede from Russia, and the governments of Poland and Germany have both formally renounced all claims to the territory.[48] But Kaliningrad is in a vulnerable geopolitical position, since it is separated from the Russian mainland by 600 miles and the two republics of Belarus and Lithuania. Communications with the region have become more difficult and costly since the erection of customs posts in the Baltic republics. The government in Lithuania also has a useful bargaining lever in its relations with Moscow, since all electricity and oil to Kaliningrad has to pass through its republic.

Kaliningrad has considerable strategic value to Moscow. It contains Russia's only western warm-water port and houses the Russian Baltic fleet. Since the withdrawal of troops began in the Baltic republics, many have been redeployed to Kaliningrad. As Kaliningrad borders Poland, the military buildup has become the main cause of tension between Moscow and Warsaw.[49] There is no desire in Poland, however, to exacerbate the problem.

The Moldova-Romania Question

Moldova's relationship to Romania likewise is an important issue because it may draw Russians into armed conflict. About 64 percent of the Moldovan population are ethnic Romanians. After the fall of Ceausescu, some ethnic Romanians expressed a desire for reunification with Bucharest. This, in turn, led Slavic Moldovans (most of whom are ethnic Russians), who made up about 25 percent of the population, to set up a secessionist "Trans-Dniester Republic" on Moldovan territory after the collapse of the USSR in December 1991. Since 40 percent of this new "republic" was Moldovan, the claim of independence was violently resisted, leading to hundreds of deaths at the height of the conflict in May-June 1992. In July Boris Yeltsin and Mircea Snegur, the Moldovan president, agreed to a cease-fire in which Trans-Dniester was accorded special status but remained within the state of Moldova. Trans-Dniester was, however, guaranteed the right of secession if Moldova reunited with Romania.

If reunification were to take place, it would result in a major political crisis. However, the risk of this happening has been exaggerated by the Russians in Moldova. Snegur has opposed reunification, and in a poll in early 1994 only 5 percent of Moldovans supported the idea.[50] Moldova has no history as a nation-state, and has shared its history at various times since 1812 with both Russia and Romania. Therefore, there is no unified view among ethnic Moldovans that Moldova's fate is inextricably tied up with Bucharest. Moreover, Romania has few attractions to the ethnically uncommitted. Living standards are lower there than in Moldova, and even without Ceausescu, Romania remains an authoritarian state that has had problems throwing off its communist past. Bucharest has also acted with circumspection on the issue. Romania was one of the first countries to recognize Moldova's independence and to open an embassy in Chisinau.

There is still the problem, however, of the Russian military. As elsewhere in the near abroad, it has acted on occasion in Trans-Dniester in apparent defiance of the political authorities in Moscow. The commanding officer of the 10,000 strong Russian 14th Army, Alexander

Lebed, has allowed his troops to get involved in the Trans-Dniester dispute on the side of the Russians. He has also publicly opposed Yeltsin's agreement to withdraw the 14th Army.[51] Lebed was able to act independently due to his close relations with influential military figures in Moscow, including Afghan veterans, the former vice-president, Rutskoi, and Defense Minister Grachev. Since the storming of the White House in October 1993, the autonomy of the military may have grown, adding to concerns in Eastern Europe.[52]

The Yugoslav Question

Such worries have been compounded by the belief in some quarters that official Russian foreign policy has converged with the military perspective.[53] Moscow's reasserting its influence in the former Yugoslavia has been, for many, the most obvious example of Moscow's new strategic perspective on foreign policy. How far has Russia acted irresponsibly in the former Yugoslavia?

In fact, the Russian government has followed the basic outlines of international policy in the former Yugoslavia insofar as that has been possible given the frequent U-turns and disputes between Western partners. Thus, Moscow has agreed that the burden of blame for the war rests with the Serbs. Therefore, it has supported key UN resolutions against the Serbs, including the imposition of economic sanctions on Belgrade since May 1992.

However, Moscow has argued that the Western view of the war has been one-sided. For Russia, the Serbs are not the only guilty party. According to Moscow, the war began because Bosnia and Croatia as independent sovereign states were unacceptable to a significant proportion of their respective populations. The conflict in the former Yugoslavia, therefore, was not a war of aggression waged by the Serbs but a civil war over national rights.[54]

As a result, the Yeltsin administration has consistently held to the view that the problems can never be solved by military force. Therefore, Moscow has supported the UN embargo on all military equipment to any of the combatants. It has also been highly suspicious of President Clinton's call for airstrikes, believing they would only escalate the conflict. Some reports suggest that Moscow has taken a more hard-line, pro-Serb stance since the December 1993 elections. The fear is that this reflects the growth of nationalism in Russia. No doubt there is some truth in this. However, the level of pan-Slavic feeling in Russia is too often exaggerated. There is little evidence to suggest that parliament is accurately reflecting Russian public opinion on events in Bosnia. Apathy rather than outrage seems the current mood.

In practice, Moscow and Belgrade have used each other during the Yugoslav crisis for their own particular purposes. Thus, the Serbs saw the support of the Russians as a constraint on the possible use of Western military power and a conduit for Serb interests in international organizations. The Russians, for their part, were able to use the Bosnian impasse as a means to reintroduce themselves as a great power on the world stage. The Russian claim to leverage over the Serbs appeared vindicated when they negotiated the Sarajevo cease-fire in February 1994. However, the limits of Russia's newfound great-power role were revealed in April 1994 in Gorazde. Russia was embarrassed both by the NATO airstrikes, which were undertaken without its prior consultation, and by the Serbs' continued bombardment of the city despite Moscow's mediation.

Like the West's, Russia's leverage was limited because of a lack of political will and military readiness to get involved in the mire of the latest Balkan war. When Russian weakness was revealed, Yeltsin condemned the Serb bombardment of Gorazde and called for a Serb withdrawal. The strategic imperatives and pan-Slavic sentiments suddenly fell away.

Conclusion

The main danger for European security lies in the possibility of the war in Bosnia spilling over into neighboring countries. This might be welcomed by the Russian ultranationalists, who could use the escalation as a justification for Russian military intervention. Such a strategy is not backed by the government. Analysis of the Russian military varies, but most accept that it is scarcely able to fight a difficult, protracted war outside the borders of the former Soviet Union.[55]

The chance of Russia seeking to reassert itself in Eastern Europe is unlikely because the region is no longer a first priority for Russian policy-makers. That is why Gorbachev earlier decided to withdraw from Eastern Europe. The region remains the Russian gateway to the West, but no one in Moscow fears that those strategic interests are currently under threat. Therefore, there is little incentive for Russian interventionism as long as the war in former Yugoslavia and the nationalist conflicts inside the former Soviet Union can be contained.

Notes

I would like to offer the most sincere thanks to Dr. Cameron Ross of Cambridge and Oberlin Universities, who helped write a first draft of this chapter.

1. *Rossiiskie vesti*, October 29, 1992, p. 1.

2. Steve Crawshaw, *Good-bye to the USSR: The Collapse of Soviet Power*, London, Bloomsbury, 1992.

3. *Washington Post*, October 15, 1990, p. A1.

4. Jeffrey Gedmin, *The Hidden Hand: Gorbachev and the Collapse of East Germany*, Washington, D.C., AEI Press, 1992, p. 19.

5. Michael McGwire, *Perestroika and Soviet National Security*, Washington, D.C., Brookings Institution, 1991, p. 321; and Gedmin, *The Hidden Hand*, p. 21.

6. Mark Frankland, *The Patriots' Revolution: How East Europe Won Its Freedom*, London, Sinclair Stevenson, 1990, pp. 111 and 118.

7. Jan T.Gross, "Poland: From Civil Society to Political Nation," in Ivo Banac, ed, *Eastern Europe in Revolution*, Ithaca and London, Cornell University Press, 1992, pp. 62–64.

8. Charles Gati, *The Bloc That Failed: Soviet-East European Relations in Transition*, Bloomington, Indiana University Press, p. 169.

9. Michael R. Beschloss and Strobe Talbott, *At the Highest Level: The Inside Story of the End of the Cold War*, London, Little Brown, 1993, p. 102.

10. Gedmin, *The Hidden Hand*, p. 64.

11. Beschloss and Talbott, *At the Highest Level*, p. 134.

12. This has become the standard view of the 1989 revolutions. See, for example: Gati, *The Bloc That Failed*, and Alex Pravda (ed), *The End of the Outer Empire: Soviet-East European Relations in Transition, 1985–90*, London, RIIA/Sage, 1992.

13. See, for example, the secret International Department document of 1991 leaked to the German newspaper *Frankfurter Allgemeine Zeitung*, June 7, 1991; and A. Bovin, *Izvestiia*, January 1, 1991, p. 5.

14. Yuri Kornilov, "The Berlin Wall—TASS comment," *Soviet News*, November 15, 1989, p. 390.

15. Mikhail Gorbachev at the 28th CPSU Congress, *Vestnik*, August 1990, p. 19.

16. Michael McGwire, *Perestroika and Soviet National Security*, p. 360. Shevardnadze also stated in an interview with Fedor Burlatsky that he was fully aware of the consequences of his actions in Eastern Europe, see: *Soviet Weekly*, May 2, 1990, p. 6.

17. *Izvestiia*, May 27, 1990.

18. Beschloss and Talbott, *At the Highest Level*, p. 219.

19. *Soviet Weekly*, October 17, 1991; Eduard Shevardnadze, *The Future Belongs to Freedom*, New York, Free Press, 1991, p. 131; and Gedmin, *The Hidden Hand*, p. 49.

20. Jonathan Steele, *Eternal Russia: Yeltsin, Gorbachev and the Mirage of Democracy*, London and Boston, Faber and Faber, 1994, p. 174.

21. *Soviet Weekly*, May 2, 1990, p. 6.

22. Archives of the general department of the Central Committee of the CPSU, Folio 89, List 9, Document 33, September 28, 1989. Source cited in Steele, *Eternal Russia*, p. 181.

23. *Frankfurter Allgemeine Zeitung*, June 7, 1991.

24. M. Marrese and J. Vanous, *Soviet Subsidization of Trade with Eastern Europe*, Berkeley, University of California Press, 1983.

25. Karen Dawisha, *Eastern Europe, Gorbachev and Reform: The Great Challenge,* Cambridge, Cambridge University Press, 1988, p. 105.

26. See, Dawisha, *Eastern Europe,* p. 197; and Zbigniew Brzezinski, *The Grand Failure: The Birth and Death of Communism in the Twentieth Century,* London, Macmillan, 1989, p. 128.

27. For a detailed summary of Gorbachev's new political thinking, see McGwire, *Perestroika and Soviet National Security.*

28. See TASS comment, November 10, 1989, in *Soviet News,* November 15, 1989, p. 390.

29. *Frankfurter Allgemeine Zeitung,* June 7, 1991.

30. Libor Roucek, *After the Bloc: The New International Relations in Eastern Europe,* London, RIIA, Discussion Paper, 40, p. 5.

31. *Rossiiskie Vesti,* February 16, 1993, p. 2.

32. *New Times International,* March 1993, pp. 16–17.

33. For details of the meeting, see *Pravda,* January 31, 1990.

34. For more details on this entire process, see Gerhard Wettig, "Moscow's Acceptance of NATO: The Catalytic Role of German Unification," *Europe-Asia Studies,* vol. 45, no. 6, 1993, pp. 953–972.

35. *Moscow News,* April 15–21, 1994, p. 4.

36. *Guardian,* April 25, 1994, p. 13.

37. *Guardian,* March 19, 1994, p. 11.

38. Bill Miller, Stephen White, Paul Heywood, Matthew Wyman, "Democratic, Market and Nationalist Values in Russia and East Europe: December 1993," paper prepared for the 1994 Annual Conference of the British Political Studies Association, Swansea, March 1994, PR6/PSA94, p. 22.

39. See, for example, Vaclav Havel's plea for NATO membership in *International Herald Tribune,* October 20, 1993, p. 4.

40. *Moscow News,* September 3, 1993, p. 4.

41. Cited in *International Herald Tribune,* November 26, 1993, p. 1.

42. *Guardian,* October 28, 1993, p. 13.

43. "Partnership for Peace: A NATO Initiative," *Background Briefing,* London, Foreign and Commonwealth Office, March 1994, p. A2.

44. *International Herald Tribune,* April 18, 1994, p. 1.

45. *International Herald Tribune,* April 18, 1994, p. 1.

46. Bill Miller, Stephen White, Paul Heywood, and Matthew Wyman, "Zhirinovsky's Voters," *Two-Wave Russian Opinion Poll,* Glasgow University, Press Release 5, February 21, 1994, p. 1.

47. Miller et al., "Zhirinovsky's Voters."

48. *International Herald Tribune,* April 23–24, 1994, p. 5.

49. See the interview with Lech Walesa in *Moscow News,* no. 13, April 1–7, 1994, p. 5.

50. *Guardian,* February 25, 1994.

51. *Izvestiia,* February 26, 1993, p. 5.

52. See also Brian D. Taylor, "Civil and Military Relations After the October Uprising." *Survival,* vol. 36, no. 1, Spring 1994, who argues, in contrast to most

analyzes, that the military has not increased its influence in Russia since the events of October 1993.

53. One example of this could be found in the address by Vytautas Landsbergis, the former president of Lithuania, to the British Political Studies Association, University of Swansea, Wales, March 30, 1994.

54. This is a controversial view of the war in some quarters, but most European governments would not argue with it. It is also close to the analyzis presented by the respected journalist Misha Glenny; see *The Fall of Yugoslavia*, Harmondsworth, Penguin, 1992.

55. See, for example, Stephen Foye, "Russia's Defense Establishment in Disarray," *RFERL Research Report*, vol. 2, no. 36, September 10, 1993, pp. 49–53; and John Erickson, "Fallen from Grace: The New Russian Military," *World Policy Journal*, vol. X, no. 2, Summer 1993, pp. 19–24.

5

Russian Policy Toward Western Europe: The German Axis

Peter Shearman

Introduction

Russia has always had an ambivalent attitude toward Europe and the West. For a complete understanding of Russia's relations with Western Europe, it is important that certain historical cognitive and ideological issues be appreciated.[1] But Russia's relations with Western Europe are also determined by a number of other factors that are external, structural, and domestic. As suggested in Chapter 1 the German question was an important factor in the development of the East-West Cold War competition. With the reunification of Germany and the end of the bipolar power structure, the question of Germany's future is again uncertain. As Simon Serfaty puts it, "Throughout the years, the future of 'Europe' has been built around, about, or against Germany."[2] Germany was central to Soviet policy in Europe too and will continue to be the pillar of Russian policy in Western Europe into the next century.

In terms of economic assistance and trade relations, Western Europe remains important for Russia both in bilateral relationships with individual countries and through the institutions of the European Union (EU). Western Europe is also important in the security realm, not only in military terms as traditionally conceived but also with regard to the securing of human rights for ethnic minorities and dealing with crime and ecology problems. This chapter focuses on three aspects of Russia's policy toward Western Europe: the importance of Germany, security issues, and relations with the EU.

The German Question

East Germany: The "Jewel in the Crown" of the Soviet Empire

The division of Germany into East and West was a reflection of the power vacuum that resulted in Europe after the defeat of Hitler's Germany in 1945. The Soviet Union sought to gain three basic objectives by creating in the eastern half of the defeated Reich a political economy modelled on that of the USSR. First were security concerns: East Germany provided Stalin with a security "buffer zone" to counter any military threat from the West—and the division of Germany ensured that a powerful German state would not again be in a position to challenge the European balance of power. Second were economic factors: Stalin's objectives were to gain economic benefits for the Soviet Union through war reparations—and modelling the GDR's economy on that of the USSR allowed Moscow to control the planning process to suit the needs of the Soviet economy. Also, given the degree of fusion of politics and economics in a Soviet-type system, integrating the East German economy into the framework of the CMEA gave Stalin additional controls over *political* developments in East Berlin. Third were ideological and societal factors: incorporating East Germany into a wider Soviet communist bloc of nations demonstrated for Stalin the legitimacy and efficacy of Moscow's leading role in an expanded "world socialist system." East Germany was critical for the Soviet leadership's perceptions of its own security and for its economic and political relations with Western Europe. As Adrian Hyde-Price put it, East Germany was the "Jewel in the Crown" of the Soviet empire.[3]

Mike Bowker's chapter in this volume describes how Gorbachev came to encourage reform in East Germany, and then ultimately to accept the inevitable forces for East German reintegration with West Germany that his own reformism stimulated. While Stalin's "ideal empire" in Eastern Europe was delivering payoffs in the early post-war period in each of the three categories listed above, by the late Brezhnev period the Soviet Union was achieving only one of its original objectives. It was still maintaining its security buffer zone, but at an increasing cost as the economies of Eastern Europe began to stagnate and Moscow was left to bail them out—in what turned out to be a failed attempt to stave off domestic discontent.[4] Finally, an overstretched Soviet Union could no longer afford to maintain a buffer zone, especially one that was of dubious worth in an age of nuclear weapons. In addition, Gorbachev recognized that Western Europe did not pose a real and present danger to the territorial integrity of the Soviet Union—on the contrary, improving relations with the countries of the region offered possibilities for assisting domestic reform and economic development.

Detente: Germany Between East and West

This was the essence of Gorbachev's conception of a "common European home": he sought to break down the ideological divisions and mutual suspicions dividing Europe in order to facilitate perestroika at home.[5] The unanticipated consequences included the collapse of communism in Eastern Europe and the unification of Germany. Western Europe, and particularly West Germany, was viewed by Gorbachev and senior figures in the Soviet Ministry of Foreign Affairs as the most promising target for trade and scientific cooperation.

The seeds of East-West detente in the early 1970s were to be found not in Washington but in Europe, with Chancellor Willy Brandt's *Ostpolitik* a key factor in stimulating the whole process. Germany and France, not the United States, were the initiators of this earlier easing of Cold War tensions—indeed, Henry Kissinger, whose name is associated with the U.S. policy of detente during this period, acknowledges this in his memoirs. Kissinger notes that Brandt's *Ostpolitik* "had effects far beyond those intended," contributing to what became "a race to Moscow," a race in which Brandt felt it necessary for the U.S. to catch up with the governments in Bonn and Paris so that Washington could maintain its leading position in the West in dealing with the Soviet Union.[6]

With increasing East-West tensions in the late 1970s there existed a "residual detente" between both sides of the iron curtain in Europe—even the "Iron Lady," Margaret Thatcher of the United Kingdom, would not give in to President Reagan's pressures to cancel the gas pipeline agreements made with the USSR in the early 1980s.[7] West Germany, too, continued to abide by its side of the pipeline agreement in the face of U.S. pressure. The Soviet Union and West Germany signed four contracts (in 1970, 1972, 1974, and 1981) for Soviet deliveries of natural gas up to the year 2008, with Bonn supplying large-diameter pipes, machinery, and equipment for the gas pipelines.

Although the Soviet Union was unsuccessful in causing serious splits between Washington and Bonn over security issues, it achieved at least partial success in the economic and diplomatic realms. West Germany was the Soviet Union's largest trade partner outside of the CMEA nations (East Germany was Moscow's largest single trade partner) and had been consistently since 1972 despite periods of rising East-West tensions. For example, whereas Soviet trade with the United States was halved between 1979 and 1980 (during the onset of renewed Cold War tensions following the Soviet invasion of Afghanistan), that with West

Germany increased. In 1985, the year that Gorbachev came to power, West Germany accounted for 5 percent of the total volume of Soviet foreign trade, whereas the United States accounted for less than 2 percent.[8]

Kissinger was concerned (along with other members of the Western alliance) that this example of German unilateralism in foreign policy would "unleash a latent German nationalism." He feared the resurgence of a "free-wheeling, powerful Germany trying to maneuver between East and West" as posing the "classic challenge to the equilibrium of Europe...."[9] This was a concern of Moscow's too, as Brezhnev nevertheless sought to capitalize on Germany's new foreign policy orientation in order to gain access to Western technology while simultaneously undermining the solidarity of the Atlantic alliance. Yet Bonn, so long as Germany was divided and the Soviet threat provided sufficient incentive for the United States to maintain its dominance over the Western alliance, was restricted in the extent to which it could engage in an independent policy toward Moscow.

German Reunification

Gorbachev facilitated and even encouraged the developments that led to the toppling of the communist regimes in Hungary and Poland. Germany was different: it was the key to unlocking the Cold War and long the "linchpin of Soviet strategy in Western Europe."[10] Moscow could not easily give up its control over East Germany, yet events by late 1989 had gone so far as to make it impossible, without risking massive military intervention, for the Soviet Union to do more than improvise policy concerning events it could no longer control. Gorbachev and West German Chancellor Helmut Kohl met together to work out the final details in the Soviet resort of Zheleznovodsk in the Caucasus. Alvin Rubinstein considers the agreement the two leaders concluded at Zheleznovodsk to have been "as dramatic as the Rapallo agreement of April 1922 and as momentous for all of Europe as the 1939 Nazi-Soviet pact."[11] The Soviet Union agreed to recognize the territorial integrity and political sovereignty of a united Germany with rights, if so desired, to remain in NATO, and to remove all Soviet troops from German soil by the end of 1994.

For its part Germany agreed to restrict its armed forces to 370,000 personnel; to renounce the right to manufacture biological, chemical, or nuclear weapons; to accept the post-war territorial status quo in Europe; and, most important for Gorbachev, to provide generous economic aid to the Soviet Union.

Both sides kept to their commitments. Yeltsin attended a ceremony in Berlin to commemorate the departure of the last remaining Soviet troops stationed on German soil on September 1, 1994, and Germany delivered billions of dollars in aid, part of which was used to construct barracks for the repatriated Russian soldiers. German economic aid to Moscow between 1989 and 1992 represented more than 50 percent of all foreign economic assistance ($50 billion, compared to $9 billion from the U.S. and $3 billion from Japan).[12]

Russia and Germany: Key Players in a New Europe

With the fall of the Berlin Wall and the disintegration of the Soviet Union, Germany and Russia have once more become the key players in a turbulent and uncertain European arena, and the question of European security and stability and levels of integration (or disintegration) will be determined to a large degree by these two states. During the Cold War the two potential revisionist states in Europe were Soviet Russia and Germany—the one with predominant military power and a history of constant territorial expansion, the other defeated but situated in the center of Europe with a potential to rise again from the ashes of defeat. The institutions of the Cold War were in part designed to manage this distribution of power and to ensure that both Soviet *and German* power were contained—what Josef Joffe referred to as "Double Containment."[13] Now, with the Cold War over, both Russia and Germany share a similar dilemma in having to reinvent themselves. Both have similar preoccupations in creating new nations out of the ruins or amalgamations of old ones. They will both look increasingly inward, but when looking outward they will see one another as the main potential threat to overall stability, but also as the main potential partner in organizing a new balance of power in Europe.

Germany is now the unquestioned economic power in Europe, and since unification it has become far more confident in the pursuit of its perceived national interests. As Josef Joffe has noted, for the first time in its history Germany is "surrounded only by friends" and is hence much more likely to translate its economic power into political influence and to more forcefully project itself onto the international arena.[14] Following defeat in the Second World War and the subsequent pressure to constrain its political and military activities during the Cold War, West Germany was effectively a "semi-sovereign state" (East Germany's sovereignty was of course even more limited). It was a time, according to the Bavarian Premier Edmund Stoiber, "when it was often considered a burden to be a German."[15] Free of Cold War shackles, Germany will once again assert its power both in Europe and on a global scale (before the end of the century Germany alongside Japan, will become a full member of the UN Security Council).

The end of the Cold War brought down the Berlin Wall, but it did not bring down with it the traditional boundaries of the nation-state. Rather, we have witnessed a resurgence of nationalism and an increase in the idea of the territorial nation-state. The two most important powers on both sides of the European continent are actively engaged in a renewed process of state-building. Europe is no longer bifurcated along military or ideological lines, but it is still nevertheless divided: it is divided along socio-economic lines. The two great powers of Russia and Germany are the polar forces on either side of the divide, and they will remain the key actors in Europe. Germany is increasingly looking eastward in its foreign policy, and when the political capital moves back to Berlin this process will be enhanced. Russia is increasingly looking westward, particularly to forging new relations with the "near abroad." Due to their political, historical, and economic interests in Central and Eastern Europe, Russia and Germany are bound to perceive each other as the *significant* other in their policy-making in the region.

A Special Relationship

In an interview in *Moscow News* in December 1993, the German ambassador in Moscow referred to a "special relationship" between Russia and Germany.[16] This is not surprising given the common interests and security concerns of the two countries. Both states lie close to regions of conflict, or potential conflict, that could spill over and lead to instability in neighboring territories. The Balkans are a case in point. Germany and Russia share a mutual interest in preventing a much wider Balkan war from developing out of the conflict in Bosnia. Both wish to prevent conflicts in Central Europe and Eastern Europe, for situated on either side of such a conflict, Germany and Russia could easily become embroiled. Both have an interest in containing conflicts in the republics of the former Soviet Union, in preventing hyper-nationalism, and in avoiding wide-scale migration and waves of refugees. It is also in the interest of both sides to prevent regional arms races, nuclear proliferation, international terrorism, and the smuggling and illegal sales of plutonium. Other states in Western Europe—and elsewhere—share these concerns. However, Germany and Russia, by dint of geography, national interests, and economic ties (and, some would add, historical, traditional, and cultural factors), have far greater direct interests than other major powers. In addition there is the mutual interest of the two governments in ensuring that Kaliningrad, the Russian enclave on the Baltic Sea that belonged to Germany before 1945 and that is physically separated from Russia by the Baltic republics, does not become an issue between them. Similarly, governments in Bonn and Moscow do not wish to make an issue out of the large numbers of citizens in Russia that claim German ancestry, many of whom wish to migrate to Germany.

That Russia's political relationship with Germany has been "special" and privileged in comparison to relations with other West European states is evidenced by the fact that Germany has acted as a lobby for Russia in international forums like the IMF. Germany was a strong proponent—often against opposition from the United States and Japan—of Russia's gaining membership in the group of leading industrial nations, making the G-7 into the G-8 (in the political sphere). Yeltsin has also gone directly through Germany in order to put Russia's case on specific issues to the West. For example, Yeltsin sent a message through Chancellor Kohl asking the West to support him in his struggle with the Russian parliament in early 1993. And as Jacob Heilbrunn noted, "Kohl was delighted when in March (1994) Boris Yeltsin called him first to confer on NATO's ultimatum on Sarajevo, before calling President Clinton."[17]

Security Issues

The Changing Security Agenda in Europe

In the post–Cold War era ethno-national identity, economic growth, and societal cohesiveness are replacing (or joining) military concerns as the main focus of European security.[18] With the end of bipolarism NATO is being transformed from a military alliance to counter the Soviet threat into an extended security community with a mission and scope yet to be fully elaborated but to include increasingly non-traditional roles. In Russia the large vote for the Liberal Democratic Party of nationalist Vladimir Zhirinovsky in the parliamentary elections of December 1993 is indicative of a mounting anti-Western Russian nationalism. Inside the Russian Federation titular nationalities in some autonomous republics are demanding complete independence from Russia. There is concern in Moscow for the well-being of the estimated 25 million Russians living in the other former republics of the USSR.

Yeltsin and Kozyrev have been forced by domestic pressures to moderate their pro-Western foreign policy and to concentrate more on dealing with these new security problems. It is tempting to apply the Weimar analogy to contemporary Russia: having lost a war (albeit a cold one) Moscow, in economic chaos, is suffering from hurt pride and a loss of national identity; extreme nationalist forces are gaining ground in an anarchic political setting by aggressively defending the interests of the Russians in the former Soviet Union. But such an analogy is misleading. The world of the 1990s is different from that of the 1930s. There is a consensus in an interdependent Europe that issues relating to ethnic minorities and citizenship are important and need to be resolved through political means, and human rights legislation and international and regional institutions exist to facilitate this. Russia is not being punished for waging the Cold War; rather, Western European states see it as in their interests to help Russia develop an effective market economy and liberal democracy. Economic reform and political pluralism are indeed the goals of the majority of Russia's new political groups. Thus any comparison to Germany of the 1920s and the rise of Hitler in the 1930s is, as Richard Sakwa states, "instructive but not wholly appropriate."[19]

Russia has not been challenging the status quo but seeking to participate in it and has been encouraged to do so by the leading Western states. On general security issues Russia and Western Europe have moved closer together in recognizing mutual interests. Russia has even participated in military cooperation in the Gulf with French and British forces in ensuring Iraq's compliance with UN sanctions. NATO, however, was one area of contention in the period 1993–1994.

Russia and NATO

With the demise of the Warsaw Pact and the collapse of the USSR, Russia has been reluctant to see any extension eastward in the membership of NATO. Military alliances are created by their potential enemies; NATO's role and function following the loss of the threat that created it (i.e., the USSR) has become controversial and uncertain. The Visegrad group of states—Poland, Hungary, the Czech Republic, and Slovakia—have the stated intention of gaining membership in NATO and the EU. Indicative of Bonn's newfound independence of action, it was the German foreign and defense ministers, Klaus Kinkel and Volker Ruhe (at a talk to the International Institute of Strategic Studies in London in March 1993), who first seriously posed the question of NATO membership being extended to these countries.

Earlier Hans-Dietrich Genscher, former long-serving German foreign minister and an important figure in Germany's *Ostpolitik*, with U.S. Secretary of State James Baker, had originated the idea to link Eastern Europe, including the USSR, to NATO through what came to be the North Atlantic Cooperation Council (NACC). The founding session of NACC took place on December 20, 1991—just as the Soviet Union was disintegrating. The result was that all of the former republics of the USSR gained automatic entry as separate members of the Council. As one commentator noted, this led to "the absurd situation where Kazakhstan now has a closer relationship with (NATO) Alliance members than does Austria."[20] Vladimir Kozin of the Russian Foreign Ministry's Department for Disarmament could still write in 1993 that NACC was a ". . . pioneer institution of post-confrontational interaction within which the idea of establishing partnership . . . can be put into practice."[21] This statement reflected a consensus that was emerging in political circles in Moscow *against* any further integration of the Visegrad states into the military structure of NATO. When leading German officials began to canvas this idea in 1993, many in Moscow were galvanized into preventing it from happening.

Thus it was surprising indeed (both to his hosts, the Western governments, and to his own Ministry of Foreign Affairs) when President Yeltsin, on an official visit to Warsaw in the summer of 1993, stated that he would not oppose Poland's eventual membership in NATO. The statement led to domestic controversy, reflected in debates on the issue in the Russian press.[22] What emerged was the articulation of a forceful policy opposed to extending NATO membership to the former Warsaw Pact states. Sergei Karaganov, the influential deputy director of the European Institute in Moscow, argued that it was not fear of an enhanced *military* threat that explained Russia's opposition to the Visegrad four entering NATO so much as the *political and psychological* consequences that would result.[23]

A Partnership for Peace

NATO was forced to work out a compromise and offered Eastern Europe, including Russia, Partnership for Peace agreements, that stopped well short of full membership in the alliance's military structures. Manfred Worner, NATO secretary general, stated that he was "well aware that stability in Europe depends on cooperation between Russia and NATO," and hence the Partnership for Peace was important for guaranteeing European security.[24] Sergio Balanzino, the deputy secretary general of the alliance, reiterated this view: "There will only be stability in Europe with and not against Russia."[25]

Opinion remained divided in Russia, but the government eventually agreed it would sign up for the partnership if Russia's great-power status was acknowledged in the agreement, thereby providing Moscow with an enhanced position vis-à-vis Eastern Europe (hence dealing with the psychological problem identified by Karaganov). Alexander Golz argued that Russia's relationship with NATO should be determined by its "status as a nuclear power with a military might far greater than those of other countries."[26] Russia joined the other East European states in signing on for the Partnership for Peace agreement in June 1994, an agreement that did in fact refer to Russia's special status in global affairs as one of the great powers in Europe.[27] The State Duma sought to prevent ratification of the agreement, condemning it as a betrayal of Russian national interests (a parliamentary vote on the issue only just failed to gain a majority) but Kozyrev, calling the deputies supporting the motion "traitors," pointed out that the agreement was not subject to ratification by the parliament. Kozyrev said the agreement reflected a new partnership between Russia and NATO and that it did not reflect a "Yalta Two" by dividing Europe into blocs but acknowledged Russia's importance to overall stability in Europe.[28]

The Partnership for Peace offers no security guarantees and allows for only fairly loose ties in the political and security realms. However, it does provide Russia with some access to NATO councils and hence an entry point to lobby for policies favored in Moscow. It does not give Russia any decision-making powers, but it does draw Russia closer to an organization originally established to counter Moscow's geopolitical ambitions. Russia will use these links with NATO in an attempt to legitimate its increasingly interventionary strategy in the near abroad in the pursuit of its national interest. Drawing Russia closer to NATO will also undermine, complicate, and possibly compromise the cohesiveness, unity, and ultimately the effectiveness of the alliance. Furthermore, it will now be impossible, without creating a political crisis in Europe, for NATO to offer full membership to the Visegrad nations without also offering membership to Russia, especially given the existing acknowledgment of Russia's special status. Far from being seen as a reflection of Russia's inferior status in global politics,[29] the agreement provides Russia with an entry point for having some influence over the West's basic security organization while retaining its own sphere of influence in the near abroad (the West having no representation, for example, in the CIS).

Western Europe and Russia's Sphere of Influence

High on the agenda of Russian security concerns are the rights of ethnic Russians living in the near abroad. Since the collapse of the USSR the Russian government has sought to use the Conference on Security and Cooperation in Europe (CSCE) as a vehicle to protect human rights against ethnic discrimination and also to legitimate its own "peacekeeping" role in the near abroad. Yury Ushakov, director of the European Department of the Russian Foreign Ministry, has suggested that the CSCE should act as the "central body" that would coordinate the activities of other regional organizations such as NATO, the CIS, and the West European Union. He proposed the creation of a new Executive Committee of ten to twelve permanent members (including Russia) with responsibility for overseeing the peacekeeping activities of the various regional groupings.[30] Kozyrev, too, has sought to gain legitimation for Moscow's intervention in conflicts on Russia's periphery through the CSCE. While justifying Russian policy with reference to universal human rights, Kozyrev also explicitly calls upon Western Europe to recognize Russia's traditional "sphere of influence"—"Russia's special role and responsibility in the former Soviet Union must be borne in mind by its Western partners and given support."[31]

Western European states share Moscow's concern about possible instability and conflict in Russia's near abroad. As Hannes Adomeit has noted, it is difficult to imagine any European country other than Russia willing to commit forces for peacekeeping on the territory of the former Soviet Union.[32] Again, it is Germany that has been the main target of Russia's attempt to gain West European acceptance of its special interests in the region. On the eve of a NATO summit in Brussels in January 1994, Kozyrev told the German press that Russia and Germany, "Europe's two major democracies," had a "historic common interest in Eastern Europe and could cooperate in stabilizing the region."[33] German Foreign Minister Kinkel in an interview in the *European* said that Russian peacekeeping activities in the CIS should be accepted "in cooperation with the CSCE" and also suggested the possibility of German military participation in such actions.[34] In an interview with *Der Spiegel* President Yeltsin said, in reference to Bosnia, that he would welcome it if "the Germans . . . send their soldiers as peace troops"—going on to say, "and not only in Yugoslavia."[35]

Russian policy toward Western Europe in the security sphere has been two-pronged: first to ensure that Russia's interests in Eastern Europe are taken into account, and second to gain acceptance of Russia's special role in the near abroad in defense of ethnic Russians and in order to maintain regional stability. A subsidiary, though important goal, is to foster cooperation in combating non-conventional threats to European security, for example, in countering terrorism and the illicit trade in plutonium. In each of these realms Western Europe has become more important than the United States in Russian diplomacy, and in Western Europe, Germany is the main target and potential partner.

The European Union and Economic Relations

Aid and Trade

As noted above, Gorbachev and Yeltsin sought to integrate the Soviet Union/Russia into the global economy and to gain access to aid and trade to assist economic development at home. Western Europe has been seen as a key to meeting these objectives. I have also noted how Germany has been both the largest trade partner for Russia and the most generous aid donor. In 1993, Germany's total trade turnover with Russia was two times as great as Russia's trade with France and the United Kingdom combined.[36] Russia's economy depends increasingly on access to West European markets. In 1993, trade with the EC accounted for 35 percent of Russia's trade with the "far abroad," and Oleg Davydov has estimated that when the Scandinavian states and Austria gain EC membership, that figure will increase to around 44 percent.[37] However, despite inducements from the Russian government for foreign capital investment in the Russian economy, West European states have been reluctant to take large risks because of the uncertainty of the political situation. Even German companies have been fairly slow to commit large investments given the chaos of the Russian economy.

German direct investment in Eastern Europe is larger than that of other West European states, tripling between 1989 and 1991. In 1993 direct German investment in the region rose 13 percent over the previous year, with Germany accounting for some 10 percent of the region's total investments.[38] For large companies such as Siemens and Volkswagen, Eastern Europe offers a very convenient investment site: close to home with an abundance of cheap skilled labor. Yet German companies are more willing to invest in Poland than they are in Russia, seeing this as much less of a risk. Indeed, if present trends continue Poland will replace Russia as Germany's largest trading partner in the East. More than half of all Poland's joint ventures have been concluded with German companies (more than five times those than with the U.S.).[39] Nevertheless, for Russia, Germany is still the most important trade, aid, and investment partner in the West. This is true also in broader relations with the European Union.

Cooperation Agreement with the European Union

Andrei Zagorsky notes that Russia's "main potentialities and its infrastructure are concentrated in its European part" and therefore Russia "cannot bypass Europe in seeking access to the world economy."[40] Under the communist party regime the Soviet Union, until Gorbachev came to power in the late 1980s, failed to recognize the EC as an actor in its own right. In the 1990s Moscow realizes the necessity to foster links to the EU in order to gain preferential trade agreements and access for Russian exports. Russia now has a separate ambassador assigned to Brussels, and in June 1994, following protracted negotiations (supervised by Alexander Shokhin for the Russian government), Moscow signed a Partnership and Cooperation Agreement with the EU. The agreement lifts trade barriers on a host of Russian goods (excluding steel, textiles, uranium).[41] During these negotiations Russian officials complained about EU members seeking merely to further their own selfish economic interests rather than seriously dealing with macro-economic issues—for example, reference was made to French intransigence in keeping Russia out of the uranium market.[42] Yet the agreement finally reached does bring

Russia much closer to Europe and links it much more tightly to the EU than before.

The agreement calls for meetings of the Russian president with leaders of the EU at least twice a year, and although it does not contain any commitment for Russia's eventual full membership (as do the agreements signed with other East European states), it does significantly enhance the prospects for Russia to improve its overall trade relations with EU members. As Jacques Santer, the Chairman of the European Commission stated, it also provides a "solid basis" for developing cooperation in banking and finance.[43] Indeed, the European Community has shown initiative in this and other areas through the European Bank for Reconstruction and Development (EBRD).

Russia and the EBRD

With the collapse of communism in Eastern Europe, it was Western Europe, under the influence of French President Mitterrand, that took the initiative in providing a mechanism to assist the transition from the communist plan to the capitalist market, which also helped to ensure the influence of the EU in the process.[44] Yelena Khalevinskaia claimed that the creation of the EBRD in May 1990 provided the EU with a potentially greater role than the U.S. or Japan in shaping regional and global economic policies.[45] This is a gross exaggeration of the bank's potential, but nonetheless the bank has achieved some of its stated objectives. Jacques Attali, then the bank's president, attended a ceremony officially opening a branch of the EBRD in Moscow in March 1993.[46]

The bank has assisted with a large number of projects in Russia. In 1993 it approved fifty-four projects worth 1.2 billion ECUs. The bank finances up to 35 percent of any single project, with the remaining investment coming from other organizations or private investors. By the end of 1993 the bank had invested 1.1 billion ECUs in the Russian Federation, including 17.5 million ECUs for technical cooperation, 86.8 million for credits, and 12.1 million for direct investment in stock. Projects funded included a power drilling company in Siberia, oil production facilities, and telecommunications. By mid-1994 there were nearly eighty projects being funded by the bank on Russian territory, including the reconstruction of the port of Vostochny in the Far East and of oil fields in West Siberia.[47]

It was announced at a meeting of the bank in Paris in August 1994 that it would allocate $100 million directly to Russian commercial banks and a further $300 million in credits to enable thirty to forty commercial banks to finance Russia's private sector.[48] Plans were also being drawn up to establish an investment fund in the Murmansk region, where Russia produces most of its rare earth materials.[49]

Understandably, given the scale of the problems facing the Russian government, the bank has come in for much criticism relating to the relatively modest and selective assistance that it has provided. The head of Russia's State Bank, Viktor Gerashchenko, complained about the EBRD's preoccupation with the "profitability" of projects "to the detriment of projects more vital for Russia." In April 1994, the president of the EBRD at the state bank's annual conference in St. Petersburg, stressed that the bank's basic principle was to abide by customary rational banking practices.[50] It is not surprising that the bank should be cautious about providing economic assistance to Russian private enterprise, and it has to be acknowledged that the level of assistance is certainly not massive. Yet the nature of assistance is significant in the banking and financial and infrastructural fields, which makes for important links between Western Europe and Russia when the latter's economy does finally take off.

Conclusion

In the political, economic, and security aspects of Russia's West European relations Germany looms large. Germany has the greatest interest in future political and economic development in Russia, hence the pattern as in earlier periods of the twentieth century—Russia and Germany as the key players in the newly emerging power structure on the European continent—will likely prevail. Germany's increasing interest in the East will also dictate that it will have to act more often unilaterally, independently of the EU. Russia's interests in the near abroad will determine that it too will act unilaterally in defense of its perceived national interests. Germany's and Russia's emerging spheres of interests are geographically proximate and will at times overlap. The relationship between Germany and Russia, the two largest states in Europe, is bound to be decisive as they continue to develop a complex web of political and economic ties.

In the wider international environment Germany and Russia are likely also to move closer to one another to counter the power and influence of the U.S. and Japan.[51] Jeffrey Simon predicts that "by the turn of the century the *Bundeswehr* will be the only European military force, other than that of Russia, capable of global air-and-sea lift projection."[52] In Europe, a Russian-German informal partnership is likely to develop.

Russia has also made important moves to integrate itself into West European political and security structures. Although only "partnership" agreements, the accords Russia concluded with the EU and NATO in the summer of 1994 have brought Russia closer to Western Europe than it has ever been before. Russia now has representation in organizations linked to the most important forums dealing with European issues in the political, economic, and security realms. In addition, Russia has signed bilateral accords for cooperation with other important West European countries, including France, Italy, Spain, and the U.K., that call for regular summits between government leaders. For example, in April 1994 on an official visit to Madrid, President Yeltsin signed a Treaty of Friendship and Cooperation allowing for cooperation between Spain and Russia in various fields, including the military. The treaty also calls for annual summits of top leaders.[53] Russian participation in West European councils is becoming institutionalized, thereby drawing Moscow to more closely identifying with the West and Europe.

Although many Russians—including members of Yeltsin's government—are disappointed in the level of aid provided by the EU and Western European states, Germany and the EU have been more generous than either Japan or the U.S. and more willing to risk investing in the Russian economy than the other two major Western powers. Unlike the United States, as Alexander Rutskoi put it following his parliamentary amnesty in March 1994, "Russia is not a guest in Europe, but a full participant in the European Community with an interest in its well-being."[54]

Russia's relations with Western Europe are likely to continue to widen and deepen, and Europe's future progress and stability depend to a great degree on facilitating this process.

Notes

1. See, for example, Paul Dukes (ed), *Russia and Europe*, London, Collins and Brown, 1991.

2. Simon Serfaty, "Defining 'Europe': Purpose Without Commitment," in Michael T. Clarke and Simon Serfaty (eds), *New Thinking and Old Realities*, Washington D.C., Seven Locks Press, 1991, pp. 127–160, p. 130.

3. Adrian Hyde-Price, "GDR-Soviet Relations," in Alex Pravda (ed), *The End of the Outer Empire: Soviet-East European Relations in Transition, 1985–90*, London, Sage/RIIA, 1992, pp. 151–167, p. 165.

4. See Valerie Bunce, "The Empire Strikes Back," *International Organization*, vol. 39, no. 7. 1985, pp. 1–14.

5. See Neil Malcolm, *Soviet Policy Perspectives on Western Europe*, London, Routledge/Royal Institute of International Affairs, 1989.

6. Henry Kissinger, *Years of Upheaval*, Boston, Little, Brown, 1982, p. 146.

7. On detente and the important role of West Germany (and the residual detente existing in Europe after 1979), see Raymond L. Garthoff, *Detente and Confrontation: American-Soviet Relations from Nixon to Reagan*, Washington, D.C., The Brookings Institution, 1985, chapters 4 and 28, pp. 106–126 and pp. 1009–

1067. See also Mike Bowker and Phil Williams, *Superpower Detente: A Reappraisal*, London, Sage/Royal Institute of International Affairs, 1988, pp. 85–94. For an excellent and detailed coverage of Soviet-German relations during the detente period see Michael J. Sodaro, *Moscow, Germany, and the West from Khrushchev to Gorbachev*, Ithaca, Cornell University Press, 1990, chapters 6–8, pp. 166–264.

8. *Vneshniaia torgovlia SSSR v 1986 g.: Statisticheskii sbornik*, Moscow, Finansy i statistika, 1987, table 5, p. 15.

9. Kissinger, *Years of Upheaval*, p. 146.

10. Edwina Moreton, "The German Factor," in Edwina Moreton and Gerald Segal (eds), *Soviet Strategy Toward Western Europe*, London, Allen and Unwin, 1984, pp. 110–137, p. 110.

11. Alvin Z. Rubinstein, *Soviet Foreign Policy Since World War II: Imperial and Global*, 4th edn., New York, HarperCollins, 1992, p. 132.

12. See Thomas Kielinger and Maz Ottei, "Germany: The Pressured Power," *Foreign Policy*, no. 91, Summer 1993, pp. 44–62, p. 52.

13. Josef Joffe, "The 'Revisionists': Germany and Russia in a Post-Bipolar World," in Michael T. Clark and Simon Serfaty (eds), *New Thinking and Old Realities: America, Europe, and Russia*, Washington, D.C., Seven Locks Press and Johns Hopkins University Foreign Policy Institute, 1991, pp. 95–126, p. 97.

14. Josef Joffe, "After Bipolarity: Germany and European Security," *Adelphi Paper*, no. 285, International Institute of Strategic Studies, London, February 1994, pp. 34–46, p. 37.

15. Quoted in *The Daily Telegraph* (London), November 3, 1993.

16. *Moscow News*, no. 51, December 17, 1993.

17. Jacob Heilbrunn, "Tomorrow's Germany," *The National Interest*, no. 36, Summer 1994, pp. 44–52, especially p. 48.

18. See Ole Waever, Barry Buzan, Morton Kelstrup, and Pierre Lemaitre, *Identity, Migration and the New Security Agenda in Europe*, London, Pinter, 1993.

19. Richard Sakwa, *Russian Politics and Society*, London, Routledge, 1993, p. 37.

20. Stuart Drummond, "Germany: Moving Towards a New *Ostpolitik*," *The World Today*, July 1993, pp. 132–135, p. 132.

21. Vladimir Kozin, "New Dimensions of NATO," *International Affairs* (Moscow), no. 3, 1993, pp. 53–61, p. 59.

22. See, for example, Viktor Shutkevich, "I ne drug i ne vrag: A kak?" *Komsomolskaia Pravda*, September 8, 1993, p. 7.

23. *New Times*, no. 6, 1994. Karaganov is one of the authors of "Strategy for Russia," a foreign policy document drawn up by the Council on Foreign and Defense Policy; see *Nezavisimaia gazeta*, May 27, 1994.

24. RIA, January 10, 1994.

25. Quoted in *The Australian Financial Review*, June 23, 1994.

26. Alexander Golz, "Russia's Role in Europe," *The Moscow Times*, May 21, 1994.

27. *The Observer* (London), June 26, 1994.

28. For Kozyrev's views on Russia's partnership with the West see Andrei Kozyrev, "The Lagging Partnership," *Foreign Affairs*, vol. 73, no. 3, 1994, pp.

59–71. For an assessment of his views on the Partnership for Peace with NATO see *RFERL Daily Report*, July 7, 1994, and *Moscow News*, no. 26, July 1–7, 1994, p. 2.

29. Russian Communist Party leader, Gennady Zyuganov, referred to the Partnership for Peace as the "political successor" to Operation Barbarossa, Hitler's military invasion of the Soviet Union in 1941. Quoted in *The Observer* (London), June 26, 1994.

30. *RFERL Daily Report*, July 15, 1994.

31. Kozyrev, "The Lagging Partnership," especially p. 69.

32. Hannes Adomeit, "Russia: Partner of Risk Factor in European Security," *Adelphi Paper*, no. 285, London, International Institute for Strategic Studies, February 1994, pp. 15–23, p. 26.

33. "A Russian-German Axis?" *Foreign Report*, London, the Economist, January 20, 1994.

34. *The European*, June 17–23, 1994.

35. Quoted in Heilbrunn, "Tomorrow's Germany," p. 48.

36. See *Russian and Euro-Asian Economic Bulletin*, vol. 4, no. 2, February 1994, Melbourne, Centre for Russian and Euro-Asian Studies, University of Melbourne.

37. *Moscow News*, no. 26, July 1–7, 1994, p. 3.

38. See *Foreign Report*, London, The Economist, December 16, 1994.

39. See John Orme, "Security in East Central Europe: Seven Futures," *The Washington Quarterly*, vol. 19, no. 3, Summer 1991, pp. 91–105, p. 94.

40. Andrei Zagorsky, "Russia and Europe," *International Affairs* (Moscow), January 1993, pp. 43–50, p. 50.

41. On the agreement see *Delovoi mir*, June 26, 1994.

42. Lyudmila Telen, "An Opening into Europe," *Moscow News*, no. 51, December 17, 1993.

43. RIA, August 12, 1994.

44. For details on the bank and its objectives see *Agreement Establishing the European Bank for Reconstruction and Development*, Brussels, Commission of the European Communities, May 7, 1990.

45. Yelena Khalevinskaia, "The European Bank: A New Partnership," *International Affairs* (Moscow), no. 6, 1994, pp. 119–126, p. 120.

46. *Izvestiia*, March 31, 1993.

47. Khalevinskaia, "The European Bank," p. 123.

48. RIA, August 3, 1994.

49. *The Moscow Times*, May 27, 1994.

50. *Segodnia*, April 22, 1994.

51. This is something Kenneth Waltz also suggests as a likely possibility in his "The Emerging Structure of International Politics," *International Security*, vol. 18, no. 2, 1993, pp. 44–79. See also Kenneth Waltz, "The New World Order," *Millennium*, vol. 22, no. 2, 1993, pp. 187–196.

52. Jeffrey Simon, "Central Europe: 'Return to Europe' or Descent to Chaos," in *European Security Toward the Year 2000*, McNair Paper 20, Washington, D.C., National Defense University, August 1993, pp. 31–52, p. 35.

53. *Nezavisimaia gazeta*, April 13, 1994.

54. Quoted in the *Guardian Weekly*, March 6, 1994.

6

Russian Policy Toward the United States

Peter Shearman

Introduction

As Chapter 1 in this volume makes clear, the foreign behavior of nation states is determined by a mixture of external systemic factors, internal bureaucratic and political factors, and psychological and perceptual factors. For the Soviet Union during the Cold War era, the United States loomed large at each of these levels. At the systemic level the United States was the main actor and challenger in strategic bipolarity. In the domestic politics of foreign policy decision-making the United States was often at the center of debates about the most appropriate conceptions, strategies, and policies to develop and pursue. Whether pertaining to relations to a specific region (e.g., Eastern Europe or the Middle East) or country (e.g., Afghanistan or France) or to a general conception of East-West relations (e.g., detente) the domestic bureaucratic political process ultimately focused largely upon the United States. At the psychological level, perceptions of the United States, as the significant other in the Cold War bipolar competition for power and influence, affected individual leaders' reasoning, judgements, and policies, from Stalin through to Gorbachev.

In a mirror-image fashion the same was true of U.S. foreign policy during the Cold War. The Soviet Union was the main external actor driving the domestic process of making foreign policy. From McCarthyism to Reaganism the perception of a "Soviet threat" among U.S. political leaders was important in formulating foreign policies. From Managua to Manila, from Greece to Grenada, and from Vietnam to Vanuatu, the perception of a Soviet threat was a critical factor in explaining U.S. foreign policies.

With the collapse of strategic bipolarity and the disintegration of the Soviet Union in December 1991, the relative stability and predictability of the Cold War gave way to uncertainty in global politics. In this chapter I will examine how global structural changes and domestic systemic changes have affected Russian perceptions about and policies toward the United States.

Increasing Saliency of Economics

From Geopolitics to Geoeconomics

Clearly, with the demise of strategic bipolarity, the collapse of the USSR, Russia's economic crisis, and the emerging multipolarity in which (geo)economics and managing trade relations are becoming more salient than geopolitics and managing the arms race, the Moscow-Washington link is no longer central to the overall dynamics of world politics. The end of the Cold War loosened the ties that bound former allies united against a common threat, resulting in increasing strains in economic relations among the main economic powers: the USA, Japan, and the European Community.

The Soviet Union's superpower status was based upon its formidable military power. In the post–Cold War era the two nuclear superpowers discussing arms control have been replaced by the seven economic powers (the G-7) discussing trade issues. Targets are no longer missile silos but import and export figures. Talk is no longer of geographical buffer zones to counter tanks but of economic tariffs to counter unfair trade. The principal currency of negotiations is not SS-20s and MX missiles but the yen, the U.S. dollar, and the deutche mark. GATT is recognized as more critical for security than START. Immediate threats to national security are seen more in terms of unilateral economic sanctions being imposed than any risk of a nuclear first strike. The risk now is trade wars rather than star wars. Post-Soviet Russia in the period 1991–1994 has manifestly *not* been one of the world's leading powers in economic terms.

The Russian economy emerged from the Cold War era in severe crisis. The external structures of world politics and economics determined that in order for Russia to compete it was necessary to both improve its domestic productive capacity and radically restructure its foreign policies. These changing structural parameters of world politics, with the growing primacy of economic issues, were partly responsible for the collapse of the Soviet system. The system failed to provide the material well-being that its leaders and ideology promised, resulting in a relatively poor quality of life for society, while the state continued to waste vast resources in the military industrial complex and on foreign Third World ventures. Fred Halliday's conception of the Cold War as an "inter-systemic" conflict between two opposing socioeconomic systems, between capitalism and communism, is interesting here.[1] One party to this conflict had to win out over the other, and in the end it was the communist bloc that *lost* the Cold War as the Soviet system was undermined by the economic, and hence social and political, strengths of the Western capitalist bloc. Because Russia was defeated by that system Russian behavior has subsequently been in part determined by it. Thus the external structural or systemic factors that impact Russian foreign policy ensure only a secondary role for Moscow in those areas of political economy that have become so significant in the wake of strategic bipolarity.

Perestroika in foreign policy in the late 1980s relied increasingly upon Moscow's relationship with Washington. The Soviet Union's superpower status was dependent upon its privileged relationship with the United States, especially in the area of arms control. Summitry between the two powers took on, if anything, added importance during this period as Gorbachev and Soviet new political thinkers sought to take advantage of the remaining leverage they had over the United States to assist them in restructuring the Soviet economy while simultaneously maintaining the essentials of the Leninist system. To the very end, Gorbachev continued to proclaim his basic faith in Leninism and the Communist Party. The structure of power in the international system was such into the 1990s that the United States was still by far the most potent state actor in the military, economic, political, and cultural realms. Given this systemic structure, and particularly given the historical and contemporary symbiosis of superpower military relations and Gorbachev's and now Yeltsin's desire to save money through defense cuts, the United States was bound to remain the main external actor for the Moscow.

Multipolarity and Russian-American Relations

As Cold War strategic bipolarism gave way to a complex multipolarity Moscow's foreign policy orientation was even more heavily focused on Washington. As the world's major economic power with the greatest influence in multilateral institutions, the United States was viewed in Moscow as the player that would be key in lobbying for Western economic assistance for a decaying Soviet economy. The importance of the United States to official Soviet policy at this time can be gauged by the high level of communications between Foreign Minister Eduard Shevardnadze and Secretary of State James Baker in the period 1989–1991.[2]

In the summer of 1991 Gorbachev succeeded in getting himself invited to the G-7 summit in London in order to argue the Soviet case for a massive injection of economic aid to stave off political crisis in Moscow. He returned to Moscow empty-handed, and it was then only a matter of weeks before the botched military coup in August which was the final blow leading to the demise of the Soviet Union in December.

With the breakup of the Union, Russia continued to place great emphasis on the United States as a potential provider of economic assistance and as the major player in global financial institutions. Russia's priority under Yeltsin has been to develop a market economy and stimulate growth, both of which require external finance and increasing integration into the global division of production, consumption, trade, and labor. For a brief period, in its attempt to achieve these objectives Russia sought to convince the United States in particular, but the West in general, that it was in the interests of the world as a whole for Russia to be integrated into the multilateral institutional framework for managing the global capitalist economy. Russian leaders argued that Russia's exclusion from global economic management would lead to increasing nationalism, a return to centralized authoritarianism, and anti-Westernism. A similar scenario was said to be likely should Russian participation not lead to large-scale economic assistance from the major capitalist powers.

Under Yeltsin's leadership Russia achieved some limited success. The Russian president was invited to participate in important multilateral forums, enabling Moscow to make its case and be seen as a major actor, sitting, as it were, at the top table with the most powerful states in the system. But in the economic realm, it soon became evident that the G-7½ was little more than the G-7 reluctantly providing Yeltsin with a stage from which he could attempt to maintain his own position in Russian domestic politics. The structure of the international political economy did not require the presence of an insignificant economic actor. On economic matters the G-7½ soon became once more the G-7, and when there was any talk of increasing the membership it came mainly from Japan calling for the inclusion of China, which, according to a revised method of U.N. reckoning, had become by the early 1990s the world's third largest economy. However, by the G-7 meeting in the summer of 1994 Yeltsin had managed to do more than wrangle an invitation for Russia to appear as a mere guest. The G-7 effectively became the "G-8" when discussing global *political* issues, recognizing Russia's place at the top table when dealing with matters ranging from nuclear proliferation to regional wars. Leading up to the meeting in Naples in June 1994, Yeltsin warned that this time Russia would "not be a beggar, as it was at the G-7 summits in Munich and Tokyo." He went on to say that "I will insist on Russia being treated as equal on political matters," acknowledging that economically Russia was not yet stable or strong enough to gain equal economic status. Moscow was satisfied at this stage to cover "half the road" to full membership. However, at the G-8 summit Yeltsin did insist that Russia be admitted to the Paris Club of nations (initially as an observer), for Russia was still a major creditor "of both developing and CIS countries."[3]

The Economic Imperative

In terms, then, of the external structural determinants of Russia's relations with the United States, in the immediate post-Soviet period these continued, as in the late-Soviet period, to be primarily related to economics and questions of aid. But these same structural changes in the post–Cold War international system have led to shifts in American priorities too. Although still the world's single largest economy, in relative terms and especially in relationship to Japan and Western Europe, the U.S. economy declined during the Cold War years. There are competing views as to the nature of America's decline, or indeed as to whether it has declined at all.[4] The important point here, however, is the perception that with the end of the Cold War America has to compete harder with the dynamic capitalist economies and should no longer, with the absence of the common Soviet threat, be required to pay disproportionate costs in maintaining international order, as it did during the Cold War. It could be argued that the United States won the Cold War against the Soviet Union to the greater economic benefit of Japan and Germany. In any event, U.S. policy-makers in recent times have focused their efforts on domestic concerns; when they have turned their attention to foreign policy, the motivation has usually been their concern about U.S. quality of life, crime, and unemployment. Bill Clinton, the first post–Cold War U.S. president, was elected to revitalize the *American* economy, not the Russian economy. The structure of the international political economy has become a major determinant of Russian-U.S. relations, and in this structure there is a marked asymmetry of power and hence ultimately of interests and policy priorities between the two states.

As the bipolar military confrontation has given way to an emerging multipolar economic contest, Russia is clearly not a first-league player. The contest is now based upon who produces the most competitive consumer goods and provides the better service and process industries, not upon who builds the biggest and most destructive bomb. A tripolarization of the global economy is envisaged as the world transits from the Bretton Woods/GATT-driven free trade system to one of managed trade and trading blocs. The three main powers in the global economy are the United States, Japan, and Germany. The United States was clearly the main economic power in the Cold War period.

The United States was able to dominate in the global economy, to set the rules of trade, and to act as overall coordinator of the world's key international financial institutions. But this was due in part to the overriding military-strategic structure of the international political system. As long as the Soviet threat existed, then the United States, as the only power with the military capacity to deter the USSR, was assured its dominant position in the "West." The end of the Cold War and the collapse of the Soviet threat has resulted also in a breakdown of consensus over managing the global economy.

Still, the United States was perceived by Russian President Boris Yeltsin and his foreign minister, Andrei Kozyrev, as the most likely source of economic aid. In 1992, the first year of Russia's new independence, foreign policy was economically driven. Economic policy was designed to integrate the Russian Federation into the global economy, dismantle the command system of centralized planning, and institute market reform. In the late Gorbachev period and in the early post-Soviet period the official governments in Moscow were clearly hoping for a Marshall Plan–type commitment to salvage the Russian economy, with the United States acting as a coordinator. But even if Presidents Bush and Clinton had wished to organize such a relief program, it would probably have been impossible to get it accepted in a Congress more concerned about America's own economy.

Although many argue that geography, geostrategic factors, military threats, and buffer zones now have much less salience in U.S. conceptions and evaluations of national security than they did during the Cold War, geography does still have relevance. Turmoil in Russia, and in the former communist states of Central and Eastern and Southern Europe, is distant from the United States and does not carry the same risk to Washington (or Japan) that it does to Western European countries. Civil wars, anarchy, conflict, and streams of refugees and illegal immigrants from across their borders make Western European states much more vulnerable to the chaos in the former communist world. It is also the case that the long-standing dispute over the Kurile Islands has prevented Russia from attracting large-scale economic aid from Japan. Germany and other members of the European Community are much more likely to commit themselves to aiding Russia out of self-interest than is Washington or Tokyo. At the structural level, then, it is perhaps to be expected that Russia would come to target the European Community for aid that the United States has been reluctant to commit.

Although the United States had played the leading role in the global capitalist economy, Western European states had always been more willing, from the 1920s through to detente in the 1960s and 70s to conduct trade relations with Moscow. Stanislav Shatalin, one of the authors of the ill-fated "500-days" economic program, which was designed to save the former Soviet economy, has referred to a misdirected emphasis on the United States. He states that in talks "Europeans have told me outright that we are carried away by Americanism."[5] Alexander Bykov recognizes that with the United States as the only real superpower, Russia is left with a lesser role to play in global affairs than the old USSR, and this role should be more balanced. He argues that Russia should pay "in particular, more attention to Western Europe, which, Germany in the first place, can better understand our needs and interests and render us tangible support."[6] According to Viktor Linnik, the United States will not come to the aid of Russia in the form of a new Marshall Plan because it would not be in America's national interest to build up a strong Russia. Whereas Western Europe and Japan were required to balance the power of the USSR and to help contain the Soviet threat, thereby warranting massive aid to rebuild their economies after World War II, Russia is only needed as a "middle-ranking power" to help the United States counter China and the Islamic world.[7]

Nevertheless, the Yeltsin administration continued to cultivate good relations with the United States in order, in part, to gain economic aid to assist in the process of transition from centralized planning to the market. Indeed, while Yeltsin was preparing for his G-8 diplomacy in Europe, Russian Prime Minister Viktor Chernomyrdin was in Washington, where he signed twenty-two documents on bilateral cooperation with the United States in a number of areas, including a $10 billion deal to develop and exploit oil and gas fields off the coast of Sakhalin.[8]

Russia's weak position in the global economy and its geostrategic location in Eurasia will determine the future direction of Russian-U.S. relations. As evidenced by trends between 1992 and 1994 Russia's political and economic relations with America, although still important, have become less significant. Moscow has directed its foreign policy more toward its immediate neighbors and the developed capitalist states of the European Community. If Russian-American political and economic relations do not make up the axis around which the post–Cold War world turns, what can we say about the significance of military-strategic relations?

Decreasing Saliency of Military-Strategic Relations

Changing Threat Perceptions

In the bipolar East-West struggle, military-strategic issues were dominant. As Eileen Crumm and James N. Rosenau have put it, "One of the notable characteristics of the U.S.-Soviet relationship is that during the Cold War it was largely confined to the areas of security and political goals."[9] The United States and the Soviet Union, as the two states with by far the largest concentrations of nuclear weapons, were superpowers in their war-making capacities. The situation was fraught with the danger that mutual antagonism in the global superpower competition could one day result in a suicidal nuclear war (Ronald Reagan used to refer to nuclear deterrence as a "suicide pact.") During the Cold War fully two-thirds of the total U.S. intelligence budget was allocated to the Soviet threat (by 1993 this had been cut to less than one-third).[10] That immediate sense of risk has now passed, but security, based upon nuclear and military-strategic issues, is, like everything else in the post–Cold War period, now complex and uncertain.

Yeltsin made it clear immediately with the collapse of the Union that Russia did not see the United States as a potential threat but rather as an ally in developing new methods of collective security. As already noted, a priority for the Russian president was garnering American economic aid, and on a visit to Washington in June 1992 he quickly agreed to cut strategic nuclear forces by half, including scrapping Russia's giant SS-18 ICBMs. Announcing the agreement, Yeltsin decried what previously had been traditional Soviet demands for parity in nuclear strength as having resulted in half of the Russian population ". . . living below the poverty line. We cannot afford it."[11] In order to better compete in the global economy Russia would give up its global military-strategic role. Of course, Soviet nuclear weapons were deployed not only on Russian territory but also in Ukraine, Belarus, and Kazakhstan, the three republics thought by Moscow to be the most loyal to the center. Overnight, three nuclear powers were born when the Union collapsed, and Ukraine in particular demonstrated a reluctance to transfer the weapons on its soil to Russia. During the Cold War the superpowers opposed the proliferation of nuclear weapons among other states, and Russia and the United States have continued to share this interest, coordinating their endeavors to prevent this from happening.

In terms of the overall balance of power and the structural features of international politics, then, Russia and the United States are no longer natural antagonists. The two countries are not tied together in complex economic interdependencies that could lead to tensions. There are no residual areas of conflict from the Cold War (save for domestic opposition to Yeltsin and Kozyrev, which is part of an ongoing struggle over policy and employs an anti-U.S. discourse). Russians and Americans have never fought a full-scale hot war against each other (indeed, they have fought on the same side in two wars during this century); there are no disputes over territorial boundaries; and no third party is seeking to play them off against one another, as so often happened between 1947 and 1991. And with neither side perceiving gains to be made through unilateral intervention in regional conflicts, there is no longer any great asymmetry of interests between them. Vladislav Chernov, while recognizing that Russian interests will not always coincide with those of the United States, argues that essentially the two states have sufficient "mutual interests" to cooperate in establishing a "stable and secure system of international relations." He refers to common interests in preventing nuclear proliferation and averting regional conflicts.[12] On his visit to Moscow (via Kiev) in January 1994 President Clinton was party to a trilateral agreement among Ukraine, Russia, and the United States on dismantling nuclear weapons still remaining on Ukrainian territory. At a press conference following the summit Yeltsin referred to Russian-U.S. relations as being "stable, well-regulated, and based on partnership."[13] Significant for Russia at the summit was Clinton's apparent acknowledgment that Russia has a legitimate right to perform a peacekeeping role in the territory of the former Soviet Union: "You will be more likely to be involved in some of these areas near you, just like the United States has been involved in the last several years in Panama and Grenada near our area."[14]

The United States as Strategic Partner?

No longer is Russia's security policy or its international political and strategic concerns linked to the "U.S. threat." This has facilitated a much greater openness in dealing with the United States over security-related issues, including exchanges of military personnel, cooperation in trying to resolve regional conflicts, a joint peacekeeping exercise in September 1994 at Totsk in the Orenburg district of the Russian Federation, coordinating measures against international terrorism and drug trafficking, and the sharing of intelligence in areas of mutual interest. The U.S. Federal Bureau of Investigation has established an office in Moscow to assist local authorities in combatting organized crime. Even with the tensions between them over the war in Bosnia the United States and Russia managed to reach agreement or compromise.

Russia's geopolitical security position in Europe altered radically between 1989 and 1991 as it lost first Eastern Europe and then the Western republics of the former Soviet Union, thereby increasing the distance between Moscow and Western Europe. NATO forces commanded by an American general were no longer perceived as a real or present danger to the territorial integrity of the state. Russia's security concerns were becoming increasingly regional, and the Yeltsin administration sought to enlist the support of the United States in many of its dealings with the former republics of the USSR. For example, whereas human rights were used as a stick to beat the Soviet Union in the Cold War, now the United States was being asked by Moscow to put its weight behind Russia's calls for the Baltic states to recognize and guarantee the human rights of resident Russian minorities.

Foreign Minister Andrei Kozyrev has argued that the world is not unipolar, or yet multipolar, for Russia and the United States are still the "prime movers" as world players. Following talks with Secretary of State Warren Christopher in Geneva in March 1993, Kozyrev stated that ". . . there is a firm understanding by the sides that no alternative exists to the strategic partnership between Russia and the USA." Kozyrev argued that Russian-American interaction was essential for seeking to resolve conflict situations throughout the world.[15]

Of course, this was an exaggeration. Russia is *not* one of the "prime movers" in global politics alongside the United States, it does *not* have a "partnership" with the United States, and Russia has effectively renounced its interests in such distant areas as Latin America and Southern Africa. Yeltsin and his foreign minister wished to enlist the United States, as clearly the most powerful actor in global politics, in support of their more limited objectives: economic reform, arms cuts, preventing nuclear proliferation, and defending the rights of Russians in the former Soviet republics. Although the United States has expressed support for each of these objectives, it has energetically committed itself only to those relating to nuclear cuts and nonproliferation, with the main result being the signing of START 2 in Moscow by Bush (on the eve of handing over the presidency to Clinton) and Yeltsin.

Potential Conflicts of Interest

Yet despite this seeming harmony of interests and the rhetoric of leaders on both sides suggesting an almost complete mutuality of national goals, there is nevertheless scope for disagreements. For example, in conflict closer to home Russia has demonstrated interests not always commensurate with those articulated by the United States. During the period under review there have been no open and serious conflicts of interest between the two sides, but disagreements have had to be resolved and compromises made.

Bosnia

In the case of the former Yugoslav republic of Bosnia, Russia's traditional mediating role in the Balkans in support of fellow Slavs (i.e., the Serbs) has come to the fore in negotiations with the United States and in the United Nations. Russia would agree to airdrops of supplies for beleaguered Muslims in the first half of 1993 only if they also applied to the Serbs. Yevgeny Ambartsumov, influential chairman of the Russian Joint Committee on International Affairs and Foreign Economic Relations of the Russian Supreme Soviet (until Yeltsin disbanded it by decree in

September 1993), has been outspoken in his support of the Serbs. He has visited Belgrade, where he held talks with Bosnian Serb leaders (but not Muslims or Croats), and participated in Russian delegations in international talks on the war in Bosnia.[16] When NATO air strikes were unleashed against Serb positions in Goradze in April 1994, Russia was not even consulted by the Americans, and it was not just Yeltsin who was piqued, expressing his annoyance personally to Clinton in a telephone conversation. Defense Minister Grachev too vented his frustration in a telephone conversation with his U.S. counterpart, William Perry. Sergei Shakhrai, Yeltsin's deputy prime minister, referred to the bombing raid as a blow to Russia's prestige.[17] The bombing raid served to galvanize the conservative opposition to Yeltsin and the government and forced a more pro-active policy on the part of Kozyrev and the Foreign Ministry in dealing directly in the Bosnian war. Through to the summer of 1994 Russia was still cooperating with the United States (and other Western states and the United Nations) in trying to broker a political solution to the conflict, but signals from all quarters in Moscow have made it clear that Russia's perceived interests and status as a great power cannot be ignored in any resolution.

Arms Trade

With regard to the international arms trade there is also a potential asymmetry of interests between Russia and the United States. For example, there have already been tensions in relations as a result of U.S. pressures on Russia not to provide a submarine to Iran (making it the first Gulf state to have one). Alexei Bausin is indignant that Americans should complain about this, and quoting the deputy commander of the Iranian navy, he asks why it is that the West can have over sixty warships in the Gulf while Iran is denied a single submarine.[18] Russia also resented American insistence that Russia should deny India the supply of cryogenic rocket engines as had previously been agreed between Moscow and New Delhi. The export of arms was a main source of hard currency earnings for the Soviet Union, but in recent years such earnings have declined. It has been estimated that whereas in 1986 the USSR sold $29 billion in arms, in 1993 the figure for Russia is between $2 and $3 billion.[19] *Izvestiia* noted that whereas Russia's share of the arms market in from 1991 to 1993 had dropped from 38 percent to 17 percent, the U.S. share had increased from 30 percent to 58 percent.[20] Russia perceives real potential in the one area where it can be competitive and has embarked upon a mission to sell its state-of-the-art weaponry.

In February 1993 Kozyrev expressed his concern directly to U.S. Secretary of State Warren Christopher that Russia should be free to legitimately participate in this lucrative market.[21] That same month Defense Minister Pavel Grachev was in Abu Dhabi, capital of the United Arab Emirates, where Russia had on display 370 of its best military systems at an international arms exhibition.[22] The Middle East and the Gulf states, especially after Iraq's invasion of Kuwait, are seen as offering the best potential markets. The following month, Vice President Alexander Rutskoi (a former commander and fighter pilot in the Soviet air force) was in Kuala Lumpur trying to sell the Malaysian air force the Russian MiG-29 fighter aircraft (a deal was finally reached in June 1994). *Izvestiia* referred to these negotiations as an important factor in the increasing competition between the American and Russian military-industrial complexes.[23] Certainly Russia began in 1993 to aggressively compete with the United States, Britain, and France in the international arms trade.

Sanctions Against Iraq

Russia has been developing its own independent policy in other areas, which could possibly lead to serious differences with the United States. Russia's policy has often been pushed in new directions by dissenters. For example, many officials in positions of influence in Russia have been uncomfortable with Moscow's policies toward Iraq since its invasion of Kuwait in August 1990. It was difficult for President Bush and James Baker during the crisis in the Gulf to ensure that Gorbachev and the Russian government were kept on the side of the coalition and gave support for the UN resolutions that ratified U.S. policy. Gorbachev himself wavered on the issue as he was faced with strong vocal calls from Defense Minister Yazov, KGB chief Kryuchkov, and Soviet Prime Minister Pavlov not to do the Americans' bidding and risk losing the heavy investments that Moscow had made in fostering good relations with an important ally in the region. Although successful in providing Soviet support for the war against Saddam Hussein, Foreign Minister Shevardnadze was later forced to resign in the face of what he considered to be in December 1990 the beginnings of a new dictatorship led by senior military officials.[24] The same institutional groupings in Moscow have never been satisfied with the way in which, in their view, Russia has followed the U.S. line on Iraq at the expense of Russia's own "national interests." Yuly Vorontsov, the former Russian ambassador to the UN who succeeded Lukin as ambassador to the United States in July 1994, has indicated that Russian policy on this could change. It is reported that the Russian Foreign Ministry has drawn up a program for lifting the sanctions.[25]

Thus there are a number of areas at the level of the international strategic setting where increasing tensions with the United States could develop. Both Russia and the United States will continue to share an interest in maintaining a stable nuclear deterrence. They will both also cooperate in managing, or where possible preventing, nuclear proliferation. But in a world moving toward complex multipolarity it is unlikely that bilateral relations will result in "partnership" or "alliance," the language of Kozyrev and the reformers. Russia's interests in various regions are certain to conflict with those of other states.

Kozyrev has stated that Russia after the Cold War no longer faced any external threats. With the demise of any perception of threat, Russia's security was based upon a "defensive" military doctrine, originally developed as part of the new thinking in the USSR under Gorbachev.[26] Yet all states have traditionally based their military forces, strategies, and doctrines on worst-case scenarios and maintained sufficient military might to deter aggression and counter any attack. The Russian military establishment has ensured that this traditional conception remains the basis for Russia's security, with the adjective "defensive" dropped from a revised doctrine that assumes potential aggressors and allows for sufficient military means to meet them. Central to this doctrine is nuclear deterrence. No serious figure in Russia today proposes the utopian project of total nuclear disarmament. At a conference on Russia's military security, Colonel General I. Rodionov, chief of the Russian armed forces General Staff Association, argued that Russia was faced with real threats to its national interests. He gave as examples Russian interests in the Middle East and around Russia's periphery and in Eastern Europe and the Far East, where Moscow's interests conflict with others "and above all those of the United States."[27] This is not to suggest the beginnings of another Cold War between Russia and the United States, but indications at the systemic level suggest that tensions will develop over some issues where interests diverge. And these tensions will be managed as and when they emerge, since there is no overall "new world order" or global institutionalized arrangement through which to settle them.

However, this examination is at the level of the international setting and assumes that the Russian state acts rationally in pursuit of its national interest, defined in terms of power and security, i.e., it assumes a personified Russian state acting according to the norms of international behavior. Yet, as was pointed out in Chapter 1 we should not ignore the domestic environment in which foreign policies are made, for other factors such as personality, power struggles, bureaucratic politics, and ideology can often be equally important. Clearly, external economic and strategic systemic circumstances have influenced the development of Russian policy toward the United States, but for a more comprehensive assessment we should now turn to the domestic setting.

Domestic Politics and Russian Policy
Toward the United States

At this level of analysis the assumption is not that we have a unitary rational actor pursuing the national interest from a set of logical choices but rather that we have a multitude of actors in a domestic competitive political environment with a mix of conflicting and mutual goals. Political and bureaucratic divisions between imperfectly rational actors with imperfect information results in a process of bargaining in order to reach a decision. The domestic setting in Russia has been very confusing because the partly reformed institutional structures of the old Soviet Union have remained in force. New political divisions have emerged both over the most appropriate process for reaching decisions— i.e., over which institutions should have competency in foreign policy— and over the general orientations and priorities of foreign policy. Here the focus is on the extent to which the domestic political process in Russia has influenced relations with the United States.

Zbigniew Brzezinski has developed an argument against a premature U.S. "partnership" with Russia that is essentially driven by domestic factors: democratic development is none too sure in the near future, and many neo-imperialists in Moscow with increasing influence are seeking to reestablish influence or control over the states of the near abroad. Hence, a policy of "geopolitical pluralism" is called for in which Russia's role in the former republics of the USSR is contained.[28] Kozyrev argues that on the contrary the "best strategic choice" for the U.S. and Russia is to forge a proper "partnership," which itself would encourage and facilitate democratic development in Russia. Nevertheless, Kozyrev notes that "it must also be understood that a firm and sometimes aggressive policy of defending one's national interests is not compatible with partnership."[29] These arguments reflect a misunderstanding of the influences of contemporary Russian domestic politics on foreign policy.

Yeltsin Versus Parliament

Much has been made in the Western media of the divisions in Russian politics between Yeltsin and the reformers on the one hand and the parliament and the conservatives on the other. The reformers have been associated with a pro-Western foreign policy orientation and seen as advocates of presidential authority; the conservatives have been described as anti-West as and advocates of parliamentary control over foreign policy. There is truth in this, but generally the picture presented has been misleading. Throughout the first two years of Russia's new post-imperial status, relations with the West, and the United States in particular, were central to domestic debates on foreign policy. Psychologically, it might be argued, it would naturally be difficult for Russians to embrace the United States, having suffered such a humiliating ideological and strategic defeat in the Cold War global competition of ideas and power. To run, cap in hand, begging for handouts from the victor in this epic struggle simply adds to this humiliation. For reasons of national pride and power, many Russians would be opposed to such a policy. Others, convinced by Leninist ideology that American neo-imperialism is the natural enemy of humanity and progress, also oppose Russia's Western foreign policy orientation. Nationalists and communists have apparently joined forces against the reformers in what reformist newspapers in Russia have dubbed an alliance of "brown and red shirts."

Domestic Politics and START-2

Yet opposition to the Russian Foreign Ministry's strong orientation toward the United States has also been utilized as a means to achieve instrumental political goals. To oppose an incumbent government, one has to offer alternatives in important policy areas, and with the collapse of the Russian empire, foreign policy has clearly been highly important and hence has become central to internal power struggles. Leading political scientist and president of the Russian Research Foundation, Andrei Kortunov, has expressed concern, for example, that internal power struggles could prevent ratification of START-2 and hence seriously undermine relations with the United States.[30]

Most senior military figures expressed support for the START treaty, and the Ministries of Defense and Foreign Affairs formed a united front to promote its ratification during parliamentary hearings. Leading experts on security drew up documents, published articles, and held talks to demonstrate that ratification of the treaty was important for the national security and economic interests of the Russian state. For example, a special report prepared for the Foreign Policy Association called upon parliament to endorse the treaty. The group that produced the report was headed by Aleksei Arbatov, a leading specialist on nuclear strategy who had previously openly criticized some aspects of the defense policies of both Gorbachev and Yeltsin.[31] Colonel General Mikhail Kolesnikov, chief of staff of the Russian army, spoke openly in support of the treaty at a seminar at the General Staff Academy.[32] Defense Minister Pavel Grachev and the top brass of the Russian military have given support to the treaty; thus it would seem that this mixture of senior government officials, security personnel, and independent expert opinion would be sufficient to see the SALT treaty's smooth ratification. But opposition to the treaty came from a number of influential sources, and whatever the final fate of the treaty, the struggle over its ratification demonstrates the salience that policy toward the United States still has in post-Soviet, Russian domestic politics. *Izvestiia* claimed that opposition to START was simply a flag for opposition to Yeltsin and the government and should be viewed in a "purely domestic political context."[33]

In the old Russian parliament, notorious for its conservatism, opposition to the treaty came from some influential factions and individuals, including Iona Andronov, vice-chairman of the parliamentary Committee on International Affairs, who referred to the treaty as an American "trick."[34] This theme of the United States somehow manipulating the Yeltsin government to accept policies detrimental to Russian national interests is one taken up by most opponents of the president.

The U.S. Factor in Domestic Power Struggles

That the United States had come to play an important role in Russia's domestic power struggles is evidenced by warnings to U.S. President Bill Clinton even from *supporters* of Yeltsin's foreign policy. For example, *Komsomolskaia Pravda* and *Izvestiia*, two important daily newspapers generally sympathetic to the government, criticized Clinton for taking too strong a stance in openly supporting Yeltsin in his struggle with the Russian legislature. The influential political columnist Stanislav Kondrashov stated clearly that Clinton's outside intervention was "counterproductive," for it simply served as "fuel for domestic conflict."[35] Given that the U.S. Congress seemed at the same time to be more uncritically supportive of Yeltsin and Kozyrev than of the Russian Supreme Soviet, it is not surprising that opponents of the president and the foreign minister should question Russia's policy toward the United States as part of a power ploy.

One's stance toward the United States has come to partially determine and define where one stands in the domestic power struggle. Elgiz Pozdnyakov has claimed that the United States has taken advantage of the Soviet collapse to ensure that Russia remains too weak to dominate the "Eurasian strategic area." He argues that the United States has been playing on the contradictions in relations between Russia and other former republics of the Soviet Union to further American national goals. Having previously, under new thinking in the late Soviet period, expressed idealist sentiments, Pozdnyakov now talks of the need for Russia to recognize its own national interests and to engage actively in "power politics" in their pursuit.[36] Another former influential "new thinker" from the Gorbachev era, Georgi Arbatov, has recently warned about the possible onset of a new cold war between Russia and the United States. His argument is similar to Brzezinski's in relation to the lack of democracy and problems for its development in Russia and how this is creating the circumstances that could lead to an aggressive foreign policy that is anti-West and designed to restore the USSR. But unlike Brzezinski, Arbatov suggests that the problem is partly of the West's own making: by seeking to impose the "worst form of Reaganomics" on Russia at a time when it would be totally unacceptable to any modern Western country, Washington is fostering conspiracy theories in Russia about American attempts to undermine the foundations of Russian society.[37] These can then be used by opponents of the Yelstin administration in a struggle for power and influence over policy. Advocating radical shock therapy and monetarist economics without backing this up with large-scale U.S. aid while simultaneously talking of a new containment strategy against Russian influence in its "near abroad," Arbatov argues, can only strengthen hard-line opponents of Yeltsin's foreign policy and improve the prospects for a new cold war.

Ambartsumov has argued that Russian foreign policy has been formulated without any overall concept of what is in Russia's national interests and in "somewhat naively utopian terms."[38] Yeltsin and Kozyrev have been attacked from many quarters—not just by the conservatives—for lacking any coherence in their foreign policies other than an apparently biased Western orientation. The National Salvation Front has criticized Russian foreign policy for being "slavishly dependent on the West, especially the USA." Ambartsumov has criticized a tendency to "copy" U.S. policies and to see the United States as a "big brother"; and Yeltsin's former ambassador in Washington, Vladimir Lukin (who was elected to the new State Duma in December 1993 and heads its Foreign Affairs Committee) warned Clinton not to treat Russia as some kind of "small, timid village idiot waiting on every word of its big brother."[39] There has hardly been a single voice among those criticizing Russian foreign policy that has not attacked a perceived pro-U.S. bias, which is said to take insufficient account of Russian national interests. "Pro-American" policies for which Yelstin has been attacked include the following: unilaterally renouncing Russian influence in the Balkans by following the U.S. lead in Bosnia; supporting after the event, without any prior warning of the impending action, U.S. bombing raids in Iraq; reneging on commitments to supply military equipment to third parties following U.S. pressure; permitting the U.S. to dictate terms relating to domestic economic reform as a condition for IMF and Western aid, thus undermining Russia's sovereignty; and undermining Russia's security by signing START-2 and thereby sacrificing nuclear parity with the United States.

Yeltsin has not been unaffected by these domestic pressures. His first trip overseas after the demise of the USSR was to the United States, Canada, the United Kingdom, and France. While in New York at a United Nations Security Council meeting of heads of state, Yeltsin made clear that he saw Russia not just as a partner of the United States but as an "ally." Just twelve months later, however, in January 1993, he stated that "the recent series of state visits to South Korea, China, and now to India is indicative of the fact that we are moving away from a Western emphasis" in Russian diplomacy.[40] Justifying his initial foreign policy focus on the United States, Yeltsin stated that it was necessary "... to lay the foundation, that is to prepare a detailed treaty on the global reduction and elimination of strategic nuclear weapons, on the basis of which it would be easier, afterward, to build relations with any country, be it from the West or East, Europe or Asia."[41] The implication was that the U.S. bias was a preliminary tactic that would facilitate Russia's later long-term economic and strategic objectives closer to home in Eurasia. Vitaly Churkin, Yeltsin's diplomatic envoy in talks on Bosnia, has stated that Russia's "channels of contacts with Belgrade will always be open" and that Russia would not support any U.S. or U.N. proposal to engage in military action against the Serbs.[42] Russian diplomats and officials from the Foreign Ministry began to put Russia's case in various bilateral and multilateral forums much more energetically than they had done in 1992. Support from the security ministries for Russia's early pro-Western policy was always more measured than that of the Foreign Ministry, and from early 1993 this too became more critical. Senior military figures and the ministers of defense, internal security, and foreign intelligence (Grachev, Barannikov, Primakov) began to articulate more pragmatic and conditional backing for Russia's policy toward the United States. Even Kozyrev, who had always been the most outspoken advocate within Russia's government of a pro-U.S. policy, now began to tone down and qualify his enthusiasm for forging a "partnership" with the United States.

The U.S. Factor in Determining the National Interest

There was a consensus in Russia that what was required to ensure coherence in foreign policy was a carefully calculated conception of what was in Russia's national interests. A number of organizations inside and outside government had been working on setting out such a coherent foreign policy concept that would serve as a general guide for establishing Russia's new place in the world. Clearly, given its powerful position in world politics and its salience in domestic power struggles, the United States would figure prominently in these conceptions. In late 1992 the Russian Foreign Ministry published a document on Russia's foreign policy concept that continued to stress the ministry's "partnership" and "alliance" with Western countries based on a "commitment to common democratic values."[43] The Russian Foreign Policy Council held a forum to discuss the document in which Kozyrev, taking up a theme that was becoming impossible to ignore, spoke of

Russia as a "great power" in Eurasia. Eurasia defined the uniqueness of Russia, straddling two continents and civilizations. More and more influential figures had seized upon this uniqueness as the determining characteristic for guiding foreign policy, seeing Russia's mission in terms of serving as a bridge between East and West. But Kozyrev still held strong to his focus on the United States, pointing out that although Russia's Eurasian location is part of its status, "Anyone who looks at the map will see that the United States is our next-door neighbor in the East." To stress his point, he added: "In the East, not the West." In fact, he repeated this three times just in case anyone should miss the point. The United States, Kozyrev was arguing, is not only Russia's largest neighbor in the East but the most significant power in the West, and it is clearly in Russia's national interest to have "the closest possible partnership and eventually allied relations with that leading Western country and our biggest Eastern neighbor."[44] Kozyrev argued that this would assist Russia's relations with the G-7 and the IMF and enhance Russia's position and status in the Asia-Pacific region given the powerful position the United States has in all three. Possibly Kozyrev was attempting to give more of a pro-U.S. slant to the Foreign Ministry's document than it warranted, but at the least he was continuing to demonstrate his own personal commitment to the West, the United States, reform, and democracy.

The Russian Security Council, then headed by Yuri Skokov, was commissioned by Yeltsin in the summer of 1992 to draw up "Guidelines for the Foreign Policy of the Russian Federation." Participants in this process included the Foreign, Defense, and Security Ministries. It has been suggested that the conservative Skokov formed an alliance with Grachev, Barannikov, and Primakov in order to negate the input from Kozyrev, and hence any pro-U.S. tendencies.[45] The document, however, does not advocate an anti-Western or anti-U.S. foreign policy orientation, although at the same time it does not privilege the United States as Kozyrev may have wished. Rather, it prescribes that Russia take its place as a world power, as a bridge between East and West, with specific interests in the "near abroad"—the former republics of the USSR. Civic Union, the centrist political opposition to Yeltsin, developed its own Concept of Russian Foreign Policy, which was adopted in January 1993. Sergei Rogov, deputy director of the Institute for the Study of the USA and Canada of the Russian Academy of Sciences, was head of the group of experts that drew up the document. It might be intuitively thought that members of this institute would have a pro-U.S. bias and act as a "U.S. lobby" in domestic debates over policy. But, as in society as a whole, one can find all manner of political opinion in the institute. Rogov had complained that Russian foreign policy lacked coherence and, significantly, despite

Kozyrev's talk of a natural alliance with the United States, that Russia lacked any real allies. He argued that neither in the economic nor in the military realm did Russia have any natural or logical partners or friends and that this should be recognized in formulating foreign policy. Russia should recognize its priorities in the "near abroad" and ensure that it maintains sufficient military capability commensurate with its status as the "world's second great power," a status the United States must acknowledge. As Alexander Rahr notes, this document reflects many of the ideas of the "Eurasian lobby."[46] Thus, again the United States was not seen as a natural partner. And again, Russian policy should be based upon a conception of its national interests in terms of great-power status in Eurasia.

Conclusion

Both at the international systemic level and the domestic politics level, and where these levels overlap, relations with the United States have become progressively more difficult and simultaneously less salient in overall conceptions of Russian foreign policy. At the outset, when Russia was suddenly faced with the task of redefining itself, the United States was the most important focus of Russian diplomacy. In renouncing the Soviet empire and Soviet foreign policy of the Cold War era, Russia dropped its commitments to weak, non-democratic allies in the "Third World" (e.g., Cuba, Angola, Ethiopia) and sought to develop a "partnership" with the old enemies of the Cold War period, that is, with the Western democracies, especially the United States. The United States was the central target for economic aid and for negotiating arms cuts. However, with the end of the Cold War the international political economy was becoming increasingly difficult to manage in the absence of strategic bipolarity, and interest in Russia's fate in the United States declined as concerns for America's own place in the global economy grew. By the end of 1992 it was becoming evident to the Russian government that the hoped for economic dividends from its strategy toward the United States were not being realized, and Russia began courting other developed states in Western Europe and among the newly industrialized countries of Asia to assist its own economic development. Although Russia and the United States share common interests in limiting or preventing nuclear weapons proliferation, in other security areas there is potential for differences and tensions (e.g., in the Balkans and in competition for the international arms trade).

Competing conceptions of what Russia's place in the world should be, and hence differences over foreign policies, have been fundamental issues in domestic politics and power struggles. At first the only groups opposing a policy orientation on the West and the United States were from among the more extreme conservatives, but by the end of 1992 most opponents to Yeltsin, and even some supporters, were criticizing Russia's dominant pro-U.S. foreign policy and calling for the development of a coherent conception of Russia's national interest. By the end of 1993 it was accepted by most political groups, including Yeltsin and the government, that Russia's essential national interests required a stronger focus on countries closer to home, particularly its nearest neighbors. However Eurasia is ultimately defined, and whatever it means for Russia's desire to remain a great power, it was now recognized that Russia and the United States would not develop an alliance and that on occasion Russian and U.S. interests could diverge. While there are groups in Russia who claim that the United States was directly and deliberately responsible for bringing Russia to its present impasse, the most vehemently anti-U.S. elements are unlikely to affect policy to any great degree. *Pravda* may carry ludicrous reports (citing former KGB chief and coup plotter Kryuchkov) accusing former Gorbachev adviser Yakovlev and some of Yeltsin's advisers of having been CIA agents, and Arbatov, resentful at no longer being part of the foreign policy establishment in Moscow, can carp about a new cold war, but Russian foreign policy is unlikely to return to an ideological Cold War confrontation with the United States.[47]

What has occurred during the early years of Russia's relations with the United States has been a search for a policy that reflects Russia's national interests. This has been particularly difficult given the radical changes in the international system and in domestic politics. At first, due to the fact that the United States was the most influential actor in the international system, Washington loomed large in Russian policy at the expense of other areas closer to home. The influential political commentator Stanislav Kondrashev summed up the situation by early 1994 when he wrote about the "honeymoon" between Russia and the United States being over.[48]

It is not simply, as the simplistic arguments of many observers claim, the pressure from neo-conservatives in Moscow has led to a more assertive foreign policy in the near abroad and an increasing tendency to challenge U.S. policy in some areas. Rather, changes in policy are due to a mix of basic geopolitical and economic realities relating to Russia's position in Eurasia and to the process of domestic politics and the institutionalization of a foreign policy system.

Relations with the United States will most probably mature into a mixture of contention and cooperation depending upon the specific issue area and its perceived importance to respective national interests. At times these interests will coincide, at other times they will diverge.

However, this should be no great cause for concern for it will simply reflect the normal parameter of relations between states in the international system.

Notes

1. Fred Halliday, "The Cold War as Inter-systemic Conflict—Initial Theses," in Mike Bowker and Robin Brown (eds), *From Cold War to Collapse: Theory and World Politics in the 1980s,* Cambridge University Press, 1993, pp. 21–34.

2. Baker and Shevardnadze developed a very close working relationship; in the first two years of the Bush presidency they met on more than twenty occasions. For an account of U.S.-Soviet relations during this period see Michael R. Beschloss and Strobe Talbott, *At The Highest Levels: The Inside Story of the Cold War,* London, Little, Brown, 1993.

3. See RIA, June 9, 1994, and *RFERL Daily Report,* June 24, 1994.

4. See, for a recent discussion on the question of American decline, the March and May issues of *Commentary* in 1992.

5. *International Affairs* (Moscow), no. 2, 1993, p. 19.

6. Alexander Bykov, "At the Crossroads of World Development," *International Affairs* (Moscow), no. 3, 1993, pp. 87–96, p. 90.

7. *Pravda,* March 10, 1993.

8. *Delovoi mir,* June 25, 1994.

9. Eileen Crumm, "From Superpower Deadlock to Ordinary Relationship: Materials for a Theory of U.S.-Russian Relations," in Manus I. Midlarsky, John A. Vasquez, and Peter V. Gladkov (eds), *From Rivalry to Cooperation: Russian and American Perspectives on the Post-Cold War Era,* New York, HarperCollins, 1994, pp. 126–144, p. 132.

10. *Economist,* quoted in *Australian,* April 4, 1993.

11. Quoted in *Time,* June 29, 1992.

12. *Nezavisimaia gazeta,* April 29, 1993.

13. RIA, January 14, 1994.

14. Quoted in Zbigniew Brzezinski, "The Premature Partnership," *Foreign Affairs,* vol. 73, no. 2, 1994, pp. 67–82, p. 70.

15. Interview with Kozyrev in *Moscow News,* March 5, 1993.

16. For an assessment of Ambartsumov's influence on Russian foreign policy during this period, see Suzanne Crow, "Yevgenny Ambartsumov's Influence on Russian Foreign Policy," *Radio Liberty Research Report,* April 29, 1992. For an interview with Ambartsumov, see *Moskovskie novosti,* February 28, 1993.

17. See *Izvestiia,* April 20, 1994, and *Rossiiskie vesti,* April 23, 1994.

18. *Rossiiskaia gazeta,* January 19, 1993.

19. Figures given by Andrew J. Pierre of the Carnegie Endowment for International Peace, *Moscow News,* no. 21, May 21, 1993.

20. *Izvestiia,* February 16, 1993.

21. *Izvestiia,* February 27, 1993.

22. *Izvestiia,* February 16, 1993.

23. *Izvestiia,* March 3, 1993.

24. For an excellent account of superpower relations during the Gulf War, see Beschloss and Talbott, *At the Highest Levels*, 1993, chapters 9–15.

25. *Komsomolskaia pravda*, June 18, 1994.

26. On new thinking see Peter Shearman, "New Thinking Reassessed," *Review of International Studies*, vol. 19, no. 2, 1993, pp. 139–158.

27. Rodionov's keynote address to the conference has been translated with a commentary by Marcy C. Fitzgerald in *Orbis*, Spring, 1993, pp. 281–288, p. 283.

28. Brzezinski, "The Premature Partnership."

29. Andrei Kozyrev, "The Lagging Partnership," *Foreign Affairs*, vol. 73 no. 3, 1994, pp. 59–71, p. 62.

30. *Moskovskie novosti*, January 31, 1993.

31. *Nezavisimaia gazeta*, March 23, 1993.

32. *Nezavisimaia gazeta*, January 11, 1993.

33. See Stephen Foye, "Russia's Fragmented Army Drawn into the Political Fray," *Radio Liberty Research Report*, March 31, 1993.

34. On this see Alexander Rahr, "Russia: Struggle Between President and Legislature Continues," *Radio Liberty Research Report*, January 28, 1993.

35. Rahr, "Russia: Struggle Between President and Legislature Continues."

36. Elgiz Pozdnyakov, "The Geopolitical Collapse of Russia," *International Affairs* (Moscow), no. 3, 1992.

37. Georgi Arbatov, "Eurasia Letter: A New Cold War?" *Foreign Policy*, no. 95, Summer 1994, p. 96.

38. *Moscow News*, February 25, 1992.

39. On the National Salvation Front's Congress see *Izvestiia*, October 26, 1992. For the Lukin quote see Vladimir Lukin, "Klinton i Rossiia: Novyi vitok," *Moskovskie novosti*, March 21, 1993. For the interview with Ambartsumov see *Moskovskie novosti*, February 28, 1993.

40. Cited in Suzanne Crow, "Processes and Policies," *Radio Liberty Research Report*, April 19, 1993.

41. Crow, "Processes and Policies."

42. *Moskovskie novosti*, March 21, 1993.

43. *International Affairs* (Moscow), no. 1, 1993, pp. 14–16.

44. *International Affairs* (Moscow), no. 2, 1993, pp. 3–20, for the verbatim report of the forum.

45. Vladimir Orlov in *Moscow News*, April 30, 1993.

46. Rahr, "Russia: Struggle."

47. *Pravda*, February 5, 1993; Arbatov, "Eurasia Letter: A New Cold War?" Arbatov does not conceal his resentment at foreign policy being conducted by a new generation of elites whom he considers to be inexperienced and ignorant of the ways of the world. Clearly he believes that he could do a much better job himself.

48. *Izvestiia*, April 6, 1994.

7

Russian Policy Toward Japan

Robert F. Miller

Introduction

When Mikhail S. Gorbachev undertook his "new political thinking" on Soviet foreign policy in 1986, it was clear that he did not intend the dismantling of the Soviet empire. His intention was to increase the effectiveness of Soviet ventures in various parts of the world—to improve the payoff, in terms of Soviet power and influence, with a lower-cost (read "less militarily assertive") and more politically, economically, and diplomatically astute kind of foreign policy.[1] Although he was increasingly aware of the economic and social ailments that were afflicting his country as late as the end of 1988, he was still acting as if he were able to deal from a position of strength in bargaining with opposing international forces in the prosecution of Soviet interests. As Paul Dibb farsightedly concluded in 1984, Soviet power was remarkably uni-dimensional—a First World military capability based on a Third World economy.[2] Nevertheless, that dimension was powerful indeed, and few in the West were prepared to deny that Gorbachev and his country were entitled to be consulted on the major world issues of the day. As late as May 1991, a few months before the collapse of the USSR, Gorbachev still found it possible to declare:

> Everyone must proceed from the fact that the Soviet Union exists. That is the first thing. That it will continue to exist. That is the second thing. That, thirdly, it is a powerful state. And, fourthly, it will remain such.[3]

Nowhere was the continuing image of the Soviet menace more evident than in the Asia-Pacific region (APR). Gorbachev's intention to become a major player in the APR, stated in his Vladivostok and Krasnoyarsk speeches in 1986 and 1988, respectively, evoked considerable anxiety in Washington and the capitals of the regional states. In these speeches

Gorbachev foreshadowed a major campaign to engage Soviet economic, political, and military power in the international relations of the region. The two major policy speeches were also clearly informed by a recognition of several features of the APR that had not customarily been given prominence by Soviet leaders: this was economically the most dynamic region in the world; the Soviet Far East was in dire need of developmental assistance—which Japan and the so-called "newly industrializing countries" of the region, especially South Korea and Singapore, were in an excellent position to supply; and Japan's growing political and military might could best be turned to the USSR's advantage by enlisting that country's involvement in the development of the Soviet Far East.

A further vital concern was the relationship with China, which until the eve of Gorbachev's historic visit to Beijing in May 1989 was still regarded as a serious danger to Soviet security interests in the Far East. Until the "normalization" of Sino-Soviet relations, which Gorbachev's visit ultimately achieved, Moscow viewed Japan as a potential counterweight to growing Chinese power, particularly if Japan could be persuaded to transfer to the USSR some of the investment and commercial resources it had been channelling into China in response to Deng Xiaoping's economic "opening" to the capitalist West.

Earlier efforts to enlist Japanese investment in Soviet Far East development in the 1960s had eventually withered on the vine during the 1970s—partly for economic reasons but also in response to the heavy-handed, military-centered Soviet foreign policy in the region under the Brezhnev regime.[4] Like the Chinese, the Japanese had responded to Brezhnev's aggressiveness with a militant anti-Soviet attitude, including enhanced reliance on the U.S. military and diplomatic presence in the region.

Given the increasing weight of Japanese economic involvement throughout the region in the 1980s and the diplomatic influence this conferred, it was clear to the "new political thinkers" in Moscow that an improvement in relations with Japan was a key to any feasible strategy for enhancing Soviet power and influence in the APR. However, it was equally clear that rapprochement with Japan depended on convincing Washington that the nature of superpower conflict in the region should no longer be viewed as a zero-sum game.

From the beginning it was evident that Gorbachev's new approach was fraught with serious contradictions, both from the standpoint of both internal Soviet power politics and from the perspectives of the major regional actors. Conservative politicians and military leaders had to be convinced of the viability of the new strategy, which included certain trade-offs—first and foremost, in return for a somewhat reduced Soviet military presence in the region, there would be a reduction of the U.S. naval presence; also, an enhancement of Soviet intelligence-gathering capabilities would be made possible by the expansion of Moscow's diplomatic and commercial representation throughout the APR.[5]

Gorbachev's approach called forth a negative reaction by the United States; and his proposals regarding mutual reductions of naval activities and the closure of U.S. bases in the Philippines in return for the abandonment of Soviet facilities at Cam Ranh Bay in Vietnam were greeted with derision. Gorbachev came to realize that he had few bargaining chips to induce the U.S. to sacrifice its military and economic dominance in the region. His efforts to recast security arrangements in the APR along European lines foundered on the rock of the major differences in the power relationships between the two hemispheres, which were evidently better understood by the regional powers than they were by him.

Even if the domestic opposition could be won over, Gorbachev had to contend with an increasingly independent Japanese position. Japanese demands for a return of the so-called northern territories—the southern Kurile islands of Iturup, Kunashir, Shikotan, and the Habomai group, all seized by Stalin at the close of World War II—had become so important a factor in internal Japanese politics that no Japanese government could afford to neglect their return as a price for the improvement of Soviet-Japanese economic and political relations. Gorbachev's historic visit to Japan in April 1991 ran into a brick wall on the northern territories issue. The lack of results showed how little bargaining power the USSR had to overcome Japanese insistence on this condition sine qua non for rapprochement.

The collapse of the Soviet Union in the wake of the failed putsch of August 19–21, 1991, eroded the ability of the successor Russian state to implement Gorbachev's strategies for enhancing Moscow's power in the APR. As time has passed, however, evidence is accumulating that certain constants of the Russian-Japanese relationship and of the countries' internal configuration of interests have remained. An examination of these constants is the major focus of this chapter.

Ideas and Structures Influencing the Russo-Japanese Relationship

Foreign Policy Actors

One of the most important institutional changes in the way the USSR conducted its foreign policies in the APR was the restructuring in 1986 of the Ministry of Foreign Affairs (MFA) under Foreign Minister Eduard Shevardnadze. The MFA apparatus, which had been inherited virtually unchanged from the reign of Tsar Nicholas II, was now transformed functionally and territorially to reflect the new assessment of changes in the relative weight of regions and individual countries. In its current incarnation as the MFA of the Russian Federation, the Division (*Departament*) for the Asia-Pacific Region now contains two separate departments (*upravleniia*). The first determines and oversees policy on the still or former communist states of China, North Korea, Mongolia, and Indochina; the second, policy on Japan, South Korea, the ASEAN states, Australia, New Zealand, and the Pacific Island states. These changes have over time given more scope for professionalism in the conduct of Russian foreign policy toward individual countries in the region.

In addition to the formal governmental agencies involved in the analysis, determination, and implementation of foreign policy, there are increasing numbers of think tanks to provide non-official expert commentary on foreign policy matters. Many of them have been hived off from academic bodies and agencies of the former foreign policy establishment, whose members were regularly called upon by the CPSU Central Committee to give advice to the decision-makers. Now these agencies, particularly those of the old USSR Academy of Sciences, are compelled to seek government contracts and private deals with foreign and domestic businessmen to supplement their resources. It is clear that the number of players involved in the foreign relations game in post-Soviet Russia is considerably larger than in the old USSR.

Foreign Ministry policy under the new constitution adopted in December 1993, along with that of the other so-called power ministries (defense and internal affairs), is maintained as a preserve of the president. That is to say, the minister of Foreign Affairs is nominated by and is accountable to him and not to the prime minister or to the two houses of parliament. Nevertheless, experience has already shown that in the highly fractured political ambience resulting from the December 1993 elections, if the president does not choose to express his position on foreign policy and security issues—and sometimes even when he does—there are plenty of other actors willing and able to declare their own agendas for Russian foreign policy. This inchoate, not to say chaotic, nature of the conduct of Russia's foreign policy has been particularly visible in relations with Japan. Various actors, from Prime Minister Chernomyrdin to high military officials and radical nationalist politicians, have vied with President Yeltsin and the MFA under Minister Andrei Kozyrev to set the tone and substance of the relationship.

Searching for a New Role

Much of this apparent confusion is a product of the transitional character of the new arrangements, of the search for a specific role for Russia in the so-called new world order, and probably of the leading incumbents as well. For the moment, as Russia reconsiders its "national interests" and its position vis-à-vis the U.S. and the West in general (certainly including Japan), ideas and domestic political point-scoring seem to be more important than structures in the formation and conduct of policy.

The signs of ferment are abundant. In October 1992 the MFA promulgated an extensive document entitled the "Concept of Russian Foreign Policy," and Yeltsin was expected to endorse it, thus indicating his support for the Kozyrev line.[6] In a key speech at the MFA on October 27, however, Yeltsin gave only lukewarm support to Kozyrev personally and criticized the ministry for not defending Russian national interests consistently enough, especially as regards the protection of Russians in former republics of the USSR. He also castigated the ministry for not carrying out essential personnel changes fast enough. Finally, he urged Russian diplomats not to be afraid of accusations of Russian imperialism and to be as active as the former USSR had been in defending the country's national security interests and its dignity.[7]

Thus, although Yeltsin had not shifted his support entirely to the conservative position, there is little doubt that the conservatives' arguments were having a growing influence on his policies. It is also worth pointing out that there are considerable numbers of prominent individuals not normally associated with the conservatives—let alone with the reactionary positions of Vladimir Zhirinovsky—in whom some of the anti-liberal or anti-Western rhetoric of the right wing strikes a responsive chord. Some of these arguments and the tenor of their presentation deserve brief comment here because they impinge directly and indirectly on Russo-Japanese relations.

First, one might mention the attitude of the conservatives on the nature of correct foreign policy decision-making. A major element of policy formation under the old regime was the existence of a body of theory— Marxism-Leninism—which purportedly exerted an orientational influence on current strategy and tactics. It set forth a coherent hierarchy of goals and national interests, to which Soviet policy-makers were always constrained at least to pay lip service. Never mind, as Gorbachev and his chief theoretician Alexander Yakovlev pointed out in their promotion of the "new political thinking," that it was precisely this "ideologization" of foreign policy that had got the USSR into the morass of over-commitment that proved to be its eventual downfall: the conservatives obviously miss the old penchant for theory. Indeed, Kozyrev, when pressed on the matter of defining Russian national interests, expressly eschewed the need for it, pointing out that Western powers seem to find no need to enshrine their conceptions of national interests in specific formal documents:

I am criticized for lacking a clear concept of Russia's foreign policy. We work on it together with scientists and experts. But I must confess that it is a futile undertaking—just like a CPSU program: if it overlooks something, it is incomplete; when complete it becomes a dead scheme. For instance, there exists the notion of the U.S. national interests. But where are they recorded? They are each time defined according to the situation. . . .[8]

Other prominent individuals, such as Vladimir Lukin, former Russian ambassador to the USA and now a leader of one of the "democratic" opposition parties, also feel the need for a more coherently conceptualized policy. He has criticized the tendency of individual leaders, such as then CIS military commander Marshal Shaposhnikov, to enunciate their own "foreign policies," attributing this to the lack of a coordinating center and clear guidelines on foreign policy.[9] An article on the fallout from Yeltsin's cancellation of his visit to Japan in September 1992 advised that it was better to wait for the further crystallization of the conceptual basis of foreign policy before planning a new visit and the resumption of negotiations on the Kurile Islands question.[10]

The eventual publication of the "Concept of Russian Foreign Policy" indicated that Kozyrev had yielded to demands for a comprehensive theoretical statement of Russia's goals and interests. Indeed, there were indications that a more independent, less automatically pro-Western line had come into force by early 1993.[11]

The "Eurasian" Myth

The content of the conservatives' theoretical challenge is no less interesting than its epistemology. Perhaps the most interesting manifestation is the reappearance of the "Eurasian" myth, which was popular among Russian émigré intellectuals in Europe during the 1920s. For the original "Eurasians," the only bad thing about the Bolsheviks was their communist ideology, and hence their alienation from the Russian national spirit. They fully approved of the Bolsheviks' campaign to recover the territories of the Russian empire lost in the wake of the First World War. The essence of their theory was that Russia was not a purely European country but a conglomerate of European and Asian peoples with a distinct identity and modes of behavior. They believed that the Russian spirit was the dominant force in this symbiotic relationship but that the Asian (by which they meant primarily the Caucasian and Central Asian geographical areas) element was also influential, creating a conception of political interests and cultural perspectives that could not be satisfied by incorporation into European civilization, which they saw as in terminal decline.[12] In essence, the "Eurasian" myth was an extension of the conservative Slavophile attack on the liberalizing "Westernizers," whose debates occupied the center of intellectual life in the Russian empire during the nineteenth century—an extension in the sense that it went beyond the Orthodox-religious cultural and geopolitical sphere of the Slavophiles.[13] Foreign Minister Kozyrev has made it clear that he has little patience for the attempt to dredge up past ideologies and apply them to the search for alternative, non-Western-oriented paths for Russian foreign policy. In an address to the Russian parliament in October 1992 he condemned those who operate "under the guise of slogans", such as a "third way," "Eurasianism," or "great-power patriotism," which he said did not conform to Russia's choice of a democratic path.[14] That position may no longer be dominant; even Kozyrev seems to have changed his tone, if not his tune.[15] It is worth remembering that Japan is considered by the Russian foreign policy community as part of the West, not of Asia.[16] Accordingly, the generally hostile attitude toward the West of the conservative neo-Eurasians and their less intellectually fastidious brethren is also directed against Japan. The same variety of arguments marshalled against selling out Russian interests for Western economic assistance has been used in relation to Japan. Moreover, since Japan is one of the few "Western" countries with which territorial issues are also at stake (another is Finland), the anti-Western antagonism on the nationalists' side is even more intense in its case.

The highly charged "debates" on the Kurile Islands were reflected in attitudes expressed by Valentin Fedorov, the hard-line former governor of Sakhalin Island, which has jurisdiction over the contested southern Kuriles. In response to a proposal by Deputy Foreign Minister Georgy Kunadze in favor of acceding to the Japanese claims, Fedorov was alleged to have said that no one with a Georgian surname (e.g. Kunadze) had any right to decide questions concerning Russia.[17] Fedorov's attitude, shared by many Russians, liberals as well as conservatives, is hardly in keeping with the "Eurasian" outlook—indeed, it makes the Eurasians look positively liberal. It suggests how salient the reawakening of Russian nationalism has become across the Russian political spectrum. Yeltsin's remark during his trip to India in January 1993 that the tsarist eagle had two heads—one looking East and the other West—was clearly meant to convey that Russian interests in the East would henceforth be vigorously pursued.

The Kurile Islands Question and Japan

Historical Background

The international legal position of the Japanese claims to Iturup, Kunashir, Shikotan, and the Habomai group of small islets is not at all clear. The original inhabitants of the islands were the aboriginal Ainu and Aleut peoples. The first international document concerning the possession of the islands was the Russo-Japanese Treaty of 1855, providing for the shared possession of an undivided Sakhalin Island and the annexation by Russia of the Kurile Islands north of Iturup, with Iturup and the other three islands to the south becoming Japanese territory.[18] The next agreement on the region, the Russo-Japanese Treaty of 1875, gave Russia full possession of Sakhalin Island in return for renunciation of claims to the rest of the Kurile chain, which became Japanese property.

With the rise of Japanese expansionism toward the end of the nineteenth century, the previously amicable arrangements ceased. As a result of the Russo-Japanese War of 1904-1905, the southern half of Sakhalin Island was annexed by Japan, thus bringing it into possession of all of the Kuriles and part of Sakhalin. This was the maximum extent of Japanese expansion in the region, attempts at encroaching on Russian territory around the borders of Manchuria having been beaten off in major battles in 1938 and 1939.[19] During WWII, under the terms of a treaty of neutrality between the USSR and Japan of April 13, 1941, there was no further movement for territorial change; that is, until the Soviets, under some pressure at Yalta from their wartime allies the USA and Britain, denounced the 1941 treaty on April 5, 1945. The swift defeat of the Japanese Kwantung Army in the following weeks left the Soviets in possession of all of Sakhalin and the southern Kurile Islands now in dispute.[20] Their right to do so had been endorsed in the Yalta agreements. Thus, the Russian position today is that the so-called illegal occupation of the Kuriles was not an arbitrary act of the USSR alone but was fully sanctioned by other major powers. It is sometimes pointed out that at the San Francisco Conference in 1951 the Japanese themselves renounced their claim to the southern Kurile Islands.[21] The Japanese qualify this position by pointing out that they did not specifically cede them to the Russians, who did not sign the San Francisco Peace Treaty.[22]

There was another complicating document on the status of the Kuriles that the Soviet side offered during the incumbency of Nikita Khrushchev, namely, the Joint Declaration of the USSR and Japan of October 19, 1956. Under the terms of this declaration, which sought to establish full diplomatic relations and open the possibilities of economic cooperation, the USSR in response to Japanese wishes agreed to the handing over of the Habomai Islands and Shikotan after the conclusion of a formal peace treaty. The Japanese signature to this declaration is being interpreted in some circles as renunciation of claims to the other two islands and as recognition that the offer to hand over the Habomais and Shikotan was an act of pure goodwill on the Soviet side and not an acceptance of Japanese legal rights to them. Other Soviet commentators point out, however, that after the ratification of the 1956 declaration the foreign ministers of the two countries exchanged letters expressing readiness to negotiate on the status of Kunashir and Iturup as well. Thus, even then it was not unthinkable on the Soviet side that all of these islands would eventually be handed back to Japan.[23]

In any event, the formal peace treaty was never signed and the Southern Kuriles remained under Soviet jurisdiction. The Japanese conclusion of a security treaty with the United States in 1960 was used by Khrushchev as a justification for not proceeding with the terms of the 1956 declaration, and the territorial question quickly became an instrument of pressure against Tokyo in the vain attempt to force Japan away from its alliance with Washington.

That is ostensibly where matters have stood up to the present. However, former Soviet Deputy Foreign Minister Mikhail Kapitsa (now head of the Institute of Oriental Studies of the Russian Academy of Sciences) has recently revealed that during a visit to Japan in January 1972, Foreign Minister Andrei Gromyko made Japanese Prime Minister Eisaku Sato a secret offer to hand over the two southernmost islands, the Hobomais and Shikotan, in return for a bilateral peace treaty. The context was the growing rapprochement between the USA, Japan, and the Chinese People's Republic, and Soviet fears of encirclement in the Far East. The proposal had clearly been sanctioned by the Soviet leadership under Brezhnev. The Japanese did not rise to the bait and never replied to the offer.[24] And the Soviet side quickly repudiated it. This proposal is good evidence that the traditional pre-Gorbachev Soviet position on territorial concessions was not as rigorously "principled" as nostalgic present-day conservatives would have us believe. But it is also true that the Soviet position in 1972 was more heavily bolstered by an image of strength than it is today, which certainly constitutes a major difference in the psychological context of Russo-Japanese relations on the Kuriles and other issues.

Contemporary Difficulties

Some Russian commentators argue that the 1956 declaration still confers a valid obligation to hand over at least the two islands in question, especially since the subsequently announced condition of Japan's renouncing the security treaty with the USA was nowhere specified in the original declaration.[25] However, when Gorbachev travelled to Tokyo in April 1991 he did not feel it expedient to be seen as conceding any obligation emanating from the 1956 declaration or any other consideration of rights. As Harry Gelman has pointed out, Gorbachev was by that time no longer in a position to be offering territorial concessions to Japan or anyone else.[26] He did, however, make the significant concession in Tokyo that the territorial issue existed and could become the object of future negotiations. The results of Gorbachev's efforts in Tokyo were generally acknowledged to have been meager. The agreements he signed did not provide the anticipated economic benefits. There can be little doubt that the reason for his failure was the weakening of the Soviet position and the Japanese understanding of that fact.

There are a number of specific political, strategic, and moral reasons for the fact that any Russian leadership continues to find it difficult to hand over the islands to Japan despite the obvious advantages that would accrue in economic and international political terms. For one thing, the approximately 25,000 Russian inhabitants of the islands have indicated their opposition to coming under Japanese rule.[27] For another, the two largest of the islands, Iturup and Kunashir, stand on either side of one of the main channels for access to and from the Sea of Okhotsk, where a major part of the Russian ballistic missile submarine fleet is stationed. Estimates of Russian troops on all of the contested islands have varied from 7,000 to 20,000—the former figure generally being accepted as the current size of the contingent.[28]

As a tripwire force, this is not a negligible component of Russian defenses in the Far East. It is said to operate a number of installations that are crucial to Russian early warning and naval blocking capabilities and that the Russians are little inclined to give up. Thus, when President Yeltsin announced on the eve of his scheduled first visit to Tokyo that Russian military forces would be withdrawn from the Kuriles within a year, he was roundly repudiated by his military advisers, most notably Defense Minister Pavel Grachev. Grachev subsequently retracted his remarks, but there is ample evidence that so-called military-patriotic elements among the opposition to Yeltsin would make substantial capital out of any summary move to reduce the Russian military presence in the Kuriles.[29]

The Dilemmas of Russo-Japanese Relations in the Transition Period

The Russian Far East

The blame for the collapse of the 1992 Russo-Japanese negotiations probably ought to be apportioned equally between the two sides. It is perhaps not difficult to empathize with Russia's ambivalence toward the emerging transition of Japan from an economic to a diplomatic and possibly military superpower. On the one hand, Russia obviously desires Japanese assistance for the development of its neglected Maritime Province and Eastern Siberia. Political and economic interests there are keen on attracting foreign commercial and development capital, and Japan is obviously the most logical source.

On the other hand, many Russians, and not necessarily only radical nationalists, fear becoming too heavily dependent on Japanese assistance. They are seeking to involve other regional investors—Chinese, South Korean, Singaporean, Thai, and even Australian—in the development of the region. Former Governor Fedorov was anxious to create a "special economic zone"—on the Chinese Shenzhen model—on Sakhalin, and he succeeded in attracting substantial interest from Japanese and South Korean businessmen.[30] He successfully delayed the signing of an oil and gas development project off the Sakhalin coast with a Japanese-American consortium in early 1992 in favor of a deal with a smaller South Korean firm that promised to provide commercial and infrastructural financing as a sweetener. Moscow scuttled this agreement, but Fedorov's intervention necessitated a review of the tendering process.[31]

Fedorov was adamant on maintaining Russian (in particular, his own) control over the development process, even threatening at one point to seek the independence of his territory if Moscow yielded to Japan on the Kuriles.[32] Both he and his neighbor, Siberian and Far Eastern "superpatriot" Vladimir Kuznetsov, then governor of the Maritime Province (*Primorskii Krai*), resorted to threats of secession to blackmail the Russian government into taking greater account of its economic and political interests. One such threat envisaged the revival of the old Far Eastern Republic idea of 1918–1923, which Lenin used to parry Japanese thrusts into the region during the Russian civil war.[33]

There are grounds for believing that Yeltsin does not find such positions on the Kuriles and other issues of the Russo-Japanese relationship entirely uncongenial. Even before his aborted visit to Tokyo—and certainly since—the Russian position in the APR had begun to harden. By the middle of 1992, after a period of chaos and disillusionment within the Russian military, the military dimension of Russian policy was beginning to occupy a more prominent place once again. A liberal Russian commentator warned that the Russian military-industrial complex still "makes up 70 percent of the country's economy, constituting its very foundation, mentality, core."[34]

The Military Dimension

After having been lulled into a sense of security by a number of signs of Russian retrenchment—the rapid winding down of the base at Cam Ranh Bay, a sharp reduction in steaming time by the Russian Pacific Fleet (RPF) and its air surveillance activities near Japan, and a spate of articles in the liberal press arguing against the maintenance of a large blue-water navy[35]—Western defense planners in the APR suddenly found themselves with a Russian "bear" far from content to remain in his den. In late April 1992 the RPF began a series of extensive naval exercises that caught the U.S. and its allies by surprise. Earlier that month the Japanese government lodged an official protest over a Russian military incursion into Japanese air space. The Russian authorities denied that the intrusion had been deliberate and promised further investigation.[36] The implication was either that local commanders were pursuing a tougher policy on their own or that the official policy was in the process of change.

A further sign of change was the surprise decision to retain the Cam Ranh Bay facilities after all, despite the fact (was it because of the fact?) that the U.S. Seventh Fleet was well on the way to removing its forces from Philippine bases and reducing its military presence in the region. Commenting on the sudden Russian decision, the pseudonymous Polish international commentator Dawid Warszawski remarked:

> In getting itself involved in the game in the South China Sea, the new Russia is seeking to remind [everyone], and not only Beijing, that it still considers itself a superpower. This is in many ways a return to the policy announced back under Gorbachev in Vladivostok of Moscow's very active involvement in Asia.[37]

Russian observers have argued that the U.S. and regional powers in the APR have welcomed the return of a Russian military presence in the South China Sea as a factor of stability in the region. The "instability" that is implicitly the object of this assessment is a combination of the anticipated reduction of the U.S. presence; recent evidence of aggressive Chinese intentions, that is, by military actions in the contested Spratly Islands; and the potential threat of growing Japanese military strength.[38] It was even suggested by some that the USA share the facilities in Vietnam with Russia as part of a unified collective security and crisis-management system in the APR.[39] There was a note of euphoria in some of these comments—at last Russia's military presence is being welcomed into the region as a factor of stability, not of disruption, as in the recent Soviet past. Similar sentiments have surrounded the sudden injection of Russian peacekeeping forces as the "sharp end" of a more assertive policy in the Balkans.

The sudden evident weakness of the Russian position had levelled the playing field in the APR in a way that the previous apparent strength could never achieve. Some Japanese circles tried to deny the change. On the military front the announcement by Japanese sources in October 1992 of Russia's alleged intention to strengthen the Pacific Fleet in a major reorganization of Russian naval power is certainly cause for concern. According to this report, Russia would be transforming its present four ocean fleets into two main fleets—the Northern and Pacific Fleets, allegedly by scaling down the now less important and operationally more problematical Black Sea and Baltic Fleets and transferring some of their capital ships to Vladivostok. Speculation had it that the second of the Kuznetsov class attack carriers, the *Varyag*, would be purchased from the Ukrainian shipyard, where these ships are built, and assigned to the Pacific Fleet.[40] An alternative rumor was that China might purchase this carrier.[41] Suggestively, news of these developments became public only after the cancellation of Yeltsin's visit. These reports eventually proved to be unfounded or ambiguous, but the mind-set behind them reflected the thinking of important elements in the Japanese strategic community that were finding it difficult to adjust to the changed circumstances in the region.

The indirect evidence of the reappearance of the military factor was similarly noted. Most of the examples involved the intensification of military equipment sales by the Russian MIC throughout the APR. The list of recent deals and offers extends from the commitment to sell India large rocket engines suitable for ICBM use and the sale of modern Kilo-class diesel-electric submarines to Iran—both of which evoked condemnations from Washington—to the offer of patrol boats to the Philippines (for bananas!), and MiG-29s to Malaysia (allegedly for coconuts!) and an attempt to engage South Korean industries in joint production ventures with the Russian MIC, not only in so-called conversion (military-to-civilian) undertakings but also in such directly military activities as the development of a multirole fighter aircraft and the production of gas-turbine engines and aircraft components.[42]

From the standpoint of Japan—and the U.S.—the most worrisome development in this area has been the sale of state-of-the-art Russian weapons systems to China, including twenty-four high-performance Sukhoi-27 aircraft, with plans for the co-production of other advanced weapons, including MiG-29s, MiG-31s, and T-72 tanks. According to a Western report of the Russian offer, "Some analysts contend that the Russian-Chinese arms deal was prompted not only by Moscow's need for money but also by mutual fear of the rising power of Japan."[43]

Russia Seeks Asian Investment in the Kuriles

Meanwhile, in the non-military area the Russians went out of their way to show the Japanese that they were not to be taken lightly. In June 1992 it was announced that South Korea had been given fishing rights in the territory around the disputed Kurile islands. The Japanese protested to both Russia and South Korea over the deal, which they characterized as prejudicial to their interests in the area.[44] Just after the cancellation of the

Yeltsin visit in September 1992, it was announced that Russia had granted a Hong Kong development company (actually a front for a Taiwanese businessman with Japanese citizenship) a fifty-year lease to build a resort and casino complex on 278 hectares of Shikotan Island. The Japanese warned that they would annul the deal when they recovered the island and demolish the complex at the expense of the Hong Kong firm.[44] The undertaking bore all the hallmarks of former Governor Fedorov's approach to development in his region, but it clearly also reflected Moscow's intention of signalling Japan that it, too, could play tough in negotiations on the islands and that it intended to remain there indefinitely. Significantly, Shikotan was one of the two islands that the Russians were least reluctant to give back. In any case, the Hong Kong interests involved in the casino evidently responded to the Japanese threat and agreed to shelve the project.[45] However, on December 8, 1992, Yeltsin issued a long-awaited decree setting up a special economic zone for the Kuriles and permitting the leasing of land to foreign investors for up to ninety-nine years. Not surprisingly, there were strong Japanese protests.[46]

Yeltsin used his visit to Seoul in November 1992 to unleash a number of fresh security and economic initiatives, none of which could have been much to Japan's liking. Most provocative to Tokyo was the offer to South Korea to participate in the development of rich sulfur deposits on the island of Iturup, thus demonstratively indicating an intention to retain the Kuriles for the indefinite future.[47] Russian and South Korean defense ministers also signed a defense protocol on November 20, calling for regular exchanges of visits by defense officials and military observers, as well as naval ship visits by the two countries. In addition Yeltsin pledged to re-examine his country's security treaty with North Korea.[48]

Japan Courts the CIS and the United States

Lest one be tempted to argue that the impetus for the hardening of the Russian position in the APR is entirely internally generated, it should be noted that the Japanese have certainly contributed to Moscow's disposition to become more assertive. In the months leading up to Japanese Foreign Minister Michio Watanabe's fateful trip to Moscow to prepare for the Yeltsin visit, where he indicated no sign of flexibility on the northern territories issue, the Japanese had been making numerous contacts with non-Russian members of the Commonwealth of Independent States, particularly the newly independent Asian republics. The implication was that if Russia did not prove amenable to Japanese wishes, Japan would make its own deals with Russia's erstwhile provinces, perhaps inducing them to apply pressure on Russia to make the desired concessions. Russian diplomats were well aware of this challenge. In May 1992, Sergei Agafonov, *Izvestiia's* man in Tokyo and a recognized expert on Japanese affairs, concluded his description of what he called the "Russian season in Japanese diplomacy" in the following words:

> Japan, no doubt, is and will be an alluring partner for the former Soviet republics. Lithuania, Latvia, and Estonia began their sovereign connections with Japan with recognition of the "legitimacy" of Tokyo in the territorial dispute. Now Kazakhstan and Kyrgyzstan are "latching on" to the territorial theme. There is reason to assume that in the near future someone else from the former "indivisible family" will promise to speak to the Russian leadership concerning the Japanese aspirations. There will be many such conversations. But the right to decide—or not to decide—the infamous problem will remain to Russia in any case. . . .[49]

The decision to cancel Yeltsin's visit was taken despite Japan's successful effort to enlist the support of U.S. President Bush and other Western leaders to apply pressure on Moscow to accede to Japan's wishes on the northern territories. Presumably such pressure was in fact exerted on Yeltsin during his trip to Washington in June. This makes the decision to call off the visit all the more striking as a demonstration of Moscow's defiance on the Kuriles issue and the general stiffening of its position in the APR. An interesting sign of the change in Russia's perceptions of the world situation and the need for greater independence in shaping its international relations was the report of the minister for foreign economic relations at that time, Petr Aven, at the aforementioned meeting in the MFA on October 27. Aven recommended that Russia cease relying so heavily on Western credits; the foreign debt was already becoming unbearable, he said, and the West was inadequately motivated to provide the kinds of assistance needed.[50] In short, the "beggar's stage" of Russia's involvement with the West seemed to be coming to an end.

Just how far and how rapidly this transformation would occur and what it would mean for the country's foreign relations with countries like Japan, which had a reputation for respecting only strength, remained to be tested. In November 1992, Yeltsin had made it clear that as far as the Kuriles were concerned, the ball was now squarely in the Japanese court. Progress would be possible, he asserted, only when the Japanese came forth with a suitably softened position on the handover of the islands.[51]

Transition to What? Prospects for Russo-Japanese Relations

Throughout this chapter I have been arguing that Russian foreign policy has been in transition toward what might be considered a more "normal" posture for Russia in international relations. Namely, it has been evolving from the chaos, self-doubt, and internal preoccupations of the immediate post-putsch period, when the ideas of Western-oriented liberal democrats prevailed in decision-making circles, to a more assertive projection of Russian state interests. Such assertiveness is linked to the growing ascendancy in policy-relevant positions of persons who, although not necessarily conservative or authoritarian, are more heavily influenced by Russian nationalism and a narrower conception of Russian patriotism. The effects of the confrontation between these two perspectives have been particularly well illustrated by the development of Russo-Japanese relations, especially over the issue of the return of the south Kurile Islands.

The Demise of Russian Power and the Liberals' Position

The position of the liberals, doggedly pursued but with diminishing conviction by Foreign Minister Andrei Kozyrev, is that honest negotiations with full consideration of the vital interests of the negotiating partners, and without bluster and threat of force, are the key to successful diplomacy in the post–Cold War era. In this approach they are continuing to operate under the basic postulates of Gorbachev's new political thinking. In the beginning Gorbachev could implicitly negotiate from a position of strength because of the aura of military power that the USSR patently still exuded. That had its negative side, of course, as the lack of Western enthusiasm for his Vladivostok and Krasnoyarsk initiatives illustrated. As the Soviet power position demonstrably weakened, however, Gorbachev paradoxically found it easier to convince his Western partners in dialogue that his offers were genuine and worth considering. Concrete achievements were relatively meager, but the promise of Western financial assistance for the country's rapidly disintegrating economy seemed to make the transformations being carried out under Gorbachev's auspices worthwhile.

Yeltsin continued to derive benefits from the relative weakness of Russia's position, at least in the sense of eliciting Western understanding and support for his initiatives in further transforming the Russian economy and the political system. However, that understanding and encouragement were not uniform among Russia's Western partners. Germany and the United States were not inclined to take much advantage of Russia's weaknesses, implicitly recognizing that the potential power of a revived Russian state could once again make it a dangerous opponent if the desired changes to the political and economic system were not firmly anchored. As Gelman argued, this change in Washington's perspective on the nature of the Russian challenge had significant effects on the U.S.-Japanese alliance and especially on Japan's confidence that it could continue to rely on the U.S. for support on such issues as the northern territories.[52]

Japan was not nearly so farsighted or accommodating when dealing with Russian sensibilities. As Sergei Agafonov argued, the Japanese worldview tends to be much more pragmatic and inspired by a shortsighted conception of realpolitik, which makes Japan prone to take advantage of momentary weaknesses on the part of its opponents to achieve specific gains.[53] This assessment is confirmed by Japanese conduct surrounding the Yeltsin visit scheduled for mid-September 1992. Foreign Minister Michio Watanabe, in his trip to Moscow to prepare for the visit, showed virtually no flexibility on the south Kuriles issue, giving little room for maneuver to Yeltsin, who had proclaimed his readiness to explore from twelve to twenty-nine different variants (!) of a possible solution to the issue. This readiness to make concessions may have been a mistake, since it made Yeltsin vulnerable to both the Japanese and his domestic opponents. Given the mounting domestic opposition, especially from the increasingly vocal military leadership, to any concessions at all on the matter, Yeltsin had little choice but to postpone his visit; the abruptness with which he did so—four days before his scheduled departure—however, did little for his reputation as a statesman.

Changing Positions in Moscow and Tokyo

Since that time, the positions of the two sides have changed substantially. The Japanese, significantly weakened by the decline in the Japanese economy during 1993 and beset by a series of political scandals that resulted in the downfall of the long-ruling LDP and its replacement by a weak seven-party coalition of reputed "cleanskins," are less able to confront the Russians from a position of self-confident strength. They have shown slightly more tactical flexibility on the Kuriles and have bowed to G-7 pressures to offer limited amounts of aid to the troubled Russian economy. They have, however, sought to target specific parts of the former USSR for most of this aid; assistance to Russia is being directed mainly at the Far East, and special attention is being focused on the Central Asian republics, which cannot be entirely reassuring to Yeltsin. Curiously, Tokyo has begun to explore the possibilities of negotiations with potential Russian alternatives to Yeltsin— hard-liners who would presumably let the Japanese know precisely what they can expect in the form of trade-offs for improved relations.[54]

Russia, meanwhile, has been pursuing in the open a fairly aggressive counter-offensive of its own, with more assertive initiatives across a broad front—from military sales to economic concessions—that are clearly designed to discomfit Tokyo. The Japanese have come to fear being diplomatically isolated by the new Russian ventures,[55] and given the present turmoil in internal Japanese politics, they perhaps realize that the Russians are giving them some of their own medicine in taking advantage of short-term weaknesses. While the relative power positions of the two countries somewhat altered during 1993 and 1994, the positions of their respective political leaders, Boris Yeltsin and Morihiro Hosokawa, ironically tended to converge at a common point of domestic weakness and vulnerability, which made it impossible for either to offer the kinds of concessions that would make genuine Russo-Japanese rapprochement possible. The best that can be said of the results of Yeltsin's visit to Tokyo in October 1993, which he finally managed to consummate after two abortive efforts, was that his meetings were surprisingly cordial and non-confrontational. By that time, Yeltsin was already vulnerable to his nationalistic rivals over the shoot-out at the White House on October 3-4 and could make no concessions. But neither was Hosokawa in a position to take advantage of his guest's discomfiture.[56]

Conclusion

Subsequent developments suggest that the stalemate in the relationship over the Kuriles and its linkage to Japanese economic assistance are likely to persist for the indefinite future.

Russia apparently intends gradually to return to center stage in the APR, using a number of traditional instruments of diplomatic, economic, and military influence. The nature of Moscow's new challenge is certainly different from that in the Soviet period. The Leninist ideological element is no longer present, and the threat of subversion through the use of surrogate powers to achieve the objectives of an expanding "world of socialism" is now absent. Nevertheless, resurgent Russian nationalism and vestigial impulses from the imperial past are emergent motivating forces that will make the Russian presence in the region a more active factor than seemed possible in the period immediately following the post-putsch collapse. The nature of the challenge is certainly different, but it is a challenge nonetheless. Russia's sudden injection of diplomacy into the crisis over North Korea's nuclear weapons program in March 1994 was a good illustration, following its remarkable successes in Bosnia and Croatia, of an increasing ability to assume a central role in international crisis management at very low cost in material and military terms. Those in Tokyo—as well as Washington, Canberra, the ASEAN capitals, and elsewhere—who have been arguing and acting as if Russia were a negligible factor in the diplomatic and security considerations of the Asia-Pacific region are obviously being compelled to rethink their assumptions.

Notes

1. I have discussed this aspect of Gorbachev's foreign policy and the nature of his new political thinking in my ill-fated, or at least poorly titled, book *Soviet Foreign Policy Today: Gorbachev and the New Political Thinking*. Sydney: Allen & Unwin, 1991, esp. chapter 1.

2. "V dva golosa," *Sovetskaia Rossiia*, May 30, 1992, p. 4.

3. For a good account of Soviet-Japanese relations during this period see Myles L. C. Robertson, *Soviet Policy Towards Japan: An Analysis of Trends in the 1970s and 1980s*. Ph.D Thesis, the Australian National University, 1987.

4. For a discussion of the enhancement of Soviet signals intelligence capabilities in the region as a consequence of expanded Soviet diplomatic and commercial involvement in the 1980s, see Desmond Ball, *Soviet Signals Intelligence (SIGINT)*, Canberra: Strategic and Defence Studies Centre, Research School of Pacific Studies, the Australian National University, 1989.

5. Suzanne Crow, "Foreign Policy 'Concept' to Appear Soon" and "Yeltsin to Speak at Foreign Ministry," *RFERL Daily Report*, no. 204, October 22, 1992.

6. John Lepingwell, "Yeltsin Criticizes Foreign Ministry," *RFERL Daily Report*, no. 208, October 28, 1992. For a more detailed discussion of Yeltsin's speech, which suggests somewhat greater support for Kozyrev, see the BBC Monitoring Service dispatch "Russia: Yeltsin Addresses Foreign Ministry Collegium," Reuters Textline, October 28, 1992.

7. Andrei Kozyrev, "And Yet Russia Is Destined to Be a Great Power," *New Times*, no. 3, 1992, p. 21.

8. Arkady Dubnov, interview with Vladimir Lukin, "It's Bad When a Country Has Three or Four Foreign Policies," *New Times*, no. 7, 1992, p. 7.

9. Sergei Agafonov, "Problema Kuril'skikh ostrovov: Pauzu luchshe zatianut'," *Izvestiia*, October 5, 1992, p. 7.

10. These emerged initially in Europe, where an inclination to support the Serbs and to oppose solutions in the Balkans favored by the Americans and the Germans was already apparent by that time.

11. The 1931 edition of the Large Soviet Encyclopaedia described the "Eurasians" as "A literary-philosophical current among the Russian counter-revolutionary emigration asserting that the Romano-German culture heretofore dominant in the West was undergoing a crisis and was disintegrating, and to replace it a new culture is appearing, whose bearer will be the Russian people, uniting around itself not only Eastern Slavdom, but also a series of non-Slavic peoples inhabiting the so-called 'Eurasia.'" Quoted in Alexander Krivopalov, "Kto ona, Vera Treil-Guchkova?," *Izvestiia*, September 22, 1992, p. 7. The article goes on to suggest that many of the emigre "Eurasians" came to work for the NKVD, which, of course, eventually made them vulnerable to Stalin's "Great Terror"—the purges of the late 1930s.

12. For recent, basically sympathetic, treatment in the Russian press of the "Eurasians" and their anti-Western theories, see I. Isaev, "Evraziistvo: Mif ili traditsiia?" *Kommunist*, no. 12, 1991; Lidiia Novikova and Irina Sizemskaia, "Dva lika Evraziistva," *Svobodnaia mysl'*, no. 7, 1992, pp. 100-110.

13. Cited by Suzanne Crow, *RFERL Daily Report*, no. 205, October 23, 1992.

14. For a good example of the subtlety and defensiveness of the shift in Kozyrev's line, see "Russia: Kozyrev Defends His Foreign Policy in Interview, Denies Playing to the Galleries," BBC Monitoring Summary of World Broadcasts, in Reuters Textline, April 5, 1994.

15. Along with South Korea and Australia, among other countries. For example, see the recent collective essay "Russia and the Challenges of the Contemporary World" by members of the Institute of World Economy and International Relations of the Russian Academy of Sciences: "Rossiia i vyzovy sovremennosti," *Mirovaia ekonomika i mezhdunarodnye otnosheniia*, no. 4, April, 1992, p. 100.

16. Cited in V. Gaidar, "Problema Kuril'skikh ostrovov: Mezhdunarodno-pravovoi aspekt," *Mirovaia ekonomika i mezhdunarodnye otnosheniia*, no. 4, April, 1992, p. 113.

17. The discussion of the legal issues here is derived from V. Gaidar, "Problema," pp. 112-115.

18. For an excellent account of Soviet-Japanese relations during the 1930s, which demonstrates the continuities in the antagonism between the two powers in the pre- and post-Soviet periods, see Jonathan Haslam, *The Soviet Union and the Threat from the East, 1933-41: Moscow, Tokyo and the Prelude to the Pacific War*, London and Birmingham, Macmillan, 1992.

19. For an interesting account of the Soviet occupation of the Kuriles and Stalin's attempt to take part of Hokkaido as well—more than two weeks after the Japanese capitulation—see Boris Slavinskii, "Sovetskii desant na Khokkaido i Iuzhnye Kurily," *Izvestiia*, May 12, 1992, p. 6. The author rejects conservative patriots' claims that the islands should not be returned because Soviet blood had been shed in their capture, since he points out that the operation took place without bloodshed on either side.

20. Gaidar, "Problema," p. 114. This argument is disputed by another Soviet commentator, who points out that the 1951 San Francisco Treaty says nothing about the transfer of the islands to the USSR. Vladimir Yeremin, "Moscow Won't Have to Make Concessions," *New Times*, no. 22, 1992, p. 25.

21. A Japanese scholar, Professor Kenichi Ito, has made a similar argument to Yeremin's in "A Japanese View of the Kuril Dispute," *International Herald Tribune*, November 6, 1992, p. 7. For an extended treatment of the San Francisco negotiations from the Japanese point of view, see Prof. Khirosi Kimura, "Sovetskii Soiuz i mirnoe uregulirovanie c Iaponiei," *Problemy Dal'nego vostoka*, no. 5, 1991, pp. 92-102. Incidentally, the Japanese claim that Shikotan and the Habomais are not part of the Kurile chain at all but rather extensions of the northernmost main island of Hokkaido.

22. Yeremin, "Moscow Won't Have to Make Concessions." The author makes the point, apparently in agreement with many Russian specialists on Japan, that the most important thing is for the Kurile problem to be solved "on the basis of justice and law." That, he says, is the defining characteristic of the genuine democrat.

23. JIJI Press Newswire, "Russia: USSR Offered Return of 2 Isles in '72," Reuters Textline, June 29, 1992.

24. For example, Gaidar, "Problema," p. 115. Deputy Foreign Minister

Kunadze presumably also at least tacitly agrees with this reasoning.

25. Harry Gelman, *Russo-Japanese Relations and the Future of U.S.-Japanese Relations*. Santa Monica, Calif.: RAND, 1993, p. 24.

26. Opinion polls have shown a 75 percent majority in favor of remaining under Russia, despite rumors of substantial cash payments from Japan for relocation. Many are clearly worried over the Japanese reputation for racial discrimination against non-Japanese. Terry McCarthy, "Russia: Kurile Islanders Tempted by a Place Under the Sun—Japan Claims Sovereignty," *The Independent*, in Reuters Textline, July 2, 1992.

27. See, for example, "Russia Gives Ground on Disputed Islands," *Sydney Morning Herald*, August 19, 1992, p. 11, which gives a figure of 20,000; Stephen Foye, "Kurile Islands," *RFERL Daily Report*, May 21, 1992, gives the more generally accepted figure of 7,000 troops.

28. John Lepingwell, "Russian Defense Ministry Affirms Kuril Withdrawal Plans," *RFERL Daily Report*, October 2, 1992; "Japan: Disputed Kuriles Spark War of Words," Reuters Textline, September 21, 1992. Contrary signals for and against proposals to withdraw troops have continued well into 1994. See, for example, Stephen Foye, "Plans for Withdrawal from Kuriles Denied," *RFERL Daily Report*, March 25, 1994, where reports in the Duma concerning secret plans to withdraw military forces from the islands are denied by MFA and MOD spokespersons.

29. For example, "C. Itoh to Open Branch Office in Sakhalin," Reuters Textline, April 6, 1992.

30. Boris Reznik, "Shel'f v tumane," *Izvestiia*, June 12, 1992, p. 2; also, Leonid Mlechin, "Rivalry for Sakhalin's shelf," *New Times*, no. 7, 1992, pp. 13-15.

31. Fiona Fleck, "Russia: Russian 'Kamikazes' in Rebellious Mood on Kuriles," Reuters Textline, September 20, 1992.

32. Viktor Serov, "Krasnoiarsk-Moskve: Idu na vy!" *Rossiiskie vesti*, no. 27, July 1992, p. 2. On Fedorov as a leader of the anti-Tokyo forces see John Helmer, "Russia: Yeltsin Decree on Developing Far East," Reuters Textline, October 13, 1992.

33. Leonid Goldin, "The Hard Road to a Common Home," *New Times*, no. 29, 1992, p. 13.

34. See, for example, Comline News Service, "Japan: Fewer JASDF Air Defense Scrambles in 1991," Reuters Textline, April 16, 1992; Andrei Aksenenko and Eduard Gams, "Can Moscow Afford to Be a Naval Superpower?" *New Times*, no. 50, 1991, pp. 21-23; Andrei Aksenenko, "The Winds Are Not Favorable for Warship," *New Times*, no. 9, 1992 pp. 20-23.

35. "Japan Protests at Russian Spy Plane Intrusion," Reuters Textline, April 10, 1992.

36. Dawid Warszawski, "Powrot do Cam Ranh," *Rzeczpospolita*, July 25-26, 1992, p. 5.

37. Dimitry Volsky, "Old Disputes in a New Asia," *New Times*, no. 36, 1992, p. 9. Volsky asserts that U.S. Secretary of State James Baker and, "even more," the ASEAN foreign ministers all welcomed the return of Russia to Cam Ranh Bay.

38. Eduard Grebenschchikov, "Subik-Bei i Kamran'—zven'ia edinoi sistemy?" *Izvestiia*, August 27, 1992, p. 5.

39. JIJI Press Newswire, "Japan: Russia to Strengthen Pacific Fleet," Reuters Textline, October 13, 1992.

40. "After the Cold War," editorial article, *Asia-Pacific Defence Reporter*, vol. XIX, no. 2/3, August-September 1992, p. 7.

41. See, for example, "Philippines: Russia Offers to Sell Gunboats to Philippines," Reuters Textline, September 15, 1992; Korean Economic Daily, 'South Korea: Trade Ministry Picks 21 Areas for Russian Defense Ventures', Reuters Textline, October 13, 1992; according to another report, Russia and South Korea have actually signed a protocol giving the latter access to Russian military technology as part of Moscow's conversion process. *Asia-Pacific Defence Reporter*, vol. XIX, no. 2/3, August-September 1992, p. 19; John Helmer, "Malaysia Prefers MIG to the F-16," *The Australian Financial Review*, December 18, 1992, p. 10.

42. *Asia-Pacific Defence Reporter*, vol. XIX, no. 4/5, October-November 1992, p. 21.

43. JIJI Press Newswire, "Japan Asks ROK to Drop N. Island Fishing," Reuters Textline, June 8, 1992; JIJI, "Japan: Government Seeks Change in ROK-Russia Fishing Pact," Reuters Textline, June 12, 1992.

44. S. Y. Yue, South China Morning Post, "Russia: Demolition Warning over Disputed Island Project," Reuters Textline, September 19, 1992.

45. "Kurile Plan Abandoned," *Far Eastern Economic Review*, November 5, 1992, p. 12; see also Margaret Harris, "Russia Riles Japan with Mystery Deal on Island," *Sydney Morning Herald*, September 17, 1992, p. 11. I am indebted to Dr. Godfrey Linge of the ANU for bringing these articles to my attention.

46. "Yeltsin Signs Decree on Developing Kurile Islands," Reuters Textline, December 9, 1992.

47. JIJI Press Newswire, Russia: "Russia-ROK Joint Projects Proposed," Reuters Textline, November 18, 1992.

48. John Lepingwell, "Russia, South Korea Sign Defense Protocol"; and "Russia to Revise Defense Pact With North Korea," *RFERL Daily Report*, November 23, 1992.

49. Sergei Agafonov, "'Rossiiskii sezon' iaponskoi diplomatii," *Izvestiia*, May 9, 1992, p. 5.

50. BBC Monitoring Service, "Russia: Minister for Foreign Economic Relations Says Russia Must Not Rely on Western Credits," Reuters Textline, October 28, 1992.

51. "Yeltsin Call on Kuriles," *Sydney Morning Herald*, November 23, 1992, p. 21.

52. Gelman, *Russo-Japanese Relations*, pp. 96-8.

53. Dr. Aurelia George has pointed out to me that the inflexibility of the Japanese position is actually limited pretty much to the Ministry of Foreign Affairs, which, for good or ill, has enjoyed a large degree of autonomy on running Japanese policy on the Kuriles and relations with Russia in general. George argues that Japanese politicians are in reality much more flexible on these issues. This is an important point and is probably one on which Russian experts on Japan experts are well versed and have informed Russian policymakers accordingly.

54. See, for example, Agafonov's account of the secret visit to Tokyo of

Mikhail Bocharov, the head of the so-called International Russian Club, who reportedly emphasized his country's determination on three lines: (1) to act as a global power, pursuing its own interests; (2) to generate its own model of economic development; (3) to deal constructively only with those countries that take a long-term perspective on relations with Russia. Sergei Agafonov, "Tokiiskii debiut 'Russkogo kluba,'" *Izvestiia*, February 2, 1993, p. 3.

55. "Japan: Watanabe Airs Fear Russia Trying to Isolate Japan," Reuters Textline, September 22, 1992. This point is also strongly argued by Gelman, *Russo-Japanese Relations*.

56. For a good treatment of the ambience surrounding the visit see Stephen Foye, "Russo-Japanese Relations: Still Traveling a Rocky Road," *RFERL Research Report*, vol. 2, no. 44, November 5, 1993.

8

Russian Policy Toward China

Eugene Bazhanov

Traditional Friends or Traditional Adversaries?

Ever since Moscow's tsars commenced their expansion into Siberia in the seventeenth century, the Russians have encountered the Chinese attempting to check their advance. The first military clashes between Russians and Chinese took place in 1652, and since then, confrontation has been continuous with only minor interruptions. The two empires competed for control in Siberia, the Far East, and Central Asia, but by the nineteenth century, a much stronger Russia secured favorable borders with China. Although it signed border treaties with Russia, Chinese officialdom nevertheless felt uneasy about "the loss" of immense territories to its northern rival.[1]

Following their seizure of power in 1917, the Bolsheviks began promoting a communist movement on Chinese territory. On many occasions the leaders of the Chinese Communist Party recognized the significant role the Kremlin played "in the victory of socialism" in China in 1949, when the People's Republic of China was proclaimed.[2] However, in the 1920s disagreements emerged between the two communist parties, later contributing to the deterioration of Sino-Soviet relations. Mao Zedong and Joseph Stalin differed on ideological issues (for example, on how to conduct the revolutionary struggle in China) and on political problems (Moscow wanted the Chinese communists to engage the Japanese armies more actively in the Far East, while Mao preferred to conserve his forces for the civil war). Moscow was perceived as the center of the international communist movement—as the "elder brother" who gave orders to the "younger brothers," openly intervening in their affairs. Mao resented this interference, particularly as Stalin attempted to elevate Mao's rivals to the highest ranks of the Chinese communist movement.[3]

159

During the Chinese civil war and throughout the first years of the PRC, tensions eased as Stalin and Mao closed ranks in their struggle for socialism in China and against world "imperialism." The accession of the revisionist Khrushchev to power in the Kremlin revived some of the old grievances while simultaneously creating new ones. Disagreements between Moscow and Beijing came to encompass a wide range of issues: the two states differed in their approach to the role of leadership in a socialist country, the ways and means of building socialism, the implications of international trends; attitudes toward the USA, interactions within the communist movement, and regional conflicts. Purely bilateral antagonisms also arose: disagreements in the military and economic spheres, and territorial disputes.[4]

Fuel was added to the fire by Mao's irritation over China's role as a "junior partner" to the Soviet Union and by Khrushchev's anger over the challenge Beijing posed to the dominant position of the Kremlin in the world communist movement. The dogmatism of the communist elites in both states, combined with their totalitarian structures, prevented management of the differences in a civilized manner.[5] By the end of the 1960s the two giant neighbors were engaged in a full-fledged cold war that occasionally erupted into genuine military engagements along their common border. China turned to, and found, allies in the West, and adversarial relations between the two communist powers became an important and (it seemed) permanent feature of world politics.[6]

In the 1980s Sino-Soviet relations changed for the better again as the post-Mao leadership concentrated its energies on modernization of the country, an objective that required a more constructive relationship with the USSR. Moscow, entangled in internal and external problems of an unprecedented magnitude, reacted favorably to Chinese overtures.[7] The advent of Gorbachev's perestroika presented real possibilities for the full normalization of Sino-Soviet relations and the development of friendly, neighborly cooperation. Chinese leaders were satisfied that Moscow had discontinued hegemonic practices toward Beijing,and that internally Gorbachev was encouraging reforms similar to those in China.[8]

In May 1989 Gorbachev and Deng Xiaoping met in Beijing and announced full normalization of bilateral relations. The mood in both capitals was euphoric, but it disappeared just a few weeks later when Chinese troops put down a pro-democracy rebellion in Tiananmen Square and Beijing's internal and external policies abruptly returned to conservatism. China and the USSR once more moved in opposite directions, relations cooled, and mutual suspicions resurfaced.[9]

However, while Soviet and Chinese societies were moving apart both ideologically and politically, communist party apparatchiks in the two countries closed ranks. Beijing was eager to help the communists retain power in the USSR. Conservatives surrounding Gorbachev used this "China card" to try and persuade their leader to retreat from perestroika and to "put the Soviet house in order." And Gorbachev himself displayed some inclination to unite with the socialist giant in the East. Nevertheless, China heartily welcomed the abortive Soviet coup of August 1991 (without admitting it publicly).[10]

Early Difficulties Following the Soviet Collapse

The beginning of relations between the new Russian state and China were not particularly auspicious. Democratic forces in Russia were euphoric, having just overwhelmed the most powerful communist regime in the world. Before the democrats lay the open road to a free and prosperous society. Victorious Yeltsin supporters regarded remaining communist regimes abroad with disgust, as clones of their Soviet father. China especially was despised because of the Tiananmen massacre of Chinese democrats in 1989 and Beijing's support of the pro-communist coup in Moscow in August 1991.

Political emoting aside, a number of factors hindered Russia's relations with China. The new Russian government focussed all its attentions on the West as the natural ally of the embryonic Russian democracy. Western states had always remained antagonistic toward the Kremlin's communist empire and had sympathized with its opponents in Moscow. The West promised to provide massive financial, technological, educational, and other forms of assistance to post-communist Russia. Yeltsin and his close associates' first priority was to make Russia a part of the "civilized family of nations." Asia was half-forgotten. Moreover, feelings surfaced that the trouble with Russia was in its being *too* Asian and that it was necessary to move the country away from its Asian roots of oriental despotism and toward the Western democratic camp.

China was both communist and Asian, the worst combination for the Westerners in the new Moscow leadership. There were no positive factors that could outweigh the negative ones insofar as China was concerned. It was not considered to be a serious economic partner. It could not become a friend interested in the promotion of political changes in Russia or in the success of its reforms. Finally, many democrats in Moscow felt that the days of Chinese communism were numbered and that it would soon collapse in the same manner as the former communist regimes in Eastern Europe. Democratically minded scholars in Russia suggested that:

Russia should stay away from the doomed authorities of communist China. In the near future the regime will collapse and will be replaced by a new democratic government. That government will not forgive us for dealing with the old authorities. At the same time it will be grateful to Americans for their tough stand against Chinese communists.[11]

Many prominent politicians shunned contacts with Chinese officials, and when Jiang Jiemin, leader of the Chinese Communist Party, visited Leningrad in May 1991, Leningrad's liberal mayor, Anatoly Sobchak, did his best to avoid meeting him. In Moscow, high-ranking officials from China were greeted with hostile resolutions by the local city council and with demonstrations by students.

Beijing, in turn, was shocked at the turn of events in "the Motherland of Lenin." At an extraordinary meeting in the aftermath of the defeat of the pro-communist coup in Moscow, Chinese leaders displayed "pessimism" and "helplessness."[12] Discomfort and fear were escalating in China for a number of reasons.

First, events in the Soviet Union were perceived as a blow to the international communist movement. Internal party propaganda channels described Gorbachev as a "traitor" and developments in the USSR as the ". . . destruction of a bastion of socialism, detrimental to the future of mankind."[13] The Chinese media expressed bitterness over the defeat of socialism in the Soviet Union, blaming it on Gorbachev's policies.[14]

Second, China was concerned about the potential global impact of instability in the former USSR. Xinhua news agency stressed on December 28, 1991, that the collapse of the Soviet Union "created concern in the world," singling out such problems as safeguarding nuclear weapons, the division of state property, and territorial disputes between parts of the defunct Soviet Union. The authoritative journal *Banyuetan* was even more direct:

> If somehow control over nuclear weapons on the territory of the disintegrated USSR is lost, it will pose a serious threat to Europe and to the whole world. . . . Besides, with declarations of independence by the Soviet republics, the probability of ethnic tensions will arise. This can lead to a civil war.[15]

Increased instability in other regions of the world was equally predicted. *Banyuetan*, for instance, stated that collapse of the Soviet empire "would undermine the balance of forces and would provoke new regional military conflicts."[16] A symposium for the China Center for International Studies (Beijing) in early December 1991 described "chaos in the Soviet Union as the main threat to regional and international peace for a considerable period of time."[17] Foreign Minister Qian Qichen was also alarmed. Writing in *Renmin Ribao*, he complained, "Disquieting situations in the former USSR will continue for a rather long time and will seriously affect stability in Europe and the world at large." The minister labelled events to the north of China as "unprecedentedly dangerous."[18]

Beijing was worried about the impact that events in the USSR could have on China itself, although publicly it preferred to sound optimistic. Jiang Jiemin, in an interview with the *Washington Times*, stated:

> . . . As for predictions by some persons that the end of the Soviet Union means socialism will be defeated in China, I want to note that they don't really understand the history and realities of China. . . . We fully believe in our future.[19]

Premier Li Peng stressed that the influence of events in Moscow on China "is not strong because internal conditions in the two countries differ."[20]

However, after the Soviet Union dissolved, the official tone in Beijing changed. A spokesman for the Foreign Ministry said at a press briefing on December 12, 1992, that his government was concerned about the impact of events in the USSR on the internal situation in the People's Republic. An urgent order was issued by Beijing to the authorities in the Xinjiang-Uigur autonomous region, bordering Soviet Central Asia and populated by similar ethnic groups (Kazakhs, Uzbeks, Kirghiz, Uigurs, and others), prescribing ". . . the highest vigilance against internal and external enemies."[21] The Chinese leadership was afraid that nationalist tendencies in Xinjiang would be spurred by developments across the border. Similarly, Beijing feared Soviet influence in Ulan Bator on the Mongolian population, and intensification of the drive toward independence in Tibet.

The Chinese Communist Party was simultaneously preparing to rebuff an anti-communist, pro-democratic campaign directed at the ethnic Chinese. Reform-minded leaders, headed by Deng Xiaoping, emphasized economic achievements as a guarantee against a collapse of the socialist system. In the political sphere, the leadership vowed to prevent ". . . political pluralism, ideological liberalization, and the spreading . . . of bourgeois values."[22] *Renmin Ribao* stressed at this time that

> with kaleidoscopic changes in the international arena, faced with a real danger from hostile forces which promote "peaceful transformation" of socialism, the younger generation of Chinese Marxist theoreticians must unleash a deep protracted struggle against bourgeois liberalization for the inheritance of the great cause of the October Revolution.[23]

Chinese leaders recommended that the Chinese mass media not publish materials about reforms in the former Soviet Union in order "to avoid undermining internal stability in China."[24] Measures were taken to reduce travel volume to Russia and other parts of the former Soviet Union. As some officials in Beijing suggested, they ". . . still remembered the influence of the Bolshevik Revolution on the Celestial Empire in the 1920s."[25]

There was an additional, strategic aspect in Beijing's concerns regarding the new regime in Moscow. Yeltsin clearly intended to fully Westernize Russia and make it an integral part of the West. If this line prevailed, it would tip the global balance of power against China and Chinese socialism.[26] At the same time, as a document of the Central Committee of the Chinese Communist Party pointed out, chaos in Russia could result in the emergence of another authoritarian, expansionist regime, threatening China.[27] Foreign Minister Qichen, echoing such an attitude, said at a meeting of the country's leadership that Russia might become "the heir to the tsars" in foreign policy.[28]

Beijing also had suspicions that Yeltsin's government would switch its allegiance to Taiwan. Taipei authorities doubled efforts, hoping to woo Russia and its neighbors with economic incentives. Russian democrats and technocrats also turned toward Taiwan. Some were so inexperienced and naive that they did not even suspect Beijing's possible reaction to the moves toward Taipei. Chinese politicians and diplomats noted with contempt that Yeltsin, together with his close associates, had been on record denouncing the People's Republic and praising Taiwan.

Following the abortive coup of August 1991 and the collapse of the USSR, that followed, almost miraculously the mood in both capitals changed. There were important motivations that put them back on the road of rapprochement and cooperation.

A Change of Mood in Russia

The initial euphoria over the victory of democracy in Russia soon died down because of a worsened economy and increasing social problems and political confrontations. The democrats' confidence and their supremacy over their domestic and foreign opponents disappeared. Disgruntled with the new democratic regime, some turned to the conservative camp. Many of the democrats resigned their high positions in government and were replaced by representatives of the old *nomenklatura*. Finally, the ideology of the ruling elites shifted to a less radically liberal, more pragmatic, position.

Against this background, relations with China did not appear as distasteful as they had six months earlier; particularly, in contrast with the ailing Russia, China kept forging ahead, increasing the speed of its development. Despite Tiananmen Square, Chinese citizens had a better deal than their counterparts in Russia. A more conciliatory approach inevitably grew in the Kremlin regarding China.

Another factor that helped smooth Moscow's policies vis-à-vis China was the growing experience of Yeltsin's team. Its members realized that one could not simply ignore a great neighbor in the East. There were a number of practical problems involved with Russo-Chinese bilateral relations, and the problems had to be dealt with daily. The border issue, the movement of people across the frontier, the sharing of river resources, the question of disarmament—these and many other problems attracted the attention of the Yeltsin government regarding its relationship with China. As one Russian official pointed out, "You can sometimes forget about friends if they live far away, but necessity makes you understand that you have to cooperate with close neighbors, even if they are different and not to your liking."[29]

At the meeting with Chinese Prime Minister Li Peng in New York on January 31, 1992, Yeltsin stressed that different social systems could not prevent two neighboring states from cooperating with each other.[30] Following his visit to China in April 1992, Russian Foreign Minister Andrei Kozyrev stated that notwithstanding some differences between the two countries, it was necessary to give priority to bilateral relations with such close neighbors.[31]

Rather unexpectedly, economic factors also stimulated the Kremlin's interest in China. At first, trade and economic cooperation between the two states slackened, as Moscow did not want to spend the little hard currency that it had on low-quality Chinese merchandise, and it had little to offer China in barter. However, under more relaxed guidelines the eastern provinces of the Russian Federation, private businessmen, and cooperative ventures quickly plunged into the Chinese market, where they found a wide variety of consumer goods that could be imported into Russia, yielding enormous profits. Exports to China also grew dramatically. China was one of those rare countries that displayed an interest in Russian machinery, equipment, and other industrial manufactures.[32]

The Chinese were eager to start joint ventures and open stores and restaurants in Russian cities. Being the progeny of the same communist system, businessmen of the two neighboring countries understood each other's customs and laws and, more important, they knew how to survive in an environment that seemed to be hostile to operators from advanced market economies. Beijing expressed a strong interest in acquiring Russian-made military equipment. Moscow, desperate for capital and worried about its troubled military-industrial complex, was eager to shower the Chinese with airplanes, tanks, ships, and guns. China has become one of the best customers of the Russian defense establishment.

Strategic considerations add to the growing involvement of Moscow with Beijing. In 1991 the victorious democrats were primarily Western-oriented. But by 1993 the Russian leadership felt disappointed. The U.S. and its allies in Europe were seen as inattentive to Moscow's needs. The promised assistance arrived in much smaller quantities, and it was noted that there were politicians in the West who would clearly prefer Russia to remain weak and engrossed with internal problems.

Under such circumstances, a natural desire developed in the Kremlin to reinforce Russia's international posture, and the Chinese connection provided a good opportunity. Russo-Chinese friendship would engender a great deal more respect for Russia. The expectation was that the West would therefore become more flexible and active in assisting Moscow. As the popular Russian magazine the *Capital* argued, "Americans will become generous when they realize that Russia can survive on its own and revive close ties with China."[33] The Chinese connection was also seen as helpful in ensuring that Japanese ambitions did not become excessively grandiose.

This positive policy toward China enjoys a solid base of support within Russia. Indeed, it is probably the *only* issue upon which there is a consensus within the turbulence of Russian society. The pro-communist and nationalist opposition is even more sympathetically inclined toward China than the Yeltsin government, as China remains communist and predominantly anti-Western. Conservatives have stated that sooner or later, Moscow and Beijing will have to jointly confront the West, particularly the United States. Both conservatives and centrists marvel at the Chinese model of development. Calls to learn from Beijing are frequently heard in the Russian parliament, at political rallies and academic conferences, and in the media. It is China's political order and government-controlled economic reforms that Yeltsin's opponents want to imitate.

Alexander Volsky (at that time leader of the most powerful opposition group, Civic Union) in a speech to his supporters in November 1992 stated, "Deng Xiaoping is a great reformer. . . . To feed a billion people, Beijing needed only two to three years. This is a fact. So why is the Chinese experience being rejected?"[34] Expounding his thesis further in an interview with *Newsweek*, Volsky said,

> Chinese people have a super-militarized economy, huge state property, etc. Our situation is much closer to the Chinese experience than to the experience of any other country. We should study their experience in

conducting a land reform, as well as their experience in state support of the private sector with the help of laws, taxation, investments etc. We don't give any support to the private sector. This is our biggest mistake. We should also study the Chinese experience in setting up free-trading economic zones.[35]

The final factor that compels Moscow to seek enhanced relations with China is the behavior of the newly independent states of the former Soviet Union. The Central Asian republics, Ukraine, Belarus, Moldova, and others have given China a great deal of attention. Visits of their leaders to China are becoming a regular feature of their international diplomatic agendas. Some of them, particularly Ukraine, look to ties with Beijing as an additional guarantee of independence from Moscow.

A Change of Mood in China

Equally forceful imperatives have induced a change of mood toward Russia in Beijing. The reformers in the Chinese leadership, although not achieving a clear-cut victory over the conservatives, have gradually gained ground since 1992. Their increasing influence is partly due to the relaxation of ideological brainwashing and political persecution as part of the promotion of economic transformation endorsed by the 14th Congress of the Communist Party in October 1992. The awkward slogan "planned socialist merchandise economy" was replaced with the more rational "socialist market economy", as cautious talk of some political reform resurfaced.

Foreign policy has also become much more flexible. China normalized relations with Vietnam, its archenemy of the 1980s, and reestablished diplomatic relations with South Africa and Israel. Beijing even went as far as to offend its only remaining ideological and military ally in the world, North Korea, by officially recognizing the government of South Korea. In a classified report of the Foreign Ministry issued in the autumn of 1992, emphasis was placed upon further bold steps in the international arena.[36]

Fears that the crisis of communism in Russia would spill over into China were also subdued. It became clear that the appalling economic and political conditions in the former Soviet Union did not encourage Chinese dissidents. Indeed, the negative Russian experience convinced many Chinese that they had much to be thankful for in their own country. A high official of the Chinese Foreign Ministry stated:

The economic problems of the USSR sent a warning to many simple Chinese, showing them that the destruction of the ruling regime would bring instead of prosperity and well-being, shortages and violence. In a country which has faced so many convulsions this century, there is no other word feared as much as "chaos."[37]

Economic considerations provided a strong impetus for improving relations with Russia. In December 1991 Beijing's minister of external economic relations and foreign trade made a study trip to Russia and a number of other former Soviet republics. His recommendations were to encourage close cooperation with China's neighbors to the north. This view was echoed by leading Chinese academic specialists, who called for economic integration of the countries of Northeast Asia ". . . to respond to similar processes in Europe and North America."[38] It was announced in January 1992 that China had adopted a program of "the march to the North," a large-scale penetration of the markets of Russia and other parts of the defunct USSR. The Chinese government noted that there was a ". . . high demand in Russia for Chinese products. They fit that market perfectly quality-wise and price-wise. China will not concede the Russian market to Taiwan, South Korea, Singapore, and Japan."[39]

Beijing saw in Russia the only big market for its surplus of consumer goods. China was also interested in exporting labor to Russia, establishing joint ventures, cooperating in agriculture, fishing, and forestry.[40] Even more significant for China were technology imports, the transfer of advanced Russian industrial components to China and the advancement of the technological level of the defense industry and military forces.

China was also guided by strategic considerations in its policy of rapprochement with its northern neighbor. Chinese scholars and journalists argued that the Soviet Union's demise "brought to an end the division of the world into spheres of influence, established at the Yalta conference." It was interpreted as beneficial to China's global interests. Analysts also noted that a direct threat to China itself from a strong Soviet Union had disappeared.

Increased significance was given to closer ties with the new Russia as a form of leverage against the U.S. and its allies. The Chinese resented U.S. sales of advanced military aircraft to Taiwan, American criticisms of human rights violations in China, and Washington's pressure regarding trade issues. Summarizing American motives, a journal of China's Foreign Ministry pointed out that

as threats to U.S. interests from the USSR have ceased to exist, Washington has decided that there is a good opportunity to promote American-type "democratization" in Asia. . . . The United States is increasing pressure on socialist countries, hoping to incite "radical changes" inside them.[41]

In September 1992 Foreign Minister Qian Qichen emphasized in a speech in camera that

> the USA's hegemonic stance, and its attempts to interfere in the internal affairs of other states pose the greatest danger to socialist China. To weaken pressure from Washington, China must broaden relations with Japan, Russia, South Korea, and other neighboring countries.[42]

Moscow's and Beijing's intentions to move closer to one another were reinforced and facilitated by the absence of serious disturbances in their bilateral relations at this time, as well as in their interactions on the international scene. Troop withdrawals from the Russo-Chinese border had been agreed upon in principle. Demarcation of the border was conducted in a calm and constructive atmosphere. An understanding had been achieved regarding how Moscow should handle unofficial ties with Taipei.

Building Up Cooperation

High-level contacts between Moscow and Beijing began slowly but progressed steadily throughout 1992–1993. In December 1991 a delegation of the Russian Supreme Soviet visited China and assured Chinese leaders of Moscow's desire to live in peace with its great neighbor, clearing bilateral relations from any ideological influence.[43] On January 31, 1992, Yeltsin met with Chinese premier Li Peng in New York while attending a UN Security Council meeting. Both sides stressed a mutual intention to strengthen cooperation and contacts.[44] Kozyrev paid his first visit to China on March 16–17, 1992. The two countries exchanged ratification papers on the agreement on the Russo-Chinese border in the East. At meetings with Li Peng and Qian Qichen, Kozyrev reiterated a desire to press on with the establishment of bilateral relations in all areas. Qian also confirmed an invitation extended to Yeltsin to visit China. Kozyrev added that the forthcoming reduction of the Russian military forces by 700,000 would include the Asian region. He also promised that the retargeting of nuclear weapons would not lead to a growth in the military potential of Russia in the East. Kozyrev also praised Beijing's decision to join the treaty on the non-proliferation of nuclear weapons.

However, Kozyrev and Qian Qichen differed on human rights issues. Kozyrev stressed that his government was anxious to promote an international accord on human rights and even encouraged a certain degree of foreign interference in Russian affairs in this area. Qian Qichen reiterated Beijing's standard position on the inadmissibility of foreign interference in the domestic affairs of other states. The two ministers came to the conclusion that in Russo-Chinese ties, ". . . elements of considerable agreement coexist with different approaches to some quite significant questions." Nevertheless, the ministers did not consider these differences a reason for tension and confrontation.[45]

The next stage in the Russo-Chinese dialogue was the arrival of Russian Deputy Premier Andrei Shokhin in Beijing on May 3, 1992. Shokhin pointed out that the main task now was ". . . to utilize the potential of Russo-Chinese cooperation, to put it into practice through concrete agreements and actions." The Russian deputy prime minister discussed different aspects of cooperation in economic and social spheres with his counterparts: the functioning of a joint committee, the preparation of a number of economic agreements, the repayment of Chinese credits to Russia, and the sending of Russian specialists to China's enterprises.[46] In Beijing in June, Russian Minister of Justice Nikolai Fedorov signed a treaty on legal assistance in civil and criminal cases. In November, Shokhin was again in China and by the end of the month, Qian Qichen arrived in Moscow for final preparations for Yeltsin's visit to China.

According to Russian Foreign Ministry officials, talks with Qian went surprisingly smoothly. Chinese diplomats stationed in Moscow agreed: the atmosphere at the talks was remarkably calm and peaceful. The two sides expressed a desire to make Yeltsin's visit a very successful one and to turn their high-level bilateral political dialogue into a regular forum. Most of the bilateral disagreements were found to be on the road to a solution. Even human rights were discussed, this time in a low-key fashion without polemics. The only international problem on which Moscow attempted to tackle China was Cambodia. Qian did not bend, confirming the usual Chinese stand. In an interview on the results of his talks in Moscow, Qian sounded a great deal more optimistic than before. He predicted that Sino-Russian relations would have "a brilliant future."[47]

Yeltsin's official visit to the People's Republic on December 17 to 19, 1992, brought Russo-Chinese relations much closer to an alliance and further away from the animosity of the 1960s and 1970s. On the eve of his trip, Yeltsin felt nervous, as he himself admitted. Since becoming leader of democratic Russia, Yeltsin had never set foot on the soil of a communist country. Not only did Yeltsin have bad memories about the Soviet communists but he had just recently wrestled with the pro-communist Seventh Congress of People's Deputies and, in the struggle, had lost some of his powers and close associates, including chief economic reformer Yegor Gaidar.

However, when the visit to China ended, Yeltsin was beaming. At a press conference in Beijing, Yeltsin explained his original feelings and how they had been transformed. He said that he had not believed in the reality of Chinese reforms. "I thought," stated Yeltsin, "that reforms existed only on paper, as decrees of the Central Committee of the CPC." Yeltsin expressed bewilderment at the fact that it was possible to satisfy the food requirements of 1.1 billion people. He came to the conclusion that the Chinese Communist Party was simply different from its "comrades" in the former Soviet Union. Yeltsin joked, "It would be a good idea to send some Russian communist to China, where he could learn how the Communist Party contributed to reforms."[48]

More than twenty documents covering all manner of cooperation were signed in Beijing. Among the most important of these was the Joint Declaration on the Foundation of Relations Between the People's Republic of China and the Russian Federation. The declaration stipulates that both Russia and China will not enter into unions and alliances aimed at harming one another. Beijing and Moscow also agreed not to permit territories to be used by third parties to undermine the security of the other. At the same time, the document makes it clear that Russia and China will not act in such a way as to harm the interests of any third country. Thus, in the final analysis, the joint declaration should not be perceived as an attempt to revive the 1950s Russo-Chinese alliance. Rather, it aims at leaving behind the legacy of mutual confrontation, according to which both Moscow and Beijing acted in collusion with other nations against one another.

Worthy of mention too is a memorandum on principles of military-technical cooperation; an agreement that Russia would construct a nuclear power station in China; Chinese food credits to Russia; and a memorandum on a drastic cut in military forces in the areas adjacent to their common border. The chiefs of the ministries of security and internal affairs accompanied Yeltsin to China and worked with their Chinese counterparts on a cooperation agreement in such areas as terrorism, organized crime, and illegal trafficking in weapons and narcotics. Just prior to Yeltsin's visit, the chief of Russia's external intelligence service, Yevgeny Primakov, also paid a visit to Beijing.[49]

In September 1994, the extent to which relations had improved was demonstrated by the visit to Moscow of Chinese leader Jiang Zemin. While in Russia Jiang concluded a number of economic agreements.

Political Relations

The Joint Declaration on the Foundation of Relations, signed during Yeltsin's stay in Beijing, provided a solid legal framework for bilateral cooperation. Moscow hoped to sign a full-scale treaty in this area, but Beijing refused for two obvious reasons. First, since the early 1980s, China has had a policy of not entering into treaties with foreign nations. Chinese leaders fear that treaties might deny China freedom of action and tie it too closely to the policies of its partner. Second, at the time of the joint declaration Beijing was afraid that projecting itself as being too close to Moscow would harm rather than facilitate relations with the U.S. and Japan and make them more reluctant to participate in the modernization of China. This situation did not change with Jiang's visit.

According to the memorandum on drastic cuts in military forces and installations in the areas adjacent to the border, the two sides agreed to establish a zone of stability, restricting military activity to a depth of 100 kilometers along the frontier. Some troops will remain inside the zone, but their numbers will be strictly limited. Large-scale cuts covered offensive weapons: tanks, armored vehicles, military aircraft, river gunboats, tactical nuclear missiles, missile launchers, and artillery. The size of border patrols will also be reduced. To avoid hardships for Russian officers and soldiers, their withdrawal from the border areas is scheduled to be completed by the year 2000.[50]

Russia, and three other CIS members who are neighbors with China (Kazakhstan, Kyrgyzstan, and Tajikistan) have successfully proceeded with negotiations on a new border agreement. The eastern side of the border has already been covered by a partial agreement. The dispute over two islands near Khabarovsk has been put aside, and the two governments have commenced with the demarcation of the border line.

On the issue of nuclear disarmament, Yeltsin, when in China, endorsed Beijing's position. Its essence was that before China joined the disarmament process, both Washington and Moscow should make further drastic cuts in their arsenals.

The Chinese leadership does not support a collective security system for Asia and the Pacific. It prefers arrangements on a bilateral basis, whereby interested parties can proceed toward measures of confidence building, the reduction of tensions, and the solution of regional conflicts. The Russian government has ceased developing large-scale projects in the security field and has demonstrated roughly the same approach as China in the field of regional security. Beijing, following Moscow's example, has recognized South Korea.

Trade and Economic Cooperation

Let us now turn to the most dynamic element of Russo-Chinese relations: trade and economic cooperation. In March 1992, the two sides signed an agreement that laid down a broad legal framework for the development of commercial and production links. Moscow and Beijing extended to one another most-favoured-nation status and put an emphasis on promoting unofficial, free-market style trade and economic cooperation. A special Russo-Chinese intergovernmental committee on trade, economic, scientific, and technical cooperation was established. It held its first session in Beijing in August 1992.

Trade made remarkable progress during 1992. In 1991 trade volume decreased by 37 percent (to $US3.9 billion) in comparison with 1990. In 1992 it shot back up and broke the record for Russo-Chinese trade. The two sides exchanged goods worth $US5.5 billion. Two-way trade again rose sharply, to more than $US7 billion, in 1993. Yet in the first half of 1994 it once more dropped significantly—by 39 percent compared to the same period in 1993.[51] Ninety percent of trade volume was outside the terms of reference of government protocols. China supplied Russia with large quantities of clothing, fabrics, foodstuffs, and utensils. Russia exported various machines and equipment, metals, and non-metallic raw materials. Trade was greatly facilitated by the legalization of barter deals and the relaxation of the border restrictions regarding direct ties between provinces and individual businessmen.

Economic cooperation also rose to new heights. The Russians agreed to supply China with $US2.5 billion worth of necessary technology and technical assistance to build a nuclear power station. China will repay this assistance with supplies of consumer goods and some equipment and machinery. The two sides agreed to construct new transportation systems across their common border. Included in this agreement is a bridge over the Amur River, and a number of highways are planned,partly to avoid paying high transit charges to the Mongolian authorities.

Concerted efforts have been made to set up a special economic zone along the Tiumen River, where the borders of Russia, China, and North Korea meet. The preparatory work and financing are being conducted under the auspices of the UN's development program. The Chinese have expressed the hope that the zone will become "a new Hong Kong." Beijing depends upon Russian natural resources, Chinese and North Korean labor, and Japanese and South Korean finance and technology.[52] There are doubts whether such an aim can be achieved, particularly as North Korea has expressed caution about the project.

Cooperation in mutual exports and imports of labor seems to be promising. Beijing is happy to send its surplus labor force to work in enterprises and to build houses and roads in the Russian Far East and Siberia.

In 1992 the Chinese government unveiled an ambitious plan to attract large numbers of highly qualified Russian scientists, engineers, and technicians. Beijing called upon domestic enterprises to create joint firms, research institutes, and information centers with their Russian counterparts.[53]

Special attention is paid by Chinese authorities to tapping Russian expertise in the nuclear industry. Besides the aforementioned agreement on construction of a huge nuclear power station, the Chinese are eager to gain Russian technology in the fields of nuclear fuel production and nuclear waste conservation. In the spring of 1992, a Russo-Chinese Center for Nuclear Studies opened in Harbin in north-eastern China. Beijing would also like to send researchers to the well-known nuclear research center in Dubna, near Moscow.[54]

Rather unexpectedly, there has been a dramatic rise in military and military-technical cooperation between Moscow and Beijing. Back in February 1992, when the Chinese leadership was still very much on its guard concerning developments in post-communist Russia, chief of staff of the United Armed Forces of the CIS, Vladimir Samsonov, paid an official visit to China. He was accorded a very warm reception that even included an audience with Communist Party leader Jiang Zemin. Samsonov confirmed further supplies of SU-27 fighter planes and the Chinese displayed great interest in importing other weapons systems.[55]

During Deputy Premier Shokhin's visit to China in May 1992, it was revealed that Moscow started deliveries of large numbers of T-72 tanks and some other weapons. The two sides discussed exports of additional quantities of military planes and battleships to China.[56] Throughout the following months, Asian and U.S. media were flooded with alarming news regarding the growing military trade between Russia and other CIS nations and Beijing. China was accused of attempting to become the dominant military force in Southeast Asia.

The Russian government preferred to keep a low profile on the matter, periodically assuring the world that it did not intend to break any international agreements on the transfer of military technology and weapons. In December 1992, Acting Prime Minister Yegor Gaidar disclosed that Russia had concluded contracts with China for exports of $US1 billion worth of weaponry.[57] Later, President Yeltsin mentioned the figure $US1.8 billion.[58] In addition, as the newspaper *Izvestiia* reported, large quantities of military technology and information were slipping into China behind the Kremlin's back.[59]

President Jiang Zemin's visit to Russia in September 1994 marked an attempt to put bilateral trading relations on a more secure and formal footing. This was the first official visit to Moscow by a Chinese leader since Mao Zedong's visit in 1957.

Conclusion: Future Uncertainties

Not everything, however, is perfect in Russo-Chinese relations. It is sufficient to look back at their difficult history of uneasy cohabitation to be cautious about their future. If our ancestors could not find the key to long-term harmony, why should we today be so sure of our ability to achieve this objective? We are no better or more clever than previous generations. Nor is the present world-system closer to being utopia than it was before.

Territorial Disputes

Among the most obvious issues for quarrels and disputes between Moscow and Beijing is their common border. As noted above, the Russian Federation and China have been moving ahead in the border legalization process. And yet the two islands near Khabarovsk remain in dispute. Constantly under attack from the nationalist opposition, the Yeltsin administration is scarcely in a position to satisfy Chinese claims on these islands, which have been inhabited and cultivated by Russians for most of the twentieth century. But Beijing is well-known for its obstinacy on territorial issues. In addition, the Chinese believe the Russians illegally gained control over the Far East and much of Siberia in the nineteenth century. Thus, from Beijing's point of view, China has already made more than its fair share of concessions by having ceased making claims on "the eastern territories."

Such feelings run extremely deep in China and there is no guarantee that at some point a new Chinese government will not resurrect old demands to restore justice and repay old debts. Such demands may become an expression of the growing nationalism and ambition of a successful post-communist China. Or territorial disputes may be used by the Chinese government to avert the attention of the populace from internal problems, if they develop. The territorial issue may also flare up as a result of a deterioration in Russo-Chinese relations for various other reasons, as was the case in the 1960s. But ultimately, Chinese expansionism in the North may be triggered by the disintegration of the Russian Federation and the emergence of splinter regions in the eastern part of the country. If Moscow loses control of these traditionally Chinese lands, it may be China that gains them.

Economic Disputes

Let us imagine that China imports (illegally and legally) increasing quantities of Russian natural resources, such as metals, natural gas, oil, and timber. Domestic demand for these products then rises, and Moscow, as well as the local Siberian and Far Eastern authorities, retaliate against China. When Russian national production of consumer goods begins to expand, measures are taken to limit imports from China, creating another area for dispute.

Economic disputes may also begin with social or political upheavals. The presence of substantial numbers of Chinese nationals on Russian territory and Russian nationals in China have already created unpleasant consequences (e.g., law-breaking by guests and harsh treatment of them by locals). Such controversies can affect bilateral relations. One should not exclude competition between Russia and China for scarce foreign funds and technology. The Chinese would certainly be envious should there be large-scale Japanese or Taiwanese investment in Russia or should Moscow be given large credit facilities. Beijing may ultimately become extremely critical of American generosity toward Russia.

Ideological Disputes

It would certainly be wrong to assume that the ideological factor has been completely removed from Russo-Chinese relations. Now, as Russia is weak, Chinese communist leaders have stopped worrying about "evil winds" blowing from the north. But this air of nonchalance may disappear rapidly if reforms in the former USSR begin to work. Simply by leading by example, Russia in its democratic development may inspire the Chinese intelligentsia with a new vigor. In addition, if reforms are successful Russian democrats will be more confident and may join the Americans in their missionary zeal to transform China into a free country.

A different scenario may develop if the Russian Federation plunges into uncontrollable chaos, which is not implausible. In such a case, neighboring China would sooner or later be flooded with refugees and might find itself in conflict with those groups and even, perhaps, with terrorist groups from the north.

To complete this sketch of the future, let us not forget that China, while seeming relatively stable and self-assured at present, may backtrack. No country has yet managed to transform a communist state into a successful market economy. Who can be certain that China will complete such a restructuring? The economic, social, and ideological problems present in China are too complex to be resolved smoothly, and chaos in China would threaten peace and stability in the entire Eurasian continent and destroy the current Moscow-Beijing entente cordiale.

The Taiwan Question

The issue of Taiwan remains on the Russo-Chinese agenda (as it does with China's relations with all governments around the world). How sensitive the issue can become was clearly shown by the events of September 1992. On September 9, it was announced that Russia and Taiwan would establish coordinating committees on economic and cultural cooperation, and they exchanged representatives to this end.

Yeltsin appointed his close aide Lobov to head the Russian committees. Lobov gave an interview during which he implied that Moscow and Taipei would develop ties similar to diplomatic ones.[60]

Beijing reacted immediately. Its ambassador sharply attacked the move in a meeting with Russian Foreign Ministry officials. First, the ambassador reminded them that Moscow and Beijing had agreed to hold consultations on Taiwan in October. Before the consultations had even started, the Kremlin had acted completely unilaterally. Second, China wanted to know why Yeltsin had created an unofficial committee by decree and why it comprised so many government officials. China also protested granting diplomatic immunity to Taiwanese representatives in Moscow and the establishment of direct air links by official Russian and Taiwanese airlines. Yeltsin, on advice from his foreign minister, corrected the error immediately. He issued a new decree on September 15, confirming adherence to Moscow's traditional "one China policy." The incident seemed to be settled. But given the strong economic interest in Taiwan, in both governmental and private spheres in Russia, new tensions between Moscow and Beijing are possible in the future.

The Wider International Context

Presently, the Chinese are quickly making economic inroads in Mongolia and the former Soviet Central Asian republics without encountering any resistance from Moscow. The situation may change in a matter of months if the democratic order collapses in Russia and the ultra-nationalist parties gain control of Moscow's foreign policy. These parties would definitely attempt to regain Russian predominance in these areas, and sooner or later they could also find themselves at odds with Beijing. China will not accept Moscow's control of Mongolia and Central Asia regardless of who controls the Kremlin. Russian nationalists may regard Chinese communists as partners in a resistance struggle against the West's supremacy in the international arena. But if they act too arrogantly, they will not necessarily find a partner in Beijing, but a very strong adversary.

Untying the "Korean knot" may also produce tensions between Moscow and Beijing. The imminent dismantling of the communist regime following the death of Kim Il Sung will not necessarily be a peaceful one. South Korea, the U.S., and Japan will inevitably be involved. If China maintains its present communist system, it is likely to defend socialism on Korean soil. In the event of Russia joining the democratic camp, its policies may collide with Beijing's interests.

The advancement of cooperation between Moscow and Washington is another potential area of friction with between China and Russia.

Beijing will be irritated if the United States neglects China and focusses U.S. attention and resources upon helping Russia reinforce democracy and its market economy. Chinese communists are certain to dislike both Moscow's endorsement of U.S. supremacy in the international arena and the Kremlin's attempts to once again rule the world in a bipolar partnership with Washington. Indeed, little choice exists for Russia in international affairs if it cares about Chinese goodwill. As I attempted to demonstrate above, this goodwill may easily disappear in the case of either of the two following scenarios: (1) if Russia becomes weak and too dependent upon the West; or (2) if the Kremlin attempts to resume hegemonic practices.

Should China continue to develop rapidly, and if Russia remains in deep crisis, Moscow may lose its present admiration for China. Jealousy, fears of Chinese ideological influence, and Beijing's encroachments upon Russian territories are bound to recur. Moscow and Beijing may again plunge into disputes concerning Indochina, the South China Sea islands, and India.

Of course, all of these problems currently appear highly hypothetical, as Russo-Chinese cooperation is on the increase. However, trouble spots in the relations between these two neighboring giants should not be overlooked.

Notes

1. For details on Russo-Chinese relations in the seventeenth to nineteenth centuries see, for example, *Mezhdunarodnye otnoshenie na Dal'nem Vostoke*, vol. 1, Moscow, 1973, pp. 14–19, 24–42, 71–3, 88–108, 216–22.

2. See E. Bazhanov, *Kitai i vneshnii mir*, Moscow, 1990, pp. 32–4.

3. See E. Bazhanov, "Sovetsko-kitaiskie otnosheniia: uroki proshlogo i sovremennost'," *Modern and Contemporary History*, no.2, 1989, pp. 3–25.

4. See E. Bazhanov, "Zakryt' proshloe, otkryt' budushchee," in *Aktual'nye problemy noveishei istorii*, 1991, pp. 200–17.

5. For details, see E. Bazhanov, "SSSR i Kitai ostavliayut v proshlom bol'shuyu ssoru," *Azia i Afrika segodnia*, no. 8, 1989, pp. 6–11.

6. A detailed description of that period may be found in E. Bazhanov, *Dvizhushchie sily politiki SShA v otnoshenii Kitaia*, Moscow, 1982.

7. E. Bazhanov, "Kurs na spokoistvie v Podnebesnoi," *Novoe Vremia*, no. 17, 1988, pp. 32–5.

8. E. Bazhanov, "Uravnenie so mnogimi neizvestnymi," *Pravda*, March 2, 1989.

9. E. Bazhanov, "Sut' peremen," *Novoe vremia*, no. 16, 1990, pp. 20–22.

10. E. Bazhanov, "Policy by Fiat," *Far Eastern Economic Review*, June 11, 1992, pp. 16–18.

11. *Vserossiiskii tsentr po khraneniyu Sovremennoi dokumentatsii* (VTsKhSD), Arkhiv 8, opis' 6, edin. khraneniia 116, list. 49–50.

12. *Central Daily News*, August 28, 1991.
13. *South China Morning Post*, October 1, 1991.
14. *Jiefangjun Bao*, December 29, 1991.
15. *Banyuetan*, no. 24, 1992.
16. *Banyuetan*, no. 24, 1992.
17. *China Daily*, December 19, 1991.
18. *Renmin Ribao*, December 16, 1991.
19. Xinhua News, November 1, 1991.
20. *Renmin Ribao*, September 18, 1991.
21. *South China Morning Post*, December 10, 1991.
22. *Renmin Ribao*, September 11, 1991.
23. *Renmin Ribao*, November 6, 1992.
24. *Kiodo Tsucin*, February 28, 1992.
25. ITAR-TASS, February 15, 1992, "AK," pp. 3–4.
26. *Kompass*, no. 40, February 28, 1992, pp. 3–4. See also *Beijing Zhoubao*, July 5, 1992.
27. *New York Times*, September 8, 1992.
28. TASS, October 2, 1991, "AK," pp. 12–13.
29. *Nezavisimaia gazeta*, September 10, 1992.
30. *Izvestiia*, February 1, 1992.
31. *Atlas*, April 6, 1992, pp. 57–8.
32. See *Izvestiia*, July 7 and 21, 1992.
33. *Stolitsa*, August 18, 1992.
34. *Rossiiskaia gazeta*, November 17, 1992.
35. *Newsweek*, no. 29, 1992.
36. *Sankei Simbun*, November 11, 1992.
37. *International Herald Tribune*, April 22, 1992.
38. *China Daily*, November 1, 1991.
39. *China Daily*, April 8, 1992.
40. *Rossiiskaia gazeta*, August 18, 1992.
41. *Guoii Quanxi Wenti Yaniiu*, June 1992.
42. *Sankei Simbun*, November 12, 1992.
43. *Kuranty*, December 24, 1991.
44. *Renmin Ribao*, February 1, 1992 .
45. ITAR-TASS, March 17, 1992, "AK," pp. 3–4.
46. *Trud*, May 7, 1992.
47. *Renmin Ribao*, November 28, 1992.
48. *Nezavisimaia gazeta*, December 18, 1992.
49. *Izvestiia*, December 18, 1992.
50. *Izvestiia*, December 2, 1992.
51. *RFERL Daily Report*, July 28, 1994, and *Australian*, September 9, 1994.
52. *Renmin Ribao*, March 30, 1992; and May 1, 1992.
53. *China Daily*, March 12, 1992 .
54. *Trud*, March 25, 1992.
55. ITAR-TASS, March 3, 1992, p. 3.
56. *Kiodo Tsusin*, May 3, 1992.
57. *Rossiiskaia gazeta*, December 4, 1992.

58. *Nezavisimaia gazeta,* December 18, 1992.
59. *Izvestiia,* December 3, 1992.
60. *Izvestiia,* September 10, 1992.

9

Russian Policy Toward the Two Koreas

Yoke T. Soh

This chapter examines Moscow's evolving policy toward the two Koreas, with particular emphasis on the period from July 1990 to July 1994. The Russian Federation, which succeeded the Soviet Union in January 1992, adopted a very different stance from the USSR in world politics, its foreign policy being directed toward a complete break with the communist dogmas that had previously influenced Soviet decision-making. Increasingly, Russian foreign policy–makers began to focus their attention on a growing domestic economic and political crisis. Most of the foreign policy issues with which they concerned themselves involved efforts to acquire aid and investment from the technologically advanced capitalist nations.

Soviet-Korean Relations During the Early Gorbachev Period

There was only limited change in Moscow's policy toward the Asia-Pacific in Gorbachev's first three years in power from 1985 to 1987. Gorbachev did not end the military and economic relationship with North Korea, which had existed since the two countries signed a treaty of friendship and cooperation in 1961. In 1984 the Kremlin was concerned about a perceived anti-Soviet coalition consisting of the U.S., China, and Japan. For this reason, the Soviets decided to resume military and economic assistance to the North. Following Kim Il Sung's 1984 and 1986 visits to Moscow, the USSR provided Pyongyang with MiG-29 and Su-25 aircraft, M-2 helicopter gunships, advanced early warning radar, and advanced nuclear technology for power generation.

The USSR also increased its economic aid to Pyongyang. The Soviets built seventy industrial projects that produced about 25 percent of North

Korea's gross output, and the volume of trade also increased from 1987 to 1988. Soviet trade on easy terms accounted for about 60 percent of North Korea's foreign trade in 1990. North Korea paid for Soviet oil sold at "friendship" rates and other products by exporting shoddy consumer goods to the USSR and by sending its workers to cut timber in the Siberian forests.[1] In addition to maintainingsubstantial military and economic ties, the USSR continued to support North Korea's unification policy and endorsed Pyongyang's call for a nuclear-free zone and for the withdrawal of U.S. troops from South Korea.

Although Gorbachev intensified Soviet–North Korean ties in his first years in power, he also demonstrated a degree of flexibility. An important aspect of Gorbachev's foreign policy was a new emphasis on the Asia-Pacific region. This was first articulated in his July 1986 Vladivostok speech when he expressed an interest in removing the dangerous tensions on the Korean peninsula and in initiating a serious dialogue between the two Koreas. Gorbachev's Vladivostok speech came to be seen as a major step toward revising the long-standing rigidity in Soviet Asian policy. In January 1988, the Soviet Union also announced its decision to participate in the Seoul Olympics despite Pyongyang's boycott.

Improvement in Soviet–South Korean Relations, 1988–1991

The Soviet Union reassessed its policy toward South Korea after President Roh Tae-woo's July 7, 1988 speech declaring the "Northern Policy" as a central focus of his foreign policy. Roh's "northward diplomacy" aimed at improving South Korea's economic and other ties with communist countries while at the same time bringing North Korea out of isolation in the international community. President Roh's declaration was well received by the Soviet Union. In his September 1988 Krasnoyarsk speech, Gorbachev expressed a willingness to develop economic relations with South Korea. Moreover, he proposed to hold multilateral discussions on reducing the military confrontation in areas adjacent to the shores of the USSR, China, Japan, and the two Koreas. President Roh responded to Gorbachev's Krasnoyarsk speech in his address to the U.N. General Assembly in October 1988, in which he endorsed the concept of a consultative conference between these states that would also include the United States.[2]

A crucial impetus to the economic exchange between Moscow and Seoul was initiated by Chung Ju-young, founder and honorary chairman of the Hyundai Business Group. On a visit to Moscow in January 1989, he signed an agreement to establish a Soviet-Korean cooperation committee with the Soviet Chamber of Commerce. To facilitate increased bilateral commercial contact, the Soviet Chamber of Commerce opened a semi-official trade office in Seoul in April, and in July the Korean Trade Promotion Corporation (KOTRA) opened an office in Moscow and consular sections were established in February and March 1990. The Hyundai Group had been active in developing joint ventures with the Soviet Union. In August 1989, Chung led a 31-member economic mission to the Soviet Union, where he signed an agreement on logging and wood processing in Siberia with the Forestry Office of the Maritime Province of Siberia. Agreement was also reached to construct a $5 billion petrochemical complex in Siberia with a U.S. company in March 1990. Soviet–South Korean trade increased from $US160 million in 1987 to $600 million in 1989.[3]

In December 1988, Moscow permitted Soviet Koreans from Sakhalin to visit South Korea with visas obtained through the Soviet Embassy in Tokyo. In June 1989, Yevgeny Primakov, then director of the Institute of World Economics and International Relations, invited Kim Young Sam, president of the Reunification Democratic Party at that time, to meet North Korea's former foreign minister, Ho Dam, in Moscow. Direct flights between Seoul and Moscow also started in March 1990.[4] That same month Kim Young Sam led an 11-member delegation, including first state secretary for political affairs, Park Chul-un, to Moscow and succeeded in paving the way for diplomatic normalization. Kim met with Gorbachev and Politburo member Alexander Yakovlev, who informed Kim that the Soviet Union no longer viewed North Korean objections as a major obstacle to improved Soviet–South Korean relations.[5]

The climax of the ongoing improvement in Soviet–South Korean relations was the summit meeting between President Roh and Gorbachev held on June 5, 1990, in San Francisco. This first ever meeting between the two countries' leaders focussed on bilateral relations and regional stability, promoting peace in Northeast Asia, particularly with North Korea, and expanding commercial and cultural relations.[6] Two months after this meeting a South Korean delegation led by Roh's chief economic secretary, Kim Chong-in, visited Moscow for negotiations with Soviet officials on economic cooperation and diplomatic normalization, which were formally announced on September 30, 1990. In October 1990, Korean officials went to the Soviet Union and met with Soviet First Deputy Premier Yury Maslyukov, who submitted a list of twenty-two joint projects that he hoped South Korean industry would undertake.[7] These developments culminated in the Moscow Declaration, signed by Presidents Roh and Gorbachev at their summit meeting in December 1990. Gorbachev and Shevardnadze officially apologized to Roh for Stalin's conspiracy with North Korean President Kim Il Sung in the 1950 Korean War, and for the 1983 Soviet missile attack that downed Korean

Air Lines flight 007 carrying 269 people over Sakhalin. The focus of the meeting was increased economic cooperation. Seoul agreed to provide $3 billion in soft loans over three years to Moscow, comprising $US1.5 billion to finance purchases of South Korean consumer goods and industrial products, $US500 million tied to purchases of South Korean capital goods, and $US1 billion in untied loans.[8]

The third Gorbachev-Roh meeting, on Cheju Island, South Korea, in April 1991, reaffirmed common perspectives on important issues such as the need for North Korea to open its nuclear facilities to international inspection. Gorbachev supported Seoul's unilateral admission into the U.N. even if North Korea continued to reject a simultaneous entry. Both countries agreed to push bilateral trade from $US900 million in 1990 to $US1.5 billion in 1991. Roh promised to release the first $US800 million in trade credits to alleviate the shortage of consumer goods in the Soviet Union and to support investment plans by the various South Korean conglomerates. Finally, Gorbachev called on Roh to negotiate a "treaty of good neighborliness and cooperation" with the Soviet Union. Roh promised to consider this after careful consultation with the U.S. and Japan.[9]

Explaining Change in Policy Toward the Two Koreas

The Soviet economic crisis was the impetus for improving relations between the Soviet Union and South Korea. Relations with Tokyo remained deadlocked because of a territorial dispute and Moscow had been looking to other Asian trade partners for capital and technology. South Korea provided a source of badly needed consumer goods and managerial skills. In addition, the USSR was explicitly targeting the newly industrialized countries in their efforts to promote the integration of the Soviet Far East and the Siberian region into the Asia-Pacific economy. For its part, South Korea saw the resource-rich USSR as complementary its economy. Because of Washington's increasing trade protectionism, South Korea needed to diversify its markets by trading with the Soviet bloc. The establishment of official relations was therefore based on these mutually advantageous economic interests.

Whereas Seoul's economic clout was crucial in accelerating the pace of diplomatic normalization with the Soviet Union, Moscow began to perceive North Korea as an unsustainable economic burden. Historically, Soviet–North Korean relations had always been troubled and were described as "a marriage of convenience and necessity" bound by practical mutual interests.[10] The USSR provided North Korea with economic and military aid out of ideological and geo-strategic considerations. Sino-Soviet detente and the improvement of U.S.-USSR relations resulted in the ending of Sino-Soviet competition over Pyongyang and diminished North Korea's strategic value to Moscow. This greatly reduced Pyongyang's leverage over its two major allies. As Suzanne Crow argued, "Moscow seems to have come to grips with the fact that its alliance with Pyongyang is neither profitable, reliable, nor compatible with enhancing Moscow's stature in the Northeast Asian region."[11] In contrast, South Korea's meteoric economic rise had a positive impact on Soviet perceptions. In the past, Soviet publications had treated South Korea as a mere appendage of the U.S. From the late 1980s, South Korea's economic achievements were applauded in several prominent Soviet articles.[12]

The change in Soviet policy toward the Korean peninsula was also influenced by security concerns. The Soviet Union viewed its improving relations with South Korea as conducive to the reduction of tensions on the peninsula. Soviet Asian specialists realized that reunification could be attained only through a gradual and peaceful process and supported the cross-recognition of the two Koreas in the meantime.[13]

The Soviet Union also publicly called on the North Korean government to open its nuclear facilities to international inspection. Russia welcomed the non-aggression agreement signed by the two Koreas in Seoul on December 13, 1991, which included mutual inspection of nuclear facilities and nuclear storage sites. A further agreement reached by the two Koreas on December 31, 1991, calling for a nuclear-weapon-free zone, also met with a favorable response from Moscow.[14] The first great power to establish diplomatic relations with both Koreas, the Soviet Union was seen as being in a good position to play a mediating role.

Impact of the August Coup and the Dissolution of the USSR

Events in the Soviet Union in the latter part of 1991 had a profound impact on Moscow's policy toward the two Koreas. These were the democratic election of Boris Yeltsin as president of the Russian Federation in June 1991, the failed coup attempt against Gorbachev in August, the dissolution of the Communist Party of the Soviet Union later that month, and the subsequent breakup of the USSR in December 1991.

In contrast to Pyongyang's obvious delight at the attempted coup in Moscow, the Seoul government was dismayed. The coup was a personal shock for Roh, who had developed a close rapport with Gorbachev. Seoul's more immediate concern was the impact of the coup on North Korea, which might have stiffened its attitude toward Seoul if the coup had succeeded. When the coup failed, Roh sent congratulatory messages separately to Gorbachev and Yeltsin. He welcomed the reinstatement of Gorbachev, calling the collapse of the coup a "monumental victory" of the Soviet people. He also renewed his invitation for Yeltsin to visit Seoul.[15] The difference between Seoul's and Pyongyang's responses was noted by Moscow. When the Soviet vice-premier, Servakov, held a briefing for foreign ambassadors in Moscow about the failed coup, the South Korean ambassador and twenty-four others were invited, but the North Korean ambassador was excluded.

The failed coup and the subsequent breakup of the USSR had a very negative impact on Russia's relations with North Korea. Yeltsin's Russian government, taking over the role of the former USSR in foreign policy, ended the limited economic aid that it had continued to provide to Pyongyang and started to enforce the January 1991 requirement that North Korea pay hard currency for Russian goods. Under Yeltsin, Russia stopped supplying North Korea with weapons, discontinued nuclear cooperation, and ended all military ties. The Soviet Union long had maintained military links to North Korea while at the same time striving to establish diplomatic ties with South Korea—despite the resultant deterioration in USSR–North Korean diplomatic relations. Exchanges of high-ranking military officials between the Soviet Union and North Korea were conducted regularly. Thus, the demise of Soviet communism and of the USSR itself further weakened the already poor relations between Moscow and Pyongyang, damaging both the economic and strategic sphere of this relationship.

Following the failed coup, Russian and South Korean publications began to express even more openly critical views on Kim Il Sung and his son and future successor, Kim Jong Il. It was revealed that the two Kims had lied about their bizarre life history. Writing in Moscow's *New Times*, Leonid Melchin, a Russian specialist on Korea, described Kim Il Sung as "cruel and cunning" and Kim Jong Il as "nothing but a spoiled child of his father's."[16] The repressive Kim Il Sung regime's appalling human rights record toward dissidents was highlighted by Yeltsin's decision to grant political asylum for the first time to a North Korean student, Kim Myung-se, in Moscow on June 16, 1992.[17] Yeltsin's decision to accept Kim in spite of strong protests from North Korean authorities implied a shift in Russian policy toward the two Koreas.

As for South Korea, the failed coup and the breakup of the USSR had a mixed impact on its relations with Moscow. One positive aspect was the exchange of visits by high-ranking South Korean and Russian military officials in the period shortly after the coup. A negative impact of the failed coup and the subsequent dissolution of the USSR was that they contributed to doubts and sagging confidence among the South Korean business community over prospects of trade with and investment in

Russia. The Seoul government was also concerned that the economic package it had promised Russia in exchange for diplomatic recognition might never be repaid. This led to a growing perception among Seoul's policy makers that Russian policy mattered less than before. Reinforcing this perception was the fact that as Moscow's influence over Pyongyang seemed to have diminished after the dissolution of the USSR.[18]

Russian Policy Toward the Two Koreas in 1992

Throughout 1992, Russian policy continued to favor South Korea. Although South Korean businessmen had complained bitterly against the harsh conditions of the Russian market, several companies, especially Daewoo, that were interested in Russia's natural resources and its military and space technology continued to look for opportunities for investment in Russia. Moscow, in turn, pressed for the resumption of the $US1.5 billion loan that was frozen by Seoul after the disintegration of the USSR. However, problems over Russia's interest payment on this loan put an obstacle in their bilateral relations. The two countries nevertheless needed each other politically. Russia played "the Korean card" to put pressure on Japan, and it supported South Korea's greater role in East Asia and the future unification of Korea. For South Korea, the Russian connection was used to put pressure on North Korea and as a counterbalance to American and Japanese influence in the region.[19]

Russia's relations with North Korea remained cool. All military shipments from Russia to North Korea had stopped, and Russian–North Korean trade plummeted following Moscow's insistence on hard currency transactions. China had established diplomatic relations with South Korea on August 22, 1992, after two years of unofficial ties at the trade level. This development was a severe diplomatic setback for North Korea, as China was its sole remaining big-power supporter. In the span of two years Pyongyang had lost both of its erstwhile allies and critical friends—the former Soviet Union and China. As these two countries accounted for around 60 percent of North Korea's foreign trade, serious economic dislocation resulted. According to South Korean estimates, North Korea's GNP shrank by 3.7 percent in 1990 and by 5.2 percent in 1991, and it continued to contract by 5 percent during 1992.[20]

In reviewing its military relationship with Pyongyang, Russia sought to modify the Treaty of Friendship, Cooperation and Mutual Assistance signed between North Korea and the former Soviet Union in 1961. When Yeltsin's special envoy, Igor Rogachev, visited Pyongyang from January 17–18, 1992, he proposed revision of the 1961 treaty. Pyongyang refused, objecting that the treaty was to remain effective until 1996. Rogachev did persuade Pyongyang to abide by the obligations of the Nuclear Non-Proliferation Treaty and accept IAEA inspections of its nuclear facilities.[21]

Kozyrev's two-day visit to Seoul on March 19–20, 1992, also focused on security and economic issues. Kozyrev assured the foreign minister of South Korea, Lee Sang Ock, that Russia would not cooperate with North Korea in the development of its nuclear program and that it had ended financial and technical assistance to North Korea in constructing nuclear power plants. Moscow had also stopped selling offensive weapons to Pyongyang. Kozyrev promised the full support of the Russian government if the question of North Korea's nuclear programs was taken up in the UN Security Council and raised the possibility of signing a friendship treaty between the two countries during Yeltsin's scheduled September 1992 visit. And Kozyrev succeeded in overcoming Moscow's diminished credibility as a result of its defaulting on $US32.5 million in interest payments to Seoul on loans previously provided: Seoul disbursed the remaining amount of more than $1.5 billion of a $3 billion loan that was frozen after the Soviet Union's collapse.

Kozyrev's visit to South Korea was followed by South Korean Foreign Minister Lee Sang Ock's visit to the three former Soviet republics Russia, Ukraine, and Kazakhstan in July 1992. Yeltsin again reaffirmed Russia's full support for inter-Korean nuclear inspections and said that there would be no Russian financial and military support for North Korea, including the supply of offensive weapons, unless Pyongyang changed its stance toward these nuclear inspections.[22] Further steps to establish security ties with South Korea took place during Russia's Deputy Defense Minister Andrei Kokoshin's visit to South Korea in October 1992.[23] To improve Russia's image before Yeltsin's departure for Seoul in November, a ceremony was held at the Kremlin on October 14, 1992, where Yeltsin turned over a deciphered transcript of the downed Korean Air Lines 747's "black box" and ten documents related to the ill-fated aircraft to a South Korean delegation headed by Deputy Minister of Transportation Chang Sang Hyon.[24]

It could be argued that at this stage there was still a degree of ambiguity surrounding Russian policy toward the two Koreas. Several news reports cautioned against the diplomacy of making a one-sided choice in Seoul's favor, the fear being that Russia would lose a chance to play an intermediary role in uniting the two Koreas. Some Russians were also irked by the South Korean Ministry of Defense's demand that Russia exclude the military clauses in the Treaty of Friendship with North Korea. In July 1992, the Russian Ministry of Foreign Affairs contradicted Yeltsin's comments at his meeting with the South Korean foreign minister by issuing a statement that the treaty with North Korea remained fully in effect.[25] These ambiguities and inconsistencies in Russian policy toward the two Koreas reflect that different spokespersons and organs adopt different positions vis-à-vis the two Korean states.

One of the highlights of Russian–South Korean relations in 1992 was Yeltsin's three-day state visit to Seoul in mid-November. After postponing his planned trip to Japan, Yeltsin had chosen South Korea as the first Asian country for a Russian state visit, thereby demonstrating that Russia assigned major importance to ties with South Korea. Yeltsin reiterated his support for the unification of the two Koreas in a peaceful manner through dialogue between the two parties and assured South Korea that Russia had already stopped the supply of offensive arms to North Korea. In a subsequent news conference, Yeltsin declared that the 1961 USSR–North Korea Friendship and Mutual Assistance Treaty "is either to be abolished or revised to a very great extent."[26] In particular, Moscow would consider repealing Article 1 of the treaty whereby the former Soviet Union pledged to aid North Korea in the event of an attack by a third party. Yeltsin proposed multilateral consultations among countries in Northeast Asia as a preliminary step for the formation of a security consultative body in the region that could mediate international disputes, and the creation of a center for regional strategic research. At the end of the Seoul visit, the joint communiqué spoke of "overcoming the consequences of the adverse period of their common history," which refers to the Soviet involvement in the 1950–1953 Korean War and the destruction of the Korean Air Lines flight 007.[27] Yeltsin promised to open the archives of that war and to provide materials to South Korean historians. As a sign of goodwill, Yeltsin then handed over to Roh the two black boxes, the cockpit voice recorder, and the flight data recorder of the KAL 007 Flight.

In return, Yeltsin hoped to increase the flow of aid that South Korea had already pledged to Gorbachev. Roh said that he would review the current aid embargo to Russia and release a further $US1.5 billion worth of trade credits on condition that Russia would pay interest in the form of aluminum ingot. Earlier, in May 1992, Russian officials had agreed on repayment guarantees on all aid, including paying the $US500 million in tied aid and some $US36.8 million in overdue interest on a $US1 billion commercial bank loan.

Russia and South Korea also signed three new agreements during the November meetings: a basic relations treaty providing a legal framework for closer economic, political, scientific, and cultural cooperation and binding both countries to common goals on human rights and market economics; a military agreement on exchange visits; and a double-taxation treaty. Yeltsin further expanded bilateral economic cooperation by presenting twenty-three potential economic projects, including the establishment of a South Korean industrial complex at Nakhodka in the Russian Far East and a feasibility study on the joint development of a natural gas pipeline from Yakutia through North Korea to South Korea backed by a consortium from the two countries.[28] Thus, Yeltsin's visit to South Korea greatly contributed to the promotion of cooperative ties between the two countries.

Recent Developments and Implications

Russian relations with the two Koreas are characterized by both positive and negative aspects in the economic, political, and military fields. Russo–South Korean exchanges remain relatively dynamic. The two sides continue to converge on most international issues, including the security of the Korean peninsula. Moscow is expanding military ties with Seoul, exchanging top military leaders and goodwill tours by naval vessels. At the end of August 1993, a Russian flotilla from Vladivostok sailed into Pusan for the first time since 1905, and there was agreement to hold joint naval exercises in 1997.[29] In contrast, relations with North Korea have continued to deteriorate, partly as a consequence of Russia's increasing ties with the South and also due to Pyongyang's stance on the nuclear issue.

Relations with South Korea

The bilateral cooperation between Russia and South Korea is best demonstrated in the trade field. Bilateral trade doubled from $US860 million in 1992 to $US1.6 billion in 1993. Russo–South Korean trade is based on an exchange of raw materials for finished goods. The $US1 billion in South Korean imports from Russia in 1993 comprised steel, fish, timber, gas, and aluminium. South Korea exported to Russia consumer electronics, cars, and heavy machinery. On the whole, trade between the two countries was established on a firm commercial basis, as the South Korean government no longer provided export credits for its companies. In early 1993, the South Korean government began to show an interest in having South Korean companies establish a presence in the CIS by approving direct investments there. One of the major South Korean companies that has found moderate success in the CIS is Samsung, whose sales surpassed $US100 million in 1993, with televisions and videocassette recorders making up more than 75 percent of the sales. In addition to its consumer-electronics ventures, Samsung is making semiconductors at a plant outside Moscow with plans to invest $US20 million in 1993 in a joint venture to make digital telephone stations in northwest Russia. In February 1993, Samsung unveiled plans to set up a dealer network in ten locations in the CIS.

Another of South Korea's big business groups, Daewoo, supplies parts for the assembly of consumer-electronics products at plants in Russia and Kazakhstan. In March 1993, Daewoo invested $US100 million in the construction of a car plant in Uzbekistan, the largest investment by a South Korean company in the CIS. The plant, which is due to start production in 1995, will make 180,000 vehicles annually. Daewoo also invested another $US45 million in 1993 in consumer-electronics and textile joint ventures in Uzbekistan and $US30 million into television and videocassette-recorder factories in Russia and plans to manufacture 5,000 buses a year in Khabarovsk. In addition to South Korean investment in assembly and manufacturing operations, there was also cooperation in technology transfers from Russia's military sector.[30]

By the end of 1993, South Korea had invested just $US26 million in Russia, $US16 million on one project, the Hyundai-Svetlaya timber project in the Russian Far East. At that point, investments stalled because the investment climate in Russia had worsened. South Korean investors in Russia were faced with difficulties such as unforgiving tax laws, conflicting decrees, and even environmental claims. In 1993, a law suit brought by a local group against Hyundai's Svetlaya timber operation in the Maritime Territory resulted in Hyundai's loss of millions of dollars when it was forced to slash operating capacity. Daewoo's plans to set up a car-assembly plant in Yelabuga, Tatarstan, foundered when the Russian government refused tax concessions. Instead, Daewoo is sticking to the plan to build a plant in Uzbekistan, where a more stable political climate has created more favorable investment conditions. Samsung Electronics declared during President Kim Young Sam's visit to Russia in June 1994 that it would invest $US200 million in telecommunications over the next two years. South Koreans also saw bright prospects for cooperation in technology transfer and in the energy and satellite fields. But the issue of Russia's debt to the South Korean government has hindered progress on joint large-scale projects such as the Sakha natural-gas pipeline, development of the Nakhodka port, and construction of a South Korean business center in Moscow.[31]

Despite a robust growth in trade between Russia and South Korea, it could be argued that the economic and political cooperation foreseen when diplomatic relations were restored in 1990 has failed to materialize. Bilateral tensions in economic relations between Seoul and Moscow led to the suspension of all further South Korean aid programs, including delivery of $US1.5 billion worth of trade credits agreed in 1991. The main reason was Russia's failure to service its debts on the $US1.5 billion in bank loans arranged by Seoul as an incentive for opening diplomatic relations. Moscow has settled part of the $US52.5 million outstanding interest payment by delivering aluminum ingots worth $US12.5 million. Seoul, which borrowed the money from international lenders and then lent it to Moscow, was forced to service debts on behalf of Russia at a relatively high interest of 1.375 percentage points above the London interbank rate. Moscow was also slow in interest payment on trade credits between November 1992 and February 1993. Russia had paid $US12.7 million in interest, leaving $US15 million in arrears. Moscow suggested that some of these debts could be settled by weapons purchases, but because of the incompatibility of Russian weapons with U.S. weapons in South Korea and Washington's strong opposition, the possibility of South Korea buying Russian weapons seems remote.[32] In December 1993, South Korea accepted a Russian offer to repay part of the Seoul-provided loans, and overdue interest on them, in the form of leasing some 23,000 square meters of land in Moscow free of charge for ninety-nine years to build a Korean trade center.[33]

The second issue straining the Seoul-Moscow diplomatic relationship has been Russia's stance on the Korean Air Lines tragedy. Russian-South Korean relations suffered a minor setback shortly after Yeltsin's visit to Seoul. Three days after the ceremony in which the "black boxes" of the downed airplane were turned over by Yeltsin, South Korean officials were furious when they discovered the boxes did not contain the critical flight data recordings and that the tapes of the pilots' voices were not the originals. The explanations by the Russian president's chief of staff, Yury Petrov, to the South Korean ambassador, Hon Soon Yen, on December 1, 1992, that Yeltsin did not know that the contents of the "black boxes" were not the original materials, clearly did not satisfy the South Korean side. Some South Koreans protested by pelting the Russian embassy in Seoul with eggs. This incident caused a scandal in the South Korean presidential elections under way at that time. The circumstances of and reasons for this 1983 tragedy still remain a mystery, and the misunderstanding over the KAL 007 issue continues to mar the relationship between Russia and South Korea.

South Korea pledged its support for President Yeltsin during his battle against the conservative Russian parliament in September, saying it believed his emergency measures reflected the Russian people's will for continued reform. South Korean officials viewed improved ties with Russia as dependent ultimately on Yeltsin's defeat of the conservatives, as the return to power by conservatives in Moscow could mean that Russian support would swing back to North Korea. South Korean companies decided to put off investment in Russia pending the parliamentary elections in Russia in December 1993 because of worries that the investment environment would worsen if the conservatives seized power and reversed the economic reforms.[34]

In Moscow, Russian officials regarded these developments as problems of transition in their relations with Seoul. Despite being plagued by numerous domestic economic and political troubles, Russia is prepared to strengthen and enlarge its role in the Korean peninsula and help reduce tension. The former Soviet ambassador to Seoul, Oleg M. Sokolov, now head of the Foreign Ministry's Disarmament and Military Technology Control Division, suggested at a seminar with South Korean scholars that Moscow supports a comprehensive arms control package negotiable between North and South Korea. Moscow's readiness to play a role stems not only from its concern over the proliferation of nuclear weapons around Russia's borders, but also from its classic role as a balancer on the Korean peninsula, together with China and Japan.[35]

Relations with North Korea

The already erratic relationship between Russia and North Korea seemed to have drifted even further after Yeltsin's visit to South Korea. Pyongyang responded to this visit by criticizing it as "diplomacy for begging."[36] North Korea tried to enlarge economic relations with the former socialist countries by concluding sixteen economic cooperation pacts in the first half of 1993. Included among them were scientific, technological, and economic cooperation treaties with Bulgaria, Ukraine, and Belarus. North Korea also attempted to improve the economic relationship with Russia. In February 1993 both countries concluded an agreement on technological and scientific cooperation. But Russia indicated that it was reviewing its relations with North Korea in terms of its own economic interests—something made clear during a closed meeting between North Korea's deputy minister of external economic affairs, Kim Jong-u, and his Russian counterpart, Mikhail Pladkov, in Moscow on August 10, 1993. They discussed matters such as the resumption of Russian investments in North Korea, North Korean debts to Russia, the renewal of the agreement on a joint lumbering venture at the Chegdomyn logging site, the opening and development of the Rajin port by expanding railroads connecting Nakhodka and Rajin, and the reciprocal opening of a trade exhibition house. It was revealed in January 1994 that the Far East–Pacific fleet, with the authorization of naval headquarters in Moscow, sold four Russian submarines—the 2,500-ton Foxtrot class vessels—to North Korea for an undisclosed price. This incident will not improve relations between Seoul and Moscow because despite Pyongyang's claims that the purchase is for scrap metal, the Foxtrot is an attack vessel and still serviceable. The spare parts of these craft could be cannibalized and used to repair North Korea's existing extensive submarine fleet.[37]

Apart from partial economic and military cooperation, Moscow-Pyongyang relations are characterized more by negative aspects, especially in the economic, trade, political, and military fields. North Korea's economic relations with Russia continue to be prickly. Moscow slashed North Korea's fishing quota in its waters for 1994 by half, from 60,000 tons to 30,000 tons, because of depletion of stocks in the Bering and Okhotsk Seas, and the need to put Russian fishing interests first.[38] The scale and form of North Korean trade with Russia has undergone the most dramatic change. Russia was the largest source of imports until Gorbachev started applying international prices in trade relations in January 1991. According to the estimate of the Bank of Korea in Seoul, North Korea's two-way trade with Russia was $US600 million in 1992. The Russian government's statistics showed trade of $US320 million during the first six months of 1993: $US270 million in North Korean imports from Russia and $US50 million in Russian imports from North Korea.[39]

One of the priorities in Russia's economic relationship with North Korea is the preservation of the timber agreement. However, the continuation of North Korean logging operations in Russia is in doubt. Under the joint venture agreement with Russia, North Korean workers numbering 17,000 to 19,000 have logged in Chita, Amur, and Chgdomyn, near Khabarovsk, in Siberia since 1966. North Korea receives 40 percent of the profits in return for providing cheap (forced) labor. A Russian delegation visited Pyongyang in May 1994 and renewed an agreement with North Korea to allow Pyongyang to continue logging in Siberia over the next five years on the condition that Pyongyang abide by Russian laws, including one relating to the human rights of North Korean loggers. The renewal of the Moscow-Pyongyang logging agreement came at a time when a growing number of North Korean loggers had been escaping the logging sites because of adverse working conditions and violations of human rights. The development of political democracy in Russia has highlighted the issue, further undermining relations with North Korea.[40]

Moscow has been applying constant pressure on Pyongyang to pay back its rising debt, which amounted to about $US5.2 billion in 1992. In an interview with ITAR-TASS on November 30, 1992, in Pyongyang, the Russian ambassador to North Korea, Yury Fadeev, depicted Russian–North Korean relations in 1992 as "complicated and painful."[41] North Korea has suggested an agreement for repayment in kind.

The military alliance between North Korea and Russia remains only nominal. The North Korea–USSR Treaty of Friendship, Cooperation and

Mutual Assistance, a military alliance signed in 1961, has become virtually a dead letter since Moscow established diplomatic relations with Seoul in 1990. Russian Deputy Minister Georgy Kunadze, during his four-day visit to Pyongyang Moscow's intention not to stick to the military alliance clause in the 1961 treaty that called for Russia's automatic military intervention in case of an attack against North Korea.

On his return to Moscow, Kunadze told the South Korean ambassador to Moscow, Hon Soon Yen, that Moscow was preparing a supplementary memorandum to Pyongyang that would provide a new interpretation of the clause in the 1961 treaty. North Korea did not object to this proposal and Kunadze invited his North Korean counterpart, Kang Sok-ju, to visit Moscow in the near future to conclude this matter. Thus, Kunadze's visit served to virtually end the existing military bonds between Russia and North Korea.

Tensions in Russian–North Korean relations are also on the rise because of Russia's solidarity with the international community in pressuring North Korea to open up its nuclear program to inspection. Kunadze also expressed worries about Pyongyang's stalling tactics on the bilateral nuclear inspection program between South and North Korea. There have been many factors indicating that Russia is opposed to Pyongyang's nuclear arms development. First, Russia supports the U.N. sanctions against North Korea in the event of its failure to fulfill the safeguards agreement with the IAEA. Second, during Yeltsin's visit to Seoul in November 1992, he declared that Russia would suspend providing North Korea with offensive weapons and nuclear materials and technology, rejecting Pyongyang's request for assistance in training uranium mine and nuclear energy experts and for the resumption of aid for the construction of nuclear power plants. And third, in December 1992 a Russian news magazine, *Vek (Century)*, reported that Russia stopped thirty-six Russian missile engineers at the airport from going to North Korea for employment. This incident created another dispute between Moscow and Pyongyang. Moscow was determined to pressure Pyongyang to abandon its intentions to develop its nuclear weapons program.[42]

The stability of the Korean peninsula was then threatened by the unexpected crisis caused by North Korea's abrupt announcement on March 12, 1993, that it was withdrawing from the NPT. Pyongyang's intention was to circumvent a demand by the IAEA to open two suspicious nuclear facilities to inspection by March 31. The Russian media labelled North Korea's withdrawal from the NPT an "unacceptable act of adventurism."[43] Yeltsin held talks on the North Korean nuclear issue with President Clinton at their summit in Vancouver, Canada, in early April 1993, and they warned North Korea to return to

NPT membership by the deadline of three months period after its NPT pullout.[44] Russia has repeatedly urged North Korea to clear doubts about its nuclear arms development program and even made eight Russian scientists working on North Korea's nuclear development program return home in May 1993. During Yeltsin's state visit to Japan in October 1993, the foreign ministers of the two countries, Tsutomu Hata and Andrei Kozyrev, issued a joint statement that expressed extreme concern over North Korea's suspected nuclear weapons program and urged Pyongyang not to follow through with its threat to withdraw from the Non-Proliferation Treaty.[45]

Russia proposed in March 1994 an international conference outside the U.N. framework for turning the Korean peninsula into a nuclear-free zone to settle the latest crisis. The proposed meeting would be attended by the two Koreas, the U.S., Japan, China, and Russia. Moscow also opposed a Security Council "statement," preferring a resolution instead. China was neutral to Russia's proposal, and the reactions of the U.S., South Korea, and Japan were unenthusiastic. In particular, the U.S. brushed aside the Russian proposal, saying it preferred U.N. action instead. The North Koreans regarded Russia's proposal as complicating the difficulties of getting Pyongyang to accept IAEA inspections.[46] A new dimension to the escalating dispute was added when Russian Deputy Foreign Minister Alexander Panov warned Western nations that Russia would provide military backing to Pyongyang under the 1961 treaty against any act of "unprovoked aggression."[47] Mr. Panov's remarks were seen as raising the stakes in Russia's efforts to prevent the West and the U.N. from adopting a unilateral approach to the latest North Korean nuclear crisis. Indeed, Russia was concerned not to be perceived as an outsider in the Asian arena and out of the political game among the other great powers in Asia in this latest escalation of tension concerning North Korea's nuclear ambitions. Thus, Russia wants a continuing role in countries that are within its traditional spheres of influence and is reasserting its right to a say in critical issues in international affairs.

Conclusion

This review of Russian foreign policy toward the two Koreas in the period 1985–1994 reveals how the favorable international environment, South Korea's economic achievements, and its timely policy enabled Roh's government to reap a spectacular success in its northern diplomacy toward the Soviet Union. It is argued that economic and security considerations were the major factors in improved Soviet–South Korean relations. Soviet–North Korean relations deteriorated after the establishment of diplomatic relations with South Korea in 1990 and eroded even more sharply after the failed coup attempt and the collapse of the USSR.

Events in 1992, especially Yeltsin's visit to Seoul served to accelerate the termination of all economic and military ties between Russia and North Korea. Since then, Russia has not been consistent in its policies vis-à-vis the two Koreas because of extreme economic hardships at home. Russia has not hesitated in maintaining cooperation with North Korea when such cooperation provides economic benefits and does not pose a serious threat to its relations with South Korea. These changes in Soviet foreign policies prompted North Korea to adopt a more open approach in foreign affairs. Pyongyang began to make overtures to Japan and the United States to improve relations and to relax its rigid stance toward the South.

The radical reduction of Russian economic and military aid after the disintegration of the USSR induced Pyongyang to sell SCUD missiles to Middle East countries and to develop its nuclear weapons program.

The sudden death of Kim Il Sung marked the end of an era. It also cast doubt on the peace initiatives in the region. Kim's death came at a time when U.S. and North Korean negotiators were just beginning talks in Geneva on the mounting dispute over Pyongyang's suspected nuclear program. The United Nations was considering economic sanctions as a response to North Korea's refusal to allow full international inspections of its nuclear plants, from which the West suspected fuel was being diverted to a military atomic program. Tensions were defused in late June 1994 when Kim Il Sung promised former U.S. President Jimmy Carter that he would freeze the nuclear program and proposed the first ever summit between North and South Korean leaders, which was slated for July 25, 1994. Talks in Geneva and the planned summit in Pyongyang were suspended after the news of Kim's death. The death of Kim Il Sung also signaled communism's first dynastic succession. For twenty years, Kim Il Sung had groomed his son, 52-year-old Kim Jong Il, to succeed him. The changeover at the top opened up a new era of uncertainty.

Indications suggested that Kim Jong Il would take over, at least initially, as leader and commander of the nation's million-strong armed forces. But there is still speculation that Kim Jong Il may have difficulty retaining power because he lacks his father's charisma, personal authority, and military credentials. He is believed to be opposed by the conservative military leadership and the old guard elements who supported his father. North Korea's economic performance will be a vital determinant of Kim Jong Il's ability to remain in office. The main challenge confronting Kim Jong Il is whether he can reverse the country's economic decline and save it from possible collapse. The North Korean economy shrunk at an average annual rate of 5.2 percent during 1990–

1994. Finally, Kim's death raised fresh hopes in the reunification of the two Koreas, but with estimated costs of reunification at $US1000 billion over ten years, any German-style unification and absorption would need to be gradual. Also, a sudden collapse of the North Korean regime with streams of refugees and huge new economic burdens to South Korea has not been ruled out—a development that would not be welcomed by Seoul, Washington, and Beijing. Much depends on what North Korea's new leaders do now. Perhaps they could be persuaded to give up their nuclear ambitions for diplomatic and economic benefits to shore up North Korea's sagging economy. The dilemma in North Korea is that it needs to introduce liberalizing economic reform and allow foreign investment to reverse decades of Stalinist central planning, but economic change carries the risk of undermining the regime and eroding its power and thus of following the path of Eastern Europe and the Soviet Union in previous years. Whether North Korea pursues reform or lingers in isolation now highlights the continuing fragility of security in Northeast Asia.[48]

Notes

1. V. Mikheev, "USSR-Korea: Economic Aspects of Relations," *Sino-Soviet Affairs*, vol. 13, no. 1, Spring 1989, p. 74.

2. Hak Joon Kim, "Emerging Relations Between South Korea and the Soviet Union," *Far Eastern Affairs*, no. 4, 1991, pp. 68–85, p. 74.

3. Carolyn McGiffert Ekedahl and Melvin A. Goodman, "Gorbachev's 'New Directions' in Asia," *Journal of Northeast Asian Studies*, vol. 8, no. 3, Fall 1989, pp. 3–24, p. 13.

4. Byung-Joon Ahn, "South Korean-Soviet Relations: Issues and Prospects," *Korea and World Affairs*, vol. 14, no. 4, Winter 1990, pp. 671–686, p. 682.

5. Shim Jae Hoon, "Diplomatic Drive: Seoul Expands Ties with Moscow, Eastern Europe," *Far Eastern Economic Review (FEER)*, April 5, 1990, p. 17.

6. Shim Jae Hoon and Susumu Awanohara, "Perestroika Pay-off: North Korea Outflanked as Gorbachev Meets Roh," *FEER*, June 14, 1990, p. 10.

7. Shim Jae Hoon, "Kremlin Connection," *FEER*, August 30, 1990, p. 28, and Hak Joon Kim, "Emerging Relations," p. 80.

8. Mark Clifford, *FEER*, February 7, 1991, p. 44.

9. Shim Jae Hoon, "Cheju Honeymoon," *FEER*, May 2, 1991, pp. 12–13.

10. Roy Kim, "Gorbachev and the Korean Peninsula," *Third World Quarterly*, vol. 10, no. 3, July 1988, pp. 1267–1299, p. 1272.

11. Suzanne Crow, "Soviet-South Korean Rapprochement," *Radio Liberty Report on the USSR*, vol. 2, no. 25, June 15, 1990, p. 11.

12. See, for example, *Izvestiia*, September 1, 1989, p. 5.

13. Mikhail L. Titarenko, "Asian and Korean Security and Stability," *Korea and World Affairs*, vol. 13, no. 2, Summer 1989, p. 288, and Yuri I. Ognev, "Soviet

Position on Peaceful Settlement and Reunification in Korea," *Sino-Soviet Affairs*, (Seoul), vol. 14, no. 3, Fall 1990, pp. 63–76, especially p. 67.

14. Gennady Chufrin, "Russian Interests in Korean Security in the Post-Cold War World," April 1992, unpublished paper, Institute of Oriental Studies, Moscow.

15. *Korea Newsreview*, vol. 20, no. 35, August 31, 1991, p. 4. For an analysis of the different responses by the two Koreas to the coup attempt, see *FEER*, August 29, 1991, pp. 10–13, *FEER*, September 5, 1991, pp. 10–13, *North Korea News*, no. 594, September 2, 1991, p. 3, and *Vantage Point*, vol. 14, no. 9, September 1991, p. 13.

16. Leonid Melchin, "Old Clients Are Not Served," *New Times*, no. 2, 1992, p. 19.

17. Alexander Chudodeyev, "Hunting Down a Compatriot," *New Times International*, May 21, 1992, pp. 26–27, and *Vantage Point*, vol. 15, no. 6, June 1992, pp. 24–25.

18. Peggy Falkenheim Meyer, "Gorbachev and Post-Soviet Policy Toward the Korean Peninsula: The Impact of Changing Russian Perceptions," *Asian Survey*, August 1992, pp. 757–772, especially pp. 770–771.

19. E. Bazhanov and N. Bazhanov, "Russia and Asia in 1992: A Balancing Act," *Asian Survey*, January 1993, pp. 91–97, especially p. 97.

20. "Pyongyang Calls for Vigorous Efforts to Boost North Korean Economy," *North Korea News*, no. 675, March 1993, pp. 6–7.

21. Interview with Gennady Chufrin at the Institute of Orientalism, Moscow, by the author in May 1992. See also "Yeltsin's Special Envoy Visits Pyongyang— Moscow Stresses Nuclear Issue Must Be Resolved," *North Korea News*, no. 615, January 27, 1992, pp. 5–6.

22. "Russia-North Korea Ideological Link Terminated," *Korea Newsreview*, vol. 21, no. 28, July 11, 1992, pp. 4–5.

23. *Current Digest of the Post-Soviet Press*, vol. XLIV, no. 41, November 11, 1992, p. 21.

24. *Current Digest of the Post-Soviet Press*, vol. XLIV, no. 41, November 11, 1992, pp. 16–20.

25. Georgy Stepanov, *Izvestiia*, July 31, 1992, p. 6, and *CDPSP*, vol. XLIV, no. 37, October 14, 1992, pp. 17–18, and *CDPSP*, vol. XLIV, no. 47, December 23, 1992, p. 21.

26. *China, North Korea: Country Report*, no. 4, 1992, p. 33.

27. Shim Jae Hoon and Ed Paisely, "Trade and Trade-off: Yeltsin's Visit Brings Profit to Seoul, Moscow," *FEER*, December 3, 1992, p. 15.

28. Hoon and Paisely, "Trade and Trade-off," pp. 4–7.

29. Eugene Bazhanov and Natasha Bazhanov, "Russia and Asia in 1993," *Asian Survey*, January 1994, pp. 87–94, especially p. 93.

30. Jeffrey Lilley, "Dancing with the Bear: South Korean Firms Forge Ahead in Russia," *FEER*, May 20, 1993, p. 56.

31. Jeff Lilley, "What Is to Be Done? South Korean Companies Find Russia a Quagmire," *FEER*, June 16, 1994, p. 77.

32. Shim Jae Hoon, "Russian Roulette," *FEER*, October 7, 1993, p. 30.

33. "Russia to Repay Loans in Form of Land Lease in Moscow," *Korea Newsreview*, vol. 22, no. 52, December 25, 1993, p. 16.

34. "Seoul Supports Yeltsin's Action," *Korea Newsreview*, vol. 22, no. 40, October 2, 1993, p. 12, and "Russian Investment Suspended," *Korea Newsreview*, vol. 22, no. 40, October 2, 1993, p. 24.

35. Shim Jae Hoon, "Russian Roulette," p. 30.

36. *North Korea News*, no. 659, November 30, 1992, pp. 2–3.

37. "Russian Navy Admits Selling Submarines to North Korea," *North Korea News*, no. 719, January 24, 1994, p. 3, and "Moscow to Sell Twelve Submarines to Pyongyang," *North Korea News*, no. 720, January 31, 1994, pp. 4–5.

38. "Pyongyang and Moscow Hold Fisheries Talks," *North Korea News*, no. 715, December 27, 1993, p. 8, and "Russia Cuts North Korea's Fishery Quota in Half," *North Korea News*, no. 716, January 3, 1994, p. 6.

39. "North Korea's Efforts at Better Relations with Russia Fruitless," *Vantage Point*, vol. 16, no. 10, October 1993, pp. 16–21.

40. "Pyongyang-Moscow Logging Agreement Renewed," *North Korea News*, no. 738, June 6, 1994, p. 6.

41. *Vantage Point*, February 1993, pp. 12–13.

42. *Vantage Point*, February 1993, pp. 11–13.

43. "Russian Media Label North Korea's NPT Withdrawal An 'Unacceptable Act of Adventurism'—Pyongyang Raises Issue of 'Russia's Nuclear Threat,'" *North Korea News*, no. 680, April 26, 1993, pp. 3–4.

44. "North Korea's Efforts at Better Relations with Russia Fruitless," p. 18.

45. "Diplomacy and Drift," *The Bulletin*, April 5, 1994, p. 47, and "A Sea of Fire?" *Asiaweek*, April 6, 1994, p. 26.

46. BBC, *Summary of World Broadcast*, Part 3, Asia-Pacific, FE/1962 D/6, April 4, 1994, and "Making Haste Slowly: Seoul, Tokyo, Play Up to Beijing on North Korean Issue," *FEER*, April 7, 1994, p. 16.

47. "Russia Backs North Korea in Dispute," *The Australian*, March 31, 1994, p. 7, and Ean Higgins, "Russian Push to Reassert Its Sphere of Influence," *The Australian*, April 4, 1994, p. 5.

48. "Son King or Sinking?" *The Economist*, July 16, 1994, pp. 13–14.

10

Russian Policy Toward Vietnam

Carlyle A. Thayer

In 1978 Vietnam and the Soviet Union cemented their long-standing relationship by signing a twenty-five-year Treaty of Friendship and Cooperation. The treaty was at heart an anti-China alliance. With the protection afforded by the treaty, Vietnam invaded Cambodia and commenced its decade-long occupation of that country. China retaliated by "teaching Vietnam a lesson" in a short, sharp border war and over the next several years kept up military pressures on Vietnam's northern border. In defiance Hanoi declared that Indochina was a "single strategic unit" linked to the Soviet Union.[1]

It was during the decade 1979–1989 that the Soviet Union became the "firm cornerstone" on which Vietnam based its foreign and domestic policies.[2] Mikhail Gorbachev's coming to power precipitated a transformation in Moscow's relations with the socialist community in general and Vietnam in particular. Vietnam was pressed to undertake domestic reforms and to adopt "new political thinking" in foreign policy.[3] It was encouraged to seek a negotiated settlement of the Cambodian conflict and to follow the Soviet lead in normalizing relations with China.[4]

In 1989–1990, when the tectonic plates on which Cold War alignments rested began to shift, communism collapsed in Eastern Europe and weakened in the Soviet Union. When the Soviet cornerstone began to crumble, leaders in Hanoi had to prepare for a drastic alteration in their bilateral relationship with Moscow. When the Soviet Union finally succumbed, it was forced to end its support for Vietnam. Vietnam in turn was compelled by circumstances to withdraw from Cambodia, sue for peace, and restructure its economy by opening to capitalist market economies.

After the collapse of the Soviet Union in December 1991, bilateral relations between Vietnam and the new Russian Federation entered a period of neglect, "some mistrust," and what was later diplomatically termed "a pause."[5] Trade plummeted as Vietnam reoriented its economy to the Asia-Pacific region. Military relations fell to an all-time low and eventually focused on squabbling over the terms for a continued Russian residual presence at Cam Ranh Bay. Close political relations became a thing of the past as new irritants arose, such as debt repayment schedules, the treatment of Vietnamese residents, and pro-democracy radio broadcasts beamed from Moscow in Vietnamese to Vietnam.

During 1992 officials in both countries made efforts to take stock of the relationship and worked to preserve those elements each felt were mutually beneficial. The state of play in bilateral relations as of early 1993 was captured by a former Soviet diplomat and his academic wife in these words:

> Ideologically, the new Russian ruling class felt no affinity with the regimes in Indochina. Strategically, the Kremlin also lost interest in the Indochinese states. Russia still maintained a military presence in Vietnam's Cam Ranh Bay, but it looked doomed. Hanoi shifted emphasis in its international relations toward cooperation with the ASEAN countries, China, and Japan. Moscow continued to participate in the United Nations effort in Cambodia but without passion, simply because it could not behave otherwise.[6]

During 1993–1994 "the pause" in the relationship was ended as Russia and Vietnam exchanged high-level economic, political, and military delegations. In June 1994, on the occasion of the visit of the Vietnamese prime minister, Russia and Vietnam renegotiated the terms of their Treaty of Friendship and Cooperation to put relations on a more equal footing. This chapter reviews these developments by tracing changes in Soviet-Russian political, military, and economic relations with Vietnam.

Political Relations

The Late-Soviet Period

Soviet-Vietnamese relations developed an "all around" character in the decade following the signing of the 1978 treaty. One major feature of this relationship was the frequency of summit meetings between party and state leaders. Until 1990 an average of two summits were held every year during the Gorbachev period.[7] In 1990 no summit was held. It was not surprising that as Vietnam moved to convene its seventh national party congress, it pressed for a meeting at the highest level with Soviet leaders in order to take stock of their bilateral relationship.

After a postponement at Moscow's request, the summit was eventually held in Moscow in May 1991. Vietnam sent two delegations, one led by its party leader, Nguyen Van Linh, and the other led by Chairman of the Council of Ministers Do Muoi. Linh held political talks with Gorbachev while Muoi held economic talks with his Soviet counterpart. The discussions between Linh and Gorbachev were later characterized as "difficult and complicated" by R. L. Khamidulin, the Soviet ambassador to Vietnam. Gorbachev volunteered to Linh that he (Gorbachev) had made the mistake of going too far with political reforms without first restructuring the economy. Gorbachev then astounded his guest by suggesting that some of the Soviet Union's reforms could be copied by Vietnam.[8]

At the same time, Do Muoi was also having a tough time in his discussions on aid and trade. He was told frankly that the Soviet economy was in such a chaotic state, with no budget having been drawn up, that it would not be possible to discuss aid. Muoi was given the further bad news that Moscow would not cancel Vietnam's 10 billion ruble debt and that Vietnam was expected to begin debt service repayments of around US$350 million per year at the commencement of 1992.[9] Vietnam's negative reaction to these developments was reflected in various reports delivered to the seventh party congress. The Central Committee's Political Report in its review of foreign affairs noted tersely that "the relations between our country and the Soviet Union are being renewed in accordance with the interests of each people." Such official reports belie what Vietnamese leaders were saying in private. Gorbachev was now described as a "traitor to the socialist cause." In August 1991, when Kremlin hard-liners attempted to seize power and oust Gorbachev, Vietnam's leaders were privately elated. They drafted a congratulatory telegram to the leaders of the coup. Only the timely intervention by the Soviet ambassador prevented its dispatch and the political embarrassment that this would have caused.[10]

The Communist Party of the Soviet Union (CPSU) was only one of four foreign parties invited to the seventh national congress of the Vietnamese Communist Party.[11] At the congress, Vietnam jettisoned its long-serving foreign minister, Nguyen Co Thach, and replaced him with a career diplomat, Nguyen Manh Cam. This proved a fortuitous decision, as Cam had previously served as Vietnam's ambassador to Moscow. He assisted in refashioning Vietnam's relations with the states of the former Soviet Union (FSU) when the Soviet Union announced its dissolution on December 26, 1991.

The Post-Soviet Period

On the very next day, Vietnam's foreign ministry announced its readiness to establish diplomatic relations with all states of the FSU.

Russia and Ukraine were singled out in separate messages sent by Foreign Minister Cam. Vietnam's "all around" relationship with the FSU enabled it to refashion relations with Moscow by building on the ties forged by tens of thousands of Vietnamese and former Soviet officials who had worked in each other's countries. One by one Vietnam was able either to reaffirm or renegotiate agreements signed prior to December 1991.

For example, as early as December 24, 1991, members of the USSR-Vietnam Friendship Association renamed their organization and began to lobby for the maintenance of existing relations. In mid-year the association sent a delegation to Vietnam to work out new forms of cooperation. Russia's Indochina specialists (academics, diplomats, and aid workers) formed a professional association and in April 1992 convened the international symposium "The Countries of Indochina and International Economic Cooperation: Potentialities and Prospects" in Moscow.[12]

The actions of these groups led to a rethink of Russian policy toward Vietnam. According to a Moscow-based academician, by May 1992 it was agreed that the precipitate Soviet withdrawal of economic and military assistance to Vietnam was a mistake.[13] While the USSR could not afford such aid and this decision was understandable, he said, it was taken with too much haste. Later in the year, no doubt responding to such internal pressures, the Russian foreign minister launched his country's first foreign policy initiative toward Vietnam and Southeast Asia (see below).

In mid-1992, on the eve of the most senior state visit to Vietnam by a Russian official, a spokesman in Moscow declared, "Our relations are friendly, but they have been depoliticized and de-ideologized."[14] This transformation in Soviet-Vietnamese relations has not been without problems, particularly evident in the political and strategic spheres, where ideology no longer serves to draw Russia and Vietnam together.

New Irritants

A number of irritants have arisen. For example, Russian attempts to take down statues of Lenin and Ho Chi Minh and to remove Lenin's body from his mausoleum in Red Square provoked Vietnamese editorial protests. Vietnam's leaders were reportedly disturbed by the decision to return East German party boss Erick Honecker to Germany for trial for his "shoot-to-kill" orders. Honecker was considered a staunch ally of Vietnam. Finally, Vietnamese leaders have little common ground with the pro-democracy movement in Russia. The official Vietnamese media often portray political instability in Moscow as a negative example for the people of Vietnam. Privately, Vietnamese officials are dismissive of Russian reform efforts.

Vietnam was angered by seemingly off-the-cuff statements by Boris Yeltsin that some American servicemen captured during the Vietnam War may have been taken to the Soviet Union and was later irritated by a series of leaks of Soviet intelligence reports on American prisoners held by Vietnam during the war.[15] Vietnam denied these reports and expressed concern that such statements could harm its warming relations with the United States. For example, Vietnamese ire was also aroused in April 1993 when an Australian researcher uncovered a 1972 document in the CPSU archives revealing that Vietnam had held more American servicemen prisoner than it had since admitted. Vietnam denounced the document as a fake designed to harm U.S.–Vietnamese relations. When the alleged Vietnamese author was asked who could have produced it, he hinted that the Russian intelligence service may have been responsible.[16] Subsequent leaks of Soviet intelligence reports on alleged American prisoners of war have served to strain relations.

Finally, Russia's seemingly lax attitude toward the activities of anti-communist Vietnamese operating on its soil became a major irritant in relations.[17] For example, overseas Vietnamese in America financially supported the operations of Voice of Freedom (or Radio Irina), which leased transmitters belonging to the Russian state radio service to beam Vietnamese-language anti-communist propaganda at Vietnam. Vietnam made several diplomatic protests and privately called on Russian authorities to close the station down. Russian officials initially replied that under their new press laws they could take no action against a private station.[18] Later, when Radio Irina broadcast the names of political prisoners held in detention in Vietnam, Vietnam's top leaders reportedly met to consider jamming the station.[19] Russian officials eventually bowed to Vietnamese pressure, and in mid-1993 Radio Irina was taken off the air.

A Renewed Warming of Relations

All aspects of Russian-Vietnamese relations—political, military, and economic—were reviewed during the course of the January 1993 visit by a delegation of the Russian Supreme Soviet. The delegation was led by S. V. Stepansin, chairman of parliament's Security and Defense Committee. The delegation met with Nong Duc Manh, chairman of Vietnam's National Assembly's Standing Committee, and Vice Premier Tran Duc Luong. Stepansin also held talks with his counterpart, Dang Quoc Thuy, chairman of the National Assembly's National Defense and Security Committee. It was clear from the discussions that bilateral relations had been depoliticized and were now almost exclusively focused on economic and trade relations.[20]

Russian-Vietnamese political relations improved markedly during the final quarter of 1993 as a result of progress in restoring economic ties (see below). Vietnam's Foreign Minister Nguyen Manh Cam visited Russia (and Ukraine, Belarus, Kazakhstan, and Uzebekistan) in October primarily to discuss how to strengthen bilateral cooperation and to arrange a visit by Vietnam's prime minister. Cam met separately with his counterpart, Andrei Kozyrev, Deputy Prime Minister Yury Yarov, and Prime Minister Viktor Chernomyrdin. Cam's visit focused heavily on economic issues, and a number of agreements and protocols were signed. On the political side, Cam and Kozyrev reached accord on regular consultations between their ministries and signed a protocol setting out visa requirements for visitors. The contentious issue of the status of Vietnamese residents who remained in Russia was raised during the official talks. Many refused to return home, preferring to engage in commercial activities instead. Some were subject to physical abuse by irate Russians. Cam was concerned to obtain guarantees of their security.

In February 1994, Nguyen Manh Cam briefly stopped over in Moscow to meet with Andrei Kozyrev to discuss the final preparations for a visit by Vietnam's prime minister. Cam also held a working session with Yury Yazov, the chairman of the Russian-Vietnam Commission for Economic, Scientific, and Technical Cooperation. They discussed areas in which bilateral cooperation should be stepped up (energy, tropical agriculture, mining, light industry, and relations between localities) and areas of contention (debt repayment and the security of Vietnamese residents living in Russia).

Russian-Vietnamese relations reached an historical high-point in June 1994 when Vo Van Kiet made the first visit to the Russian Federation by a Vietnamese prime minister (he also visited Ukraine and Kazakhstan; putting off a visit to Belarus at the last minute). The visit had been postponed from the previous year due to turmoil in Moscow. Kiet's visit produced some turbulence of its own. Despite the historic nature of talks between the two prime ministers, Kiet and Chernomyrdin, the signing of a new "cornerstone document" to replace the 1978 Treaty of Friendship and Cooperation was delayed because of unresolved differences over a number of issues (e.g., debt repayment, Vietnamese workers, Russian military presence at Cam Ranh, and the operations of Vietsovpetro, a joint venture). According to official spokesmen, the new document sets out a "new framework for relations" (as of this writing the official text has yet to be released). A scheduled meeting with President Boris Yeltsin was cancelled on the lame excuse that he was "busy with urgent state affairs." Kiet did not go home empty handed, however, as three economic agreements were signed (agriculture, fisheries, and capital investment). Interviewed on his return about the significance of his visit, Kiet replied:

> My visit was intended to help create conditions for renewed cooperation between Vietnam and these countries [Russia, Ukraine, and Kazakhstan].

We renewed and restored all the relations we had in the period from 1992 to early 1993 and from 1993 to early 1994. Vietnam and these countries signed a number of agreements. We signed with the Russian Federation a new treaty to replace the old one which was signed with the former Soviet Union. We successfully surmounted this hurdle.[21]

The new treaty, though based on the same old friendly spirit, does not follow the old pattern of doing business. The two sides will now conduct business in accordance with the new principles of relations.

Military Relations

The Economic Imperatives

The disintegration of the Soviet Union during 1990–1991 had a major impact on Soviet-Vietnamese military relations. The Soviet Union's fall from superpower status meant the reduction of military forces stationed abroad, including in Vietnam. The Soviet Union's weakening economic position resulted in the ending of its subsidized military aid program to Vietnam. Moscow now requested that all military assistance be paid for in hard currency.

In May 1991, during the course of a summit in Moscow, Soviet and Vietnamese leaders argued over the issue of hard currency payments for Soviet military aid. According to Ambassador Rashid Khamidulin, "Military cooperation will continue, but under a form that is under discussion. We continue to reduce our presence at the Cam Ranh Bay naval and air base and we no longer maintain a strong permanent naval or air presence there."[22] Vietnam had reportedly asked Moscow for $US350–400 million in annual rent for Cam Ranh Bay, an amount equal to the past annual Soviet supplies of military equipment and training.[23] Moscow suggested paying $US40 million instead.[24] Soviet officials have resisted linking the rental question with the issue of Hanoi's debt repayments.

During 1991, the Soviets drew down their forces at Cam Ranh Bay, regrouped those remaining into one residential area, and began returning vacated buildings to Vietnamese control.[25] At year's end Interfax news agency reported that the last major warship, the 8,000-ton destroyer *Admiral Spiridonov*, had returned to Vladivostok. The number of Soviet submarines declined from twenty to only two or three.[26] The number of personnel stationed there dropped from a high of 4,000 to 1,000 or less by mid-1992. In mid-May 1992 formal military cooperation was brought to an end with the return to Russia of the last military adviser posted to Vietnam.[27]

Irritants in the once warm bilateral relationship led Vietnam to restrict the movements and curtail privileges of Russian personnel stationed at Cam Ranh Bay. They were now required to show Vietnamese guards written permission from the Vietnamese commander to leave the base. A Vietnamese military source stated that this was because Russia was no longer seen as a reliable military partner. "Vietnam wants the Soviets to leave," he said:

> It's nonsense for them to stay now. In the past, we were the same society, both socialist. We had a special relationship. The Soviet Union provided military equipment and technology and training. But since Gorbachev said last year that all military supplies had to be paid for in dollars, that relationship ended.[28]

Security and the Asia-Pacific Region

In 1992 Russia formulated a new foreign policy for Southeast Asia and the Asia-Pacific region (APR). This new policy was announced by Foreign Minister Andrei Kozyrev at the post-ministerial conference of the Association of South-East Asian Nations (ASEAN) in Manila in July 1992. It followed a series of provocative Chinese moves in the South China Sea.

Kozyrev proposed a number of confidence-building measures for the APR, including limitations on the scale of naval exercises and restraint in the conduct of such exercises in international straits and areas of intensive navigation and fishing; initiation of a multilateral dialogue on establishing a crisis management system in the region to avert the buildup of military tensions; and negotiations to form an international naval force to provide freedom of navigation. Within the Southeast Asian region, Kozyrev stated Russia's willingness "to develop cooperation in the military and military-technological area with the ASEAN states with the aim of maintaining their security at the level of reasonable sufficiency." He also proposed the transformation of Subic and Cam Ranh "into logistic support centers for naval activities."[29]

Kozyrev's initiative was designed to redefine Russia's role in the APR as a great power by taking advantage of regional concerns about China's future intentions. As such it posed a dilemma for Vietnam. Up until this point Vietnam had been preparing for a Russian departure from Cam Ranh. Plans were afoot to convert the facilities to commercial use. Vietnam was also unsure if a continued Russian military presence would deter China from further land-grabbing in the Spratly archipelago.

Immediately after Kozyrev launched his initiative in Manila, Vice Premier V. A. Makharadze paid the highest-level visit to Vietnam by an official of the Russian government. Makharadze discussed mainly economic and trade issues, but he and members of his entourage also raised military matters.[30] These talks were preceded by discussions in Manila between Kozyrev and his Vietnamese counterpart Nguyen Manh Cam.

The Question of Cam Ranh Bay

Both Kozyrev and Makharadze raised with the Vietnamese the question of a continued Russian naval presence at Cam Ranh Bay. Kozyrev spoke to the press in Manila and went so far as to say that "negotiations had begun," while Makharadze confined the issue to private discussions. Kozyrev made clear that it was Russia's view that Cam Ranh should not be closed "if the Vietnamese agree and other countries in the region take it as a center of stability." He also noted that "we are not necessarily rushing to leave. New terms for preserving the facility will, of course, be determined."[31]

Vietnam reacted negatively to these developments. On August 6, at a regular press conference in Hanoi, spokesperson Ho The Lan when asked by the *Akahata* correspondent to comment on Kozyrev's statement replied, "We have read carefully the official speech of Russian Foreign Minister Kozyrev at the consultative meeting with the ASEAN foreign ministers in Manila on July 22. We found no such passage [proposing that Cam Ranh be transformed into a common base for the ASEAN naval forces] as mentioned by the correspondent, so we have no grounds to make any comment thereupon." When asked by a correspondent of a Japanese news agency to comment on Russia's wish to continue to use the Cam Ranh base[32] she said, "Cam Ranh is a port of Vietnam. Under an agreement reached previously between Vietnam and the former Soviet Union, Vietnam allowed Soviet vessels to enter the port for logistical supply. Nowadays, the situation has changed. Vietnam holds that the two countries should meet to discuss a new agreement suitable to the situation in each country as well as developments in the region and the world. I think the Russian side shares this view."

Foreign Minister Cam denied outright reports that Russia and Vietnam had begun negotiations for a renewed Russian naval presence in Vietnam. Cam stated that since changes in the FSU, "we have not met to discuss a new basis for our relationship. . . . [There is only] an agreement in principle to discuss the issue towards the end of the year [1992]."[33] According to Radio Irina, however, Vietnam and Russia were scheduled to hold talks in Moscow in August, and Vietnam had issued an ultimatum: "either the radio station or the military base."[34]

At the end of the month the Russian ambassador to Vietnam foreshadowed talks later in the year.[35] He said Russia hoped to have continued use of Cam Ranh Bay under "new and different terms." He also reiterated Russia's offer to help Vietnam develop the base into a combined military-civilian facility.

In November 1992 a Russian vice minister for defense paid a quiet visit to Hanoi to initiate discussions on Cam Ranh. Russia proposed that it be permitted to maintain a small military presence at the naval base and that other areas of Cam Ranh Bay could be opened to commercial activity. Russia also offered to pay $US60 million in annual rental, with the sum deducted from Vietnam's outstanding debt of $US10–11 billion. Vietnam countered by demanding hard currency payments of $US360 million a year and rejected commercialization. The meeting proved inconclusive and both parties agreed to meet in Moscow in mid-December.[36]

The December talks were aborted as a result of President Boris Yeltsin's visit to Beijing in mid-month and press reports that Moscow had agreed to arms sales to China valued at $US1.8 billion and including twenty-four Su-27 fighter aircraft.[37] Vietnam, nevertheless, agreed to permit Russia to continue using the naval base at Cam Ranh pending further negotiations. In March 1993, Le Mai, Vietnam's deputy foreign minister, granted a rare interview on the subject of Cam Ranh:

Q: At a meeting of ASEAN foreign ministers in Manila last year, the foreign ministers of Russia and Vietnam reportedly held talks on leasing the military facilities at Cam Ranh Bay to the Russian navy. Can you elaborate on the outcome of the talks?

A: There was a meeting between the Russian and Vietnamese foreign ministers, but there was nothing about an agreement or talks or negotiations about Cam Ranh.

Cam Ranh has always been a Vietnamese military base. In the past, we gave some facilities to the Soviet naval fleet there.

Since then, the situation has changed. The role of military bases all over the world is not as important as in the past. So, that is not much of a priority for discussions between Russia and Vietnam, or between Vietnam and other countries.

Q: But, is the Russian Navy currently leasing the military facilities at the military base at Cam Ranh Bay? Reportedly, the Russian military presence at present has been reduced.

A: We are giving them some facilities, which they are using occasionally.

Q: A top Vietnamese leader was quoted in the press as saying that Vietnam would be willing to offer the military facilities at Cam Ranh Bay to Western countries. Is the offer still open?

A: That appears to be a misquotation. Vietnam's ideas are that the best would be not to have any foreign country using any military base.

Q: Are you saying that it is Vietnam's policy not to have any foreign bases on its soil?

A: Yes, that is our very strict position. We don't want to have any foreign military bases on Vietnamese soil. It is best for small countries like ours not to have foreign military bases on our soil.

That is why Cam Ranh has always been a Vietnamese base, and we are maintaining our sovereignty over that base.

But, I think the best thing to do is turn Cam Ranh into commercial use for economic development.

Q: Has Vietnam developed some ideas about the conversion of Cam Ranh military base for commercial use?

A: Of course, we are talking about that. But you see, it takes some time. For instance, we have several ports such as Danang and Vung Tau, but we do not have enough money to put into these commercial ports.[38]

The issue of Russia's presence at Cam Ranh was raised during the course of Foreign Minister Nguyen Manh Cam's visit to Moscow in October 1993. During discussions, Russian officials informed the Vietnamese of their desire to maintain facilities at Cam Ranh and also to develop unspecified "military cooperation" with Vietnam. Detailed discussions were held the following year during the March visit by General Dao Dinh Luyen, chief of staff of the Vietnam People's Army. General Luyen's delegation was the first publicly announced military visit since the collapse of the Soviet Union. Luyen held discussions with Col. Gen. Mikhail Kolesnikov, chief of the General Staff. The two sides discussed possible cooperation in the maintenance, modernization, and production of military equipment, but no details were made public. The Russian press noted that "in the very near future an agreement on bilateral military and technical cooperation will be signed."[39] The question of Cam Ranh featured again in April 1994 when Deputy Prime Minister Yury Yazov was in Hanoi for economic discussions. The terms of Russia's continued presence at Cam Ranh and the provision of military spares for the Vietnamese army was raised later, during talks between prime ministers Vo Van Kiet and Viktor Chernomyrdin in June 1994. No subsequent announcement has been made that any agreement was reached.

Russia's new interest in prolonging their stay at Cam Ranh Bay and turning over its facilities for commercial use raises difficult questions for Vietnam. On the strategic level, Vietnamese leaders are casting about for a strategy to deal with China. They are concerned about Chinese naval modernization and provocative actions in the Gulf of Tonkin and Spratly

Islands. Cam Ranh Bay houses one important military asset, a functioning signals intelligence (SIGINT) station. This could prove vital to Vietnam in the event of hostilities with China over the Spratly Islands.[40] The SIGINT station has the ability to monitor Chinese communications around Hainan Island, where the South Sea fleet is based.[41]

Western observers believe the SIGINT station is still functional.[42] Cam Ranh also serves as a Net Control Station for other Russian HF (high frequency) DF (direction finding) stations in Vietnam as well as for Vietnamese SIGINT sites. The Russian facilities at Cam Ranh include a satellite communications intercept system, two Fix 24 HF DF antennae, and a Park Drive communications link with Vladivostok and Moscow.

But Vietnamese leaders are reportedly not sanguine about Russia's ability to act as a counterweight to China. Russian public statements have been far from reassuring. For example, Foreign Minister Kozyrev is on record as stating with respect to the Spratly issues that "it is evident that they should be solved by political means. We are encouraged by the idea to start a joint economic development of disputed territories rather than to continue territorial claims."[43] The Russian ambassador was hardly reassuring to the Vietnamese when he stated, "We have to ensure that this question [Spratly Islands] doesn't turn into a conflict. . . . Of course, Russia won't interfere in this question, but it's important that it not become an explosive issue."[44]

Vietnam is also anxious to ensure a continued supply of military equipment and spare parts for its armed forces at affordable prices. As these forces were originally equipped by the Soviet Union, Russia would be the obvious source.[45] But here the issue is complicated by Vietnamese indebtedness to Russia and the poor state of its economy. Vietnam faces the further complication of responding to a Chinese offer to sell arms.[46]

Vietnam has limited bargaining power. Its military is dependent on Russian equipment and systems and needs Russian cooperation if the Vietnam People's Army is to be modernized. Moscow has pointed out that continued Russian military cooperation is essential if Vietnam is to maintain and strengthen its armed forces. Vietnam has responded by pointing out that any future Russian development as a regional power is tied to access to Cam Ranh. One defense journalist has argued that a compromise agreement is likely in which Moscow retains its military presence through at least partial payments in new arms and spare parts.[47] Western intelligence sources have since revealed that following Vo Van Kiet's visit to Russia, Vietnam took possession of two Tarantella-class speed patrol boats for use in the South China Sea.

Finally there are commercial considerations. Cam Ranh is situated in Khanh Hoa Province. Local authorities there have expressed the view that the Russians should leave and that the facilities should be converted to civilian use, benefitting the local economy. Foreign business interests have reportedly proposed constructing a container port. Local Vietnamese economists have called for the base to be converted into a ship repair center but they are presently opposed by the military.[48]

Economic Relations

In 1990 Moscow informed Vietnam that as of January 1991, aid would be drastically curtailed and all commercial relations would be conducted in hard currency at world market prices. Soviet-Vietnamese economic relations deteriorated sharply that year. Economic chaos in the USSR caused Moscow to fall short of its commitments to deliver vital supplies of petroleum, oil, steel, and cotton. This hurt Vietnamese industry, which was dependent on these materials. At the same time, Soviet companies backed out of between 20 to 60 percent of signed contracts to buy Vietnamese shoes, textiles, clothes, handicrafts, and light industrial products. For its part, Vietnam defaulted on at least a quarter of its commitments.

Shortfalls in the supply of fertilizer, for example, led to a decline in rice production. This caused the market price to double. Oil and steel prices nearly trebled, while unemployment and inflation both increased. At the same time, Russia demanded that Vietnam pay dollar salaries for thousands of its experts and technicians on various projects negotiated under past cooperation agreements. Vietnam lacked the cash, and many were forced to return home. The number of Soviet experts stationed in Vietnam dropped from 14,000 in 1989 to 8,000 by mid-1991.

Trade stagnated due to changes in the Soviet political system and government structure and because of the lack of an effective bilateral trade mechanism. In August 1991, Vietnamese officials announced that trade with all socialist countries had fallen to 15 percent of total trade. Trade with the FSU as a percentage of total trade dropped from over 60 percent in the 1980s to 50 percent in 1990 and to a low of 14 percent in 1991. The imbalance shifted from 4:1 in Russia's favor in the mid-1980s to 2:1 in 1990 and came close to parity the following year.

Attempts to place transactions on a hard-currency basis failed and some bilateral payments were made in U.S. dollars while others were made in rubles. In late 1991 the International Monetary Fund estimated the combined impact of the loss of Soviet and Eastern European aid and trade at 7 percent of Vietnam's GDP.[49]

In 1991 both sides attempted to stop the downward trend and to establish relations at a more business-like level. In late January, for example, Vietnam and the USSR signed two agreements, one on trade and another on aid. Under the terms of the former agreement, future trade was to be shifted from the government level to the local level and between individual companies. Trade was to be calculated at international market prices with payment in hard currency. Bilateral trade was to be balanced and the two-way total cut to less than $US1 billion in 1991.

The Soviet aid program was now scaled down to $US100 million in credits and $US10 million in grants.[50] Moscow also sought to recalculate Vietnam's 10 billion ruble debt into hard currency and get Vietnam to pay interest on 6 billion rubles that was due between then and the end of 1995. To soften the blow, the Soviet Union promised a clearing system under which Vietnamese debt at the end of 1991 would be rolled over to 1992.

Forging New Relations

In July, Vietnam and the Soviet Union negotiated an oil agreement. And in August, on the eve of the anti-Gorbachev coup, both sides signed an agreement on economic and commercial relations. Despite these positive developments, domestic chaos forced Moscow to suspend all assistance, including the package agreed to in January. Plans drawn up in the expectation that some aid would be forthcoming now had to be scrapped. According to a Vietnamese economic commentator, "In economic terms 1991 was a critical time for Vietnam. If we survived that year, we can survive anything."[51] In 1993 Russia resumed lending to Vietnam, providing a loan valued at $US40 million to assist in the completion of projects begun before the collapse of the Soviet Union (most notably the Hoa Binh, Vali, and Uong Bi electric power plants, Lao Cao apatite plant, and the Bim Son cement factory). In March 1994, during the course of a visit to Moscow by Le Xuan Trinh (see below), Russia reaffirmed this commitment and extended it to cover a lighting system for Hanoi.

In the aftermath of the dissolution of the Soviet Union, Vietnam moved quickly to limit the damage to its economic relations with Russia. A mission was quickly dispatched to Moscow in order to determine which agreements signed in the past would be honored and to work out new terms where necessary. In April 1992, for example, a delegation of the Vietnam Institute of Sciences paid a working visit to Russia to restore and develop scientific and technical cooperation. A preliminary agreement was reached.[52] Vietnam's minister of science, technology, and the environment paid a working visit to Russia in September 1993. The following month, during the visit to Moscow by Vietnam's foreign minister, an agreement on cultural and scientific cooperation was signed. In mid-1994 it was reported that the two sides had completed their eighteenth joint investigation under the terms of a 1980 agreement that the Russian Federation had agreed to respect.

Vietnam was also understandably concerned to guarantee the future of some 2,000 Vietnamese who were studying or taking graduate courses in twenty universities in different republics of the FSU.[53] As a result of discussions in Hanoi in February 1993, the two countries signed an agreement on cooperation in the field of higher education for 1993–1995. Under its terms Vietnam and Russia agreed to exchange students, staff, and information and to maintain a variety of institutional links.[54] An agreement on academic cooperation between the Russian Academy of Sciences and the Vietnam National Center for Social Sciences was reached in December 1993. It provides for cooperation in training, joint research programs, and the exchange of scientific information.

After the collapse of the USSR, the Russian Federation claimed 80 percent of the debt owed by Vietnam and left it to the other republics to determine their share. Russia also assumed responsibility for obligations entered into by the USSR. For example, in April 1992, Russia and Vietnam signed an agreement to complete the Hoa Binh hydroelectric project.[55] In December, Russian Ambassador R. L. Khamidulin announced that Russia would continue to assist in putting into operation a sixth generator at Hoa Binh by September 1993 and then would proceed to install two additional generators.[56] These commitments were reiterated during the course of Deputy Prime Minister Yury Yarov's visit to Vietnam in May 1993. A year later (April 1994) Yarov presided over a ceremony inaugurating the installation of the eighth and last generator at the Hoa Binh complex. In the meantime, Russian Deputy Premier Alexander Shokhin and Vietnam's minister of power engineering, Thai Fung Ne, agreed to extend cooperation to include Russian involvement in building a new power plant. The Russian side agreed to carry out design work, provide experts, and supply equipment; Vietnam stated it would take charge of construction.[57]

Russia also assumed control of some thirty joint venture partnerships negotiated with Vietnam covering sea foods, gold mining, rubber planting and processing, garments, essential oil, shampoo, molds for car tires, and spectacles, with a total capital investment of $US50 million. A number of new joint ventures were also formed, particularly in sea products. One of the most successful is Ha Long-Primco, located in Nakhodka. This enterprise produces agar-agar, a gelatinous seaweed product used in food industry and in medicines.[58] In September 1992, Vietnam and Russia agreed to jointly explore maritime resources and to develop links between enterprises specializing in sea products.[59] An agreement on cooperation in fishing was signed in June 1994 during the course of Vo Van Kiet's visit to Moscow.

The most successful joint venture is Vietsovpetro, which is engaged in offshore oil exploration in the Bach Ho (White Tiger) field, the only offshore field to produce commercial amounts of oil and gas. In 1991 Vietsovpetro tapped 3.9 million tons of crude oil, a production figure that rose to 5.35 million tons the following year and 6.3 million tons in 1993.[60] In late 1992 an agreement was reached granting the Russian Federation the status of legal successor to the Soviet Union and validating agreements reached in 1991 before the USSR's collapse. This cleared the way for Vietsovpetro to join Petrovietnam, a state-owned company, in a cooperative arrangement with Australia's Broken Hill Petroleum and Petronas Carigali of Malaysia to develop Dai Hung (Big Bear) oil field.[61] The status of Vietsovpetro became an issue in 1993 as Vietnam, increasingly disenchanted with what it felt was outdated and inefficient Russian technology, sought to dissolve the joint venture. This was resisted by Russia, which recognized the value of its involvement in Vietnam's only productive oil field.

Another example of the continuation of past relations is the protocol agreement reached in May 1992 on the status of Vietnamese "guest workers." It has been estimated that as many as 50,000 Vietnamese laborers lived in the USSR when it collapsed,[62] with as many as 32,000 resident in Russia. Russia agreed to safeguard the interests of these workers in conformity with an agreement on labor cooperation signed in 1981. Further, Russia guaranteed conditions for Vietnamese workers to complete their labor contracts and to provide compensation to those workers forced to return to Vietnam before the expiration of their contracts.[63]

The behavior of Vietnamese guest workers as well as racially motivated attacks by individual Russians has become a growing irritant in the bilateral relationship. In December 1992, for example, *Rossiiskie vesti* reported that the Vietnamese accounted for one-third of all criminal offenses committed by foreigners and that nearly half of all convicted foreigners who were imprisoned were Vietnamese.[64] Two Russian academics have provided this assessment:

> The behavior of Vietnamese students and workers in Russia developed into a serious problem, as did their treatment by the Russian populace and authorities. The Vietnamese organized themselves into skillful mafia groups that speculated, smuggled merchandise across the border, stole property, engaged in blackmail, prostitution, and other criminal activities. Gangs of locals retaliated by harassing Vietnamese in different ways, and the police concentrated on driving Vietnamese out of the country.[65]

The issue of Vietnamese workers in Russia has been a continuing source of irritation in Moscow-Hanoi relations. It was the subject of discussions between trade union organizations in August 1993 and during Foreign Minister Nguyen Manh Cam's visit to Russia in October. According to Cam, "Vietnam asked the Russian state and government to take measures to ensure the protection of Vietnamese working or currently on assignment in Russia."[66] The following year the Russian press reported violent clashes between Moscow police and Vietnamese residents and rising resentment against the "guest workers." In May, in a positive vein, the Russian Federal Immigration Agency and the Vietnamese Businessmen's Association reached an agreement on reciprocal employment of each other's nationals. The security and safety of Vietnamese residents in Russia featured in talks between Vo Van Kiet and Viktor Chernomyrdin in June 1994 and was one of the contentious issues that led to a delay in a scheduled document-signing ceremony.

Redefining Economic Relations

The development of economic relations between Vietnam and Russia took a major step forward in July 1992, when Vietnam's Vice Premier Tran Duc Luong led a delegation to Moscow and his Russian counterpart, V. A. Makharadze, paid a return visit. Major agreements were negotiated, including a protocol for 1992 on economic cooperation and barter trade. Total trade volume was targeted to reach $US800 million, split evenly. Both parties agreed to compile a series of documents to be signed in the future, on the principles of cooperation in the fields of investment, taxation, banking, transport, communications, science and technology, and manpower. They also agreed to cooperate in such diverse sectors as fuel, energy, agriculture and food industry, consumer goods, fishery, education and training, communications, and culture.

Immediately after Luong's tour, Russian Vice Premier Makharadze paid a historic visit to Vietnam, where he attended the first meeting of the inter-governmental Commission for Trade, Economic, Scientific and Technological Cooperation. Several major agreements were signed: an addendum to the protocol on goods exchange signed previously in Moscow and cooperation in such areas as science and technology, banking, labor, communications and transport, post and telecommunications, civil aviation, and fishing.[67] The two sides also agreed to sign in future agreements covering investment promotion and protection, avoidance of double taxation, and navigation.

The July exchange visits completely redefined Vietnam's relations with the Russian Federation. Speaking at a Hanoi news conference, Makharadze said that relations between Russia and Vietnam "should not and cannot be built on the old basis, that is, between a big brother and a younger one."[68] Thereafter both sides moved deliberately to refashion their bilateral relations by reviving and encouraging economic links forged in an earlier period, drawing upon the knowledge and expertise of Russians with Vietnamese experience and Vietnamese with Russian experience.

Two subsequent meetings of the inter-governmental Commission for Trade, Economic, Scientific and Technological Cooperation have been held. The second meeting convened in Hanoi on May 24–27, 1993, between the deputy prime ministers of Russia and Vietnam, Yury Yarov and Phan Van Khai. Both sides noted that existing economic relations had not reached their potential and that it would be necessary to encourage direct links between regions and individual enterprises to step up the volume of goods exchanged. Three areas were singled out: energy, agriculture, and consumer goods. The two sides discussed further cooperation in oil and gas extraction and prospecting on Vietnam's continental shelf and specifically committed Vietsovpetro to a drilling operation in the Thanh Long (Soaring Dragon) field.

Yarov noted that Vietnam has consistently met its obligations to supply goods in payment for Vietnam's debts to Russia. He called on Vietnam to accept "non-traditional" methods of repayment, specifically to allow Russia to re-invest the debts owed it in joint enterprises in selected sectors of the economy. Yarov also reaffirmed that Russia would continue to assist in completing projects such as the Hoa Binh plant, built with Soviet aid. Four agreements were signed dealing with air and maritime transportation, avoidance of double taxation, a framework for trade, and banking services.

The third meeting of the inter-governmental commission was also held in Hanoi in April 1994. Russia was once again represented by Yury Yarov. The two sides signed an agreement on cooperation in communications and reached final agreement on an accord to promote investment.

In 1991, apparently as a stopgap measure, Vietnam agreed to begin repaying to the Russian Federation that proportion of debts that it owed to the former Soviet Union. This was confirmed by the Russian ambassador, who announced in late 1992 that Vietnam had begun making repayments on its debts, estimated at 9.67 billion rubles. He said, "Vietnam has stated its readiness to repay its debt. It's a small amount, but the process has begun. That's very important."[69]

According to Russian sources, Vietnam repaid $US45 million in goods in 1991—mainly rubber, vegetables, fruit, coffee, tea, shoes, and carpets. In 1992, Vietnam repaid Russia in goods worth 200 million "dollar-rubles."[70] According to Victor Kozlov, the head of Russian Trade Mission in Hanoi, Vietnamese repayments were small compared to the amount due but represented "an encouraging sign." "The agreed figure for 1992, the obligation by the Vietnamese party, was fulfilled in a good way. They are trying to repay the debt," he noted.[71] Kozlov also revealed, "It is impossible for Vietnam now to pay what is falling due, according to the scheduling. In our opinion, the debt repayment in 1993 will be higher than in 1992, but we will take into account Vietnam's possibilities"[72] Russia also pressed Vietnam to consider "non-traditional" forms of repayment, such as reinvesting its debts in joint enterprises such as rubber plantations.

During the course of Nguyen Manh Cam's visit to Moscow in October it was noted that at the current rate of repayment, by year's end Vietnam would have paid off 500 million rubles in debts since 1991. Repayment was valued in goods and services—food, clothing, other goods, provision of labor, and free rent for office space in Hanoi. It was also revealed that Vietnam owed Russia an additional $US200 million in hard currency, but Russian officials said they expected Vietnam to pay off all credits that had reached full term by the end of the year.[73] In March 1994, Le Xuan Trinh, a senior Vietnamese official, announced that Vietnam had agreed to repay $US110 million in debt, consisting of $US60 million in the form of goods (rice, meat, and clothing) and $US50 million from bank accounts kept by Vietnamese workers in Russia.[74] Russia agreed to commit $40 million in loans (see above). During Vo Van Kiet's historic visit in June 1994, an impasse was reached once again on the vexing question of an appropriate exchange rate for Vietnam's ruble debt. At present, by mutual agreement, Vietnam continues to make repayment "on the basis of its capacity."

The Russian-Vietnamese economic relationship will never be as lopsided or as important as it was in the decade following the 1978 Treaty of Friendship and Cooperation. Trade figures released for 1992 revealed that two-way trade had reached $US260 million, far short of the $US400 million target that had been assigned to each party. Payment was made by letters of credit, as both countries were short of hard currency.[75] The value of two-way trade picked up slightly in 1993 and was valued at $US300 million.[76]

Conclusion

The Soviet-Vietnamese relationship, as symbolized by the 1978 twenty-five-year Treaty of Friendship and Cooperation, was at heart an anti-China alliance. For over a decade it served as the cornerstone of Vietnam's security and foreign policy. With the disintegration of the Soviet Union, Vietnam began to rethink its dependent relationship. When the USSR collapsed Vietnam adopted an "omni-directional" foreign policy, declaring that it wanted to make friends with all countries regardless of social systems.

After the signing of the October 1991 Cambodian peace agreement, Vietnam normalized its relations with China and all six members of the Association of South-East Asian Nations. In July 1992, Vietnam not only attended the twenty-fifth meeting of the ASEAN foreign ministers as an officially invited observer; it also formally acceded to the 1976 Bali treaty. In July 1994, the ASEAN ministers agreed to admit Vietnam as a full member, a development that is expected to occur before the next scheduled ASEAN summit set for late 1995.

Vietnam has rounded out its "omni-directional" foreign policy by making prime ministerial forays into Oceania (Australia and New Zealand) and Europe and by developing robust economic relations with Taiwan, Hong Kong, and South Korea. In the aftermath of the lifting of the U.S. embargo, Vietnam and the United States have agreed to establish liaison offices in each other's capitals.

Relations between Vietnam and the former Soviet Union have been depoliticized and deideologized as a result of the collapse of the USSR. The downward slide in relations has been halted and traditional economic and commercial ties are being restored. These are now being forged on a more pragmatic basis. The question of debt repayment and the status of Vietnamese residents in Russia, however, remain major stumbling blocks.

Military relations between Russia and Vietnam, including a continued Russian naval presence at Cam Ranh Bay and the sale of equipment and hardware, are the subject of ongoing discussions. The durability of Russian-Vietnamese ties will depend on Moscow's ability to maintain political stability, continue the trade relationship without disruption, and prevent the mistreatment of ethnic Vietnamese from becoming a major issue. The former Soviet Union no longer looms as large in political, economic, or military terms in the eyes of Hanoi as it once did. Nevertheless, Russia, as a member of the UN's Security Council and a major player in the Asia-Pacific region, is important to Vietnam in its own right. Russia views Vietnam as a possible stepping stone back into the Southeast Asian regional economy and as a key country in any new Asian security arrangements likely to emerge following the inaugural meeting of the ASEAN Regional Forum in July 1994.

Notes

1. General Hoang Van Thai, "Ve Quan He Hop Tac Dac Biet Giua Ba Dan Toc Dong Duong," *Tap Chi Cong San* 1, January 1982, pp. 17–24.

2. For background to this period see Ramesh Thakur and Carlyle A. Thayer, *Soviet Relations with India and Vietnam, 1945–1992*, Delhi, Oxford University Press, 1993, which is an updated version of the co-author's *Soviet Relations with India and Vietnam*, London, Macmillan, 1992.

3. Carlyle A. Thayer, "The Soviet Union and Indochina," in Roger E. Kanet, Deborah Nutter Miner, and Tamara J. Resler, eds., *Soviet Foreign Policy in Transition*, Cambridge, Cambridge University Press, 1992, pp. 236–55.

4. Carlyle A. Thayer, "Kampuchea: Soviet Initiatives and Regional Responses," in Ramesh Thakur and Carlyle A. Thayer, eds., *The Soviet Union as an Asian Pacific Power: Implications of Gorbachev's 1986 Vladivostok Initiative*, Boulder, Westview Press, 1987, pp. 171–200, and Carlyle A. Thayer, "Prospects for Peace in Kampuchea: Soviet Initiatives and Indochinese Responses," *Indonesian Quarterly*, vol. 17, no. 2, 1989, pp. 157–72.

5. Vo Van Kiet used the expression "some mistrust" during his June 1994 visit to Russia; ITAR-TASS news agency reported by World Service, Moscow, June 10, 1994. The expression "pause" was used by various Russian spokesmen including Deputy Prime Minister Y. Yarov during the course of a visit to Vietnam; ITAR-TASS, reported by World Service, Moscow, April 15, 1994, and Reuters, Hanoi, June 8, 1994.

6. Eugene Bazhanov and Natasha Bazhanov, "Russia and Asia in 1992: A Balancing Act," *Asian Survey*, vol. XXXIII, no. 1, January 1993, pp. 100–101.

7. Carlyle A. Thayer, "Civil Society and the Soviet-Vietnamese Alliance," in Chandran Kukathas, David W. Lovell, and William Maley, eds., *The Transition from Socialism: State and Civil Society in the USSR*, London, Longman, 1991, p. 215.

8. *Straits Times*, June 22, 1991.

9. *Far Eastern Economic Review (FEER)*, May 30, 1991, p. 8.

10. Based on discussions with knowledgeable sources in Hanoi in November 1991. See also Kathleen Callo, Reuters, Hanoi, October 14, 1992.

11. The others were the Lao People's Revolutionary Party (LPRP), the Khmer People's Revolutionary Party (KPRP) and the Communist Party of Cuba. The permanent representative of the Japan Communist Party in Hanoi also attended.

12. I attended this meeting.

13. Discussion held in Kuala Lumpur with a senior fellow at the Institute for Far Eastern Studies, Academy of Sciences, May 1992.

14. Agence France Press (AFP), July 14, 1992.

15. Reuters, Hanoi, *Business Times* Singapore, September 9, 1993, and *International Herald Tribune*, September 23, 1993.

16. John Rogers, Reuters, Hanoi, April 19, 1993; for background on the document see Thomas W. Lippman, "A Researcher's Dream Find on U.S. POWs Turns into a Nightmare," *The Washington Post*, April 25, 1993.

17. Viktor Pritula, *Pravda*, June 30, 1993.

18. Reuter, Hanoi and Vietnam News Agency, August 27, 1992.

19. *FEER*, December 3, 1992, p. 6.

20. Vietnam News Agency (VNA),January 9 and 15, 1993.

21. Remarks by Vo Van Kiet to correspondents enroute back to Hanoi; Voice of Vietnam, Hanoi, June 18, 1994.

22. AFP, April 22, 1991.

23. *Komsomolskaia pravda*, October 17, 1990.

24. Kathleen Callo, Reuters, *Nation* and *Sunday Times*, February 23, 1992.

25. Peter Wilson-Smith, Reuters, Cam Ranh, August 13, 1992; Reuters dispatch

from Cam Ranh, *The Jakarta Post*, August 14, 1992. BBC, Dateline East Asia August 27, 1992, in Singapore, *Foreign Broadcast Monitor*, 198/92, August 27, 1992, p. 4. A 1,000 figure was provided by Russian Ambassador Khamidulin, but he was unsure of the number because it changed often. A Vietnamese naval lieutenant estimated that the number of Russians could be as low as 400–500.

26. Reuters, Cam Ranh, *Jakarta Post*, August 14, 1992; William Branigin, *Washington Post*, September 9, 1991.

27. *FEER*, June 4, 1992, p. 9.

28. Kathleen Callo, Reuters, Cam Ranh, *Nation* (Bangkok), and *Sunday Times* (Singapore), February 23, 1992.

29. ITAR-TASS, Moscow World Service, July 22, 1992.

30. Based on discussions in Hanoi in July 1992.

31. AFP, Manila, July 22, 1992; and Cameron Stewart, Manila, *Australian*, July 23, 1992.

32. VNA in English, 1451 MT, August 6, 1992.

33. In October 1992 a well-placed Vietnamese source, quoting a Russian Embassy official, told the author that an unannounced Russian military delegation had arrived in Hanoi that month to open negotiations.

34. Russian Radio in Russian, August 4, 1992.

35. Reuters, Hanoi, *The Nation* and *The Straits Times*, August 28, 1992, and VNA, August 27, 1992.

36. Robert Karniol, "Trade Dispute Halts Cam Ranh Talks," *Jane's Defence Weekly*, March 20, 1993, p. 12.

37. Karniol, "Trade Dispute Halts Cam Ranh Talks."

38. Harish Mehta interview with Le Mai, vice foreign minister, *Business Times*, March 10, 1993.

39. ITAR-TASS quoted by Radio Mayak, March 2, 1994.

40. Robert Karniol, "Russia Seeks to Keep SIGINT Link," *Jane's Defence Weekly*, September 12, 1992, p. 27.

41. Reuters, Hanoi, *Nation*, and *Straits Times*, August 28, 1992.

42. Robert Karniol, "Russia Seeks to Keep SIGINT Link," and Derek da Cunha, "Signals Intelligence Keeps Ties Between Russia, Vietnam Going," *The Straits Times*, October 14, 1992.

43. Dispatch from Manila, *Straits Times*, July 23, 1992.

44. Reuters, Hanoi, and VNA, August 27, 1992.

45. A knowledgeable Russian source told the author in May 1992 that the Russian Foreign Ministry had agreed to continue selling arms to Vietnam provided that a mutually acceptable form of payment could be worked out.

46. Jacques Bekaert interviewed on BBC, Dateline East Asia, July 31, 1992, in Singapore, *Foreign Broadcast Monitor* 176/92, August 1, 1992, pp. 8–9.

47. Karniol, "'Trade Dispute Halts Cam Ranh Talks."

48. "Staying On," *FEER*, January 21, 1993, p. 9.

49. Data to this point in this section are found inInternational Monetary Fund, *Vietnam—Recent Economic Developments*, December 5, 1991, p. 1. See also *Nhan Dan*, July 25, 1992.

50. Murray Hiebert, "Deeper in the Red," *FEER*, February 21, 1991, p. 46.

51. Barry Wain, "Vietnam Weathers Economic Transition," *Asian Wall Street*

Journal, August 3, 1992.

52. VNA, May 4, 1992.

53. Xuan Chinh, "How do Vietnamese Workers Fare in the CIS?" *Sunday Vietnam News*, 351, July 19, 1992, p. 5.

54. ITAR-TASS, Hanoi, February 18, 1993.

55. Dispatch from Hanoi, *Business Times* (Singapore), May 2–3, 1992.

56. VNA, December 10,1992.

57. RIA News Agency, Moscow, January 12, 1993.

58. *Voice of Vietnam Network* in Vietnamese 2300 GMT, September 28, 1992, and ECO-TASS, October 26, 1992.

59. Agreement was reached during the visit to Russia by a delegation from the Ministry of Aquatic Products led by Minister Nguyen Tan Trinh. Trinh met with V. P. Korenskii, chairman of the Commission for Fisheries of Russian Federation. VNA, September 28, 1992.

60. VNA, December 25, 1992, and May 4, 1994.

61. Radio Australia, December 29, 1992.

62. Kawi Chongkitthawon, *The Nation*, January 11, 1992; Sophie Quinn-Judge, "Cash 'n Carry Cadres," *FEER*, May 21, 1992, pp. 32–33. According to another source, the figure for Vietnamese residents in Russia ranges from 50,000–100,000, of whom about 16,000 are workers. Their contracts are due to expire in 1995; see, Jeffrey Lilley, "In Capitalist Clothes," *FEER*, June 10, 1993, p. 60. A later estimate places the total number of Vietnamese at 200,000 "due to illegal immigration"; see: AFP, Hanoi, *The Jakarta Post*, November 2, 1993.

63. VNA, October 2, 1992.

64. Quoted by Associate Press (AP), Moscow, *The Straits Times*, December 5, 1992.

65. Bazhanov and Bazhanov, "Russia and Asia in 1992: A Balancing Act."

66. AFP, Hanoi, *The Jakarta Post*, November 2, 1993.

67. *Voice of Vietnam*, July 31, 1992.

68. *Sunday Vietnam News*, 365(16), August 2, 1992, p. 1.

69. Reuters, Hanoi, December 10, 1992.

70. "Dollar-ruble" is an accounting term used by Vietnam and the former Soviet Union. Vietnam's ten billion ruble debt to the former Soviet Union is in "convertible rubles" which was valued at more than one U.S. dollar when it was in circulation. It ceased to exist in 1992.

71. Quoted by Kathleen Callo, Reuters, Hanoi, January 12, 1993.

72. Kathleen Callo, Reuters, Hanoi, January 12, 1993.

73. John Rogers, Reuters, Hanoi, October 27, 1993, citing the Russian trade representative in Hanoi.

74. Reuters, Hanoi, March 7, 1994.

75. *Lao Dong*, September 3, 1992.

76. Voice of Vietnam, Hanoi, June 15, 1994.

11

Russian Policy Toward India: A Relationship on Hold

Ramesh Thakur

Our states' fundamental interests coincide. Both our countries firmly adhere to democratic principles. Both our countries deeply wish to ensure that beneficial tendencies in today's world do not go into reverse. Both our countries are equally interested in strengthening each other's stability and territorial integrity. And we firmly and unswervingly support India's position on Kashmir.
—President Boris Yeltsin in a speech to the
Indian parliament, January 29, 1993[1]

Relations that developed between India and the Soviet Union from the mid-1950s onward were broad, deep, and durable.[2] In the 1990s India has to deal with a Russia that is Eurocentric, economically dependent on Western largesse, with neither the interest nor the resources to give aid to poorer countries. Russia's new friendships will be guided by calculations of commercial profits rather than political gains. Reflecting Russia's new foreign-policy goals, Yeltsin's administration lacks an India orientation: not one member of the Yeltsin delegation visiting India in January 1993 had been there previously.[3]

In this chapter I examine the impact of the breakup of the Soviet Union on Russia's relations with India. The intimacy of the Indo-Soviet relationship had been based on conjunctions of political, military, and economic interests. In approaching relations with India through the distorting prism of the history of Soviet relations with the Third World, the new leaders of Russia lost sight of the distinctive features of past Soviet relations with India, the balance of advantages to both countries in the previous relationship, and the possibilities of establishing a mutually advantageous balance in the new international order.

The same point was made by Ruslan Khasbulatov, then speaker of the Russian parliament and political rival of President Boris Yeltsin, after leading a fifteen-strong parliamentary delegation to India in August 1992. Interviewed on Russian television on August 13 upon his return to Moscow, Khasbulatov observed that India was unique in having had "very correct relations" with the former Soviet Union: "Relations were harmonious, relations were deep, relations were, frankly speaking, cordial, very good." Therefore, attempts to revise relations with India were "completely unacceptable" not just to Russia but also to the other former Union republics.[4] By January 1993 the Yeltsin government too had apparently come around to this point of view. The speech quoted at the start of this chapter could just as easily have been made by Mikhail Gorbachev in the heyday of the old Indo-Soviet relationship.

Yet there is no doubt that the breakup of the Soviet Union in 1991 had the potential to cause serious damage to the hitherto healthy relationship between Moscow and New Delhi. I shall argue that in the new international disorder (1) some previously convergent interests between Moscow and New Delhi have dissipated and (2) there is potential for a clash of some redefined interests. But in addition, (3) some previous differences have now disappeared, (4) some interests that were common have survived the transition to the new era and (5) fresh complementarities are also emerging. For the time being, though, the relationship is probably best described as having been put on hold, as both countries confront a continuing circle of crises of more pressing urgency.

Fading Conjunctions

In the 1980s Moscow began to reassess the costs and risks of opportunities for further penetrations in the Third World. Benefits were uncertain, gains remained elusive, but the cost was substantial. Soviet statements and writings dwelt upon three sets of concerns: the escalating costs of supporting Third World clients, the dubious political and economic records of many of these clients, and the damage caused by links to unsavory regimes to other Soviet interests, in particular to U.S.-USSR relations.

Russia's leaders concluded that a major contributor to the economic impoverishment of the FSU had been its rate of military buildup. Military links with Third World countries had also alarmed the West. For both reasons, defense was reined in as an instrument of foreign policy. The Soviet Union acquired a dominant position among India's major arms suppliers in the 1960s and maintained it until its demise in 1991. The disintegration of the Soviet Union therefore had a deleterious effect on the military relationship between Moscow and New Delhi.

In the 1950s Soviet policy was driven by the desire to resist Western efforts at encircling the Soviet Union with a ring of military pacts; in the efforts at encircling the Soviet Union with a ring of military pacts; in the 1960s and 1970s the main Soviet motive was containment of the People's Republic of China. In both cases, the emergence of a regionally dominant India was in the Soviet interest "as a counterbalance to the USA and China."[5] Soviet concerns about checking U.S. alliances and containing Chinese influence dovetailed with the Indian foreign policy of nonalignment. Each concern is now largely irrelevant. After the failed coup of August 1991 the Soviet Union collapsed into a collection of impoverished states. In the new international situation, Russia attached higher priority to relations with the United States than with former Third World clients, including India.

A similar change took place in India's relations with the United States. Four factors transformed the basis of the relationship between India and the United States and brought forth the promise of greater harmony: the end of the Cold War, the start of a new cooperative relationship between Moscow and Washington, Moscow's withdrawal from Afghanistan, and the resulting downgrading of Pakistan's strategic and political importance to the United States. A flurry of high-level defense visits in both directions culminated in joint India-U.S. naval exercises in May 1992. Both India and Russia have also greatly improved relations with Beijing.

The end to major power rivalries has had another odd effect on the foundations of the Moscow–New Delhi relationship. The end of the Cold War empties the concept of nonalignment of any substantial meaning.[6] India has lost a major ideological value as an exemplar of good relations between the leading socialist regime and a leading Third World country. Nor should we discount the importance of the demonstration effect of Soviet marketing success in India. According to a senior Soviet official, Indo-Soviet relations were an example of cooperation between socialism and Third World nationalism: "The close and diversified economic ties between the USSR and India are helping to break down capitalism's international technological monopoly."[7] (In a delicious irony, the Soviet daily *Izvestiia* blamed the economic crisis afflicting India in 1991 on an economic system based on socialism, autarky, and protectionism.)[8]

Following Stalin's death in 1953 India became the Soviet Union's largest developing-country trading partner. The economic relationship between India and the USSR was dynamic and multifaceted. In entering into economic links with India, the Soviet Union had sought to erode Western influence, export the socialist-Soviet model of development to a leading Third World country, and secure an outlet for its own expanding economy. India was a reliable partner in economic cooperation, never having defaulted on credit repayments. Indo-Soviet cooperation permitted reliable acquisition, on soft terms, of machinery and equipment needed for the development of the Soviet economy.

These advantages notwithstanding, Soviet trade with India plateaued in the 1980s, and problems mounted in Indo-Soviet trade relations during 1991. Russia continued to import Indian goods prices in rupees, and India continued to maintain its delivery schedules. But many Soviet enterprises let India run short of items for which it had become reliant on Soviet suppliers; parts from the FSU often failed to reach India's construction sites. The bilateral trade gap widened even further with the collapse of international oil prices in the mid-1980s. The problems in Indo-Soviet trade had mounted to such an extent that India's Ministry of Commerce took some radical measures to control exports to the Soviet Union. India closed trading accounts with the Soviet Union on December 28, 1991, and new accounts were opened in the name of the new CIS republics. By January 1992, Moscow owed $1 billion in technical credits to India.[9] A commentator noted on Russian TV on May 3, 1992, that Moscow was not only leaving friends in the lurch but also creating an image as an unreliable trade partner. By contrast, India had managed to find $5 million worth of humanitarian aid for the FSU.[10]

Oil deliveries to India from the FSU fell short by $1.5 billion in 1991,[11] as a result of which technical credits declined.[12] President Yeltsin explained during his visit to India in January 1993 that the main reason for the disruption to oil deliveries was the UN sanctions on Iraq. Oil had previously been trans-shipped via Iraq because direct shipment from Russia to India entailed prohibitive transportation costs. Therefore, India investigated the possibility of using Saudi Arabia or the United Arab Emirates as an alternative re-exporter.[13] The problems affecting oil deliveries were exacerbated by the fact that the most convenient port for shipping Russian oil to India was Odessa in Ukraine, which is now independent.

Fresh Disjunctions

The demise of the USSR has created fresh difficulties between Russia and India. For example, Moscow's search for widened international trading relationships will put India in direct competition with any number of other Third World countries for the same products. Indian interests as an aid recipient had converged with Soviet interests as an aid donor. In particular, Moscow was the most important source of assistance to the large public sector in India. With the collapse of the Soviet Union and the economic chaos characterizing the successor states, India and Russia found themselves competing for scarce resources in the world's capital markets.

The Gulf War offered three lessons for Indian defense policy that were inimical to the Delhi-Moscow military relationship: the previous history of uninterrupted delivery of Soviet arms during a war is no assurance of continued deliveries in future conflicts, Soviet war-fighting doctrines have critical flaws, and the technological gap between Soviet and U.S. weapon systems is widening to dangerous dimensions for Indian security.

In the new era of U.S.-Russian cooperation on nuclear disarmament, Moscow attached greater importance to nonproliferation objectives than it had previously. The disincentives to public disagreement with India on the Non-Proliferation Treaty (NPT) and a South Asian nuclear-weapons-free zone (NWFZ) were removed. Russia joined the West in putting pressure on India to renounce the nuclear option and stabilize the nuclear-free status of South Asia. In November 1991, Russia caused consternation in India by supporting a joint Pakistani-Bangladeshi NWFZ resolution in the Disarmament Committee of the UN General Assembly.

Outstanding problems in the Indo-Soviet relationship include the rupee-ruble exchange rate and the related issue of repayment of previous credits. The old ruble-rupee arrangements had enabled India to purchase Soviet arms without expending hard currency. But Soviet authorities tended to apply double standards in establishing dollar values for ruble-rupee currency transactions. In an agreement signed in 1978, the value of the ruble was fixed at a "final" rate for the purpose of calculating India's debt to the USSR. The rupee has depreciated steadily since then, effectively multiplying the debt. For years, India argued that the terms of the 1978 agreement were being unfairly applied, penalizing it for the international weakness of the rupee without a matching penalty for the ruble.

A Russian delegation visiting India in May 1992 insisted that the total sum of payments could not be readjusted on the basis of the current ruble-dollar exchange rate.[14] The larger issue was the Russian objective of moving away from any political underpinning of its external trade and placing it on a commercial basis without incurring any financial costs of commercialization of its international economic relationships. India saw no reason to exempt the rupee-ruble exchange rate from commercial calculations. With the weakness of the ruble being officially recognized in 1992, the balance of negotiating power shifted to India.

Both Russia and India understood that "the 1978 exchange rate does not reflect the current economic realities at all."[15] The value of the ruble fell to 250 rubles to the dollar in September 1992, 350 in October, and 570 by the time of Yeltsin's visit to India in January 1993. Against the rupee, the 1978 protocol had fixed the value of the ruble at 31 rupees; while Yeltsin was in Delhi, the real value of the ruble was 10 paise (one tenth of a rupee). Yeltsin said it was a principal item of discussion during his visit.[16] It was agreed that the calculations of the applicable exchange rate would be based on the rate existing on January 1, 1990. The agreement gave a 32 percent net advantage to India. First Vice-Premier Vladimir Shumeiko explained that India would repay 230 billion rubles over twelve years in rupees and the remainder of 140 billion rubles in interest-free installments spread over forty-five years.[17] Yeltsin acknowledged that the outcome was not fully satisfactory from Russia's point of view. Instead, it "is a compromise" that "is not to the detriment of Russian interests." This was especially so because India at least paid its debts.[18]

Dissipating Disjunctions

If previously convergent interests between Moscow and New Delhi have begun to diverge and new competitive interests have come to the fore, then the reverse is also true. The Indo-Soviet relationship was an ideological misfit from the start. The double mismatch—of a parliamentary democracy and a communist regime, and a mixed economy and a command economy—has now been removed. In his address to the Indian parliament on January 29, 1993, Yeltsin remarked that India's experience had proven that democracy is not restricted to European civilizations, that freedom, democracy, and human rights are universal values. "India is the world's major democratic federative state," he said, and its "experience of constructive interaction between all branches of power" is of great importance to Russia.[19] At a press conference on the same day, Yeltsin reiterated that India is one of the outposts of democracy in Asia and the Pacific.[20]

Similarly, Yeltsin acknowledged that the Indian model of a mixed economy is also of great practical interest to Russia. India had chosen to fuse various forms of state ownership and free enterprise and to harness old traditions as well as imported modern ways. Experience of reform had already convinced Yeltsin that Russia too would have to establish an appropriate mix of economic principles and systems, bearing in mind that the people had forgotten the meaning of private property and political pluralism.

Enduring Complementarities

India's support for a range of international Soviet initiatives was useful diplomatically because of India's influential role in world affairs. Trade between India and the USSR was substantial and genuine, not a disguised subsidy as with so many Third World clients. Militarily, India was not an object of international opprobrium, as were Vietnam and Iraq for using Soviet-supplied weapons to invade and occupy a neighboring country. India was one of a few clients privileged enough to have been given state-of-the-art armaments. The Soviet practice of permitting India to manufacture Soviet-sourced military equipment under license too was notable for its rarity. Soviet weapons involved in action in Third World conflicts have sometimes been alleged to have performed poorly. Soviet weaponry in Indian hands was useful to Moscow in demonstrating the weapons' effectiveness in a Third World context.

Yet by 1990 there was a perceptible end-of-era sense about the Indo-Soviet relationship. There was "much anguish" in India as a result of the post-glasnost critical attention in the Soviet media to Indian opposition to the NPT, the lease of a Soviet nuclear-propelled submarine to India (which has since been returned), soft-currency trade and debt repayment arrangements, and the fragility of the Indian government.[21]

India's pusillanimous response to the 1991 coup could have contributed to the Yeltsin administration's perception of India as just another Third World client of the old Soviet Union. When Mikhail Gorbachev was a prisoner of party hard-liners, Prime Minister P. V. Narasimha Rao delivered lectures in India's parliament about the instructive example of over-enthusiastic reformers. The restoration of constitutional authority in Moscow was hailed in the Indian parliament on August 23 by unanimous euphoria. One member attacked the official response as "blinkered timidity and ineptitude"; another confessed that "our heads hang in shame before the people of the Soviet Union."[22] This mattered because the Yeltsin government of successor-state Russia remembered who had stood up to be counted and who had stayed on the sidelines.

The disappearance of the Soviet Union created a vacuum for Indian foreign policy, a problem that was alleviated by ongoing friendly feelings between the countries. A Soviet scholar had argued in 1990 that to jeopardize a tried and tested friendship with India would be "stupid, fallacious, and short-sighted."[23] Among many Indians too there remains a matching goodwill toward a country that stood by them through good times and bad and that is now experiencing its hour of need. In the winter of 1990–1991, India sent a million tons of wheat as a loan and 20,000 tons of rice as a gift to a Soviet Union facing severe food shortages: "the least that it can do for a staunch friend and unwavering ally of long standing," said a major Indian newspaper.[24] In 1992 an elder statesman among Indian commentators noted that "the afterglow of four decades of Indo-Soviet friendship is still to be found in Russia, Kazakhstan, the Ukraine and several other republics of the Commonwealth [of Independent States]."[25] In 1993 Yeltsin himself acknowledged in Delhi that the peoples and politicians of India and Russia "have a great accumulated wealth of political goodwill and diplomatic traditions."[26]

Just as India was caught off balance in adjusting to the changed political reality in Moscow, so a rapid restructuring of the economic relationship would cause painful dislocations in both countries. Protective measures were needed, therefore, to insulate the Indo-Russian relationship from the full blast of international competition. The first ever rupee-payment trade protocol between India and Russia was signed on February 22, 1992.[27] On May 4, they signed a five-year trade and economic cooperation agreement according most-favored-nation (MFN) treatment to each other. They agreed to look for mutually advantageous solutions to all outstanding problems and to make all payments in freely convertible currencies unless otherwise specified. A second agreement was signed on the establishment of an intergovernmental commission on trade, economic, scientific, and technical cooperation. Russia would renew the export of oil, newsprint, and military equipment. India would open a 2.5 billion rupee technical credit for exporting tea, coffee, tobacco, and spices.[28] In other words, both the structure (bilateral framework agreements) and substance (the products being traded) of economic exchange between Moscow and New Delhi marked a continuity from the days of the Soviet period.

India as a Major Player in Asia

A second measure of permanence in Delhi-Moscow relations lies in the geopolitical underpinning of Russia's diplomatic activity in Asia. The Yeltsin-Kozyrev combine seemed to launch Russia's foreign policy with a Western orientation. Peter Shearman has conceptualized Russian interests in terms of three concentric circles comprising the former Union republics, the West, and the Third World.[29] Initially consigned to an insignificant role on the periphery of Russia's foreign policy, the third circle regained visibility during 1992. When President Boris Yeltsin and Foreign Minister Andrei Kozyrev did begin to focus more sharply on their Asian neighbors, the London *Economist* produced a tortuous argument on why the shift to Asia should not be interpreted as a threat to Western interests.[30] An article by Elina Nikolayeva in *Moskovskii komsomolets* on January 30, 1993, ridiculed a similarly blinkered news report on the BBC for highlighting the problems of India's debt to Moscow ("poor, poor Russia!") and arms sales to India ("bad, bad Russia!").[31]

By virtue of size, location, military power, and economic potential, India is and will remain a major Asian player. The three giants of Asia are China, Japan, and India. China is more influential internationally than India, larger in size, more populous, with an enviable economic growth record over the past dozen years. It is also a permanent member of the UN Security Council. Japan's rise as a global player of the first order and the preeminent player in the Asia-Pacific has been phenomenal.

Both China and Japan are more crucial than India to Russia from a security and an economic point of view. But Russia's search for normalized relations has been more successful with China than with Japan.[32] Geopolitics ensures that Russia, China, and Japan will keep alternating between the poles of cooperation and conflict. By contrast, there is neither a history of, nor any realistic potential for, military or territorial conflict between India and Russia. This was noted by Yeltsin at a joint press conference with Narasimha Rao in New Delhi on January 29, 1993.[33]

India's importance began to register with the new Russian administration as its foreign policy attention shifted from the Atlantic to Asian-Pacific horizons. When I. K. Gujral was selected as India's ambassador to the USSR in 1976, he had an interesting briefing session with Prime Minister Indira Gandhi. Gandhi asked him to bear in mind that India was indispensable to the Soviet Union for its Asian diplomacy.[34] The crisis of confidence afflicting Indo-Russian relations in 1991–1992 threatened to reverse decades of patient work. A report on Russian TV on May 8, 1992, noted that if Moscow stopped supplying India with military items, the U.S. and its NATO allies would quickly fill the vacuum. The discussions on joint Indo-U.S. naval exercises were "a threat to Russia's geopolitical interests in South Asia, the more so as we have seriously weakened our positions in other regions."[35]

Before, during, and after his visit to India in January 1993, Yeltsin, playing on Indian sensibilities, sought to convince his hosts that Russia's western-oriented foreign policy did not mean that Moscow could ignore Asia and the Pacific. The initial focus on the West, he said, arose from the urgent need to achieve substantial nuclear disarmament in order to enhance global security. Now that nuclear weapons had been cut, Russia's policy was "equally balanced between West and East." Russia was a Eurasian country, with 10 million sq km of its 17 million sq km total territory lying in Asia. Russia, he said, was very conscious of this fact.[36] Having put relations with the United States on an even keel, Russia was turning its attention eastward. "No strong eastern policy is possible without India or without taking into consideration India's interests, its global weight and its authority," said Yeltsin at a press conference in New Delhi on January 29, 1993.[37]

Emerging Complementarities

The stability of the Indo-Soviet relationship was partly attributable to the long reigns of Jawaharlal Nehru, Nikita Khrushchev, Leonid Brezhnev, and Indira Gandhi. Mikhail Gorbachev and Rajiv Gandhi tried to give fresh momentum to a flagging relationship.[38] In 1991, Gorbachev lost his country and his office, and Gandhi lost his life. It took time for the new leaders at the helms of the Russian and Indian ships of state to acclimatize to the choppy waters of the new international relations. Once they did, they realized that it still made sense to coordinate their actions in order to ensure a smoother passage for both ships of state.

There is scope for a more genuine economic partnership between Moscow and New Delhi than in the past. At the press conference in Delhi on January 29, 1993, Yeltsin acknowledged that India had achieved great successes in many spheres over the previous few decades. Consequently, Russia was now ready "to cooperate with India as before—cooperate, not assist. This terminology is new and of fundamental importance."[39]

In January 1992 India agreed to grant 32 billion rupees worth of technical credits to Russia to pay for Indian goods;[40] the credits would be repaid with Russian oil, petrochemicals, and fertilizers. India also decided to open a special "tea representation" in Moscow as the base from which to seek market penetration in other former union republics.[41] In November 1991, the Indian deputy commerce minister said that rupee settlements in India's trade with the CIS would terminate in 1994–1995. After that date, India intended to build its economic relations with the sovereign republics on the principles of a market economy.[42]

Both India and Russia are struggling to achieve economic success by means of a market-oriented liberalizing economy functioning within a multiethnic, multiparty competitive federal democracy. The basis of the Indo-Soviet economic relationship lay in the degree to which Soviet capabilities had matched Indian needs. The two economies were mutually compatible. With increasing sophistication and modernization of the Indian economy, this situation began to chagnge and structural adjustments became necessary in the Indo-Soviet economic relationship but proved painfully difficult to implement. However, a modernized, dynamic, and vibrant Indian economy could prove even more useful to post-Soviet Russia developing a market economy. Success for Russia in its quest to forge closer links with Western economies could also turn ameliorate the growing gap between the needs and stages of the Indian and Russian economies. If economic reforms succeed in bringing prosperity to Russia, then of course it can re-emerge as a great power. Should that be the case, then a new entente could be re-established between a Russia and India no longer divided along ideological lines.

Islamic Fundamentalism

Changing international relationships have brought India and Russia closer to the United States on some issues. Interests that they have in common include the promotion of pluralist democracy and a market economy, opposition to terrorism and drug trafficking, avoidance of an India-Pakistan war, and establishment of peaceful and secure borders. Parallel interests on land are reinforced by convergent interests at sea. All three countries have a stake in ensuring freedom of the high seas, safety of the sea lanes of communication around the entire rim of the Indian Ocean from Africa to Indochina, and peace and stability around the Indian Ocean littoral.

They are also united in opposition to fundamentalist religious and other ethnic movements. Part of the reason for India's relatively soft reaction to the Soviet invasion of Afghanistan was a shared fear of Islamic revivalism in a proximate region. These fears have by no means abated in the changed regional and international situation. India and Russia share an interest in moderating the resurgent fundamentalism of Islam, which could threaten the secular identity and territorial integrity of both states.

During a visit to India in January 1992, U.S. Senator Larry Pressler warned of the possibility of a threat from the confederation of nine Islamic states: five republics of the FSU (Azerbaijan, Kazakhstan, Kyrgyzstan, Tajikistan, and Uzbekistan) and Afghanistan, Iran, Pakistan, and Turkey.[43] Even short of the spread of Islamic fundamentalism, Russia, India, and the United States share an interest in stabilizing the situation in the interconnected regions of Afghanistan and Central Asia. Guerrillas seeking to infiltrate from Afghanistan into Tajikistan or vice versa continue to cause incidents along the border, and Russian troops have become progressively more involved in protective duties in Tajikistan.

Developments in Central Asia and Afghanistan concerned India first because of the damaging aftereffects of the disintegration of the Moscow-New Delhi axis, second because of the desire to counter Pakistan's rising influence, third because of the goal of containing the spread of Islamic consciousness, and fourth because of the need to insulate Muslim-majority Kashmir from the turmoil to the north. Indian responses to the ferment in Central Asia were shaped not simply by calculations of present geopolitical realities and fears of importing religious turbulence but also by memories of historical invasions of the subcontinent from the north.

Governmental authority has crumbled completely in Afghanistan, with former mujahideen groups engaged in a bitter civil war. If Afghanistan unravels, turbulence will spread into proximate Kashmir and add to the difficulties of the Indian government. The border between Afghanistan and Central Asia is porous and the conflicts in the region involve ethnic groups spread across several political frontiers. The ongoing conflicts also threaten the safety and welfare of large numbers of Russians left stranded in the Central Asian republics with the breakup of the Soviet Union.

Military Ties

Central Asia, and in particular the disturbed situation in Tajikistan, figured on the agenda of discussions between the two countries' defense ministers during Sharad Pawar's week-long visit to Russia in September 1992.[44] This meeting symbolized the successful restoration of ties between Moscow and New Delhi. There remains a complementarity of interests between Russia as an arms seller and India as an arms purchaser. The question of spare parts became especially acute for India's fleet of MiG-29s in early 1992. MiGs account for about three-quarters of the Indian Air Force (IAF). India was confronted with uncertainty about the CIS republics' ability and willingness to continue supplying spare parts to the IAF.

In May 1992, Russia's Economy Minister Andrei Nechayev said that India wanted Russia to continue providing defense supplies in return for trade credits.[45] However, the new credits would be at double the existing interest rate and with one-tenth of the payment being made in advance.[46] He also said that Russia had agreed to a new investment credit for the construction of nuclear power stations in India.[47] Further evidence that relations between Moscow and New Delhi were on an upswing again came in an interview of Russia's ambassador to India, Anatoly Drukov. On July 6, 1992, Ambassador Drukov informed the *Asian Defence Journal* that Russia was prepared to produce frontline aircraft, tanks, armored cars, and other military equipment for use in India and also for export to third countries. "The idea has been under discussion, but I think we have now to move from an exchange of views to the concrete deal, the contract," he said.[48]

By the end of 1992, Moscow had begun to reassess and reverse its declining role in the global arms market, partly in order to earn hard currency, partly in order to salvage a contracting defense industry, partly in response to of the growing influence of the military in Kremlin policy-making and partly because it was clear that the major Western powers had not halted the arms trade. India again began to loom large in Russia's military consciousness because it was the biggest market for Russian military hardware and also because it offered the best prospects for a major new base from which to export license-manufactured equipment to other Asian-Pacific recipients. Moscow's new plans meshed neatly with India's drive to expand arms exports so as to earn hard currency, cut defense costs by exploiting economies of scale, and perhaps gain political influence around the region.

There was a spate of high-level military cooperation discussions between Russia and India in the final four months of 1992. Defense

Minister Sharad Pawar visited Russia for seven days in September 1992. ITAR-TASS reported that among other things, he was interested in purchasing an improved version of the MiG-29 fighter.[49] On September 7, he met with Russian Defense Minister Pavel Grachev to try to map out how best to restore military links.[50] On September 8, Secretary of State Gennady Burbulis acknowledged that Russia had inherited "considerable obligations" toward India for the deliveries of spare parts and armaments. He assured Pawar that India remained "a priority" for Russia.[51] On returning to India, Pawar described his Russian visit as extremely successful.[52]

By this time Russia was also having to cope with competitive pressures between its first circle of interests (relations with the former Union republics) and its third circle (former Third World clients). It was reported in January 1992 that Ukraine was prepared to sell weapons to India. Kiev, which was a major weapons manufacturing center in the FSU, had previously fulfilled many of the long-term defense contracts between India and the USSR and was prepared to resume this role.[53] Pawar travelled to Ukraine in October 1992 in search of closer military cooperation. He held discussions with President Leonid Kravchuk, Defense Minister Konstantin Morozov, and officials in the military-industrial and conversion complex. It was agreed that Ukraine would supply armaments and spare parts in return for medicine, cloth, and partial payment in hard currency.[54] In December 1992, Indian Defense Ministry officials said that Russia, reacting to a Ukrainian offer to sell an aircraft carrier from its disputed Black Sea fleet, had offered to sell India an aircraft carrier for US$458 million on attractive terms: half under barter terms and the balance on easy cash payment.[55] During Sharad Pawar's visit to Moscow in December, India finalized an agreement for the purchase of twenty MiG-29M and six MiG-29UM Fulcrum multirole fighters, as well as related spares and support package, the total deal being worth US$466 million.[56]

The problem of supplies of Russian military equipment and spares to India was addressed during Yeltsin's visit. Defense Ministers Pavel Grachev and Sharad Pawar signed a new agreement on military cooperation on January 28, 1993. Deliveries would be resumed at previous levels, and product support and comprehensive services needed for maintenance, repair, and modernization were guaranteed. The agreement envisaged cooperation in defense science and technology, training visits, exchange of personnel, and joint research and development projects. Russia also offered to help in the construction of a large plant in India for manufacturing military spares. Russian and Indian specialists discussed possible co-production of components for Tupolev airliners by the state-owned Hindustan Aeronautics Ltd.[57] Pawar told the Press Trust of India that the new agreement would "greatly relieve pressure on the Indian armed forces."[58]

The resumption of military links between India and Russia was helped by Russian realization that its unprecedented cooperative international behavior was not sufficient to bring about an end to Western arms sales and by the consciousness of Russia's awareness of its comparative advantages in this sector. Both arguments were relevant to Moscow and New Delhi dispute with Washington over the sale of rocket technology. Having already put several satellites into orbit, often with Moscow's help, India has ambitions of someday rivalling the major Western powers in launching satellites. India's more modest goal of space autarky is to be able to place satellites at a geosynchronous orbit permanently above the country. It could ultimately produce the rockets by itself, but the time scale would be seriously lengthened without the Russian technology and equipment and there would be the risk of cost overruns.

In January 1991 India agreed to purchase Russian rocket technology and equipment from Glavkosmos, the Russian space agency, in preference to American and French tenders. The contract called for the first two engines to be designed and fabricated in Russia, the third and fourth in India. India said that it needed the 12-ton cryogenic engines to build powerful rocket boosters to place advanced weather and telecommunications satellites in orbit. It promised to use the material for peaceful purposes only and to refrain from transferring it to third countries.

The United States pressured Russia to cancel the Indo-Russian rocket deal. A report in *Izvestiia* on May 6, 1992, noted that if Moscow disregarded the U.S. warning, it risked the loss of $4 billion worth of aid. But if it went back on the deal, it would lose a profitable contract whose fulfillment would enable the acquisition of consumer goods from India. Glavkosmos staff, agreeing that the engines could not be used for military purposes, felt that the U.S. goal was not to enhance international security but to protect its own space industry from international competition.[59] Russian government adviser Mikhail Maley insisted that Russia, whose people had to face serious food and other scarcities, could not afford to be more moral than Western countries, which were still selling their military products on world markets.[60] On May 11, 1992, Washington—insisting that the technology was dual-use, capable of being diverted to military uses and therefore prohibited under the Missile Technology Control Regime (MTCR)—imposed trade sanctions on both Russia and India.

A New Friendship Treaty

President Yeltsin paid his first visit to India on January 27–29, 1993. By then Russia was self-consciously attempting to harmonize its foreign policy directions. In an interview in August 1992, Foreign Minister Kozyrev said that it was time for Russia to boost its foreign policy activities in the East, to normalize relations with Japan and South Korea, and to take note of China and India within Russia's geopolitical framework.[61] Moscow's Radio-1 reported on January 25, 1993, that the forthcoming Yeltsin visit was designed to show that "Russia is continuing to redress the balance between the Western and Eastern directions of its policies."[62]

Two days before the start of the visit, there was an item on the Russia TV channel in Moscow discussing the state of Russo-Indian relations and the impending trip by Yeltsin.[63] Yeltsin said that his visit would mark the start of a qualitatively new relationship, preserving the positive elements from previous relations and building on the accumulated goodwill. Moreover, the forthcoming visit to India "should be seen as a major demarche by this great country and as part of our efforts towards forming Russia's new Asian policies." Interestingly, Yeltsin spoke of India and China in the same breath as the "major, great states" of Asia; South Korea, for example, was "a very strong state." In response to a question, Yeltsin said that while in the past relations between Moscow and New Delhi had formed a counterweight against China and the United States, the new ties would not be directed against any third country.[64]

The most important diplomatic achievement of the Yeltsin visit was the signing of a new friendship treaty and several other agreements for strengthening bilateral ties in a number of fields. Unlike the 1971 Treaty of Peace, Friendship and Cooperation, the 1993 Treaty of Friendship and Cooperation does not contain any clauses (1) requiring military consultations in the event of a threat to Russia's or India's security, (2) proscribing the parties from joining military alliances directed against each other, and (3) forbidding each party from providing assistance to a third party engaged in armed conflict against the other party. (Hence the significance of the dropping of "Peace" from the title of the treaty). Instead, it calls vaguely for regular consultations on all matters and for coordination in dealing with any developing threats to peace. Both parties are to refrain from actions that might damage each other's security. The treaty also envisages cooperation on trade and economic relations; environmental protection; arts, culture, education, sports, and tourism; health care and social security; and combating crime, drug trafficking, and terrorism. Like its 1971 predecessor, the 1993 treaty has a life span of twenty years with automatic five-year extensions after that date and is subject to a twelve-month notice of withdrawal by either party.

By January 1993 Russia's relationship with India had improved substantially. This can been seen if consideration is taken of Moscow's changing relations with Pakistan—India's traditional enemy. By mid-1991 Pakistan was exploring the possibility of buying military spare parts and missiles from Moscow and developing trading links. In November, Moscow disappointed India by endorsing a Pakistani proposal on establishing a nuclear-weapon-free zone in South Asia. For most of 1992, Russia sought to improve relations with Pakistan in order to enhance the prospects for stability in Afghanistan and Central Asia.[65] Appearing on television in Moscow two days before his visit to India in 1993, Yeltsin said that the NPT was not on the agenda of his discussions in India.[66] During his visit, Yeltsin said that Russia fully supported India's stand on Kashmir. The state was an integral part of India, and Russia would continue to support India's unity and territorial integrity.[67] In his address to the Indian parliament on January 29, Yeltsin declared: "We do not intend to give Pakistan any military-technical aid [applause]."[68]

Time seemed to stand curiously still in the bilateral relationship following the Yeltsin visit. The main reason for this was the different agendas and priorities that have preoccupied the two governments. Not surprisingly, the Yeltsin administration has been most concerned with internal challenges culminating in the assault on parliament but then re-emerging in a different manifestation after the fresh parliamentary elections of 1994. The next items on Moscow's order of priorities were relations with the near abroad, that is, the former Soviet republics; with the West; and with Japan and China. Russian leaders simply have not had the luxury of being able to focus on relations with India. Having coped successfully with the collapse of the Soviet Union in 1991, India too had other more pressing domestic, regional, and international issues to concern it in 1993–1994.

There were some signs of efforts by both sides to limit damage to the bilateral relationship. On the economic front, for example, Russia decided to purchase agricultural commodities worth $300 million to reimburse India's debt for state credits.[69] An Indian toothpaste manufacturer decided to set up a joint venture project in Russia. And on November 6, an agreement was signed for a joint Russo-Indian development of a small, fourteen-seater civilian aircraft.[70] And yet while India's global exports increased by around one-fifth from 1991–1992 to 1992–1993, those to the former Soviet Union, including Russia, fell by 64.4 percent.[71]

On the political front, Foreign Secretary J. N. Dixit paid a two-day visit to Russia in October 1993 and said that Russia was one of India's most important partners in all spheres. But he also acknowledged that the two had "minor disagreements" on the issues of the NPT, human rights, and national minorities.[72] Then, in an effort to reenergize relations, Indian Prime Minister Narasimha Rao paid an official visit to Russia on June 30, 1994. During his visit a number of agreements were signed, as well as a declaration on developing further bilateral relations. Prime Minister Chernomyrdin noted that mutual trade had been dwindling and spoke of the need to restore it to its previous level.[73]

On the military side of the relationship, an agreement on arms cooperation was signed in New Delhi in March 1994 for the supply of $100 million worth of spare parts to India's army and air force. Discussion was also under way for the purchase by India of thirty MiG-29 fighter-interceptors.[74] This followed a joint Indo-Russian naval exercise in the Arabian Sea on February 18–22, 1994. The Indian navy had already conducted bilateral exercises with U.S., Australian, and some Asian navies over the previous two to three years.

Remaining Uncertainties

The state of uncertainty in relations can best be described by returning to the story of the rocket engines. President Yeltsin said at a press conference in Delhi in 1993 that the cryogenic engines deal would be fulfilled despite pressure from other countries.[75] The Indian press believed that Russia's determination to proceed with the cryogenic engines deal was indicative of its long-term interest in cooperating with India[76] and that the persistent U.S. opposition to the sale had served to strengthen Yeltsin's conservative-nationalist opponents in Russia.[77] An alternative interpretation is that pressing ahead with the deal would have allowed Yeltsin to demonstrate a degree of independence from Washington despite Russia's financial dependence on the United States.

It was not to be. On July 16, 1993, Moscow finally announced capitulation to the intense U.S. pressure. While the rocket engines would be supplied, there would be no transfer of technology. The reversal provoked recriminations in Russia as well as India. In order to secure agreement with Washington, Yeltsin had replaced the obdurate Deputy Premier Alexander Shokhin[78] with the more accommodating Yury Koptev, head of the Russian Space Agency (a rival of Glavkosmos). On July 21, Alexander Dunayev, head of Glavkosmos, told a session of the Supreme Soviet Committee on International Affairs and Foreign Economic Relations that as the government had no right to freeze an essentially commercial contract, he would simply ignore its decision.[79] Ruslan Khasbulatov, chairman of the Russian parliament, called the decision a "national disgrace."[80] Prime Minister Viktor Chernomyrdin, whose planned visit to the U.S. had to be cancelled in June because of the rocket controversy, was freed to reschedule the visit. Russia was also motivated by the desire to gain access to the lucrative Western market in space services. *Pravda* reporter Vladislav Drobkov pointed out that this was a mere "possibility." Against this "bird in the bush" Russia was losing the "bird in hand" of a firm contract and its reputation as a reliable partner. Moreover, President Yeltsin himself had confirmed the deal and insisted that a third country would not be allowed to impose its terms on Russia and India. His credibility now lay in ruins. Drobkov noted that Americans, in contrast, were exulting in the success of their pressure tactics.[81]

This, however, was not the end of the matter. In a television interview as late as September 12, 1993, N. I. Leontyev, chief designer of the cryogenic engine, insisted that [the charges that] "handing over this technology will develop the military might of India does not correspond to reality."[82] India continued to make payments to Russia as per the 1991 contract and by September 1993 had handed over $5 million for work done. In an interview on September 7, Shokhin said that the U.S.–Russian memorandum of understanding on rocket technology exports, signed by Chernomyrdin in Washington on September 2, would force Moscow to confront its partial contradiction with the rocket deal with India.[83] In the end Moscow and Delhi renegotiated their contract, replacing the technology component with additional engines. The 1991 contract had called for the supply of two engines plus rocket technology. The new agreement, signed in India in March 1994, dropped the technology transfer but increased the number of engines to be supplied to India to seven.[84]

India, fearing that the cancellation of the deal would set back its satellite program by two to four years, blamed the mess squarely on the United States.[85] An editorial in a major English-language daily condemned "this astonishing act of meddlesome diplomacy" by the U.S.[86]

India drew a threefold lesson from the episode. First, it confirmed U.S. clout in setting the terms of technology transfer to developing countries. Second, it demonstrated a newly forged U.S. ability to break the continuity of Russo–Indian relations. Washington was believed to have brutally exploited Russia's economic vulnerability to coerce it into retreating from an international agreement. And third, in view of Russia's demonstrable vulnerability to U.S. pressure, it required a reassessment of Russia's credibility in honoring contractual obligations. And so, at the time of writing, the Indo-Russian relationship remains essentially on hold.

Notes

1. BBC, *Summary of World Broadcasts (SWB)*, FE/1601 C1/3, February 1, 1993.

2. See Ramesh Thakur and Carlyle A. Thayer, *Soviet Relations with India and Vietnam*, London and New York, Macmillan and St. Martin's Press, 1992.

3. BBC, *SWB*, FE/1601 C1/3, January 26, 1993.

4. BBC, *SWB*, SU/1461 A1/4–5, August 17, 1992.

5. Yeltsin at a press conference in New Delhi; ITAR-TASS on January 29, 1993, in BBC, *SWB*, FE/1601 C1/4, February 1, 1993.

6. See Ramesh Thakur, "India After Nonalignment," *Foreign Affairs*, 71, Spring 1992, pp. 178–80.

7. Igor Khotsialov, "USSR-India: New Trends in Trade and Economic Relations," *Foreign Trade* (USSR), 3/1988, p. 12.

8. As reported in the *Hindu Weekly* (Madras), July 20, 1991, p. 4.

9. *Financial Times* (London), February 7, 1992.

10. BBC, *SWB*, SU/1372 A3/2, May 5, 1992.

11. Report on Russian TV on May 3, 1992, in BBC, *SWB*, SU/1372 A3/2, May 5, 1992.

12. Technical credits effectively converted Indo-Soviet trade into barter deals. The old agreements used to approve trade in advance. The country that failed to export sufficient goods gave technical credits instead: deliveries of goods in exchange for other goods.

13. ITAR-TASS on January 29, 1993, in BBC, *SWB*, SU/1601 A1/3, and FE/1601 C1/5–6, February 1, 1993.

14. ITAR-TASS on May 3, 1992, in BBC, *SWB*, FE/1372 A1/2, May 5, 1992.

15. Radio Mayak, Moscow; BBC, *SWB*, SU/1597 A1/4, January 27, 1993.

16. Interview with ITAR-TASS on January 28, 1993, in BBC, *SWB*, SU/1601 A1/1, January 30, 1993.

17. Radio Moscow on January 28, 1993, in BBC, *SWB*, SU/1601 A1/1, January 30, 1993.

18. Interview with ITAR-TASS on January 28, 1993, in BBC, *SWB*, SU/1601 A1/1, January 30, 1993.

19. Text of speech reproduced in BBC, *SWB*, FE/1601 C1/1–3, February 1, 1993.

20. ITAR-TASS on January 29, 1993, in BBC, *SWB*, FE/1601 C1/4, February 1, 1993.

21. C. Raja Mohan, "Indo-Soviet Relations—The Return of Common Sense," *Hindu Weekly*, August 18, 1990, p. 9.

22. *Hindu Weekly*, August 31, 1991, p. 6.

23. Tatiana Shaumian, "Thirty-five Years Later," *New Times*, vol. 32, no. 90, August 1990, p. 7.

24. Editorial in the *Hindu Weekly*, December 22, 1990, p. 8.

25. Bhabani Sengupta, "Former Friends: Time to Rebuild India-Russia Ties," *Statesman Weekly* (Calcutta), February 29, 1992, p. 12.

26. BBC, *SWB*, FE/1601 C1/4, February 1, 1993.

27. *Statesman Weekly*, February 29, 1992, p. 6.

28. All-India Radio on May 4, 1992, in BBC, *SWB*, FE/1373 A1/2–3, May 6, 1992, and ITAR-TASS on May 5, 1992, in BBC, *SWB*, FE/1375 A2/2–3, May 8, 1992.

29. Peter Shearman, "Russia's Three Circles of Interests," in Ramesh Thakur and Carlyle A. Thayer, eds., *Reshaping Regional Relations: Asia-Pacific and the Former Soviet Union* Boulder: Westview, 1993, pp. 45–64.

30. *Economist*, January 16, 1993, pp. 25–26.

31. In BBC, *SWB*, SU/1601 A1/2–3, February 1, 1993.

32. For details, see Tsuyoshi Hasegawa, "Japan," and Gary Klintworth, "China and East Asia," in Thakur and Thayer, eds., *Reshaping Regional Relations*, pp. 101–23 and 125–52.

33. ITAR-TASS on January 29, 1993, in BBC, *SWB*, FE/1601 C1/4, February 1, 1993.

34. I. K. Gujral, "Trends in Indo-Soviet Relations," in Satish Kumar, ed., *Yearbook on India's Foreign Policy 1983–84*, New Delhi, Sage, 1986, p. 163.

35. BBC, *SWB*, SU/W0230 A/10, May 15, 1992.

36. Speech to the Indian parliament on January 29, 1993, in BBC, *SWB*, FE/1601 C1/2–3, February 1, 1993; interview with ITAR-TASS on January 29, 1993, in BBC, *SWB*, SU/1601 A1/3, February 1, 1993; press conference in New Delhi on January 29, 1993, in BBC, *SWB*, FE/1601 C1/6, February 1, 1993.

37. ITAR-TASS on January 29, 1993, in BBC, *SWB*, FE/1601 C1/4, February 1, 1993.

38. See Thakur and Thayer, *Soviet Relations with India and Vietnam*, pp. 49–53.

39. ITAR-TASS on January 29, 1993, in BBC, *SWB*, FE/1601 C1/4, February 1, 1993.

40. Russia's Radio on January 28, 1992, in BBC, *SWB*, SU/1291 A3/2, January 30, 1992.

41. BBC, *SWB*, SU/WO257 A/5, November 20, 1992.

42. TASS on November 18, 1991, in BBC, *SWB*, SU/1234 A3/3, November 20, 1991.

43. *Statesman*, January 12, 1992.

44. ITAR-TASS on September 7, in BBC, *SWB*, SU/1484 C2/5, September 12, 1992.

45. Russia's Radio on May 6, 1992, in BBC, *SWB*, SU/W0230 A/9, May 15, 1992.

46. ITAR-TASS on May 3, 1992, in BBC, *SWB*, FE/1372 A1/2, May 5, 1992.

47. Russia's Radio on May 6, 1992, in BBC, *SWB*, SU/W0230 A/9, May 15, 1992.

48. *Asian Defence Journal*, August 1992, p. 96.

49. BBC, *SWB*, SU/1471 A1/3, August 28, 1992.

50. ITAR-TASS on September 7, in BBC, *SWB*, SU/1484 C2/5, September 12, 1992.

51. Interfax on September 8, in BBC, *SWB*, SU/1483 A1/3, September 11, 1992.

52. ITAR-TASS on September 14, in BBC, *SWB*, SU/1487 C3/5, September 16, 1992.

53. Radio Mayak on January 25, 1992, in BBC, *SWB*, SU/1289 B/6, January 28, 1992.

54. ITAR-TASS on October 12 and 14, and Radio Ukraine World Service on October 16 and 17; in BBC, *SWB*, SU/1511 A1/2, October 14, SU/1513 C2/3, October 16, and SU/1516 A1/3, October 20, 1992.

55. BBC, *SWB*, SU/1567 A1/5, December 18, 1992; *Asian Defence Journal*, January 1993, p. 154.

56. Edmond Dantes, "An Indepth Look at the Asia-Pacific Air Forces and Future Procurement," *Asian Defence Journal*, January 1993, p. 23.

57. BBC, *SWB*, FE/1600 A1/4, January 30, 1993 and FE/1601 C1/7, February 1, 1993.

58. BBC, *SWB*, FE/1601 C1/7, February 1, 1993.

59. *Izvestiia*, May 6, 1992, in BBC, *SWB*, SU/W0230 A/8, May 15, 1992.

60. ITAR-TASS on May 7, 1992, in BBC, *SWB*, SU/W0230 A/17, May 15, 1992.

61. ITAR-TASS report on August 4, 1992 in BBC, *SWB*, SU/1451 August 5, 1992.

62. BBC, *SWB*, SU/1596 i, January 26, 1993.

63. See BBC, *SWB*, SU/1597 A1/1–4, January 27, 1993.

64. BBC, *SWB*, SU/1597 A1/2–3, January 27, 1993.

65. For details of Islamabad-Moscow relations in 1991–1992, see Ramesh Thakur, "South Asia," in Thakur and Thayer, eds., *Reshaping Regional Relations*, pp. 174–76.

66. BBC, *SWB*, SU/1597 A1/3, January 27, 1993.

67. General Overseas Service of All-India Radio, 2100 GMT, January 29, 1993.

68. BBC, *SWB*, FE/1601 C1/3, February 1, 1993.

69. BBC, *SWB*, SUW/0298 WC/8, September 10, 1993.

70. BBC, *SWB*, SUW/0307 WC/4, November 12, 1993.

71. *India Today*, March 31, 1994, p. 87.

72. BBC, *SWB*, SU/1823 B/10, October 19, 1993.

73. RIA, July 1, 1994.

74. Radio Moscow on March 28, 1994; in BBC, *SWB*, SU/1959 S1/5, March 30, 1994.

75. ITAR-TASS on January 29, 1993, in BBC, *SWB*, FE/1601 C1/4–5, February 1, 1993.

76. See "Russia Firm on High-tech Deal," *Times of India*, January 29, 1993.

77. See "Cryogenic Deal Strengthens Yeltsin's Foes," *Times of India*, February 5, 1993.

78. On May 5, 1993, for example, Shokhin said that Russia would continue to denounce U.S. dishonesty in the world arms market, such as opposition to the purchase of Russian planes by Malaysia; BBC, *SWB*, SU/1682 C2/1, May 7, 1993.

79. BBC, *SWB*, SU/1749 A1/2, July 24, 1993.

80. BBC, *SWB*, SU/1747 i, July 22, 1993.

81. BBC, *SWB*, SU/1747 A1/4–5, July 22, 1993.

82. Moscow TV on September 12, in BBC, *SWB*, SU/1795 S1/2, September 16, 1993.

83. Interfax on September 7, in BBC, *SWB*, SU/1793 B/4, September 14, 1993.

84. Radio Moscow on March 25, 1994; in BBC, *SWB*, SU/1959 S1/5, March 30, 1994.

85. See K. K. Katyal, "India Regrets Decision," *Hindu Weekly*, July 24, 1993, p. 1.

86. *The Hindu* (Madras), July 19, 1993.

12

Russian Policy Toward Latin America and Cuba

Yuri Pavlov

Introduction

During the Soviet period, Latin America, like Africa and Asia, was viewed in Moscow as a region promising revolutionary upheavals and hence opportunities for undermining Western domination and spreading Soviet influence. The ruling Communist Party of the Soviet Union (CPSU) as a matter of established routine channelled secret subsidies to Latin American communist parties through Soviet security agents, maintaining links with local revolutionary leaders who, it was hoped, would one day come to power in their respective countries. These hopes seemed to come close to fruition, albeit temporarily, only in Chile. In most cases such practices simply played into Washington's hands, bringing hostility toward the USSR on the part of oligarchic Latin American regimes while simultaneously facilitating American hegemony in the region as the defender of the status quo. Nevertheless, flirting with the Soviet Union was a useful means of demonstrating independence in the face of overwhelming U.S. influence in the region. The establishment of diplomatic relations with the USSR was also in some cases part of the political deals struck by Latin American governments with local left-wing political parties.

Ironically, the only successful Soviet-style socialist transformation in Latin America was carried out in Cuba, not by communists but by "petty bourgeois" left-wing radicals (initially without any Soviet assistance). Soviet leader Nikita Khrushchev saw Cuba as a "beacon of socialism" in the Western hemisphere, and his emissary, Anastas Mikoyan, confirmed in conversation with E. Che Guevara in Havana in 1962 that the Soviet Union had "... enormous moral and military stake" in the island and wanted to preserve it as a "... base of socialism in Latin America."[1] This was partially the reason for Moscow's attempt to turn Cuba into its forward missile base, the other factor being the desire to diminish U.S. superiority in nuclear strike capability. Most salient for Moscow in its relationship with Cuba was the provision of the USSR's first strategic foothold in the Western hemisphere. Despite increasing economic costs, Cuba was viewed as an important political and military asset in the Cold War confrontation with the United States.

On the commercial side, the Soviet Union's policy in the region was not a complete failure either. Even dictatorial anti-communist military regimes in Latin America appreciated an alternative source of exports for their grain, meat, wool and other agricultural products. As a consequence of the disastrous performance of collectivized agriculture, the USSR became in the 1960s a large importer of these products. Defying pressure from Washington to impose trade sanctions against the Soviet Union following its invasion of Afghanistan, Argentina and Brazil increased exports of grain to the USSR in the early 1980s. Moscow, in turn, did not make an issue out of the repressive internal policies of the regimes in Argentina, Bolivia, Brazil, Peru, or Uruguay, particularly if they pursued a nationalist anti-American foreign policy. The one exception was Chile after General Pinochet took power in a coup against the leftist Salvador Allende in 1973; but even there, Soviet-made Lada cars made sizable inroads into the local car market.

However, the USSR accounted on average for only slightly more than 1 percent of total Latin American foreign trade (excluding Cuba). As for the Soviet-Cuban trade turnover, by 1990 it constituted 72 percent of Cuba's total foreign trade and 7 percent of the Soviet Union's. Moscow's politically motivated decision to replace the United States as the main buyer of Cuban sugar and as the principal supplier of Cuba's needs in oil resulted eventually in Cuba's heavy dependency on the USSR for a wide range of its critical products. Moreover, the Soviet Union itself came to depend, to a substantial degree, on imports of Cuban sugar, citrus fruit, and nickel concentrate (respectively accounting for 30, 40, and 20 percent of internal consumption).

Latin America and New Thinking in Foreign Policy

Mikhail Gorbachev's "new political thinking" led to a substantial revision of Soviet policy in Latin America. The "Complex Plan of the Development of the USSR's Relations with Latin America," approved by the Soviet leadership in March 1987, provided for a series of practical steps designed to raise the level and increase the frequency of political contacts with Latin American countries. The Soviet Foreign Ministry was allocated the task of preparing the preliminary groundwork for the first visit of a Soviet leader to the South American continent. Economic aspects of this program were further elaborated in the "Long-Term Concept of Trade and Economic Cooperation of the USSR with Latin American Countries," approved by the CPSU Central Committee in December 1987.

The "Complex Plan" still carried visible hallmarks of the traditional Soviet policy in Latin America, stipulating that Latin American countries should be encouraged to distance themselves from the United States while giving support to Cuba and Nicaragua—and that efforts should be intensified to propagate in the region a socialist path of development. However, as Soviet perestroika progressed, such notions became increasingly irrelevant to the demands of the moment and were conveniently relegated into the background. In a survey of the foreign policy and diplomatic activity of the Soviet Union during the period 1985–1989 that he presented to the Supreme Soviet in October 1989, Foreign Minister Shevardnadze noted that the "new line" of Soviet policy toward Latin America "takes account of the great political diversity of the states in the region and builds on coinciding or close positions on many global and regional problems" and that "we are rediscovering Latin America" while Latin America, in turn, was "discovering the Soviet Union in its new quality deriving from perestroika."[2]

Democratic reforms in the USSR coincided with a similar process of the restoration and consolidation of democratic institutions in Latin American countries. In the period 1987 to 1991 there was a flurry of diplomatic activity and high-level political contacts between Moscow and Latin American capitals. The presidents of Argentina, Brazil, Mexico, and Uruguay visited the USSR, signing with the Soviet president joint political declarations and comprehensive programs for the development of trade and economic cooperation. However, both the Soviet Union and its Latin American partners experienced serious economic difficulties that affected their capacity to implement these programs. Due to the falling production of oil and other export products, the Soviet side repeatedly failed to meet its long-term commitments for the purchase of substantial quantities of wheat from Argentina, wool from Uruguay, bauxite from Jamaica, and consumer goods from Peru.

The reforming Soviet Union no longer acted intentionally against U.S. strategic or economic interests in the region. Its cooperation with the United States in promoting political settlements of civil conflicts in Nicaragua and El Salvador signified a radical shift in Moscow's attitude toward guerrilla movements in developing countries. This coincided with positive shifts in U.S. policy in Latin America. Washington ceased viewing the internal turmoil and upheavals in the countries of the region exclusively through the prism of the Cold War confrontation and embarked upon a course designed to assist the development of democratic institution-building.

The Cuban Connection

Thus Soviet-American rivalries in Latin America were significantly reduced. However, there still remained the problem of Cuba, which was still in the Gorbachev era on the Soviet payroll despite Castro's critical attitude to Soviet reforms and his categorical refusal to democratize his regime. Cuba continued to utilize Soviet-supplied resources for indulging in activities contrary to U.S. interests. Far from discarding the Soviet Union's close ties to Cuba, Gorbachev undertook an official visit to Havana in April 1989 during which he signed a Treaty of Friendship and Cooperation between the two countries, reaffirming and formalizing their special relations. Shevardnadze's survey of foreign policy included a special section on Cuba with reference to "a high degree of trust and understanding" between Soviet and Cuban leaders and an optimistic forecast that Soviet-Cuban cooperation would "continue to strengthen, helping to fully unlock the potential of socialism in our two countries and to resolve the problems that humanity is encountering today."[3]

Responding to the deepening crisis of the Soviet economy and mounting internal political pressure to cut Moscow's massive economic and military aid to Third World clients, Gorbachev took steps designed to reduce Soviet subsidies to Cuba but leave Soviet-Cuban political and military ties intact. As the Russian foreign minister commented later, "Relations with Cuba, Iraq, Libya, and North Korea only underwent cosmetic changes: they simply toned down the wording of congratulatory telegrams."[4] All Soviet dignitaries who travelled to Cuba after Gorbachev's visit—some of whom headed the later August 1991 coup attempt in Moscow—went out of their way to reassure Fidel Castro of the invariable Soviet support for his regime and to dispel his fears that the Soviet Union was considering abandoning its loyal socialist ally.

Soviet insistence on maintaining friendly relations with Cuba despite the growing political oppression in that country bordered on the absurd: fearing negative reactions in Havana, Soviet authorities denied legal protection to many Cubans studying in the USSR who refused to return to their country. A Cuban psychologist who successfully defended his doctoral thesis at Moscow State University saw the degree cancelled at the insistence of the Cuban embassy in Moscow as a punishment for his application to be allowed to stay in the Soviet Union.

Understandably, the failure of the August coup and the removal of the CPSU from power in Moscow produced shock and consternation in Havana. Cuba would henceforth be deprived of the multibillion dollar system of subsidies and guaranteed sources of energy supplies that had kept its inefficient economy afloat. The Cuban leadership faced the grave consequences of having modelled Cuba's post-revolutionary development on the Soviet prototype and having become totally dependent upon trade and aid from the USSR and the East European socialist countries. To add insult to injury, in the presence of U.S. Secretary of State James Baker, and without any prior warning to Castro, Gorbachev publicly announced Moscow's decision to withdraw the Soviet combat brigade from Cuba, which had been deployed there for the past twenty-nine years. This was in September 1991. Explaining this decision, Soviet Foreign Minister Boris Pankin said that the Soviet brigade in Cuba was a ". . . symbol of a past epoch in international and Soviet-U.S. relations."[5]

In contrast to the Cuban regime, all democratic governments and political parties in Latin America joined Western nations in denouncing the August coup attempt in Moscow. There were no longer fears in Latin American capitals of the potentially destabilizing consequences of closer contacts and wider exchanges with the Soviet Union. Latin American communist parties and other left-wing radical groups were left in disarray.

Emerging Symmetry of Interests

In Latin America Russia inherited some well-developed political and cultural ties but only very limited trade and economic relations. By the end of 1991 the Soviet Union had diplomatic relations with twenty-two countries in the region and embassies in sixteen. While these countries, excepting Cuba, had never been a priority in Soviet foreign policy objectives, and most probably will not become one of Russia's—and the same is true of Russia's place in Latin American foreign policy thinking—there does exist a number of objective factors that stimulate mutual interests in extending contacts. Russia and Latin America actually have a lot in common in their respective histories: of political oppression; despotic, dictatorial, or one-party rule; the lack of long-established traditions and experience of democratic government; respect for law; and individual freedoms (with the notable exception of Costa Rica). This creates major obstacles for consolidating democratic institutions, particularly in prevailing conditions of widespread poverty and economic underdevelopment.

There are other similarities in historical, cultural, social, and economic backgrounds that in the opinion of Sergei Stankevich, a former adviser to President Boris Yeltsin and now a leading member of the Russian parliament's Foreign Affairs Committee, make the Mexican, Chilean, and Argentine experiences of privatization more useful for Russia as a model than those of Poland and other East European countries.[6] Former Russian Vice President Alexander Rutskoi, who visited Argentina, Brazil, and Venezuela in June 1992, also noted a certain affinity of political and economic processes in Russia and certain Latin American countries. Rutskoi saw Russia's national interests in Latin America as being served by a more active political and economic presence in the region, and by close and effective cooperation in ensuring peace and stability and in finding solutions for ecological and other global problems. Sergei Filatov, Yeltsin's chief of staff, who headed the Russian parliamentary delegation to Mexico in October 1992, said the experience of Mexico's political development could be very useful as a model for building a new, democratic Russia.[7]

Economic Complementarities

Long-term prospects for the development of Russian economic relations with Latin America are not as bleak as they may first appear when judged by the present trade figures and the economic situation in Russia. There are several important factors that make the economies of Russia and Latin American countries in some ways complementary. Russia possesses rich natural resources; a well-developed heavy and mechanical engineering industry; and sophisticated space, nuclear-energy, and defense-related technologies. It will continue to depend on the importation of reasonably priced consumer goods, foodstuffs, and agricultural raw materials for many years to come. In a number of Latin American countries, quite the reverse is the case—they require not only stable overseas markets for their agricultural and manufactured products but also the above-mentioned technology, machinery and equipment, which Russian industry will be able to provide at a lower cost than will Western suppliers.

There exists, then, a solid foundation for establishing economic ties and mutually advantageous cooperation in a number of areas. Argentina, Brazil, Bolivia, and some other Latin American countries have already had a positive experience of such cooperation with the Soviet Union in these fields. In some of them Russia and leading Latin American countries are already able to compete successfully with the United States, Japan, and Western Europe; in others they acquire this competitiveness by pooling their resources and technical know-how.

It should be noted, however, that for all its predominant economic weight in the former USSR and the prevalent role it played in foreign trade (accounting for about 80 percent), Russia finds it difficult to replace completely the Soviet Union's economic presence in Latin America. For instance, the tractors that are popular with farmers in Chile and other countries of the area,are produced in Belarus. The same is true of the BELAZ heavy trucks for the mining industry. The production of air conditioners, which the USSR exported to Cuba, was monopolized by one factory in Baku, capital of Azerbaijan. There is already a competition in Latin American markets between the Beloruss producers of the BELAZ and the producers of KAMAZ heavy trucks, manufactured in Naberezhnye Chelni in Tatarstan, and between the producers of the Belarus tractors in Minsk and tractors manufactured in Vladimir, in Russia.

In an interview in *Latinskaia Amerika*, Georgy Mamedov, Russian deputy foreign minister, who toured the countries of the region in November 1992, characterized this competition among Russia and other former Soviet republics as a normal phenomenon in the world of free enterprise, but he spoke in favor of the coordination of their commercial activities in the region and for mutual help in getting established in Latin American markets. This proposition appeared logical and attractive, but it was hardly realistic, since these republics find it difficult to normalize economic relations and to coordinate trade policies even inside the Commonwealth of Independent States (CIS). Mamedov also talked about the experience of Latin American economic integration which could serve as a useful model for Russia and other members of the Commonwealth of Independent States in helping to find solutions to the problem of preserving a single economic space while maintaining the political independence of former constituent parts of the USSR. Mamedov noted that while Russians still need economic concessions on the part of the West to be able to enter Western markets, with Latin America they can cooperate from the beginning as equal partners, and that makes this region one of the most promising markets for Russia in its period of transition to a free enterprise economy.[8]

Originally, Russian businessmen travelled to the area with little cooperation on the part of Russian trade missions and embassies in Latin American countries, but their substantial contribution to the development of Russian trade and economic cooperation with these countries came to be appreciated by the Russian official establishment. Moscow now follows the practice of Latin American governments, inviting Russian businessmen to accompany official delegations visiting the regions, although it has yet to learn how to effectively defend their interests in foreign markets.

One example of this is the transformation of the Moscow Credit-Consensus Bank—one of the leading Russian commercial banks—into the Russian–Latin American Bank for Economic Cooperation, with the participation of over twenty Russian enterprises, commercial banks, and Russian joint ventures with West European companies. As noted by

Alexander Krysin, chairman of the board of directors of the new bank, in the past ten years Latin American businesses invested abroad from $400 to $450 billion, and the Russian economy could well benefit from such investment.[9]

Latin America represents an attractive export market for Russian machinery and equipment—it is less restrictive and demanding than West European and North American markets. Lada is one of the most popular cars in the region. A number of hydro-electric plants built on South American rivers and lakes are equipped with Russian-made turbines. Latin American countries were also one of the main sources of imported foodstuffs and raw materials for the Soviet Union, particularly when the United States was "punishing" it through economic sanctions. For instance, in 1981 the USSR took 80 percent of Argentina's grain exports, worth $3.4 billion. It imported sizable quantities of meat from Argentina; soybeans from Brazil; meat and wool from Uruguay; bananas from Equador; coffee from Brazil, Colombia, and Costa Rica; tin concentrate from Bolivia; bauxite from Jamaica; and footwear and other consumer goods from Peru.

If anything, the re-emergence of Russia as an independent state and the dislocation of its trade and economic ties with other former Union republics and East European countries augmented, rather than reduced, its interest in doing business with Latin America. As was pointed out by former Russian Vice President Rutskoi, who became an active advocate of the Russia's "rediscovery" of that region: "The mutually complementary nature of Russian and Latin American economic spaces and the export-import and technological conjuncture of the Latin American markets . . . create a good outlook for mutually beneficial trade, economic, scientific, and technical exchanges." In his opinion, the countries of the region can become ". . . one of the channels of satisfying urgent needs of Russia's population in food and other products" and, as Russia's economy recuperates, ". . . an important market for Russian industrial products."[10] In April 1993, a Russian trade and economic delegation headed by Sergei Glazyev visited several Latin American countries to discuss the problem of Moscow's debt, inherited by Russia from the USSR, and the opportunities for setting up joint enterprises. Apart from government officials, the delegation included private Russian businessmen. In Buenos Aires, Glazyev said that for Russia, Latin America was a promising region for the development of all forms of cooperation, and in Montevideo he proposed that Russia repay its $50 million debt to Uruguay by supplying equipment and technology rather than cash. The proposal was accepted.[11] Vladimir Shumeiko, chairman of the upper chamber of the Russian parliament, gave an address to the Senate of the National Congress of Venezuela on May 31, 1994, in which he expressed confidence in increasing economic and trade relations between Russia and the Latin American countries.[12]

Due to the disastrous state of the Russian economy, this trade diplomacy will not quickly result in greater volumes of trade and investments. Yet more commercial deals are being concluded between Russian and Latin American firms than ever before, preparing the ground for future growth. Russia is too weak economically, and too backward technologically, to stand up against the U.S., Japanese, and West European competition in Latin American markets for manufactured products. There are, however, three important fields in which Russia can already compete successfully with Western technology: nuclear energy, space-related technologies, and, especially, arms production.

Exporting Arms

Now that purchases of Russian arms by Latin American governments cannot any longer be regarded in Washington as a potential threat to U.S. strategic interests in the area or interpreted as a demonstration of political disloyalty to the United States, as was the case with the Peruvian military government in the 1980s, there may be more interest in the region in acquiring Russian weapons, known for their reliability, simplicity in servicing, and competitive prices. There are indications of such interest in countries that never before considered this possibility. Visiting Russia in October 1992, the Argentine defense minister stated that his government's project of modernizing the armed forces required advanced technologies, including communications satellites and flight safety technology. Argentina intended to develop cooperation with Russia in such fields as physics, chemicals, and nuclear power.[13] Prospects for Russian arms sales in Latin America were also discussed during Deputy Foreign Minister Mamedov's visit to the region in November 1992.

Exporting arms has become an important issue on the agenda of high-level Russian–Latin American meetings. Since Russia began to drastically reduce its defense industrial establishment, which employed until recently nine million workers and accounted for half of the total industrial production of the country, it has been trying to compensate for the loss of government orders by increasing the sales of arms and military technology abroad. Weapons remain Russia's most competitive export commodity, and the Yeltsin government has been under heavy political pressure not only from the influential military-industrial complex and other conservative forces but also from its own supporters,to take more energetic steps to ensure more export orders for Russian arms, both to stave off mass unemployment in defense industries and to gain hard currency.

When Western powers object to certain Russian military-related sales in pursuit of commercial or political interests in certain areas, the Russian government finds itself in a politically precarious position of having to choose between the Western negative reaction and the ire of the Russian conservative opposition, which accuses the government of submissiveness to the West. There have been, for example, such conflicts of interest in some Russian exports to India, Iran, and China. This could also happen in relation to Latin America.

Human Rights, the OAS, and the CIS

Russia and the United States are already collaborating, together with other democratic countries, in the U.N. Human Rights Commission in bringing international pressure to bear upon governments of the region that practice systematic violations of human rights on political, religious, or racial grounds. Such pressure was partially successful in Guatemala, Peru, and El Salvador although it has not succeeded so far in influencing the policy of the present Cuban regime. In September 1994, Russia gave its support in the United Nations to the U.S. action to restore the democratically elected president in Haiti, who had earlier been overthrown in a military coup. Speaking in Geneva on February 12, 1992, Foreign Minister Kozyrev noted that following democracy's victory over totalitarianism, Russia's domestic interests were identical with international standards in the sphere of human rights. He proposed to resort to the imposition of economic sanctions on states found guilty of violating human rights.[14]

Reflecting this proximity of political interests of Russia with those of the democratic states of the Western hemisphere, the Permanent Council of the Organization of American States decided in May 1992 to grant it observer status in the OAS. The Russian Foreign Ministry welcomed this decision as a testimony to "... the growing confidence of the international community and, in particular, states of Northern and Latin America, to Russia's course towards fuller integration with world economic and political systems." It expressed hope that Russia's participation in OAS structures would give a fresh impetus to the development of its comprehensive mutually beneficial relations with American states. It noted that Russia was ready, using its positive experience, to render every possible assistance to the OAS member-states "... in their elaboration of steps to create a reliable regional security system" and expressed hope for a mutually beneficial cooperation with the OAS. The Foreign Ministry added that in the process of Russia's economic and political renovation, it intended to use the experience of the OAS member-states in the realization of similar reforms.[15]

Both the Russian Federation and the Commonwealth of Independent States—if it survives as a regional organization—would certainly benefit from establishing contacts and exchanges with the OAS. The CIS has much to learn from the rich experience of American states in setting up and operating regional mechanisms designed to render peaceful solutions to territorial disputes and other problems similar to those currently threatening its own existence. Of particular interest for the CIS will be the recently initiated collective efforts of the OAS to promote the consolidation of democratic institutions and to discourage the interruption of normal constitutional processes and violations of human rights among its members. Such problems have already arisen in Azerbaijan, Georgia, Tajikistan, Moldova, and other former Soviet republics. Equally instructive is the experience of Latin American economic integration—study and analysis of this complex and difficult process can help to find answers to some of the problems that the CIS countries encounter in their efforts to preserve the common economic space that existed in the USSR.

A distinctive feature of Russia's policy toward Latin America is that in contrast to its policy toward the West, it causes no internal political controversy—the democrats and the political opposition, including neo-communists, agree that the Russian economic presence in the region should be maintained and expanded, and political contacts developed. It has no pro-American or pro-Western tinge that irritates the opposition and nothing that could be interpreted as detrimental to Russia's national interests. Moreover, the expansion of Russian influence and presence in Latin America is seen in Moscow as an effective way of strengthening its position vis-à-vis Washington, of confirming Russia's status as a great power. It is not accidental that *Pravda*, which expresses the views of the communist opposition, has given extensive positive coverage to the problems of Russian relations with Latin America, particularly in the economic field.

The Cuban Question Reconsidered

De-ideologization of Political Relations

This cannot, however, be said of Russia's relations with Cuba, which became a subject of debate not only between the government and the opposition but also inside the government and the academic community. President Yeltsin stated in his speech to the U.S. Congress on June 17, 1992, that Russia "... has corrected the well-known imbalances in its relations with Cuba" and that the latter has become just one of Russia's Latin American trade partners.[16] Indeed, most "imbalances" have been removed. The Russian attitude toward Cuba has changed radically compared to Soviet policy, which proceeded from the "fraternal and indestructible friendship and solidarity" with Cuba based on a common ideology and objectives formulated in the preamble of the Soviet–Cuban Treaty of Friendship and Cooperation concluded in Havana by Gorbachev and Castro in April 1989.[17] The Yeltsin government completed the process of the de-ideologization of Soviet-Cuban relations that was initiated by Gorbachev and then Soviet Foreign Minister Pankin in September 1991 and ended Moscow's economic assistance and subsidies to Cuba.

As far as political relations with Cuba are concerned, the question immediately arose as to what extent the treaty corresponded to the changed nature of Russian-Cuban relations. As reported by Interfax on December 28, 1991, the Russian Foreign Ministry, when confirming Russia's commitment to observe all treaties and agreements concluded by the former Soviet Union with foreign countries, expressed misgivings with regard to the expediency of some of these documents, naming, specifically, treaties with only three countries: Iraq, North Korea, and Cuba. It did not make any sense to negotiate new political agreements with regimes that were becoming international outcasts. It was thought in Moscow to be expedient to postpone any decision relating to the Soviet-Cuban treaty, but for all practical purposes it had become a dead letter.

An important role in the radical change of Moscow's policy toward Cuba was played by the Russian democratic press and well-known parliamentarians and public figures, including Alexei Surkov, Sergei Yushenkov, Yuri Karyakin, Sergei Kovalev, and Yuri Afanasyev. They were instrumental in establishing in October 1991 in Moscow the Committee for the Defense of Human Rights in Cuba and in organizing unprecedented public hearings on Cuba's human rights record in Russia's parliament. In February 1992, Sergei Kovalev, a former Soviet dissident, who was appointed Russian representative in the U.N. Human Rights Commission in Geneva, issued on behalf of the Russian government a public apology for Moscow's past support of Castro's oppressive regime and voted in favor of the resolution condemning violation of human rights in Cuba. This caused an indignant reaction in Havana. Hoping to influence Cuba's inflexible negative position on the issue and to prevent another confrontation in Geneva, the Russian Foreign Ministry tried to engage Cuban officials in bilateral discussions, presenting them with a list of political prisoners in Cuba and asking to clarify the charges against them. The Cuban delegation to the conference on human rights refused to enter into such discussions, whereupon in March 1993 the Russian delegation in the U.N. Human Rights Commission supported again the resolution condemning the Castro regime for systematic violations of human rights.

Despite Havana's protests, high-level contacts have been established by the Russian government with leaders of the Cuban exile community in the United States and Spain. In December 1991 Russian Foreign Minister Andrei Kozyrev received a delegation from the Cuban-American Foundation (CANF)—one of the most influential Cuban exile organizations in the United States—and stated that Moscow intended to expand contacts with representatives from all political forces in Cuba, as well as with the government. Kozyrev did not want Russia to find itself in a situation analogous to the former Soviet Union in its relations with Eastern Europe, where it failed to make contacts with political opposition figures—for example, Lech Walesa before he became president of Poland. CANF was allowed to open an office in Moscow. There were also contacts made with Carlos Montaner, leader of the Cuban Liberal Union in exile.

Economic and Trade Relations

In January 1992 Russia cut off completely its cheap loans for Cuban purchases of Russian goods and military equipment and stopped paying preferential prices for Cuban sugar. As a result of protracted negotiations an agreement was reached to exchange 800,000 tons of Russian oil for 500,000 tons of Cuban sugar during the first three months of 1992. This deal was renewed in April-June, resulting in Russia importing in 1992 only 1 million tons of Cuban sugar in exchange for 1.6 million tons of oil at world market prices. Deliveries to Cuba of all other commodities were stopped. In a telling episode in St. Petersburg on January 15, 1992, President Yeltsin, speaking at a public meeting at a maritime commercial port, informed dockers of his decision that 50,000 tons of foodstuffs destined for Cuba would be kept for St. Petersburg residents.[18] Russian-Cuban trade in 1992 amounted to a mere fraction—7 percent—of what it was in the previous year.[19]

This caused difficulties not just for Cuba. Since half of domestic beet sugar production in the USSR was accounted for by the now independent Ukraine, and only one-third by Russia, the latter's dependence on imported sugar increased, and in 1992, apart from the above-mentioned transaction, it had to buy additional quantities of Cuban sugar at elevated prices from other former Soviet republics that had moved quicker than Russia in establishing direct trade links with Cuba. As a result, the communist opposition accused the Yeltsin government of neglecting national interests by reducing trade with Havana too drastically in order to please Washington. In November 1992 the Russian government signed a trade agreement with Cuba—Russia was one of the last former Soviet republics to formalize its trade relations with the island. Despite its falling oil production, Russia agreed to increase in 1993 its sales of oil to Cuba to 2.3 million tons in order to be able to import 1.5 million tons of sugar and agreed to consider the possibility of supplying, in addition, 1 million tons of petroleum products in exchange for Cuban nickel concentrate and cobalt.

A Renewed Debate over Cuba

Russian policy toward Castro's Cuba was debated in May 1992 at a symposium in Moscow ("Russia-Cuba: Prospects of Relations in New Conditions") sponsored by the Institute of Latin American Studies and the Institute of International Economic and Political Studies. Most Russian Cubanologists criticized the initial decision of the Russian government to radically curtail political, economic, and military ties with Cuba and called for "civilized forms of cooperation" with Havana on the human rights issue, separating existing differences on this issue from bilateral relations between the two countries in order not to enter a "zone of political confrontation." Several participants, however, castigated Fidel Castro for mass violations of human rights. Dr. Karen Khachaturov, president of the Russian Committee for Cooperation with Latin America, asserted that by going "from one extreme to another" in its relations with Cuba, Moscow was damaging Russia's prestige in Latin American countries, creating the image of an ". . . an unpredictable and impulsive partner, who may take the same attitude tomorrow to any other country." He argued that Russia would do better to follow the example of Ukraine, the Central Asian republics, and the Baltic states, which develop their relations with Cuba "without any vociferousness." Dr. Vladimir Borodayev called for the continuation of military cooperation with Cuba, asserting that with changing Russian defense capabilities due to the disintegration of the USSR and the process of disarmament, the Russian electronic intelligence base at Lourdes and naval facility at Cienfuegos were more important for ensuring Russia's national security than before.

Dr. K. O. Leino, after citing figures illustrating the dynamics of Moscow's economic assistance to Cuba (from $5–6 billion annually in the late 1980s, when it constituted 10 percent of the Soviet Union's balance of payments' deficit and 25 percent of Cuba's GNP, to $2.1 billion in 1991 and to zero in 1992), set forth arguments against a complete cessation of Russian technical assistance and against Cuba's replacement by other suppliers of sugar. He argued that the continuation of economic cooperation with the island, albeit on a commercial basis, would help to secure some repayment of Cuba's debt to the USSR, which amounted to 16.7 billion rubles, or $380 million, in 1991. Dr. Gennady Zyukov argued that Russia would probably need in the coming years from 5 to 6 million tons of imported sugar and would also require Cuban citrus fruits and nickel concentrate.[20] In March 1993 Zyukov's views on Russia's sugar supply were disputed at an international seminar on this problem in Moscow. The Russian government informed the participants of its plans to increase, with Western technological assistance, Russia's own sugar production and to reduce its dependence on imported sugar.[21]

Speaking in this debate, Alexei Yermakov, deputy head of the Russian Foreign Ministry's Department of Central and South America, said that Russian-Cuban relations were going through ". . . a complicated and painful period of transition to a new quality, . . . of a serious revision of priorities and parameters of cooperation, based on a strict parity, mutual respect and account of realities." Yermakov affirmed that recently Russian foreign policy, including that toward Cuba, was characterized by a tendency of making "balanced decisions." He referred to the exchange of personal messages between Boris Yeltsin and Fidel Castro on the problems of bilateral relations, which ". . . should be developed on a de-ideologized basis, with due account of mutual interests, on an equitable mutually advantageous foundation." He advocated the continuation of relations with Cuba in all spheres, including military cooperation, criticized U.S. policy toward Cuba, and stated that a bill, reestablishing American sanctions against foreign cargo ships calling on Cuban ports, ". . . was, in essence, an attempt to exert pressure on Russia."[22] Finally, Yermakov, echoing the sentiments of other participants at the symposium, expressed an opinion that some reports on Cuba published in the Russian press ". . . contradict Russia's national interests."[23]

Later the same official, who became the Russian Foreign Ministry's spokesman on the Cuban problem, told the press that "the period of the greatest difficulties in relations between Cuba and Russia is in the past, and now both sides are moving to a greater mutual understanding and mutual cooperation."[24] In September 1992 Moscow and Havana came to an agreement on the withdrawal of the Russian motorized brigade from the island—the Cuban side dropped its original insistence on linking this problem with the liquidation of the U.S. naval base at Guantanamo and agreed that the brigade should be withdrawn by July 1993.

Problems and Prospects

The agreement on the removal of the Russian brigade removed a major obstacle to the improvement of political relations between the two countries. However, apart from the human rights issue, which became a thorn in these relations, there remained problems caused by Russia's inability to continue its technical assistance in the construction on the island of about eighty economic projects. The most important and expensive of them—the nuclear power plant at Juragau—had already cost $1.1 billion and was nearing completion. When completed, it was expected to satisfy 10 percent of the Cuban domestic demand in electricity. Havana asked Moscow to continue its participation in the construction of the power plant and to guarantee the supply of uranium. The Russian side agreed in principle but imposed financial conditions that the Cuban side found unacceptable. Whereupon Fidel Castro, without any prior warning to Moscow, made a surprise announcement in September 1992 that the Cuban government would suspend construction of the plant.[25] Russia's reaction was restrained. A Foreign Ministry spokesman stated that first it was necessary to discuss the problem with Cuba and that the suspension of the project could ". . . entail serious economic problems for both countries and will make it necessary to solve complex technical issues."[26] The problem was that the maintenance of the equipment already installed required almost as much expense in hard currency as the completion of the construction. If the project collapsed, then Russia would lose its right to ask for repayment of Soviet investment in the project. This was also true of other uncompleted projects of Soviet-Cuban cooperation. Consequently, in July 1993, Russia agreed to provide Cuba with $350 million in credit for the completion of twelve of these existing projects and an additional $30 million specifically for conserving the Juragua power plant.

Moscow's new pragmatic course toward Havana was confirmed by Russia's agreement in December 1993 to increase further in 1994 sales of oil to Cuba (up to 2.5 million tons) and to resume deliveries of other raw materials, chemicals, agricultural machinery, equipment, and spare parts for the modernization of Cuba's sugar industry, which would enable Cuba to fulfill increased commitments to supply sugar and nickel concentrate to Russia.

There were also substantial shifts in Russian-Cuban military links. Despite discrete attempts by Washington to persuade Moscow to liquidate completely Russia's military presence in Cuba, the Yeltsin government negotiated with Cuba the right to maintain the Russian intelligence-gathering facility at Lourdes, near Havana. Russia paid the rent with spare parts for Russian-made weapons used by the Cuban armed forces. In November 1993 a high-level Cuban military delegation visited Moscow for confidential discussions with the Russian Ministry of Defense—the first such talks since the disintegration of the Soviet Union. The delegation was received by Defense Minister Pavel Grachev, who announced his intention to travel to Cuba in 1994. Commenting on this visit, Moscow's *Izvestiia* said, "The Russian military still regard Castro brothers as their allies."[27]

Different explanations were given for the reasons behind the Yeltsin government's decision to keep the base serviced by Russian military technical personnel. Vice Premier Shokhin referred to its importance in maintaining communications with Russian embassies in Latin America. Russian diplomats in Washington pointed out that the Lourdes radio-electronic center was essential for monitoring the observance by the U.S. side of Russian-U.S. strategic arms reduction agreements, alluding to the continuing existence of similar U.S. radio-electronic facilities in several countries bordering the former USSR.[28]

Whatever the explanations, one of the key elements was the "correction" of Russian foreign policy by making it less "pro-Western." This was ordered by Yeltsin against the objections of Foreign Minister Kozyrev and was designed to neutralize the domestic opponents of the Western-oriented foreign policy—found not only in the opposition but also within the president's own government, reflecting growing nationalist sentiments in Russian society generally. The possibility should not be excluded that more serious negative consequences will follow if Yeltsin's authority is undermined by the conservatives in the Russian parliament or if there is a conservative victor in the next Russian presidential election. In that case the resulting deterioration or renewed tensions in Russia's relations with the United States could be accompanied by attempts of the new rulers in Moscow to play again the "Cuban card" against Washington, provided that Castro is still in power in Havana.

Barring this eventuality, any further substantial progress in Russian diplomatic relations with Cuba will become possible only after radical internal political changes on the island. In the absence of such changes, they will be limited primarily to trade and economic cooperation and will be characterized by a cool political climate as Castro's regime continues its present policy of preserving the status quo and fighting political opposition with police brutality and imprisonment. There is no chance of returning to the close political ties that existed prior to the August 1991 coup attempt in Moscow.

There is, however, one important aspect of present Russian policy toward Cuba that is a continuation of the traditional Soviet stand throughout the whole period of the Castro regime. As before, Moscow advocates an end to Washington's hostility to the Castro regime and a normalization of U.S.-Cuban relations. Furthermore, Russian diplomats have suggested that Moscow could play a useful intermediary role in bringing about the improvement in relations. The reasoning behind this position is the same old belief that by changing its policy toward the present Cuban regime, Washington would deprive Fidel Castro of his best justification for resisting democratic reforms and clamping down on political dissent and would facilitate a peaceful evolution of Cuba toward democracy and a market economy. Russian democrats who support this view tend to forget recent Soviet history: Nobel Prize laureate Andrei Sakharov was in favor of Western economic and political sanctions against the Brezhnev government for invading Afghanistan and violating human rights in the Soviet Union, and this international pressure was an important factor in bringing about positive changes in Soviet internal and foreign policies.

In the economic field the determining factor will be Russia's ability to restore its industrial capacity and, in particular, to reverse the present downward trend in its oil production, allowing an increase in oil, machinery, equipment, and consumer goods exports to Cuba in exchange for sugar, citrus fruits, nickel, pharmaceutical products, rum, and tobacco. Russian state-owned enterprises are already looking for opportunities to establish joint ventures with Cuban state organizations, especially in Cuban industries that were developed or re-equipped with Soviet assistance. This is regarded as one of the possible ways of getting some benefits from huge Soviet investments into the island's economy, which have still not been written off in Moscow as irretrievably lost. The same consideration applies to the problem of Cuba's debt to Russia—there are hopes that the renewal of extensive economic cooperation with Cuba will increase the chances of its repayment.

Notes

1. *Mezhdunarodnaia zhizn'*, January 1993, p. 98.
2. *Mezhdunarodnaia zhizn'*, January 1993, p. 143.
2. *Mezhdunarodnaia zhizn'*, January 1993, p. 143.
4. *Moscow News*, June 7–14, 1992.
5. *Granma*, September 13, 1991.
6. *The North-South Agenda*, Paper no. 5., University of Miami, North-South Center, September 1993, p. 12.
7. *Latinskaia Amerika*, no. 10–11, 1992, pp. 4–5, and FBIS-SOV-92-203, October 20, 1992, p. 13.
8. *Latinskaia Amerika*, no. 10–11, 1992, pp. 36–41.
9. *Pravda*, December 2, 1992.
10. *Latinskaia Amerika*, no. 10–11, 1992, p. 5.
11. FBIS-SOV-93-070, April 14, 1992, p. 23; FBIS-SOV-93-072, April 16, 1993, pp. 16–17.
12. RIA, June 1, 1994.
13. *Rossiiskaia gazeta*, October 20, 1992.
14. *Izvestiia*, February 15, 1992.
15. FBIS-SOV-92, May 18, 1992, p. 20.

16. *New York Times*, June 18, 1992.

17. *Pravda*, April 6, 1989.

18. FBIS-SOV-92-011, January 16, 1992, p. 51.

19. Radio Havana Commentary, December 1, 1992, FBIS-LAT-92, December 2, 1992, p. 1.

20. *Latinskaia Amerika*, no. 10–11, pp. 57–62.

21. *Finansovye Izvestiia*, March 5–7, 1993.

22. *Latinskaia Amerika*, no. 10–11, pp. 54–57.

23. *Latinskaia Amerika*, no. 1–11, pp. 54–57.

24. *Izvestiia*, September 3, 1992.

25. *Izvestiia*, September 3, 1992.

26. *Granma*, September 9, 1992.

27. *Izvestiia*, December 1, 1993.

28. *Nezavisimaia gazeta*, November 4, 1992.

13

Russian Policy Toward Central Asia and the Middle East

Amin Saikal

Introduction

The one certain thing about Soviet foreign policy in the Cold War era was its highly monolithic character. This was true of Soviet behavior in general and toward specific regions in particular. Although Moscow tried to show some sensitivity to the individual particulars of different regions, its overall policy approach toward each region was still guided, in one way or another, by its superpower rivalry with the United States and its commitment to certain broad ideological goals. Central Asia and the Middle East—the region stretching from Afghanistan to Morocco—proved to be a high-priority area in this respect. The same, however, cannot be said about *Russian* foreign policy. Ever since the disintegration of the USSR and the emergence of the Russian Federation as fledgling democratic successor to the Soviet Union, Russia's policy approach to this region has been marked more by fluidity and diversity than certainty and predictability. It has been grounded partly in the foreign policy changes initiated in the Soviet era under Mikhail Gorbachev but more firmly in post-Soviet Russia's turbulent, divided, internal politics. It has, nonetheless, been motivated by an overall direction and purpose in the conduct of Russia's relations with the region.

The aims of this chapter are threefold. The first aim is to examine what Russia under Boris Yeltsin has so far tried to achieve that could be identified as Russia's overall objectives in Central Asia and the Middle East. The second is to look at the Russian policy approach in pursuance of these objectives. The third is to highlight some of the fundamental problems and dilemmas facing Moscow, with a view to envisaging Russia's future policy directions in the region.

Policy Priorities

Of course, it is never easy to identify accurately a state's national interests and therefore foreign policy priorities and objectives. The task becomes even more difficult when that state is in the midst of a breathtaking transformation, redefining its national identity and interests and the course of political and socio-economic development. In this case, the best way to study Russia's policy toward Central Asia and the Middle East is not through any theoretical mode of analysis or through scrutiny of canonical texts but rather through identification of the broad trends and specific policy actions that have emerged as dominant in Moscow's pursuit of its relations with the region.

Russian behavior toward Central Asia and the Middle East in the post-Soviet period began by in part reflecting a divide between two rival groups that sought to control Russian foreign policy: the "Atlanticists" and the "Eurasians." In general, the "Atlanticists," led by President Yeltsin and his foreign minister, Andrei Kozyrev, emphasized the significance of Russia's democratic and capitalist transformation and its identification with the North and partnership with the West as necessary conditions for this transformation and Russia's effective participation in the creation of a new world order. As such, they felt that Russia's conduct of its relations with the South should be premised upon these imperatives. The "Eurasian" lobby, whose main spokesman emerged in the person of Russian State Counsellor Sergei Stankevich, opposed the idea of exclusive alliance with the West and criticized "Atlanticists" for abandoning the South. They argued that Russia's natural and traditional allies were in the South rather than in the West. They warned against alienating China, the Muslim world—especially importantly its Middle Eastern component—and India and urged that Russia develop its relations with the South on the basis of its own assessment of political developments, that is, independently of Western perceptions, in that part of the world.[1] Various versions of this vision subsequently gained currency among the opponents of Yeltsin inside and outside the Supreme Soviet, which attempted to exert greater legislative control of foreign policy.

The struggle between these competing visions, which soon found supporters in the foreign, defense, and trade ministries, laid an important foundation for diversity in Russia's policy approach toward Central Asia and the Middle East. As the struggle intensified, however, Yeltsin and Kozyrev found it necessary to embrace some of the formulations of their opponents by emphasizing the need for "adaptation in the world community," for the maintenance of Russia's status as "a great power, . . . with global and regional interests," and for good relations with both East and West on the basis of what best served "Russian national interests" as "the only ideology of ... foreign policy."[2] What as a consequence emerged to govern Russia's behavior toward the region was a blend of the competing visions, which in essence produced no new approach but, in many ways, a development of the policies, with all their dilemmas and contradictions, that were inherited from Gorbachev. By mid-1992, it became discernible that the Yeltsin government's approach to Central Asia and the Middle East centered on achieving four major objectives, embodying what could be described in broad terms as Russia's national interests.

The first was to substantiate Russia's claim to be the democratic legal successor to the former Soviet Union, especially to its international obligations and assets as well as some of its superpower status.

The second was to provide leadership for the former Soviet republics—or what were called "the near abroad"—within the framework of the Commonwealth of Independent States (CIS) and maintain a degree of influence over them so as to protect Russia's security and interests, especially against any form of hostile radicalism and conflict on Russia's borders. The main concern here was to deter or, if possible, to prevent Islamic radicalism from gaining strength in the Central Asian republics (where significant ethnic Russian minorities are located) and among Russia's own secessionist Muslim minorities, especially in Chechnya and Tatarstan.

The third was to secure Russia as much foreign exchange, investment, and market access as possible to aid the processes of domestic political and economic reforms, with a serious attempt to expand the sale of both Russian military and non-military goods to the region as a main source of capital.

The fourth was to develop Russia's partnership with the West in such a way as to preserve the degree of influence in Central Asia and the strategic parity with the United States and the West in the Middle East that Russia's claim of great power status warranted. Moscow proposed to do this through a measure of non-confrontational competitiveness and the carving out of a role whereby Russsia could serve as a bridge between the West and opposing interests in the region.

The pursuit of these objectives, while setting some sort of loose framework for Russia's conduct of its relations with Central Asia and the Middle East, has produced different outcomes with individual constituent states of the region. It has also confronted Russia with problems and dilemmas of a kind to which Gorbachev's Soviet Union had fallen prey. To illustrate this, it is important to survey the development of Russian relations, in both bilateral and multilateral terms, with the region.

Policy Approaches

Afghanistan

In the case of Russia's relations with Afghanistan, these policy approaches have led Russia to build on what it inherited from the Soviet Union. Russia's claim to be the ruling successor of the Soviet Union and the international recognition of such a claim, together with Moscow's apprehension about Islamic radicalism and concern about many of the Central Asian republics' cross-border religious and ethno-linguistic ties with Afghanistan, have proved to be major obstacles in this respect. They have inhibited the Yeltsin government from playing an important role in helping to stabilize post-Soviet Afghanistan and in putting Afghan-Russian relations on a new, fruitful course of development to contribute to regional stability.

In the wake of the collapse of the Soviet Union there were several issues with which Russia needed to deal urgently if it were to make a good start with Afghanistan. They included, most importantly, the questions of Soviet maintenance of Najibullah's government in Kabul; the return of Soviet prisoners of war (some three hundred, according to Moscow, but possibly no more than thirty in reality); the threat of a spread of Islamic radicalism from Afghanistan to the former Soviet Central Asian Muslim republics, especially Tajikistan; and the demand of the Afghan Islamic resistance forces, the mujahideen, for war reparations in the order of some $100–150 billion[3] from the Soviet Union and the return of thousands of Afghan children and youth who had been forcibly sent to the USSR by the Kabul communist government to be trained as future cadres. Clearly, these were issues that Moscow wished to avoid, but its claim to be the successor of the Soviet Union could not but draw it effectively into them.

Although the problem of Najibullah's government was quickly solved with the discontinuation of Soviet aid and the mujahideen takeover of Kabul in late April 1992, Russia could not or did not want to respond effectively to the other problems. Initially, Foreign Minister Andrei Kozyrev's trip to Kabul within a few days of the inauguration of the mujahideen's Islamic government in early May, and his formal apology for Soviet aggression, generated a degree of optimism about the future of Afghan-Russian relations. However, it soon became clear that the trip could not amount to anything more than a goodwill gesture primarily designed to secure a speedy release of Soviet prisoners of war and to discourage the mujahideen from supporting their Islamic counterparts in Tajikistan or, for that matter, elsewhere in Central Asia.

Russia's inability to discuss, let alone to pay, war reparations and its active opposition to the rise of Islamic radicalism in Tajikistan placed the mujahideen government in an uncomfortable position and made it wary of Moscow's intentions. Although the Afghan government was dominated by the Islamic moderate mujahideen group of Jamiati Islami Afghanistan (the Islamic Society of Afghanistan) under the leadership of President Burhanuddin Rabbani and his chief military commander, Shah Massoud, the predominantly Afghan Tajik ethnicity of the group could not allow it to be indifferent to the cause of Islamists in Tajikistan. As the power struggle widened in Tajikistan between the communists and a coalition of opposition democrats and Islamists, who wrested power from the communists for a short time in Dushanbe in September 1992 only to be overpowered by the communists in December, the Afghans and Russians found themselves involved on opposite sides of the conflict. While Russia accused the mujahideen of arming the Tajik Islamists, Kabul opposed Russia's active role in guarding the Afghan-Tajikistan border and providing military support to the Tajik communists, both directly and in cooperation with the ruling communists of Uzbekistan—another northern neighbor with which Afghanistan shares a long border and considerable ethnic ties.

Two more factors complicated the situation even further. The first was Kabul's perception of Russia's indirect support through Uzbekistan for a former Najibullah-allied warlord from Afghanistan's Uzbek minority, General Abdul Rashid Dostam. Despite his initial defection shortly before the fall of Najibullah to Commander Massoud, which proved instrumental in the mujahideen's final victory, Dostam increasingly displayed dubious loyalty to the Rabbani government. He absorbed many of the Afghan communists and gathered much military power under his control in his northern ethnic enclave of Mazar-i-Sharif in Afghanistan. The second was the mujahideen infighting that rocked the Islamic government in Kabul shortly after its establishment. With the rebel leader, Gulbuddin Hekmatyar, shelling Kabul in opposition to Rabbani and Massoud from August 1992, the infant mujahideen government found little opportunity to consolidate and manage Afghan domestic and foreign affairs effectively.

As Russia, like many other states, decided to pull out all its diplomatic staff from Kabul in late 1992 because of intensified fighting, direct Kabul-Moscow diplomatic contacts were also reduced substantially, leaving the Russian consulate in Mazar-i-Sharif, which closely liaises with General Dostam, as the main point of contact between the two sides. The situation in Kabul did improve following a March 1993 agreement among the mujahideen leaders. However, before the year ended, while supported directly by Uzbekistan and indirectly by Russia, Dostam switched sides and forged an alliance with Hekmatyar. The extent of this alliance became evident when on January 1, 1994, Hekmatyar and Dostam launched a joint blistering attack on Kabul to topple President Rabbani's government. Although unsuccessful in their attempt, they inflicted a protracted war on the already battle-ravaged capital, causing horrendous human and material losses and confronting the dwindling Kabul citizens for the first time in the fifteen-year long conflict with a distinct possibility of massive starvation. In the fight for Kabul, while Moscow failed to condemn Dostam's actions, Uzbekistan reportedly increased its logistic and material support for him.[4]

Iran

In contrast, Russia has had considerable success in pursuing its objectives with the Islamic republic of Iran. The two sides have found enough in common to enable them even to use their differences to one another's advantage. The Russo-Iranian relationship has rapidly reached an all-time high, with Iran becoming not only an important trading partner and lucrative arms customer but also an important fulcrum of Moscow's interests in the region. Despite the inherent contradictions in the relationship between Russian democracy and Iranian theocracy, it appears that Moscow has scored well through reliance on the Islamic republic to advance some of its regional objectives. Although the foundation for this development was laid in the later years of the Gorbachev era, the Yeltsin government has played a significant part in building on that foundation. A number of factors seem to have underpinned this development.

Both Russia and Iran have national vulnerabilities and regional concerns and objectives that can be best addressed through cooperation rather than through isolation from one another. Squeezed by American opposition and regional apprehension involving most of its Arab neighbors and Turkey, the Islamic regime has increasingly found it difficult to endure its international isolation, growing domestic economic difficulties, and therefore sense of national insecurity, on the one hand, and to cope with active areas of instability around it—from Afghanistan to Central Asia and from Transcaucasia to the Gulf—on the other. To address these concerns, the regime has had little choice but to rationalize, in many cases, the Islamic content of its foreign policy and to forge close ties with those powers that can be receptive to it without necessarily requiring changes in the regime's domestic base of legitimacy. No power has had as much need as Russia to find access to the Iranian market and resources and to enlist the support of Iran for manipulating and containing Islamic radicalism and national conflicts in Central Asia and Transcaucasia. Russia's new relationship with Iran also will encourage the

Arab states (especially the Gulf's oil-rich ones) and Turkey to defer to Russia as the only power with the leverage to restrain Iran from destabilizing the region further.

Thus, it is not surprising that both Tehran and Moscow have found it mutually expedient and rewarding to strengthen their ties as much as possible. To look at it from Moscow's perspective, friendship with Iran has already brought several important benefits. First, it has sold and agreed to sell the country billions of dollars worth of arms, earning Russia some of the hard currency it badly needs. Whereas in 1991 Russia sold to Iran $1 billion worth of weapons, it was reported that in 1992 it signed contracts for another $4–10 billion of arms sales to the country over the next five years. The deals have involved the following weapon systems: 3 Kilo-class diesel electronic submarines, the first of their kind to be introduced to the Gulf region; advanced MiG fighters and Sukhoi SU-24 fighter bombers; and T-72 tanks, missile launchers, and long-range guns.[5] Furthermore, lucrative contracts for Russia's involvement in Iran's industrial development, particularly in the fields of steel and petrochemical industries, were concluded. As the trade ties expanded, in 1992 the two sides also agreed to set up a joint ministerial economic commission to help them make further strides in their economic relationship.

In the regional sphere, Iran continued its pledge not to do anything that could undermine Russia's ability to maintain and strengthen the CIS and to pursue an active security role in Central Asia and Transcaucasia. In effect, Tehran undertook, as the Iranian Foreign Minister Ali Akbar Velayati subsequently commented, to approach the former Soviet republics "through the Moscow gate."[6] It refrained from fuelling Islamic radicalism in the region, providing little or no strategic help to Islamic forces in Tajikistan or any other Central Asian republic. Similarly, in the case of neighboring Azerbaijan, which shares with Iran extensive sectarian and cross-border ethnic ties and where instability could have serious effects on the Iranian northern province of Azerbaijan, Tehran worked hard to prevent an all-out war between that state and Iran's Christian-populated neighbor, Armenia, over Nagorno-Karabakh. It also labored strenuously to limit Afghans from aiding the Tajik Islamists by continuously helping a group of Afghan Shia to wage armed opposition to the Islamic government in Kabul and thus keep it weak with deepening domestic preoccupations.

However, while supporting the idea of a collective Gulf security scheme with the participation of Iran, Russia managed its Iranian connection with a necessary degree of caution. It did not want its friendship with Iran to undermine its new partnership with the West, to jeopardize its chances of gaining access to markets and sources of capital in the Gulf's Arab states, or to limit unnecessarily its opportunity to play a major power role in the Arab-Israeli peace process. It managed this in several ways.

Economic, Political, and Strategic Interests in the Gulf

First of all, Moscow defended its arms sale, which attracted much criticism from the West, particularly Washington, and caused apprehension among Iran's Arab neighbors, on the grounds that Iran was a "friendly neighbor" and that Russia for both economic and security reasons had every right to sell arms to the country as long as it did not threaten the security of third countries. Moreover, Moscow claimed that sale of some of the weapons—most importantly the three Kilo-class submarines—was in fulfillment of previous contracts. Major General Sergei Karaganov of Defense Export refuted Western criticisms by claiming that ". . . we are operating in the arms market strictly within the rules established by the United Nations and we try not to disrupt the balance of power or to harm the security of third countries. Incidentally, Iran is not on the list of states to which arms sales have been prohibited by the international community, and we have the right to sell it a wide range of goods."[7]

Second, Moscow concurrently embarked on a campaign to expand its ties with the members of the Gulf Cooperation Council (GCC), that is, Saudi Arabia, Kuwait, the United Arab Emirates (UAE), Bahrain, Qatar, and Oman, for three main objectives. One was obviously to secure a share in the market and resources of the GCC and to gain wider support against Islamic radicalism in the former Soviet Central Asian republics and, indeed, among Russia's own Muslim minorities. Another was to reassure the United States and its Gulf allies that the expansion of its ties with Iran was not intended in any way to undermine their position. The third was to back its own position as a major-power player, especially in the post–Gulf War settlements in the region.

Capitalizing on what can be best described as Gorbachev's uneasy abandonment of the Soviet Union's long-standing ally, Iraq, and support for the U.S.-led international coalition's military campaign to reverse Iraq's August 1990 invasion of Kuwait,[8] Foreign Minister Kozyrev moved swiftly to affirm Russia's position in favor of the post–Gulf War status quo in the region. He emphasized Russia's support for the independence of Kuwait and the U.S.-driven UN sanctions against Iraq until Baghdad had fully complied with the terms of the Gulf War cease-fire agreement, which was signed in early April 1991. He also stressed Russia's commitment to the promotion of stability and order, which would ensure the sovereignty and security of all states in the region.

While stressing the importance of the Gulf as an area of serious economic and strategic interest to Russia, Kozyrev paid a working visit to the GCC countries in late April 1992. He described the central purpose of his visit as more than just to secure markets and financial assistance. He reportedly said:

> I am not hiding the fact that our visit is part of a drive for markets, including arms markets. We have created a huge military-industrial complex. And now we need to find profitable markets for selling Russian armaments. In the past our country relied on just a handful of states in the region—Iraq, Iran, Libya, etc. But that was an extremely unfortunate choice. Now we prefer to deal with stable, moderate regimes, and these are the ones with which we are trying to develop military cooperation.

Yet he also made it clear that this in itself was not enough.

> We had to assert ourselves in the region, to show that Russia remains a great power that is prepared to engage in mutually beneficial cooperation, that it is not standing there with an outstretched hand.[9]

In tangible economic and military terms, Kozyrev's visit did not produce a great deal in the short run, as only Oman promised to invest (to the tune of $500 million) in the development of Russia's oil and gas industry and (another $100 million) in the modernization of the country's oil fields. This, nonetheless, laid a foundation for greater understanding and some economic and military cooperation between Yeltsin's government and its GCC counterparts. It provided an opportunity for Moscow to underscore Russia's claim to major-power status and to reassure the GCC leaders that it was conscious of their concerns about the sale of Russian arms to Iran—a subject with which Kozyrev was confronted in most of the GCC capitals, most importantly, Riyadh. In Kuwait and the UAE, where misgivings about the Iraqi and Iranian threat were voiced most strongly, Kozyrev confirmed Russia's willingness to assist in strengthening their defense and security capabilities.

In return, he found that the GCC leaders had no interest in helping secessionist Muslim minorities in Russia. Reportedly, King Fahd of Saudi Arabia told him that "no matter what the religious convictions of a person in Russia are, for us he is first and foremost a citizen of the Russian Federation, and he should be loyal to his motherland,"[10] although this did not imply that Saudi Arabia would refrain from continuing its efforts to counter Iranian attempts to gain influence among Muslims in Central Asian states and in Afghanistan.

To press Russia's objectives further, Russian Defense Minister Pavel Grachev headed a twenty-member military delegation that visited the Gulf in early February 1993. During his tour of the UAE he declared that the Gulf was "of extreme importance to Russian interests," that Russian military and technical relations with the region were aimed at strengthening security and stability of the region, and that Russia would not allow such cooperation to be used for violating regional security.[11] To alleviate the UAE's concern about Russia's supply of arms to Iran—with which the Emirates have been locked in a feud over the three strategic islands of Greater and Smaller Tumbs and Abu Musa and whose unilateral annexation of the last island in January 1993 alarmed the UAE and their GCC partners as a pointer to Iranian regional ambitions—Grachev signed a protocol of understanding and coordination as a basis for a defense agreement with the Emirates. Earlier Moscow had publicly pledged its support for the UAE and readiness to defend them against Iran if necessary. [12]

Similarly, the Russian defense minister visited Kuwait and Bahrain in mid-February to discuss expansion of military and technical ties. In Kuwait, Grachev signed a memorandum of understanding on a possible defense pact similar to the ones that Kuwait signed with the United States, Britain, and France following its liberation from Iraqi occupation. Although the prospects for Kuwaiti purchase of Russian arms remained dim, the Russians still hoped for more positive developments in this respect once that pact was signed. Earlier, the minister had attended an International Defense Exhibition in Abu Dhabi, where the Russians had put on an impressive display of their most sophisticated arms, including anti-missile missiles, in the expectation of securing substantial purchases by the GCC member-states.[13] Moreover, in late February 1993, an official Russian delegation visited Bahrain—a country that has traditionally feared an Iranian threat—in order to widen Russia's Gulf ties. The visit did not result in any major bilateral agreement, but the deputy governor of the Bahrain Monetary Agency, Sheikh Ibrahim bin Khalifa al Khalifa, announced that his Agency was ready for "constructive and fruitful" cooperation with Russia.[14]

Third, Moscow sought to complement its policy of friendship with the U.S. Gulf allies with a number of other important measures. It steadfastly maintained its support for the Western powers in their confrontation with Iraq, backed them in their dispute with Libya over alleged Libyan involvement in the Lockerbie air disaster of 1989, and cooled its friendship with the Soviet Union's most important client in the Middle East, Syria.

Restructuring Relations with the Radical Arab States

With regard to Iraq, the Yeltsin government found it necessary for the strengthening of its partnership with the United States, international credibility, and changed regional position in favor of Iran and moderate Arab governments to weather the pressure of its domestic opponents and enforce Iraq's continued international isolation for as long as the UN Security Council deemed it imperative. In September 1992, when another round of military confrontation loomed large between Iraq and the United States over Baghdad's frequent attempts to defy UN Security Council resolutions, it condemned Baghdad's behavior. It even hinted at a possible readiness to contribute to any fresh military action against Iraq should it become necessary.

The only time the Yeltsin government showed some differences with the United States over Iraq was when in a series of punitive air strikes in January and June 1993, the United States attacked a factory and baby food plant in Baghdad at the cost of civilian lives. Moscow joined Britain and France to express its disapproval of the U.S. shelling of the target in the Iraqi capital. This coincided with the arrival of a small group of Russian paramilitary volunteers in Baghdad in late January as a gesture of solidarity with Iraq against American bombing, fueling speculation that Russia might try to end Iraq's isolation. However, the Russian Foreign Ministry quickly denied any change in Moscow's position and called for legal actions against the right-wing extremist Vladimir Zhirinovsky for sponsoring the paramilitaries.[15] With the United States and its industrialized allies considering a substantial package of economic aid to Russia in April to help Yeltsin in his market reforms and power struggle with legislative hard-line opponents, Yeltsin had little reason to become pliable toward Iraq. And once the aid package was approved, he could stand up to those critics who argued that the loss of the Iraqi market had cost Russia billions of dollars notwithstanding the fact that even before the UN sanctions Iraq had faced serious difficulties in paying its foreign debts and still owed $5 billion to the Soviet Union.

Another former close Soviet friend whose market Russia has lost as a result of the Yeltsin government's foreign policy changes and compliance with the UN sanctions is Libya. It is estimated that Russia's total loss from supporting sanctions against Iraq, Libya, and Yugoslavia has been around $16 billion, with Libya accounting for about one-third.[16] Russian-Libyan relations had actually run into serious difficulties before Russia joined the Western powers in the UN Security Council to impose sanctions against Libya in March 1992 (over Tripoli's refusal to hand over two of its officials to the U.S. and Britain for questioning about their alleged involvement in the mid-air explosion of a Pan Am passenger plane over Lockerbie, Scotland, in 1989). This was mainly due to the fact that Libya, like many other former Soviet friends, questioned Russia's claim to be the ruling successor of the USSR and dragged its feet in paying Russia for the debts that it had accumulated to the Soviet Union. When the UN sanctions were imposed, Russia's relations with Libya were reduced and the issue of repayment of debts also reached a dead end. This development, nonetheless, came at an opportune time for the Yeltsin government. Its compliance with the sanctions against Libya provided it with an opportunity to substantiate further its credentials with the West and its regional allies and to make clear that its friendly relations with Iran, with which Libya was one of the few Arab countries to maintain a cordial relationship, signified nothing more than the degree of pragmatism that Russia needed to have in its policy toward the region.

Similarly, the Yeltsin government showed few qualms about a lapse in its ties with Syria, which had once provided the pillar upon which Soviet Middle Eastern policy rested. Of course, the Moscow-Damascus relationship had began to experience serious difficulties under Gorbachev. From the late 1980s Moscow had demanded that Syria pay in hard currency for its arms purchases and had also made a rapid move toward re-establishing diplomatic relations with Israel in the hope of cooperating with the United States for a peaceful settlement of the Middle East conflict. Syria's inability to meet the demand and its apprehension about a change in Soviet Middle Eastern policy put Syrian-Russian relations on a difficult course. When, following the breakup of the USSR, Russia took a new direction and asked Syria to pay its accumulated debts, Damascus expressed reluctance to recognize the legality of Russia's succession to the Soviet Union and concern about the consequences of Russia's changing position.

The problem came to a head in mid-October 1992 when a Russian delegation, led by the head of the Ministry of Foreign Economic Relations, Petr Aven, visited Damascus to discuss the problem. Questioning once again

> ... [the] very legality of talks about debts with Russia as the successor to the USSR, the Syrian side reportedly proposed the setting up of a joint commission to "study questions of Russian legal succession" and investigate in general terms whether Damascus owes Moscow anything. . . .[17]

This brought the negotiation to an unhappy end, causing Russian-Syrian relations to hit an all-time low. Russia declined to meet old arms contracts, for which Syria had not paid, and refused to sign new ones; and, as Petr Aven put it, "Political dialogue with Syria was interrupted for quite a long time."[18] Thus, Russia ceased to cultivate close ties with Syria in its pursuit of a new regional and international role.

Policy Toward Jordan and the Arab-Israeli Problem

The opposite happened with Jordan, although Jordan was not traditionally a close friend of the Soviet Union and its relations with the country were limited. With the change in Russia's national direction and the relative marginalization of Jordan in the Arab world as a result of its sympathy for Iraq in the Gulf War, the situation changed for both sides in favor of better relations. While concerned about Russia's growing ties with Iran given King Hussein's long-standing opposition to the Islamic regime in Tehran, Jordan welcomed Russia's new direction and raised no difficulty in recognizing it as the successor to the USSR. As a result, when the Russian delegation visited Jordan following its tour of Syria in mid-October 1992, it encountered no resistance to bilateral relations.[19] King Hussein met the delegation personally, and he could not but have rejoiced at the thought that Syria no longer enjoyed special support from a superpower to pursue its radicalism of the past.

During this time, Russia maintained solidarity with the United States for a peaceful settlement to the Arab-Israeli conflict. The Yeltsin government built upon Gorbachev's initiative of building close cooperation with the United States to reinforce Russia's involvement in peace talks that had begun between Israel and the Palestinians and Arab states in late 1991 under the co-chairmanship of the United States and the Soviet Union. Of course, it is true that Russia had little option but to move in this direction given its growing vulnerability to the West and loss of influence with the Soviet Union's former friends. However, it approached the issue in such a way as not to be sidelined and treated lightly by any of the parties involved in the process. It waged a sustained campaign to win the confidence of Israel, removing all the barriers created by the Soviet Union to the normalization of relations with the country, and to reassure the Palestinians and Arab states that despite all the difficulties in Russia's relations with them, it was still in their interest to encourage rather than undermine Russia's participation in the peace process.

Meanwhile, at no point did Russia attempt to use its commitment to the peace process, as marginal as it may have grown, to irritate the United States and its allies, as Gorbachev had done when he tried to broker a settlement between Washington and Baghdad just prior to the start of the Gulf War. Thus Moscow showed no hesitation in supporting the peace accords signed between the Palestine Liberation Organization (PLO) and Israel in September 1993, which came about as a result of their secret negotiations with no Russian hand in the process. Andrei Kozyrev appeared to be making a special effort to make it clear that the days of using the Arab-Israeli conflict for regional gains had gone and that what Russia now wanted was equal participation in regional markets and resources through cooperation with the West and its regional allies. By the same token, Kozyrev sought to dispel the Western and Israeli concern about Russia's relationship with Iran. The downturn in the relations between Moscow and Damascus could not have come at a better time in this respect.

Policy Dilemmas and Anomalies

It is important to note that in the process of formulating the above policy approach to the Middle East, the Yeltsin government could not avoid some important anomalies. Many of these anomalies, however, had their roots mainly in regional contradictions that Moscow has not been able to address successfully. The biggest one, which could trouble Russia in almost the same way as it did its Soviet predecessor, is embedded in the difficulty of conducting relations with Iran and the rest of the region on a balanced and beneficial basis. Given the moderate Arab governments' deep-seated apprehension of, and the U.S. and Israeli opposition to, the Iranian Islamic regime, it is unlikely that Moscow will be able to sell its Iran policy to them successfully. No matter how many assurances Russia gives about its Iranian connection, they may not be sufficient to ease the distrust and rivalry that have grown to govern the Arab states' relations with Iran and thus to allow Russia to promote its regional interests on as wide a scale as is politically and economically worthwhile. It is worth remembering the failure of the United States in this respect when in the early 1970s Washington tried during the rule of the Shah, within the framework of the Nixon Doctrine, to forge close ties between Iran and Saudi Arabia. This leaves Russia with little hope for success. Moscow's emphasis on a regional collective security system in the Gulf, with the inclusion of Iran, goes against the very strategy of isolation that GCC and the U.S. have sought to enforce vis-à-vis Iran. As the situation stands, Moscow's present approach is likely to confront it with very difficult policy choices sooner or later.

Similarly, Moscow's approach runs the risk of endangering Russia's relations with Turkey. Despite their public disclaimers, Iran and Turkey are locked in serious rivalry for influence in Central Asia and Transcaucasia. While Turkey has revived its pan-Turkic ambitions and campaigned hard to persuade the Turkish-speaking republics in the region that its secular model of development offers them the best hope for a better future, and while in this it has had the support of the United States, Iran has spared no effort to counter this development. It has made strenuous efforts to convince the former Soviet Central Asian republics of the value of its model of Islamic change and development and of its position as the most resource-rich state in the region. Should the Russo-Iranian relationship continue its present course of development, Turkey may find itself with little choice but to move to undermine the basis of such a relationship.

Nor is Russia's Iran policy likely to help its overall goal of moderating or neutralizing the forces of radical Islam in the former Soviet republics, or within the Russian Federation itself in the long run, although Moscow has probably overestimated the current Iranian influence in this respect, for two reasons: first, with the exception of Azerbaijan, all the Muslim Central Asian republics are dominated by Sunni Islam; and apart from Tajikistan, which is mainly Persian-speaking, they are all predominantly Turkic-speaking, with former communists still in power (except in Kyrgyzstan). Thus, Iran—where radical Shi'ite Islam dominates politics and society and Persian is the national language—stands little chance of being emulated in the region.

Second, although Iran is in a position to cause problems in Afghanistan, it is severely constrained in its ability to secure a compliant government in Kabul. Afghanistan is a predominantly Sunni Muslim state with a history of distrust in its relationship with Iran. This has become abundantly clear since the establishment of the mujahideen government, which has sought to distance itself from the Iranian regime in its moderate ideological disposition and political orientation. In fact, Afghanistan and Turkey have more in common with the peoples of Central Asia than does Iran. A deterioration of Russia's relations with Turkey on top of its restrained ties with Afghanistan could make Russo-Iranian friendship quite taxing and counter-productive.

There is no doubt that, despite Russia's transformation in search of a new national direction and its disruptive consequences for foreign policy formulation, the Yeltsin government has managed to pursue a somewhat consistent policy pattern in support of a number of discernible objectives in its behavior toward Central Asia and the Middle East. This certainly has not amounted to what can be described as a coherent, clear Central Asian–Middle Eastern policy, but it has given a fairly recognizable direction to the conduct of Russia's relations with the region. It has primarily centered on Russia's changing national and international circumstances, but with a clear eye on the need to lay the foundations for a long-term Central Asian–Middle Eastern policy. In this, however, the Yeltsin government has not been able to avoid certain actual and potential anomalies that have arisen partly from the contradictory dynamics of regional politics and partly from the way Moscow has sought to approach these dynamics in pursuit of its objectives. As a result, Russia's approach to the region contains the potential to entrap it in some serious dilemmas and difficult foreign policy choices, which, if not managed properly, could be costly for Russia in terms of both its regional and international interests. However, it is too soon either to draw firm conclusions or to make firm predictions in this respect.

Notes

1. For a succinct discussion of these two schools of thinking, see Alexander Rahr, "'Atlanticists' Versus 'Eurasians' in Russian Foreign Policy," *RFE/RL Research Report*, vol. 1, no. 22, May 29, 1992, pp. 17–22.

2. See "Yeltsin Criticizes Work of Russian Foreign Policy," BBC, *Summary of World Broadcasts*, (SWB), SU/1524, October 29, 1992, A1/3-4.

3. The mujahideen leaders have often mentioned a figure of $150 billion. However, the figure of $100 billion is also quoted by Western sources. See "Mission Called 'Success'," FBIS-SOV, May 18, 1992, p. 10.

4. Reuters, February 28, 1994; Amid Rashid, "Push for Peace: Neighbors Gear Up to Broker a Tajik Settlement," *Far Eastern Economic Review*, February 3, 1994.

5. Stephen Blank, "Russia and Iran in a New Middle East," *Mediterranean Quarterly*, vol. 3, no. 4, 1992, pp. 125–26.

6. "Velayati on Visit to Soviet Republics," FBIS-NES, December 9, 1992, pp. 65–66.

7. *The Current Digest of the Post-Soviet Press*, vol. XLIV, no. 30, 1992, p. 17.

8. For a discussion of Gorbachev's policy stand on the Kuwait crisis, see Galia Golan, "Gorbachev's Difficult Time in the Gulf," *Political Science Quarterly*, vol. 107, no. 2, 1992, pp. 213–30.

9. *The Current Digest*, vol. XLIV, no. 18, 1992, pp. 15–16.

10. *The Current Digest*, vol. XLIV, no. 18, 1992, p. 18.

11. Reuters, February 3, 1993.

12. Reuters, October 17, 1992.

13. Reuters, February 17, 1993.

14. Reuters, February 24, 1993.

15. Reuters, January 27, 1993.

16. See the Summary of Russian Foreign Ministry Statement in BBC, *SWB*, SU/1559 Al/3, December 9, 1992.

17. For the text of the report of the visit of the Russian delegation, see BBC, *SWB*, SU/1521, Al/1-3, October 26, 1992.

18. BBC, *SWB*, SU/1521, Al/1-3, October 26, 1992.

19. BBC, *SWB*, SU/1521, Al/2-3, October 26, 1992.

14

Russia's New Agenda in Sub-Saharan Africa

Robert G. Patman

In March 1992, Andrei Kozyrev completed the first official visit to the African continent by a Russian foreign minister. The five-day visit, according to Kozyrev, showed that Russia was not relinquishing the "global role" of the former Soviet Union (FSU) in the region.[1] This claim, however, did little to quell widespread African complaints about Russian disinterest and was belied by the political and economic realities constraining Russian policy toward Africa. In the 1960s Africa was seen as strategically important to the Soviet Union in its zero-sum Cold War competition with the United States and ideological rivalry with China. In the 1970s the USSR capitalized on its growing military power to achieve significant gains in sub-Saharan Africa. Using Cuba as a proxy, Moscow helped to promote Marxist regimes in Angola, Ethiopia, Guinea-Bissau, and Mozambique. However, by 1983, the rising costs of preserving these gains prompted the Soviet leadership to reexamine its role in Africa. This reassessment found full expression in Mikhail Gorbachev's "new thinking" after 1985. In a sweeping transformation of Soviet policy toward sub-Saharan Africa, Gorbachev sharply reduced Moscow's support for socialist-oriented states while calling for political compromises to end regional disputes. These changes, which amounted to a major Soviet retreat, had profound consequences for Africa's political power structure.

By the time of the abortive coup in Moscow in August 1991, Africa had become a region of peripheral importance for the Soviet Union. In a dramatic reversal of the situation in the 1970s Gorbachev had, in the words of one Russian specialist, presided over the "collapse" of the USSR's African policy.[2] But while Moscow's deepening economic crisis made relations with the West a top priority for Gorbachev, his government also struggled to preserve some remnants of the USSR's superpower "prestige" and "influence" in Africa.[3] All this changed, however, with the attempted coup against Gorbachev and the subsequent dissolution of the USSR. The task of this chapter is to assess the impact of these events on Russian policy toward Africa. To do this, I will consider Yeltsin's inheritance in Africa, the new Russian approach to the continent, and the overall priorities and the emerging pattern of relations with a focus on Moscow's relations with South Africa, Angola, and Somalia. Consideration will also be given to Russia's military and economic relations with Africa.

Yeltsin's Inheritance

Russian interest in sub-Saharan Africa preceded the 1917 Bolshevik revolution, but it was not until Nikita Khrushchev's reassessment of the Third World in the mid-1950s that the Soviets became sensitive to the anti-Western political and economic potential of African nationalism. Khrushchev enthusiastically supported African decolonization in the 1960s and provided material support to a number of national liberation movements and newly independent states.[4] But these efforts were not an unqualified success. In 1960, Moscow suffered a reversal through its inability to provide military support for the militant nationalist leader Patrice Lumumba during the crisis in the Belgian Congo (now Zaire). Between 1965 and 1968, three Soviet-backed African leaders—Ben Bella of Algeria, Kwame Nkrumah of Ghana, and Modibo Keita of Mali—were overthrown. In each instance, their successors turned away from the USSR. The lesson this provided for the Brezhnev leadership was that the volatility of African politics made its "natural allies" on the continent rather unreliable.

Yet, if by the early 1970s Moscow's ideological optimism about Africa had subsided, the USSR's confidence in its own ability to influence events in the Third World had markedly increased. The most decisive ingredient in this metamorphosis was the perception by the Brezhnev government in 1969-1970 that there had been a major shift in the correlation of forces in favor of socialism.

Two factors were central to this perception. First, the Brezhnev government, thanks to a massive military buildup after 1964, attained rough parity with the United States in strategic nuclear weapons. Second, tumultuous events in the United States, including racial violence, political assassinations, growing inflation, and, above all, the "Vietnam syndrome," convinced many Soviet leaders that the United States had begun a period of irreversible decline as a global actor. These developments, in Moscow's view, facilitated a more active Soviet role in the Third World.[5]

Africa provided a number of opportunities for Moscow to exploit its new global reach. The catalysts were the collapse of Portugal's African empire and the overthrow of Emperor Haile Selassie in Ethiopia. When Portugal withdrew from Angola in 1975, the Soviets successfully intervened in the ensuing civil war. The USSR mounted a large-scale air and sea operation, involving the transportation of arms worth an estimated $300 million and around 15,000 Cuban troops, to ensure the victory of the Movement for the Popular Liberation of Angola (MPLA) over its Western and Chinese-backed rivals.[6] Then, in 1977–1978, Moscow decisively intervened in the Horn of Africa, where two of its allies, Ethiopia and Somalia, had become embroiled in a war over the disputed Ogaden territory. Having come down on the side of Ethiopia, the Kremlin launched a massive operation on behalf of the Mengistu regime, ferrying in over $1 billion worth of arms, around 12,000 Cuban troops, and 1,500 Soviet military advisers.[7] Within months, the Somali army was driven from the Ogaden. The ability to supply arms also enabled Moscow in 1976 to win out over Beijing in the race for influence with the FRELIMO liberation forces in the former Portuguese colony Mozambique. And by the late 1970s the USSR had concluded long-term treaties of friendship with the Marxist-Leninist regimes in Angola, Mozambique, and Ethiopia.

The USSR had become a key regional actor in sub-Saharan Africa, but the long-term costs of its involvement were enormous. First, Moscow was drawn into intractable local conflicts. Its allies in Angola, Mozambique, and Ethiopia were all engaged in civil wars that impoverished their economies and made them dependent on Moscow for arms for which they could not afford to pay. Second, Moscow's African policy aroused suspicions in the West that the USSR was using detente as a cover to expand its influence. In 1980, the Carter administration established a rapid intervention capability through bases in Oman, Kenya, and Somalia and upgraded existing military facilities at Diego Garcia. President Reagan upped the ante by giving aid to anti-communist insurgents in Angola and Ethiopia. Third, the political and economic returns of Moscow's huge military investment in sub-Saharan Africa were meager. The economies of Angola, Mozambique, and Ethiopia were so badly damaged by unrelenting civil wars that prospects for social and economic development were virtually nil. But Moscow was not in a position to bail out its allies. In 1983–1984, Angola and Mozambique independently negotiated cease-fires with South Africa and began to look more to the West for economic assistance. The dreadful Ethiopian famine of 1984–1985 further highlighted Moscow's economic limitations as an ally, as Western governments and voluntary agencies provided the bulk of emergency food aid to Addis Ababa.[8]

The Impact of Gorbachev's New Political Thinking

Soviet pessimism about the Third World was reflected in policy under Mikhail Gorbachev after 1986. Convinced that Brezhnev's international policy had become dangerously detached from the USSR's internal needs, Gorbachev as a matter of urgency sought to improve Soviet relations with the technologically advanced West and a rapidly modernizing China. The new agenda assumed the modern world was "interconnected and interdependent."[9] By relaxing the traditional Marxist-Leninist worldview, the new Soviet leadership gradually embraced such "revolutionary" ideas as common human values, mutual security, the de-ideologization of interstate relations, the "profitability" maxim for foreign relations, and the political settlement of regional disputes.

In Africa, Gorbachev's new political thinking had profound repercussions. Moscow reversed its previous hostility to U.S. diplomacy in southern Africa. Joint Soviet-American efforts in the region culminated in the Brazzaville and New York accords, signed in December 1988 by Angola, Cuba, and South Africa.[10] These U.N.-supervised accords paved the way for the election of a South West African People's Organization (SWAPO) government in November 1989 and the formal independence of Namibia. Following this achievement, Moscow pressed for a political solution to the civil war in Angola. Eduard Shevardnadze, the Soviet foreign minister, and James Baker, the U.S. secretary of state, again worked together to assist the MPLA-UNITA peace negotiations that had resumed in April 1990. This process eventually led to the signing of an Angolan peace settlement in late May 1991. The agreement envisaged the creation of a single Angolan army and the holding of nationwide multi-party elections at the end of 1992.[11] Meanwhile, Gorbachev backed President Joaquim Chissano's policy of negotiating with the rebel Renamo movement, and the USSR was one of ten countries represented in a Joint Verification Commission established in December 1990 to monitor a tentative cease-fire in Mozambique.[12] Gorbachev warmly welcomed the Ethiopian-Somali peace accord of April 4, 1988, and thereafter advocated a negotiated settlement to the civil war in northern Ethiopia.

The growing Soviet emphasis on the peaceful resolution of regional conflicts was paralleled by a steady reduction of military commitments in Africa. In Angola, the largest importer of Soviet military hardware in sub-Saharan Africa between 1986 and 1990, this became evident only in 1990 when Moscow began to phase out its 1,000-strong contingent of military advisers. Then with the May 1991 peace settlement, the Soviet Union terminated the delivery of arms to the MPLA regime.[13] In Ethiopia,

Moscow served notice to Mengistu in November 1987 that arm supplies would cease in December 1990.[14] But EPLF military successes in early 1990 accelerated the disengagement process. In April of that year the USSR began to withdraw its 1,500 military advisers from Ethiopia, and by the time of Mengistu's exit the Soviet naval base on the Dahlak Islands had been closed.[15] At roughly the same time, Soviet military advisers left Mozambique, and shipments of arms were reduced to transfers of light weapons and spare parts.

A variety of factors pushed Moscow toward military disengagement. First, the end of the Cold War in the late 1980s undermined the rationale of military involvement. In Angola, for instance, developments such as the negotiated withdrawal of the South Africans and the end of Pretoria's occupation of Namibia seriously diminished the prospects of external aggression against Luanda. Similarly, in the Ethiopian case, the thaw in relations between Mengistu and the Bush administration in 1989 and the suspension of all U.S. military assistance to neighboring Somalia during the same year weakened the logic of any external threat to Addis Ababa. Second, with the advent of glasnost in Soviet foreign reporting, the huge cost of Moscow's military aid program in Africa became a focus for severe criticism inside the USSR. In March 1990, *Izvestiia* revealed that Ethiopia, Angola, and Mozambique were among the Third World countries with massive debts to the USSR (they owed 2,860 million, 2,029 million, and 809 million rubles, respectively).[16] The newspaper pointed out that the bulk of these debts related to military expenditure.

Another dimension of the new political thinking that had a significant effect on sub-Saharan Africa was the de-emphasis on ideology in diplomatic relationships. But if Moscow was losing "old friends" on the continent, it was expanding links with the richer, capitalist countries. The most striking example was South Africa. In March 1990, Foreign Minister Shevardnadze held a private meeting with President de Klerk while attending Namibia's independence celebrations. The meeting occurred when international economic sanctions against South Africa were still in place. Although Shevardnadze insisted afterward that there had been no weakening in the USSR's opposition to apartheid, the event spotlighted the dramatic shift in Soviet strategy from support for ANC-led armed struggle against apartheid to backing a solution through political dialogue.[17] In February 1991, the two countries upgraded their relations through the establishment of diplomatic "interest sections";[18] in June, a Soviet Union–South Africa Society was created; and in August, a Soviet deputy foreign minister made a historic visit to Pretoria because changes in the country were "becoming more and more irreversible."[19]

The final aspect of the new political thinking that left its mark on sub-Saharan Africa was the drive for "profitability" in Soviet foreign policy.

The Gorbachev government decreed that economic relations should be based on the principles of "mutual benefit and mutual interest."[20] When Soviet ventures were deemed to be unprofitable they were either "commercialized" or simply dropped. In Angola, for example, a third of all joint projects were abandoned.[21] The Soviet decision to conduct all foreign trade in hard currency from January 1, 1991, aggravated the situation further. Countries like Guinea, Ethiopia, and Mozambique, accustomed to trading with Moscow on a barter basis, were severely hit by this reform, as they had little hard currency to spare.

Moreover, Soviet attempts to diversify trade in Africa were undermined by the contracting Soviet economy and competition from the newly industrialized countries. The exception was perhaps South Africa. In May 1990, Moscow and De Beers, the large South African corporation, formalized a secret 30-year relationship in a $5 billion marketing deal.[22] The deal gave De Beers exclusive rights to the sale of 95 percent of the diamonds exported by the Soviet Union.

But generally Moscow's new economic strategy was impeded by the problem of Africa's debt. By December 1991, African countries owed the USSR 13,936 million rubles, or nearly 16 percent of the total foreign debt outstanding to the USSR.[23] The publication of these figures caused a political storm in Moscow. Gorbachev's then major rival, Boris Yeltsin, who was elected president of the Russian Federation in June 1990, condemned the squandering of national resources.[24] It was in this climate that Soviet foreign aid to sub-Saharan Africa and the rest of the Third World was slashed. In 1989, 12,500 million rubles were allocated for aid; in 1991 the amount had fallen to 400 million rubles.[25]

Gorbachev's new political thinking gradually relegated sub-Saharan Africa to the margins of Soviet foreign policy. At the time of the abortive coup of August 1991, the USSR was well on the way to disengaging from long-standing alliances in the region but had only just begun the process of advancing a new political strategy in Africa. For the Soviet leadership there were other priorities. These included the deepening economic and social crisis at home, the revolutionary upheavals in Eastern Europe, and the Gulf War.

Russian Perspectives on Africa

With the dissolution of the Soviet Union in December 1991, a new Russian foreign policy emerged amid considerable domestic discord. For President Boris Yeltsin and his foreign minister, Andrei Kozyrev, the policy had three basic parameters. First, there was the task of consolidating Russia's diplomatic status as the successor-state to the Soviet Union. Second, it was necessary to maintain "the positive gains achieved by the Gorbachev-Shevardnadze diplomacy," particularly in the field of Moscow's relations with the United States. Third, as "a completely different country from the Soviet Union," Russia would project its own interests on the international stage. In geographical terms, these interests were divided by Kozyrev into three priorities. An absolute priority for Russian diplomacy was the protection of state interests in "the near abroad," a term that refers both to the former Union republics and to neighboring states such as China. The second major priority was to move toward an alliance relationship with the West. This goal, however, was subject to some revision. In late 1993, the Yeltsin government, mindful of the nationalist challenge of Vladimir Zhirinovsky, abandoned the "romantic" notion that partnership with the West would be devoid of conflict. A third priority was relations with the Third World without ideological constraints and consistent with the "real national interests of Russia."[26]

So what did this pragmatic perspective mean for Africa? Initially, the answer seemed to be one of almost complete indifference to the continent. Internally, Kozyrev's repeated claim that Russia was a "great power" was challenged inter alia on the grounds that Moscow was neglecting Africa.[27] Nor did Kozyrev's tour of Africa in late February 1992 silence this line of criticism. Externally, Russia's "Atlanticist" foreign policy galvanized the African diplomatic community in Moscow—represented by the ambassadors of Senegal, Ghana, Zimbabwe, and Madagascar—to seek assurances from Yegor Gaidar, then the acting prime minister, that Russia was not "turning away from Africa."[28] Equally, during visits to Benin, Ghana, Nigeria, Ivory Coast, and Senegal in late 1992 and early 1993, officials from the Russian Foreign Ministry's department for Africa and the Middle-East, Viktor Posuvalyuk and Grigory Karasin, heard repeated calls for a more vigorous Russian policy in Africa.[29]

The Russian Foreign Ministry in late 1992 unveiled a working document on the Russian approach toward Africa. According to a deputy foreign minister, Boris Kolokolov, Russia viewed Africa "as a continent of problems but also a continent of the future." "The Russian Federation," noted Kolokolov, "has both political and economic interests in Africa, but . . . mutually beneficial relations with that continent can be assured only by getting rid of what was characteristic in the past—the ideological blinkers and the wasteful nature of the ties for Russia." The document also stated that Russia would continue cooperation with the West in promoting conflict resolution but reserved the right to sell arms to African countries "for defensive needs." It was claimed African states had a rising interest in relations with Russia because they recognized that "the world should not be lopsided" through U.S. and Western domination.[30]

The General Pattern of Relations

The overall trend in Yeltsin's African policy was one of accelerated retreat tempered by a measured targeting of diplomatic attention on southern Africa. The key factor in this trend was the failing Russian economy. In April 1992, Moscow decided to close Russian embassies in nine African countries—Burkina Faso, Equatorial Guinea, Lesotho, Liberia, Niger, Sao-Tome and Principe, Togo, Somalia, and Sierra Leone. Six months later the consulates in Mozambique, Angola, Madagascar, and the Congo were added to this list.[31] The Russian government stressed that the closures were caused by purely financial considerations. But a number of those African states affected interpreted the actions as a political snub.[32] This perception reflected other strains in Russian-African relations. For one thing, there were increasing reports of racist attacks on African students in Russia.[33] This, along with the steeply rising costs of studying in Russia, provided the context for an ugly incident in Moscow in August 1992 when police shot dead a Zimbabwean student, and 350 African students rioted "Los Angeles" style in the city. Almost immediately afterward Zimbabwe expressed its displeasure by cancelling plans to purchase MiG-29 fighter planes from Russia.[34] More generally, African ambassadors in Moscow adopted a collective stand of studied neutrality during the political showdown between President Yeltsin and his hard-line opponents on October 3–4, 1993.[35]

In addition, Russian's standing in Africa was damaged by the handling of the debt problem. By January 1993, thirty-two African countries owed Moscow a total of 14,000 million rubles.[36] Ninety percent of this debt was for military deliveries. In October 1991 Boris Yeltsin had placed a ban on all foreign aid.[37] This step was dictated by a growing public outcry against Moscow's "generous" assistance to developing countries. The Russian government, confronted with a $US70,000 million external debt of its own and a chronic shortage of hard currency, demanded the repayment of Africa's debt. Such pressure caused considerable resentment in Africa, particularly among the poorer, formerly socialist-oriented countries. When, for example, Kozyrev visited Angola in February 1992, President Dos Santos was reported to have flatly refused to pay what the Russians now said was a $4,000 million debt. The Angolan refusal was based on the argument that the debt was largely military in nature—and thus a function of Moscow's old strategic rivalry with the United States—and it was owed not to the Russian Federation but to the former Soviet Union.[38]

To some extent, these negative aspects of Russian-African relations were magnified by the decline of Moscow's diplomatic activism on the continent. It was in the Horn of Africa where Russia's slump from superpower status was most evident. In December 1992, Russia served as co-author for the UN Security Council resolution endorsing a U.S.-led intervention in Somalia—the one-time strategic ally of the former Soviet Union—to ensure the delivery of food aid in the conflict-ridden country. However, Moscow did not participate in this "extraordinary" operation and made its offer of medical aid conditional on UN financial support.[39] Meanwhile, in neighboring Ethiopia, Russia had very little to show for the former Soviet Union's $10 billion military investment between 1977 and 1990.[40] The new transitional government largely ignored Russia and instead established good relations with the United States, a point confirmed by Washington's pledge in September 1992 to provide Addis Ababa with $161 million in aid over the next three years.[41]

The exception to this otherwise passive phase of Russian diplomacy was southern Africa. When Foreign Minister Kozyrev toured Africa at the end of February 1992, he visited Angola and South Africa. The choice of Angola as Kozyrev's first stop in Africa was "no coincidence." Despite the unresolved debt problem, Kozyrev said Angola was one of "the richest countries in Africa" and presented "great opportunities for developing mutually beneficial cooperation."[42] Moving on to South Africa, Kozyrev "discovered" a new friend and "a very serious new economic partner"[43] The visit heralded the restoration of diplomatic relations between Moscow and Pretoria, an event that was condemned by the South African Communist Party (SACP) and also Yeltsin's pro-communist opponents within Russia.[44] Undeterred, Yeltsin ordered the promotion of South African ties and received President de Klerk in a state visit to Moscow in early June 1992.

Political and Diplomatic Relations

Angola

Angola was a unique case as far as Russian policy in sub-Saharan Africa was concerned. Although it was often depicted in Yeltsin's Russia as a failed "showcase of socialism,"[45] the Russian leadership believed Angola had enormous economic potential and could, in Kozyrev's words, emerge as "a democratic, dynamic, developing state." Situated in southern Africa, Angola shared a border with "Africa's superpower," South Africa. Therefore, despite the great changes in both the former Soviet Union and Angola, Moscow decided to try and rebuild its interests in this African country rather than simply phase them out as in Ethiopia.

Kozyrev signalled Russia's concern with Angola by making it his first destination during his brief tour of Africa in late February 1992. But there was little to justify Kozyrev's conviction that Russian-Angolan relations were "moving in the right direction." First, there was deadlock over the question of Angola's debt to Moscow. The two sides simply agreed to continue the search for a "civilized solution to this problem,"[46] the absence of which obstructed economic cooperation between Russia and Luanda. Second, while Kozyrev coupled the announcement of the closure of the former Soviet military mission in Angola with a pledge to continue military ties "on an economic basis," Luanda did not respond to the Russian offer of "expert technical support" in the formation of a new national army. Instead, this task was undertaken with British, Portuguese, and French advice.[47]

The resumption of the Angolan internal conflict, following UNITA's refusal to recognize the MPLA's election victory in September 1992, further limited the prospects for bilateral cooperation. Moscow was forced to evacuate many of its 600-strong contingent of military and economic specialists from the country. The Yeltsin government deplored the renewal of hostilities but exercised restraint in its pronouncements on the crisis until the Clinton administration belatedly recognized the MPLA as the legitimate government in May 1993.[48] Thereafter, Russia, along with its partners to the Lisbon accords, Portugal and the U.S., declared that "the terrorist actions" of UNITA were responsible for the breakdown of the peace process. While continuing to reaffirm its support for UN efforts to secure a cease-fire in Angola, Moscow resumed "limited deliveries of defensive arms" to the Angolan government in September 1993.[49] But if Moscow rekindled an old connection, the new objective of a "mutually advantageous partnership" with Luanda looked a remote possibility.

South Africa

After the failure of the August coup attempt in Moscow in 1991, relations between Russia and South Africa gained a steady momentum. In a little under two years, South African Foreign Minister Pik Botha visited Moscow, his Russian counterpart journeyed to Pretoria, the two countries restored diplomatic relations after a thirty-six year break, and President de Klerk visited Moscow.

The groundwork for the breakthrough in Russian–South African relations had been laid during the Gorbachev era. In mid-August 1991, USSR Deputy Foreign Minister Valery Nikolaenko had visited South Africa and observed that it was in the Soviet Union's "national interest" to have good relations with "regional powers" like South Africa.[50] But the Yeltsin government saw rapprochement with South Africa as the key to establishing a broader political and economic Russian presence on the African continent in the long term. It is instructive that the first Russian ambassador to South Africa, Yevgeny Gusarov, emphasized that Pretoria was a regional power with which relations "are an important direction of Russian foreign policy, aiming to strengthen Russian positions on the African continent [as a whole]."[51]

The new Russian strategy was shaped by a variety of factors. For one thing, Moscow, no longer constrained by the remnants of Marxist ideology, recognized that South Africa was in, Kozyrev's terms, "our natural partner."[52] Commentators and government officials detected a certain symmetry in the economies of the two countries. Together they produced around 80 percent of the world's gold, platinum, and other precious metals and minerals. This fact, according to one of Yeltsin's aides, meant the two countries had a "unique possibility of influencing the world markets of raw materials."[53] By the same token, South Africa was capable of becoming Russia's largest market in Africa and the "natural gateway" to the markets of the entire southern African region.[54]

In addition, Moscow felt unable to ignore the pace of change in de Klerk's South Africa. Since coming to power in 1989, President de Klerk had freed the leader of the African National Congress (ANC), Nelson Mandela, cancelled the ban on black political parties, and instituted the Convention for a Democratic South Africa (CODESA). While these reforms were incremental in nature, they convinced Kozyrev that "there will be no return to apartheid."[55]

Furthermore, with the demise of the CPSU after August 1991 and the subsequent breakup of the Soviet Union, the position of certain political forces, resisting the policy of rapprochement with South Africa, was systematically weakened. The USSR Foreign Ministry, which according to Boris Piliatskin, the *Izvestiia* correspondent, had opposed the planned visit of de Klerk in December 1991[56] (it was cancelled on the initiative of Pretoria), underwent a vigorous shake-up in personnel when Russia became the legal successor to the Soviet Union. Moreover, while Yeltsin and Kozyrev were fully prepared to run the risk of offending the ANC and the SACP and their Russian supporters to expand ties with South Africa—"We have gotten used to listening to the advice of Communists and doing the opposite"[57]—they were careful to preserve some political continuity in their new strategy. First, Kozyrev stressed that the restoration of relations with Pretoria was consistent with a rejection of racial discrimination. It was argued that high-level contacts with the present reformist South African government would further stimulate Pretoria's development away from apartheid and toward democracy. That is why Moscow backed de Klerk's policy.[58] Second, the Russian government persistently made the point that it recognized Nelson Mandela and the ANC as expressing the interests of the black majority. It is interesting that Kozyrev only officially announced the resumption of diplomatic relations with South Africa only after consultations with Mandela in Johannesburg.[59] Equally, when President de Klerk visited

Moscow in June 1992, Yeltsin resisted South African pressure to rescind an invitation to Mandela to visit Russia and, in an assessment of the positive changes in South Africa, singled out both the contribution of his visitor and the "activity of the opposition leader, Nelson Mandela."[60]

As related, Kozyrev travelled to Pretoria for talks in late February 1992. "If someone had told me five years ago that I would welcome the Russian Foreign Minister to our capital, I would have laughed in his face."[61] These were the words with which Pik Botha greeted Kozyrev. Significantly, the normalization of Russian–South African relations provoked a public disagreement between Mandela, who voiced measured approval, and his SACP allies, who denounced this step as "premature and counter-productive."[62]

In June 1992, President de Klerk paid a two-day visit to Moscow at the invitation of the Russian government. In a joint communiqué covering the talks, Yeltsin expressed support for South Africa's desire to get back into the United Nations, welcomed "the dismantling of apartheid," and attached prime importance to the process of democratization in South Africa, saying that it "could have a beneficial effect on the entire region."[63] In exchange for this diplomatic support, de Klerk promised Russia 100 million rands in revolving credit and agreed to conclude a series of agreements on trade and economic cooperation.[64] The de Klerk visit sparked furious criticism from Yeltsin opponents inside the Russian Unity parliamentary block,[65] but Yeltsin himself expressed satisfaction with the completion of what he called "the period of establishing first contacts."[66]

Since then, new nuances in Moscow's South African policy have appeared. Concerned about the level of violence in the South Africa but encouraged by the prospect of nonracial elections, Russia increasingly emphasized its ANC connection. In early May 1993, Boris Kolokolov, the Russian deputy foreign minister, visited South Africa and held talks with both de Klerk and Mandela. During his stay, Kolokolov stressed that it was necessary to "be aware in what directions the South African process is developing."[67] Within a month, a high-ranking ANC delegation arrived in Moscow, the first to do so since the collapse of the CPSU. It had talks with top officials in the Russian Foreign Ministry, Ministry of Foreign Economic Relations, and other departments. This, along with the lifting of all political and economic restrictions on ties with Pretoria, indicated that Moscow was preparing for the new political realities after the general election in April 1994.

Somalia

The U.S.-led humanitarian intervention in Somalia, Operation Restore Hope, provided a vivid example of the limitations of Russian diplomacy in Africa after the Cold War. The Russian government backed the deployment of the U.S.-dominated military force and helped to draft UN Security Council Resolution 794 in December 1992. Grigory Karasin, then the head of the Russian Foreign Ministry Africa Administration, explained that Moscow believed sending a sizable military contingent to Somalia under the UN flag was an extraordinary measure, "but there was no other way out."[68] The same official, however, conceded that the U.S. president did not consult the Russian leadership in advance about the decision to launch a large-scale action in Somalia.[69] And apart from a conditional offer of medical assistance, Russian involvement was minimal.

While such marginalization was perhaps inevitable given the scale of Russia's domestic problems, a number of commentators were concerned that Moscow's public support for the U.S.-dominated operation in Somalia diminished its international standing still further. Although the Russian Foreign Ministry upheld the UN line against the Somali warlord, Gen. Mohammed Farah Aideed, in the summer of 1993, writers in *Rossiiskaia gazeta*, *Krasnaia zvezda* and *Moskovskie novosti* condemned the U.S. for turning a humanitarian operation into "a bloody slaughter"[70] in Mogadishu. It was interesting, therefore, that on October 12, 1993, the Yeltsin government welcomed the U.S. decision to correct its "error" in Somalia and abandon the search for a military solution.[71] By distancing itself from U.S. policy in Somalia, the Russian leadership seemed to be trying to counter the impression that Moscow had ceased to be relevant in African conflict resolution.

Military Relations

According to the Stockholm International Peace Research Institute, African arms imports (from all sources) in 1990 fell by 60 percent in comparison with 1982.[72] It is safe to assume that Soviet arms exports to the continent were affected by this trend. Under Yeltsin, the downward shift initially continued. First, Russia completed the process of de-ideologizing its arms trade and now sold military products or expertise on a purely commercial basis. As a consequence, Moscow either lost some of its traditional markets (Mozambique, Ethiopia) or saw its market share greatly reduced (Angola). Second, and related to this point, a number of African states already had huge military debts to Russia and therefore were in no position to buy additional weaponry. Third, Russia faced competition from other CIS nations, most notably from Ukraine, in the arms market in Africa.[73]

However, indications suggest that Russia was trying to reverse its decline as an arms exporter to Africa. "Today, trading in arms is a necessity for us," President Yeltsin told the *Izvestiia* newspaper on February 22, 1992. In relation to Africa, Russian arms exporters, in a quest for new markets, targeted the Western-oriented states on the continent because they were in a relatively better position to pay. South Africa seemed to be a special target. After Kozyrev's visit in February 1992, a high-level Russian trade delegation travelled to Pretoria. The delegation had a strong military complexion, including senior air-force officers and representatives of the military aerospace design industry.[74] Apparently, the South Africans were interested in the possibility of purchasing MiG-29 engines and installing them in their Mirage fighter fleet. Then, in August, following a meeting with the South African ambassador in Moscow, Defense Minister Pavel Grachev noted that "in the long term" bilateral business cooperation in military-related areas "is quite possible."[75] By the end of 1993, representatives of South African military-industrial concerns envisaged joint ventures with Russia in areas such as submarines and military aviation.[76]

Economic Relations

While Moscow's economic ties with Africa always lagged far behind political and military relations, they reached a new low under Yeltsin. Only around 2 percent of Russia's foreign trade turnover in 1992 was accounted for by Africa.[77] And behind this figure lay a decline in both the share and absolute volumes of trade. In 1985, 7 percent of Soviet exports to developing countries went to Africa; by 1991 the figure had dropped to 1.6 percent.[78]

The deterioration in the Russian economic position in Africa reflected Yeltsin's new political priorities. The ban on foreign aid and Moscow's own increasing preoccupation with attracting aid and investment from the West further marginalized Africa as an economic concern. Trade with the former Soviet Union's allies on the continent collapsed. Between January and September 1990, exports to Ethiopia, Angola, and Mozambique were 210.3 million, 123.2 million, and 80.6 million rubles, respectively. They fell to 3.2 million, 61 million, and 1.7 million rubles, respectively, during the same period in 1991.[79]

Thus far the impact of the emerging Russian private sector has been very limited. Out of the hundreds of registered joint ventures with foreign partners, only a few involve African countries. Around a dozen Russian private fishing companies have established joint ventures with Africa or other foreign firms in various African coastal areas.[80] Other Russian joint enterprises in Africa include a shipping company in Liberia, a trucking company in Tanzania, and an agricultural and food processing venture in Mozambique.[81] Such a modest track record prompted Professor Yuri Popov to exclaim: "There is still too much prejudice among our officials and business executives against Africa . . . . in the new economic and trade offensive."[82]

If that mentality existed, it clearly applied less to southern Africa. Moscow sought cooperation in two related areas. The first was precious metals and minerals. In the summer of 1992, De Beers opened an office in Moscow.[83] Then, in October, Moscow received a De Beers delegation, with the talks centering on a new diamond deal. The move followed reports that Russia, desperate for hard currency and angered by its "colonial" agreement with De Beers, was exporting rough and cut diamonds in apparent contravention of its May 1990 agreement with De Beers.[84] By January 1994, De Beers indicated that it wished to amicably settle the problems of diamond sales with the Russian government.[85] The need for coordination was also stressed in the gold industries of the two countries. In April 1992, the South African ambassador to Moscow, Gerrit Olivier, visited a gold center in Novosibirsk and met with representatives from forty Russian firms in Siberia.[86] Twelve months later, a nineteen-strong group of managers of gold and diamond enterprises in the Urals and Siberia visited mines controlled by the Anglo-American Corporation and De Beers and discussed the possibility of joint ventures with South African companies.[87]

The second area of economic interest was science and technology. A number of agreements were concluded. Moscow used South African technology to combat the effects of radioactive soil from the Chernobyl nuclear accident; [88] a major Russian manufacturing firm, Sovluksgvant, established a solar power joint venture with a South African company in December 1991; [89] Russia leased four Russian planes with Russian crews to South African Airways in January 1993 to transport cargoes;[90] in February 1993, Russia sold the South African navy a scientific research vessel for $13.2 million;[91] and in September 1993, Russia and South Africa signed a scientific agreement facilitating cooperation in areas such as biotechnology, pharmaceuticals, energy, and ecology. These links were expected to be further boosted by a reciprocal most-favored-nation status agreement concluded in October 1993.[92]

By way of contrast, Russian-Angolan economic ties stagnated. The aforementioned problem of Angola's debt was the main impediment. Nevertheless, Moscow confirmed that it retained an economic interest in the country. In January 1992, a Russian ship delivered a new turbine for Angola's $2 billion Capande hydroelectric dam, a joint Russian-Brazilian-Angolan project described by the World Bank in 1991 as the key to Angola's post-war reconstruction.[93] Work on the dam continued despite the resumption of the civil war.

Conclusion

With the breakup of the Soviet Union in December 1991, the Yeltsin government completed the process of disengagement in Africa begun by its predecessor and steered Russia in a very selective and interest-oriented approach toward the continent. It is clear that Russia has targeted southern Africa as its main priority in sub-Saharan Africa. In particular, Moscow has pinpointed South Africa as the state most likely to offer Russia a "mutually advantageous relationship." According to one Russian observer, the rapprochement between Russia and the largest and richest African state confirms that Russian foreign policy is now based on the old, pragmatic principle that although the country "does not have eternal friends," it does have "eternal interests."[94]

However, it would be wrong to exaggerate the possibilities for Russian–South African relations. Economic cooperation has only just begun to be established. Given the geographical distance between the two countries and the fact that both are passing through considerable political turmoil, it is difficult to envisage large-scale economic links in the near future. For despite South Africa's economic potential, its economy does not rival that of the European Community, the United States, and Japan.[95] These economic giants are likely to be higher priorities for Russian foreign policy-makers than Pretoria.

Beyond South Africa, the prospects for Russia in Africa appear limited. Unlike the high-growth Asia-Pacific region and rapidly reviving Latin America, the economies of sub-Saharan Africa are undermined by internal conflicts, high population growth, devastating droughts, the AIDS epidemic, and the reduction of high levels of international aid. Thus, the commercial possibilities for expanding Russian exports, including arms, to the region are generally moderate. It is likely that Russia will confine its interest to the wealthier African states.

There remains, however, a possibility that Russia, after a period of adjustment to power, will seek a higher political profile in Africa. Grigory Karasin, the head of the Russian Foreign Ministry information department, said African states realize that from the political viewpoint they cannot do without Russia "if only because the latter is a permanent member of the UN Security Council."[96]

Certainly, since late 1992, Russian diplomacy has assumed greater visibility on the continent. But even if Moscow still views itself as a great power, it is difficult to envisage an enhanced Russian political role in Africa during the post–Cold War era without a major revival of its economic fortunes.

Notes

I wish to thank Cairine Meier and Nathan McConnell for their research assistance in the early stages of this project. In addition, I would like to acknowledge the generosity of Pierre Botha of the Africa Institute of South Africa for making available a large number of documents from the institute's files during the preparations for writing this chapter.

1. Interfax, February 25, 1992, *Foreign Broadcast Information Service* FBIS-SOV-92-038, February 26, 1992, p. 27.
2. A. Kiva, "Afrika: I zdes' zanovo?" *Literaturnaia gazeta*, no. 21, May 29, 1991.
3. Ye. Titov cited in TASS, July 19, 1991 in BBC, *Summary of World Broadcasts (SWB)*, SU/1131 A5/1, July 23, 1991.
4. Margot Light, "Moscow's Retreat from Africa," *Journal of Communist Studies*, vol. 8, no. 2, 1992, p. 25.
5. Robert G. Patman, *The Soviet Union in the Horn of Africa: The Diplomacy of Intervention and Disengagement*, Cambridge, Cambridge University Press, 1990, p. 109.
6. Arthur Jay Klinghoffer, "The Soviet Union and Angola," in Robert H. Donaldson (ed.), *The Soviet Union in the Third World: Successes and Failures*, Boulder, Westview Press, 1981, p. 113.
7. Patman, *The Soviet Union in the Horn of Africa*, p. 223.
8. Robert G. Patman, "Soviet-Ethiopian Relations: The Horn of Dilemma," p. 118.
9. Mikhail Gorbachev, quoted in *Izvestiia*, November 3, 1987.
10. Mark Webber, "Soviet Policy in Sub-Saharan Africa: The Final Phase," *The Journal of Modern African Studies*, vol. 30, no. 1, 1992, p. 6.
11. Interfax, May 30, 1991, FBIS-SOV-91-105, May 31, 1991, pp. 24–25.
12. Mark Webber, "Soviet Policy in Sub-Saharan Africa," p. 13.
13. Statement of USSR Ministry of Foreign Affairs, TASS, May 4, 1991.
14. Patman, "Soviet-Ethiopian Relations: The Horn of Dilemma," p. 122.
15. *Izvestiia*, May 11, 1991.
16. *Izvestiia*, March 1, 1990.
17. W. Raymond Duncan and Carolyn McGiffert Ekedahl, *Moscow and the Third World Under Gorbachev*, Boulder, Westview, 1990, p. 175.
18. *Izvestiia*, February 27, 1991, *Current Digest of the Soviet Press (CDSP)*, vol. XLIII, no. 9, 1991, pp. 21–22.
19. Soviet Television, August 15, 1991, *SWB*, SU/1155 A5/1, August 20, 1991.
20. "The Soviet Union's Co-operation with Developing Nations in the Future," interview with V. Burmistrov, *Foreign Trade*, no. 10, 1990, p. 12.
21. Webber, "Soviet Policy in Sub-Saharan Africa," p. 26.
22. *The Star*, August 17, 1990; Interfax, October 19, 1992, FBIS-SOV-92-203, October 30, 1992, p. 13.
23. *Moscow News*, no. 48, 1991.
24. *Moscow News*, no. 9, 1991.

300   *Robert G. Patman*

25. *Izvestiia*, January 15, 1991.

26. A. Kozyrev interview, *Krasnaia zvezda*, November 26, 1992; A. Kozyrev, *Izvestiia*, March 11 1994; *Kommersant*, January 19, 1994, FBIS-SOV-94-012, January 19, 1994, p. 9.

27. *Pravda*, January 18, 1992, *CDSP*, vol. XLIV, no. 3, 1992, p. 25.

28. *Izvestiia*, November 10, 1992, *CDSP*, vol. XLIV, no. 45, 1992, p. 16.

29. ITAR-TASS, December 23, 1992, *SWB*, SU/1573 A1/4, December 29, 1992; *Rossiiskaia gazeta*, January 29, 1993.

30. Moscow Radio World Service, December 7, 1992, FBIS-SOV-92-236, December 8, 1992, pp. 8–9.

31. Interfax, April 27, 1992, FBIS-SOV-92-083, April 29, 1992, pp. 18–19, Interfax, November 13, 1992, FBIS-SOV-92-221, November 16, 1992, pp. 16–17.

32. Ibid., p. 17.

33. "Black Bashing," *West Africa*, October 8–14, 1990, pp. 2606–2607; Tim Wall, "Soviet Demise Brings Africa New Challenges," *Africa Recovery*, April 1992, pp. 18–19.

34. Ostankino Channel 1 TV, Moscow, August 12, 1992, *SWB*, SU/1459 A1/2, August 14, 1992. Ostankino Channel 1 TV, Moscow, August 23, 1992, *SWB*, SU/1468 A1/2, August 25, 1992.

35. "Russia's Africa Policy," *West Africa*, November 22–28, 1993, p. 2123.

36. Moscow Radio World Service, January 24, 1993, *SWB*, SU/1599 A1/4, January 29, 1993.

37. *The Guardian*, October 29, 1991.

38. *Izvestiia*, March 7, 1992; Charles Quist Adade, "Russia to Swap African Debts for Food," *New African*, July 1992, pp. 32–33.

39. ITAR-TASS, December 2, 1992, FBIS-SOV-92-233, December 3, 1992, p. 4; ITAR-TASS, December 8, 1992, FBIS-SOV-92-237, December 9, 1992, p. 1.

40. Patman, "Soviet-Ethiopian Relations: The Horn of Dilemma," p. 125.

41. "US Signs First Development Assistance Agreement," *Friends of Ethiopia Newsletter*, 1/7, November 1992, p. 1.

42. *Rossiiskaia gazeta*, February 28, 1991, FBIS-SOV-92-040, 28 February 1992, p. 18; Radio Moscow in Afrikaans, February 27, 1992, *SWB*, SU/1319 A5/1, March 3, 1992; Radio Mayak, March 2, 1992, *SWB*, SU/1320 A1/1, March 4, 1992.

43. Kozyrev quoted on Russian television, March 2, 1992, *SWB*, SU/1320 A1/2, March 4, 1992.

44. *Nezavisimaia gazeta*, March 3, 1992, FBIS-SOV-92-044, March 5, 1992, p. 24.

45. *Pravda*, November 18, 1991.

46. Radio Moscow in Afrikaans, February 29, 1972, FBIS-SOV-92-041, March 2, 1992, p. 18.

47. Moscow TASS International News Service, February 27, 1992, FBIS-SOV-92-041, March 2, 1992, p. 17; ARB, November 1991, pp. 10359–60.

48. ITAR-TASS, May 21, 1993, FBIS-SOV-93-098, May 24, 1993, pp. 17–18.

49. Interview with Leonid Safanov, director of the Russian Foreign Ministry's Africa Department, *Nezavisimaia gazeta*, September 22, 1993, FBIS-SOV-93-184, pp. 14–15.

50. Soviet Television, August 15, 1991, *SWB*, SU/1155 A5/1, August 20, 1991.

51. Radio Moscow World Service, November 27, 1992, *SWB*, SU/1556 A1/3, December 5, 1992.

52. Kozyrev quoted by Interfax, February 25, 1992, FBIS-SOV-92-038, February 26, 1992, p. 28.

53. Vyacheslav Kostikov, head of the Russian president's press service, quoted in Interfax, June 1, 1992, *SWB*, SU/1397 A1/1, June 3, 1992.

54. President F. W. de Klerk quoted on Johannesburg SAPA, June 1, 1992, FBIS-SOV-92-106, June 2, 1992, p. 10.

55. *Izvestiia*, March 3, 1992, FBIS-SOV-92-047, March 10, 1992, p. 17.

56. *Izvestiia*, December 31, 1991, FBIS-SOV-91-003, January 6, 1992, pp. 3–4.

57. Kozyrev quoted in *Izvestiia*, March 2, 1992, *CDSP*, vol. XLIV, no. 9, 1991, p 19.

58. *Nezavisimaia gazeta*, March 3, 1992, *SWB*, SU/1321 A5/1, March 5, 1992; *Izvestiia*, March 3, 1992, FBIS-SOV-92-047, March 10, 1992, p. 17.

59. *Izvestiia*, March 3, 1992, FBIS-SOV-92-047, March 10, 1992, p. 17.

60. Russia's Radio, June 1, 1992, *SWB*, SU/1397 A1/2-3, June 3, 1992, ITAR-TASS, June 1, 1992, *SWB*, SU/1397 A1/1, June 3, 1992.

61. *Izvestiia*, March 3, 1992, FBIS-SOV-92-047, March 10, 1992, p. 16.

62. *Nezavisimaia gazeta*, March 3, 1992, *SWB*, SU/1321 A5/1, March 5, 1992.

63. ITAR-TASS, June 1, 1992, *SWB*, SU/1397 A1/2, June 3, 1992.

64. Ostankino TV, June 1, 1992, FBIS-SOV-92-106, June 2, 1992, p. 7; Interfax, June 1, 1992, *SWB*, SU/1397 A1/1, June 3, 1992.

65. Sergei Baburin, one of the leaders of the Russian Unity parliamentary block, condemned de Klerk's visit as "premature" because he did not believe change was irreversible in South Africa and thought it was in Moscow's "national interests" to strengthen ties with the ANC. Interfax, June 5, 1992, FBIS-SOV-92-112, June 10, 1992, p. 28.

66. ITAR-TASS, June 1, 1992, FBIS-SOV-92-106, June 2, 1992, p. 11.

67. ITAR-TASS, May 9, 1993, FBIS-SOV-93-088, p. 13.

68. ITAR-TASS, December 2, 1992, *SWB*, SU/1556 A1/3, December 5, 1992.

69. *Pravda*, December 5, 1992, FBIS-SOV-92-236, December 8, 1992, p. 9.

70. *Rossiiskaia gazeta*, June 19, 1993; *Krasnaia zvezda*, June 24, 1993; *Moskovskie novosti*, July 25, 1993.

71. Interfax, October 12, 1993, *SWB*, SU/1823 B/7, October 19, 1993.

72. Leonid L. Fituni, "Russia's Arms Sales to Africa: Past, Present, and Future," *CSIS Africa Notes*, no. 140, September 1992, p. 1.

73. Interfax, August 13, 1992, FBIS-SOV-92-158, August 14, 1992, p. 9. *Komsomolskaia pravda*, February 26, 1992, *SWB*, SU/1321 A512, March 5, 1992.

74. "Arms Deals Will Be First of Russia-SA Trade Links" *SouthScan*, vol. 7, no. 9, March 6, 1992, p. 69.

75. ITAR-TASS, August 11, 1992, FBIS-SOV-92-156, August 12, 1992, p. 20.

76. *Krasnaia zvezda*, December 15, 1993, FBIS-SOV-93-241, December 17, 1993, pp. 48–49.

77. ITAR-TASS, August 17, 1992, *SWB*, SU/W0244 A/3-4, August 21, 1992.

78. Fituni, "Russia's Third Discovery of Africa," p. 3.

79. Figures adapted from *Foreign Trade*, 11–12, 1992, pp. 52–53.

80. Fituni, "Russia's Third Discovery of Africa," p. 3.

81. ITAR-TASS, April 20, 1992, *SWB*, SU/W0279 A/6, April 30, 1993; *New Times*, April 17–23, 1990; Fituni, "Russia's Third Discovery of Africa," pp. 3–4.

82. Professor Yuri Popov quoted in Charles Quist Adade, "Why Do We Need Africa?" *New African*, August 1992, p. 49.

83. "Moscow Visit Alerts Diamond World," *Africa Analysis*, September 4, 1992, p. 11.

84. Under the terms of the May 1990 agreement, De Beers had the exclusive rights to market 95 percent of the diamonds exported by the former USSR; Interfax, October 19, 1992, FBIS-SOV-92-203, p. 13; Interfax, July 20, 1993, *SWB*, SU/WO290 A/14, July 16, 1993.

85. *Ostankino*, Channel 1 TV, January 14, 1994, *SWB*, SUW/0316 WD/10, January 21, 1994.

86. *Izvestiia*, April 16, 1992, FBIS-SOV-93-079, April 23, 1992, p. 19.

87. ITAR-TASS, April 26, 1993, SWB, SU/WO279 A/14, April 30, 1993.

88. Radio Moscow World Service, November 27, 1991, *SWB*, SU/1246 A5/1, December 4, 1991.

89. Radio South Africa, December 2, 1991, *SWB*, ME/1245 B/9, December 3, 1991.

90. Radio Moscow World Service, January 24, 1993, *SWB*, SU/W0266 A/27, January 29, 1993.

91. ITAR-TASS, February 20, 1993, *SWB*, SU/W0270 A/7, February 26, 1993.

92. *Rossiiskiie vesti*, September 16, 1993, FBIS-SOV-93-181, September 21, 1993, p. 16; *Izvestiia*, October 29, 1993.

93. ARB, March 1992, p. 10517.

94. Russian Television, November 9, 1991, *SWB*, SU/1226 A5/3, November 11, 1991.

95. *Izvestiia*, March 2, 1992, *CDSP*, vol. XLIV, no. 9, 1992, p. 19.

96. *Rossiiskaia gazeta*, January 29, 1993.

About the Book

This book brings together leading experts on Russia's foreign relations, providing the most comprehensive coverage of contemporary Russian foreign policy currently available in a single volume. Detailed case studies of relations with specific countries and regions are complemented by chapters that examine the process of decision-making and conflict among domestic institutional actors.

About the Editor
and Contributors

Peter Shearman, senior lecturer in political science at the University of Melbourne, is the author of *The Soviet Union and Cuba* (1987) and (with Phil Williams) *The Superpowers, Central America and the Middle East* (1988).

Eugene Bazhanov, deputy director of the Diplomatic Academy, Russian Ministry of Foreign Affairs, Moscow, is the author of many articles and books on China and Russian foreign policy.

Mike Bowker, lecturer in politics at the University of East Anglia, U.K., is the author (with Phil Williams) of *Superpower Detente: A Reappraisal* (1988) and (with Robin Brown) *From Cold War to Collapse: Theory and World Politics in the 1980s* (1993).

Neil Malcolm, previously director of the Russian and CIS Foreign Policy Program at the Royal Institute of International Affairs in London, is director of the Russian and East European Research Centre, University of Wolverhampton, and the author of *Soviet Policy Perspectives on Western Europe* (1989) and *Russia and Europe: An End to Confrontation* (1993).

Robert F. Miller, senior fellow in political science, Research School of Social Sciences, The Australian National University, is the author of *Soviet Foreign Policy Today: Gorbachev and the New Political Thinking* (1991) and *The Developments of Civil Society in Communist Systems* (1992).

Robert G. Patman, lecturer in politics, University of Otago in New Zealand, is the author of *The Soviet Union in the Horn of Africa: The Diplomacy of Intervention and Disengagement* (1990).

Yuri Pavlov, previously Soviet ambassador to Chile, lecturer in Russian Foreign Policy, University of California at Santa Barbara, is the author of *Soviet-Cuban Alliance 1959–1991* (1994).

Wynne Russell worked for six years as a Soviet analyst for the U.S. government and is currently completing a doctoral thesis at the University of Melbourne on Russian foreign policy toward the near abroad.

Amin Saikal, director of the Centre for Middle Eastern and Central Asian Studies, The Australian National University, is the author of *The Rise and Fall of the Shah* (1983) and (with William Maley) *The Soviet Withdrawal from Afghanistan* (1989).

Yoke T. Soh is completing her doctoral thesis at the University of Melbourne on Soviet relations with North and South Korea.

Ramesh Thakur, professor of international relations and director of Asian studies at the University of Otago in New Zealand, is the author (with Carlyle A. Thayer) of *Soviet Relations with India and Vietnam* (1992*)* and *India After Nonalignment* (forthcoming).

Carlyle A. Thayer, professor and head, Department of Politics, Australian Defence Force Academy, University of New South Wales, is the author of *War by Other Means: National Liberation and Revolution in Vietnam* (1989) and (with Ramesh Thakur) *Soviet Relations with India and Vietnam* (1992).

Index

Administration for CIS Affairs, 34
Administration for the Community
    Countries, 34
Adomeit, Hannes, 103
Afanasyev, Yuri, 258
Afghanistan, 270–272, 281
    Soviet invasion of (1979), 12, 18, 235,
        248
    See also Central Asia/Middle East
Africa
    and African National Congress (ANC),
        287, 293, 294
    and Andrei Kozyrev, 283, 288–289,
        290–292, 293–294
    Angola, 12, 16, 283, 285, 286, 287, 288,
        290, 291–292, 296, 297
    and apartheid, 293–294
    Benin, 289
    and Boris Yeltsin, 288–291, 293–294,
        295–296
    Burkina Faso, 290
    Congo, 290
    and economics, 287–288, 290–291, 296–
        298
    Equatorial Guinea, 290
    Ghana, 289
    Guinea, 288
    Guinea-Bissau, 283
    Ivory Coast, 289
    and Leonid Brezhnev, 284, 286
    Lesotho, 290
    Liberia, 290
    Madagascar, 289, 290
    and Marxism-Leninism, 283, 286
    and Mikhail Gorbachev, 283–284, 286–
        288
    and military, 286–287, 292, 294–296
    Mozambique, 283, 285, 287, 288, 290,

    296
    and natural resources, 293, 297
    Niger, 290
    Nigeria, 289
    political relations of, 291–295
    Principe, 290
    Russian perspectives on, 288–289
    and Russian policy, 286–288
    and Russian relations, 290–291
    Sao-Tome, 290
    Senegal, 289
    Sierra Leone, 290
    Somalia, 285, 287, 290, 291, 294–295
    South, 167, 286, 287, 288, 291, 292–294,
        298
    and South African Communist Party
        (SACP), 291, 293–294
    and South West African People's
        Organization (SWAPO), 286
    and Soviet policy, 283–285
    Togo, 290
    and United States, 284, 286, 287, 291,
        294–295
    Zimbabwe, 289, 290
African National Congress (ANC), 287,
    293, 294
Agafonov, Sergei, 149, 151
Agencies, policy-making
    and Andrei Kozyrev, 28–29, 32, 33–34,
        35–36, 37, 38, 39, 40, 43
    Communist Party of the Soviet Union
        (CPSU), 14–15, 17, 24–26, 29–30, 33,
        75, 78, 138, 203, 247
    legislature, 39–43
    and Marxism-Leninism, 15–16, 139
    Ministry of Defense (MOD), 27–28, 33,
        36–39, 125
    presidency, 25, 26–32
    process for, 26–28

and Soviet legacy, 23–26, 44
See also Ministry of Foreign Affairs
(MFA)
Aideed, Farah, 295
Albania, 76. *See also* Central/Eastern
Europe
Allende, Salvador, 248
Ambartsumov, Yevgeny, 40–41, 42, 64–
65, 120–121, 127
Analysis and Forecasting
Administration, 34
ANC. *See* African National Congress
Andronov, Iona, 126
Angola, 16, 283, 287, 288, 290, 291–292,
296, 297
and Movement for the Popular
Liberation of Angola (MPLA), 12,
285, 286, 292
and National Union for the Total
Independence of Angola (UNITA),
286, 292
See also Africa
Apartheid, 293–294
APR. *See* Asia-Pacific Region
Arbatov, Aleksei, 125
Arbatov, Georgi, 126–127
Argentina, 248, 249, 251–252, 255. *See also*
Latin America
Armenia, 53. *See also* Commonwealth of
Independent States (CIS); Near
abroad
ASEAN. *See* Association of South-East
Asian Nations
Asia-Pacific Region (APR), 135–138, 208–
209. *See also specific countries*
Association of South-East Asian Nations
(ASEAN), 138, 202, 208–213, 220
Attali, Jacques, 105
Australia, 138
Aven, Petr, 149, 278–279
Azerbaijan, 53, 67(n1), 235, 273, 281. *See
also* Commonwealth of Independent
States (CIS); Near abroad

Bahrain, 274, 276. *See also* Central Asia/
Middle East
Baker, James, 100, 113, 122, 251, 286
Balanzino, Sergio, 101

Baltic states. *See* Commonwealth of
Independent States (CIS); Near
abroad; *specific states*
Baturin, Yury, 66
Bausin, Alexei, 121
Belarus, 53, 56, 66, 67(n1), 118, 167, 205–
206
and geopolitics, 80–81, 85
See also Commonwealth of
Independent States (CIS); Near
abroad
Bella, Ben, 284
Belorussia. *See* Belarus
Benin, 289. *See also* Africa
Berlin Wall, 74, 75, 77, 97–98. *See also*
Germany
Besancon, Alain, 62
Bipolarity, 2, 9, 10, 11–12, 15–16, 111–113,
117–119
Bipolycentrism (Spanier), 12
Black Sea Fleet, 40, 42, 56–57, 63–64, 67
Bolivia, 248, 252. *See also* Latin America
Bolshevik Revolution (1917). *See* Russian
Revolution (1917)
Borodayev, Vladimir, 260
Bosnia, 87–88, 98, 119, 120–121, 152. *See
also* Central/Eastern Europe
Botha, Pik, 292, 294
Brandt, Willy, 12, 95, 100
Brazil, 248, 249, 252. *See also* Latin
America
Brest-Litovsk Treaty, 4–5, 15, 16
Brezhnev, Leonid, 14, 17, 94, 96, 136, 143,
233
and Africa, 284, 286
and Brezhnev Doctrine, 72–74
Britain, 82, 100, 103, 107, 122
Brzezinski, Zbigniew, 5, 124, 126–127
Bulgaria, 76, 79. *See also* Central/Eastern
Europe
Burbulis, Gennady, 27–29, 33, 237
Burkina Faso, 290. *See also* Africa
Bush, George, 3, 116, 120, 122, 149, 287
Bykov, Alexander, 116–117

Cambodia, 170, 201–202, 220
Cam Ranh Bay, 202, 207–213
CANF. *See* Cuban-American Foundation
Capitalism, 3–4, 15–17, 105, 112–113

Carter, Jimmy, 197, 285
Castro, Fidel, 250–251, 258, 260, 261, 262,
    263
Central Asia/Middle East, 56, 66, 159,
    177
  Afghanistan, 12, 18, 235, 248, 270–272,
    281
  and Andrei Kozyrev, 268–269, 270,
    274–275, 280
  Bahrain, 274, 276
  and Boris Yeltsin, 268–269, 277–279,
    280–282
  and Commonwealth of Independent
    States (CIS), 269
  and economics, 273–279
  and Gulf Cooperation Council (GCC),
    274–276
  and Gulf region, 274–276
  and Gulf War, 228–229, 274
  Iran, 121, 147, 235, 272–274, 280–281
  Iraq, 100, 122–123, 274, 277
  Jordan, 279–280
  Kuwait, 274, 276
  Libya, 276, 277–278
  and military, 273, 274–276
  Oman, 274, 275
  and Palestine Liberation Organization
    (PLO), 279–280
  Qatar, 274
  and Russia's policy approach, 267,
    270–280
  and Russia's policy dilemmas, 280–282
  and Russia's policy objectives, 268–269
  Saudi Arabia, 274
  and Soviet policy, 267
  Syria, 276, 278–279
  United Arab Emirates (UAE), 274–276
  and United States, 269, 274, 277–281
Central/Eastern Europe
  Albania, 76
  and Andrei Kozyrev, 82–83
  and Bill Clinton, 87
  and Boris Yeltsin, 71, 78, 82, 84, 85, 86–
    88
  Bosnia, 87–88, 98, 119, 120–121, 152
  and Brezhnev Doctrine, 72–74
  and Britain, 82
  Bulgaria, 76, 79

  and communist collapse, 74–76
  and economics, 76–78, 80–81, 83–84
  and European Union (EU), 83–84
  and France, 82, 95
  and geopolitics, 10, 76–77, 80–81, 85–86
  Hungary, 72–74, 76–77, 79, 81, 82, 83,
    96, 100–101, 102
  and Joseph Stalin, 10–11, 75–76, 77, 94
  and Kaliningrad, 80, 85–86, 98
  and Marxism-Leninism, 72, 77
  and Mikhail Gorbachev, 71–80, 88, 94–
    95
  and military, 10–11, 76–77, 78–83, 85–
    88
  and Moldova-Romania relationship,
    86–87
  and nationalism, 71, 80–81, 84–85
  and natural resources, 76, 78
  and North Atlantic Treaty
    Organization (NATO), 78–80, 82–83
  Poland, 8–9, 10–11, 72–74, 75, 76, 79, 80,
    81, 82, 83, 86, 96, 100–101, 102, 104
  post-revolutionary period, 77–80
  post-Soviet period, 80–84
  Romania, 76, 86–87
  and Russian threat, 84–88
  Russia's role in, 71–72
  Slovakia, 81, 82, 83, 100–101, 102
  and Soviet withdrawal, 71–77
  subsidization of, 76–77
  and United States, 77, 80, 81, 83
  Yugoslavia, 40, 41, 42, 76, 87–88
Central East European Free Trade Area,
    83–84
Central Europe. *See* Central/Eastern
    Europe
Central European Initiative
    (Pentagonale), 83–84
Chamberlain, Neville, 7
Chang Sang Hyon, 188
Chernomyrdin, Viktor, 32, 117, 138, 206,
    211, 217, 241–242
Chernov, Vladislav, 118–119
Chile, 248, 251–252. *See also* Latin
    America
China
  and Andrei Kozyrev, 165, 169–170
  and arms trade, 147
  attitude toward Russia, 167–169

and Boris Yeltsin, 161, 164–166, 169–171, 172, 174, 175, 177
and economics, 117, 165–166, 168, 172–173, 175–176
and future Russian relations, 174–178
and geopolitics, 172, 175, 232–233
and global politics, 177–178
and G-7 group, 114
and ideology, 176
and India, 227, 232–233, 239
and Israel, 167
and Japan, 136, 138
and Joseph Stalin, 159–160
and Korea, 167, 173, 177, 187
and Mikhail Gorbachev, 160–161, 162
and military, 147, 169, 171, 172, 174
and natural resources, 173, 175
and nuclear weapons, 172, 174
and political relations, 171–172
and Russian cooperation, 169–171
and Russian relationship difficulties, 161–164
Russia's attitude toward, 164–167
Russia's friends/adversaries, 159–161
and South Korea, 167, 177
and Soviet policy, 11, 19
and Taiwan, 164, 176–177
and Tiananmen Square, 74, 160, 161, 165
and Ukraine, 167
and United States, 11, 12, 166, 168–169, 172, 177–178
and Vietnam, 167, 201–202, 208, 210, 211–212, 219–220
Chissano, Joaquim, 286
Christian Democrats, 79
Christopher, Warren, 120, 121–122
Chung Ju-young, 182–183
Churchill, Winston, 10
Churkin, Vitaly, 128
CIS. *See* Commonwealth of Independent States
Clinton, Bill, 87, 99, 195–196, 292
and domestic politics, 3, 115, 116, 119, 120, 121, 126, 127
and Partnership for Peace (PFP), 83
CMEA. *See* Council for Mutual Economic Assistance

CODESA. *See* Convention for a Democratic South Africa
Cold War
and bipolarity, 111–113, 117–119
and detente, 12–13
and Germany, 93, 96, 97–98
and ideological changes, 1–2, 18–19, 112–113
and nuclear arms race, 10
onset of, 9
and United States, 1–2, 9, 18–19, 111–112, 115–116, 117–119
Comintern, 5
Commission for Trade, Economic, Scientific and Technological Cooperation (Vietnam), 217–218
Commonwealth Affairs Department, 60
Commonwealth of Independent States (CIS)
Armenia, 53
Azerbaijan, 53, 67(n1), 235, 273, 281
Belarus, 53, 56, 66, 67(n1), 80–81, 85, 118, 167, 205–206
and Central Asia/Middle East, 269
and China, 174
formation of, 53–57, 67(n1)
Georgia, 53–54, 59–60, 61, 67(n1)
and Japan, 148–149
Kazakhstan, 53, 58, 67(n1), 118, 149, 172, 205–206, 235
Kyrgyzstan, 53, 149, 172, 235
and Latin America, 253, 257
and Ministry of Cooperation, 35, 44
and policy-making agencies, 29, 30, 32, 34–35, 38, 40, 41, 43
and Russian nationalism, 85
Tajikistan, 53–54, 172, 235, 270–271, 281
Turkmenistan, 53
Uzbekistan, 53, 191, 205–206, 235, 271–272
and Western Europe, 102–103
See also Moldova; Near abroad; Ukraine
Communist Party of the Soviet Union (CPSU)
International Department of the Central Committee, 14–15, 17, 24–26, 29–30, 33, 75, 78, 138

and Latin America, 247
and Vietnam, 203
"Complex Plan of the Development of
the USSR's Relations with Latin
America" (1987), 248–249
"Concept of Russian Foreign Policy"
(Ministry of Foreign Affairs), 38, 65,
139, 140
Conference on Security and Cooperation
in Europe (CSCE), 65, 82–83, 102–103
Congo, 290. *See also* Africa
Constitution, Russian, 27
Convention for a Democratic South
Africa (CODESA), 293
Council for Mutual Economic Assistance
(CMEA), 71, 77–78, 94, 95
Council of Baltic States, 83–84
Council of the Federation, 43
Council on Foreign and Defense Policy,
44–45
Council of Ministers, 27
CPSU. *See* Communist Party of the Soviet
Union
Crawshaw, Steve, 72
Crimea, 31, 32, 40, 42
and Russian citizens, 59, 60
See also Central/Eastern Europe
Croatia, 87–88, 152. *See also* Central/
Eastern Europe
Crow, Suzanne, 185
Crumm, Eileen, 117
CSCE. *See* Conference on Security and
Cooperation in Europe
Cuba, 249, 257–264
and economics, 248, 250–251, 259–262,
264
and Fidel Castro, 250–251, 258, 260,
261, 262, 263
and Mikhail Gorbachev, 250–251, 258
and military, 251, 260–261, 262–263
missile crisis of, 11
and natural resources, 259–260, 262
and Soviet ideology, 16
Treaty of Friendship and Cooperation
(1989), 250, 258
and United States, 250–251, 259, 263–
264
See also Latin America

Cuban-American Foundation (CANF),
259
Czechoslovakia
and economics, 81
and Germany, 7–9
and military, 76, 79
and nationalism, 81
and natural resources, 78
and North Atlantic Treaty
Organization (NATO), 82, 100–101
and Visegrad group, 81, 83, 100–101,
102
See also Central/Eastern Europe

Daewoo, 191
Dang Quoc Thuy, 205
Dao Dinh Luyen, 211
Davydov, Oleg, 104
Dawisha, Karen, 76
de Klerk, 287, 292–294
Deng Xiaoping, 136, 160, 163, 166
Detente, 11–13, 17–18, 95
and Ostpolitik (Brandt), 12
Dibb, Paul, 135
Dixit, J. N., 240–241
Do Muoi, 203
Donaldson, Robert H., 7
Dos Santos, 290
Dostam, Abdul Rashid, 271–272
Drobkov, Vladislav, 242
Drukov, Anatoly, 236
Dunayev, Alexander, 241

Eastern Europe. *See* Central/Eastern
Europe
East Germany, 73–74, 76
and East-West detente, 95–96
and economics, 81
and geopolitics, 94–95
and reunification, 75, 80, 93, 96–97
and Western Europe, 94–95
See also Central/Eastern Europe;
Germany; Western Europe
EBRD. *See* European Bank for
Reconstruction and Development
EC. *See* European Community
Ecology, 93
Economics
and Africa, 287–288, 290–291, 296–298

and arms trade, 121–122, 147, 236–238, 255–256, 273, 274, 276, 286–287, 295–296
and capitalism, 3–4, 15–17, 105, 112–113
and Central Asia/Middle East, 273–279
and Central/Eastern Europe, 76–78, 80–81, 83–84
and China, 117, 165–166, 168, 172–173, 175–176
and Cuba, 248, 250–251, 259–262, 264
and Czechoslovakia, 81
and East Germany, 81
and European Bank for Reconstruction and Development (EBRD), 105–106
and European Union (EU), 83–84, 93, 103–107, 112
and Germany, 81, 103–104, 106–107, 115
and India, 227–228, 229–230, 231–232, 234, 239–241
and Japan, 112, 115, 117
and Korea, 181–185, 189–193, 196–198
and Latin America, 248, 250–251, 252–255, 259–262, 264
and multipolarity, 113–115, 120
and New Economic Policy (NEP), 5
and North Korea, 181–182, 184–185, 196–198
and Poland, 81, 104
and Russian Revolution (1917), 3–4
and Russia's near abroad, 54, 55, 66–67
and South Korea, 182–185, 189–193, 196–198
and Soviet collapse, 18–19
and United States, 3, 112–117
and Vietnam, 202, 205–208, 213–219
and Western Europe, 93, 94–97, 103–107, 115
El Salvador, 249
EPLF. *See* Eritrean People's Liberation Front
Equatorial Guinea, 290. *See also* Africa
Eritrean People's Liberation Front (EPLF), 287
Estonia, 53, 67(n1), 149
and geopolitics, 80–81
and military, 66, 80
and Nazi-Soviet pact (1939), 8–9
and Russian citizens, 59, 66, 69(n14)
See also Commonwealth of Independent States (CIS); Near abroad
Ethiopia, 16, 283, 285, 286–287, 288, 291, 296. *See also* Africa
EU. *See* European Union
Eurasia, 140–141, 153(n11)
European Bank for Reconstruction and Development (EBRD), 105–106
European Community (EC), 41, 77, 117
European Union (EU)
and economics, 83–84, 93, 103–107, 112
and Hungary, 83
and Western Europe, 93, 103–107

Fahd, King, 275
Far East, 136, 143, 144–145, 159, 175
Federal Assembly. *See* Legislature
Fedorov, Valentin, 141, 145, 148, 170
Filatov, Sergei, 252
Five Year Plan (1986–1990) (Gorbachev), 13–14
Foreign Affairs Committee, 40
Foreign Intelligence Service (SVR) (Russian), 29, 82
Foreign Ministry. *See* Ministry of Foreign Affairs (MFA)
Former Soviet Union (FSU), 203–204
France, 100, 103, 104, 107, 122
and Central/Eastern Europe, 82, 95
and Germany, 7–9
FRELIMO. *See* Mozambique Liberation Front
FSU. *See* Former Soviet Union
Fukuyama, Francis, 19
Fundamentalism, 234–235

Gaidar, Yegor, 84, 174, 289
Gandhi, Indira, 233–234
Gandhi, Rajiv, 233
GATT. *See* General Agreement on Tariffs and Trade
GCC. *See* Gulf Cooperation Council
G-8 group, 114–115, 117
Gelman, Harry, 143, 150–151
General Agreement on Tariffs and Trade (GATT), 112, 115

Genscher, Hans-Dietrich, 100
Geopolitics
 and Afghanistan, 12
 and Belarus, 80–81, 85
 and Central/Eastern Europe, 10, 76–
  77, 80–81, 85–86
 and China, 172, 175, 232–233
 and East Germany, 94–95
 and Estonia, 80–81
 and geoeconomics, 112–117
 and India, 232–233
 and Kaliningrad, 80, 85–86, 98
 and Latvia, 80–81
 and Lithuania, 80–81, 85
 and Moldova, 80–81
 and national security, 4–6, 8, 10, 12, 13,
  57, 76–77, 80–81, 85–86, 94–95, 98,
  112–113, 116, 119, 172, 232–233
 and Nazi-Soviet pact (1939), 8
 and Poland, 86
 and Soviet state consolidation, 4–6
 and Ukraine, 80–81
Georgia, 53–54, 67(n1)
 and military, 59–60, 61
 and Russian citizens, 59
 See also Commonwealth of
  Independent States (CIS); Near
  abroad
Gerashchenko, Viktor, 106
Gerasimov, Gennady, 74
Germany
 and Berlin Wall, 74, 75, 77, 97–98
 and Czechoslovakia, 7–9
 East, 73–74, 75, 76, 80, 81, 93, 94–97
 and East-West detente, 95–96
 and economics, 103–104, 106–107, 115
 and France, 7–9
 importance of, 93–99, 103–104, 106–107
 and Kaliningrad, 80, 85–86, 98
 and nationalism, 96, 98
 and Nazi-Soviet pact (1939), 8–9, 96
 and North Atlantic Treaty
  Organization (NATO), 11, 79–80, 103
 and reunification, 75, 80, 93, 96–97
 and Soviet foreign policy (1917–1991),
  7–9, 11
 West, 75, 80, 93, 95–97
 See also Western Europe
Ghana, 289. *See also* Africa

Glazyev, Sergei, 254
Golz, Alexander, 101
Gorbachev, Mikhail
 and Africa, 283–284, 286–288
 and Central/Eastern Europe, 71–80,
  88, 94–95
 and China, 160–161, 162
 and Cuba, 250–251, 258
 and Five Year Plan (1986–1990), 13–14
 and India, 233–234
 and Japan, 135–137, 143–144, 150
 and Korea, 181–184, 185–186
 and Latin America, 248–249, 250–251,
  258
 and perestroika, 18, 95, 113, 160–161,
  249
 and Soviet ideology, 16–17
 and United States, 113, 122, 125
 and Vietnam, 201–203
 and Western Europe, 94–96, 103
Grachev, Pavel, 36, 62, 87, 121, 122, 125,
  144, 237, 262, 276, 296
Great Patriotic War, 8–9
Great War (1914–1918), 3–4
Gromyko, Andrei, 143
Grosz, Karoly, 72
G-7 group, 80, 99, 112, 113–115, 129, 151
Guevara, E. Che, 247
"Guidelines for the Foreign Policy of the
  Russian Federation" (Russian
  Security Council), 129
Guinea, 288. *See also* Africa
Guinea-Bissau, 283. *See also* Africa
Gujral, I. K., 233
Gulf Cooperation Council (GCC), 274–
  276
Gulf of Tonkin, 211–212
Gulf War, 228–229, 274
Gusarov, Yevgeny, 292–293

Habomai Islands. *See* Kurile Islands
Halliday, Fred, 18, 112–113
Heilbrunn, Jacob, 99
Hekmatyar, Gulbuddin, 271–272
Hitler, Adolph, 94
Ho Dam, 183
Holzman, Franklyn, 23–24
Honecker, Erich, 73–74, 75, 204
Hong Kong, 147–148

Hon Soon Yen, 192, 195
Hosokawa, Morihiro, 152
Ho The Lan, 209
Hungary
  and European Union (EU), 83
  and nationalism, 81
  and North Atlantic Treaty
    Organization (NATO), 82, 100–101
  and Soviet withdrawal, 72–74, 76–77,
    79, 96
  and Visegrad group, 81, 83, 100–101,
    102
  See also Central/Eastern Europe
Hussein, Saddam, 122
Hyde-Price, Adrian, 94
Hyundai Group, 182–183

IAEA. *See* International Atomic Energy
  Agency
ICBM. *See* Intercontinental Ballistic
  Missile
Ideology
  and Cold War, 1–2, 9, 18–19, 112–113
  imperialism, 3–4, 10–11, 15–16
  Indo-Soviet, 230
  Marxist-Leninist, 3–5, 6–7, 9, 10–11, 14–
    17, 19, 72, 77, 125, 139, 152, 283, 286
  realism, 1, 2–3, 5, 6, 9, 12–13, 14, 15, 18,
    41
  and Soviet foreign policy, 15–17
  Western influence on, 17–18
IFPC. *See* Interdepartmental Foreign
  Policy Commission
Imperialism, 3–4, 10–11, 15–16
India
  and Andrei Kozyrev, 232, 239
  and arms trade, 121, 147, 236–238
  and Boris Yeltsin, 225–226, 228, 229–
    230, 231, 232–233, 234, 239–240, 241–
    242
  and China, 227, 232–233, 239
  and clashing Soviet interests, 228–230
  and economics, 227–228, 229–230, 231–
    232, 234, 239–241
  and emerging Soviet interests, 233–234
  and fading Soviet difficulties, 230
  and fading Soviet interests, 226–228
  and geopolitics, 232–233
  and Islamic fundamentalism, 234–235

and Japan, 232–233
and Mikhail Gorbachev, 233–234
and military, 226–227, 228–229, 230–
  231, 233, 236–238, 239–241
and natural resources, 228
and nuclear weapons, 229, 233, 240
and Pakistan, 235, 240
role in Asia, 232–233
space industry of, 238, 241–242
and surviving Soviet interests, 230–232
Treaty of Friendship and Cooperation
  (1993), 239–241
and uncertain Soviet relations, 241–242
and United States, 226–227, 234–235,
  238, 241–242
Indochina, 138
INF. *See* Intermediate Nuclear Forces
Intercontinental Ballistic Missile (ICBM),
  118, 147
Interdepartmental Foreign Policy
  Commission (IFPC), 28, 30–31, 33, 44,
  45
Intermediate Nuclear Forces (INF), 13
International Affairs Committee, 40, 43
International Atomic Energy Agency
  (IAEA), 188, 195–196
Iran, 235, 272–274, 280–281
  and arms trade, 121, 147
  See also Central Asia/Middle East
Iraq, 274, 277
  and arms trade, 122
  sanctions against, 122–123
  and United Nations, 100
  See also Central Asia/Middle East
Israel, 167
Italy, 107
Iturup Island. *See* Kurile Islands
Ivory Coast, 289. *See also* Africa

Japan
  and Andrei Kozyrev, 138–140, 141, 150
  and China, 136, 138
  and Commonwealth of Independent
    States (CIS), 148–149
  and economics, 112, 115, 117
  and Eurasian myth, 140–141, 153(n11)
  and Far East, 136, 143, 144–145, 175
  and G-7 group, 114
  and India, 232–233

and Korea, 136, 138, 147–148, 152
and Kurile Islands, 137, 141–144, 145,
147–149, 152
and Liberal Democratic Party (LDP),
151
and Marxism-Leninism, 152
and Mikhail Gorbachev, 135–137, 143–
144, 150
and military, 144, 145–147
and Russian relation influences, 137–
141
and Russian relation prospects, 149–
152
and Russia's transition period, 144–149
and Russo-Japanese Treaty, 142
and Soviet strategy, 135–137
and United States, 136–137, 143, 146–
147, 148–149, 150–151
and Yeltsin, 138–140, 141, 144, 145,
148–152
Jiang Zemin, 162, 171, 174
Joffe, Josef, 97
Joint Declaration on the Foundation of
Relations Between the People's
Republic of China and the Russian
Federation (1956), 142–143, 171
Jordan, 279–280. *See also* Central Asia/
Middle East

Kadar, Janos, 72, 74
KAL. *See* Korean Air Lines
Kaliningrad, 80, 85–86, 98
Kang Sok-ju, 195
Kapitsa, Mikhail, 143
Karaganov, Sergei, 101, 274
Karasin, Grigory, 289, 295, 298
Karyakin, Yuri, 258
Kazakhstan, 53, 67(n1), 118, 149, 172,
205–206, 235
and Russian citizens, 58
See also Commonwealth of
Independent States (CIS); Near
abroad
Keita, Modiba, 284
Kennan, George F., 15
KGB (Committee of State Security), 25, 33
Khachaturov, Karen, 260
Khalevinskaia, Yelena, 105

Khamidulin, Rashid, 203, 207, 215
Khasbulatov, Ruslan, 61, 225–226, 241
Khrushchev, Nikita, 8, 15, 16, 142–143,
160, 233, 247, 284
Kim Chong-in, 183
Kim Il Sung, 177, 181–182, 183, 186, 197
Kim Jong Il, 186, 197
Kim Jong-u, 193
Kim Myung-se, 186
Kim Young Sam, 183, 191
Kinkel, Klaus, 100, 103
Kirghizia. *See* Kyrgyzstan
Kissinger, Henry, 75, 95–96
Kohl, Helmut, 73–74, 79, 80, 96, 99
Kokoshin, Andrei, 188
Kolesnikov, Mikhail, 125, 211
Kolokolov, Boris, 289, 294
Kondrashov, Stanislav, 126, 131
Konigsberg. *See* Kaliningrad
Koptev, Yury, 241
Korea
and Andrei Kozyrev, 188, 196
and Boris Yeltsin, 185–186, 188–190,
192–193, 195–196
and China, 167, 173, 177, 187
and economics, 181–185, 189–193, 196–
198
and Japan, 136, 138, 147–148, 152
and Joseph Stalin, 183, 198
and Korean Air Lines (KAL), 183–184,
188, 189, 192
and Mikhail Gorbachev, 181–184, 185–
186
and military, 181–182, 184, 185, 186,
188, 193–198
and natural resources, 182, 190, 192,
194
1992 policy, 187–190
and North developments, 193–196
and nuclear weapons, 182, 184, 185,
188, 193, 195–196
and policy explanations, 184–185
and South developments, 190–193
and South (1988–1991), 182–184
and Soviet August coup, 185–187
Treaty of Friendship, Cooperation and
Mutual Assistance (1961), 187–189,
194–195

and United Nations (UN), 184, 196
and United States, 182, 196
Korean Air Lines (KAL), 183–184, 188,
189, 192
Korean Trade Promotion Corporation
(KOTRA), 183
Kortunov, Andrei, 125
KOTRA. *See* Korean Trade Promotion
Corporation
Kovalev, Sergei, 258
Kozin, Vladimir, 100–101
Kozlov, Victor, 218–219
Kozyrev, Andrei
and Africa, 283, 288–289, 290–292, 293–
294
and Central Asia/Middle East, 268–
269, 270, 274–275, 280
and Central/Eastern Europe, 82–83
and China, 165, 169–170
and India, 232, 239
and Japan, 138–140, 141, 150
and Korea, 188, 196
and Latin America, 256, 259, 263
and policy-making agencies, 28–29, 32,
33–34, 35–36, 37, 38, 39, 40, 43
and Russia's near abroad, 56, 60–63,
64–65, 102–103
and United States, 116, 118, 120, 121–
122, 123, 124, 126–127, 128–130
and Vietnam, 206, 208–209, 212
and Western Europe, 99, 101–103
Kravchuk, Leonid, 63–64, 237
Krenz, Egon, 74
Krysin, Alexander, 253–254
Kuchma, Leonid, 66
Kunadze, Georgy, 141, 195
Kunashir Island. *See* Kurile Islands
Kurile Islands, 137, 141–144, 145, 147–
149, 152
Kuwait, 274, 276. *See also* Central Asia/
Middle East
Kuznetsov, Vladimir, 145
Kyrgyzstan, 53, 149, 172, 235. *See also*
Commonwealth of Independent
States (CIS); Near abroad

Latin America
and Andrei Kozyrev, 256, 259, 263
Argentina, 248, 249, 251–252, 255

and arms trade, 255–256
Bolivia, 248, 252
and Boris Yeltsin, 255, 257, 261, 262–
263
Brazil, 248, 249, 252
Chile, 248, 251–252
and Commonwealth of Independent
States (CIS), 253, 257
and Communist Party of the Soviet
Union (CPSU), 247
and "Complex Plan of the
Development of the USSR's
Relations with Latin America"
(1987), 248–249
Cuba, 11, 16, 248, 249, 250–251, 257–
264
and economics, 248, 250–251, 252–255,
259–262, 264
and Fidel Castro, 250–251, 258, 260,
261, 262, 263
and human rights, 256–257, 258, 260
Mexico, 249, 251–252
and Mikhail Gorbachev, 248–249, 250–
251, 258
and military, 247–248, 251, 255–256,
260–261, 262–263
and mutual Russian interests, 251–252
and natural resources, 259–260, 262
and Organization of American States
(OAS), 256–257
Peru, 248
and Soviet policy, 247–248
and Soviet policy revision, 248–250
and United States, 247–248, 249–251,
259, 263–264
Uruguay, 248, 249
Latvia, 53, 67(n1), 149
and geopolitics, 80–81
and military, 66, 78
and Nazi-Soviet pact (1939), 8–9
and Russian citizens, 59, 69(n14)
See also Commonwealth of
Independent States (CIS); Near
abroad
LDP. *See* Liberal Democratic Party
(Japan)
LDPR. *See* Liberal Democratic Party of
Russia
League of Nations, 7

Lebed, Alexander, 86–87
Lee Sang Ock, 188
Legislature, 39–43
Legvold, Robert, 24
Leino, K. O., 260
Le Mai, 210–211
Lenin, Vladimir, 3–5, 6–7, 10–11, 15–16.
  See also Marxism-Leninism
Leontyev, N. I., 242
Lesotho, 290. *See also* Africa
Le Xuan Trinh, 214, 219
Liberal Democratic Party (LDP) (Japan),
  151
Liberal Democratic Party of Russia
  (LDPR), 38, 84–85, 99
Liberia, 290. *See also* Africa
Libya, 276, 277–278. *See also* Central
  Asia/Middle East
Ligachev, Yegor, 75
Linnik, Viktor, 117
Li Peng, 163, 165, 169
Lisbon Protocol, 64
Lithuania, 53, 67(n1), 149
  and geopolitics, 80–81, 85
  and military, 59, 66, 78
  and Nazi-Soviet pact (1939), 8–9
  See also Commonwealth of
    Independent States (CIS); Near
    abroad
Lobov, Oleg, 30, 177
Lukin, Vladimir, 40, 43, 122, 127, 140
Lumumba, Patrice, 284

Madagascar, 289, 290. *See also* Africa
Makharadze, V. A., 208–209, 217–218
Malaysia, 147
Maley, Mikhail, 238
Mamedov, Georgy, 253
Mandela, Nelson, 293–294
Mao Zedong, 159–160, 174
Maritime Province, 144–145
Marrese, M., 76
Marx, Karl, 5, 6, 9. *See also* Marxism-
  Leninism
Marxism-Leninism
  and Africa, 283, 286
  and Central/Eastern Europe, 72, 77
  and Japan, 152

and policy-making agencies, 15–16,
  139
and Soviet policy (1917–1991), 3–5, 6–7,
  9, 10–11, 14–17, 19
and United States, 113, 125
Mashchits, Vladimir, 35
Maslyukov, Yury, 183
Massoud, Shah, 271
Mazowiecki, Tadeusz, 73
McGwire, Michael, 75
Melchin, Leonid, 186
Mexico, 249, 251–252. *See also* Latin
  America
MFA. *See* Ministry of Foreign Affairs
MFN. *See* Most Favored Nation
MIC. *See* Military Industrial Complex
  (Russian)
Middle East. *See* Central Asia/Middle
  East
Mikoyan, Anastas, 247
Military
  and Africa, 286–287, 292, 294–296
  and arms control, 64, 112–113, 120,
    125–126
  and arms trade, 121–122, 147, 236–238,
    255–256, 273, 274, 276, 286–287, 295–
    296
  and bipolarity, 2, 9, 10, 11–12, 15–16,
    111–113, 117–119
  and Cam Ranh Bay, 202, 207–213
  and Central Asia/Middle East, 273,
    274–276
  and Central/Eastern Europe, 10–11,
    76–77, 78–83, 85–88
  and China, 147, 169, 171, 172, 174
  and Cuba, 251, 260–261, 262–263
  and Czechoslovakia, 76, 79
  and Estonia, 66, 80
  and Georgia, 59–60, 61
  and India, 226–227, 228–229, 230–231,
    233, 236–238, 239–241
  and Intermediate Nuclear Forces
    (INF), 13
  and Iraq sanctions, 122–123
  and Japan, 144, 145–147
  and Latin America, 247–248, 251, 255–
    256, 260–261, 262–263
  and Latvia, 66, 78
  and Lithuania, 59, 66, 78

and Ministry of Defense (MOD), 27–28, 33, 36–39, 125
and Moldova, 59–60, 61, 62, 63, 66, 69(n17)
and North Korea, 181–182, 184, 185, 186, 188, 193–198
and Russian citizenship, 58–60
and Russian Pacific Fleet (RPF), 145–147
and Russia's near abroad, 54–55, 56, 57–60, 61, 62, 63–64, 66, 67, 68(n10)
and Soviet superpower status, 12–13, 13–14
and Strategic Arms Limitation Talks (SALT), 125–126
and Strategic Arms Reduction Talks (START), 64, 112, 120, 125–126
and Strategic Defense Initiative (Star Wars), 13
and Ukraine, 54–55, 57, 59–60, 63–64, 66, 68(n10), 118–119, 237
and United States, 117–120
and Vietnam, 202, 207–213
and Western Europe, 93, 94–95, 96–97, 98, 99–100
and West European Union (WEU), 83
See also Nuclear weapons
Military Industrial Complex (MIC) (Russian), 147
Ministry of Cooperation, 35, 44
Ministry of Defense (MOD), 27–28, 33, 36–39, 125
Ministry of Foreign Affairs (MFA), 95, 125
and Asia-Pacific Region (APR), 137–138
and Central/Eastern Europe, 82
and Commonwealth Affairs Department, 60
"Concept of Russian Foreign Policy," 38, 65, 139, 140
and policy-making, 25, 27–31, 33–36, 37–42, 44–45, 60–63, 64–65, 67, 125, 128–129
and Russian Revolution (1917), 5
and Russia's near abroad, 60–63, 64–65, 67
Ministry of Security, 27–29

Missile Technology Control Regime (MTCR), 238
Mitterand, Francois, 75, 105
MOD. *See* Ministry of Defense
Modrow, Hans, 79
Moiseev, Mikhail, 79
Moldavia. *See* Moldova
Moldova, 40, 53–54, 167
and geopolitics, 80–81
and military, 59–60, 61, 62, 63, 66, 69(n17)
and Romania, 86–87
and Russian citizens, 59
See also Commonwealth of Independent States (CIS); Near abroad
Molotov, Vyacheslav, 8
Mongolia, 138, 177
Montaner, Carlos, 259
Morozov, Konstantin, 237
Most Favored Nation (MFN), 232
Movement for the Popular Liberation of Angola (MPLA), 12, 285, 286, 292
Mozambique, 283, 285, 287, 288, 290, 296. *See also* Africa
Mozambique Liberation Front (FRELIMO), 285
MTCR. *See* Missile Technology Control Regime
Multipolarity, 113–115, 120

NACC. *See* North Atlantic Cooperation Council
Nationalism
and Central/Eastern Europe, 71, 80–81, 84–85
and Czechoslovakia, 81
and Germany, 96, 98
and Hungary, 81
and Russia, 62–63, 81, 84–85, 98, 99–100, 114, 150, 152
and Vladimir Zhirinovsky, 71–72, 84, 289
and Yugoslavia, 81
National security. *See* Geopolitics; Military; Nuclear weapons
National Union for the Total Independence of Angola (UNITA), 286, 292

NATO. *See* North Atlantic Treaty
  Organization
Natural resources
  and Africa, 293, 297
  and Central/Eastern Europe, 76, 78
  and China, 173, 175
  and Cuba, 259–260, 262
  and Czechoslovakia, 78
  and European Bank for Reconstruction
    and Development (EBRD), 105
  and India, 228
  and Korea, 182, 190, 192, 194
  and Latin America, 259–260, 262
  and North Korea, 182, 194
  and Vietnam, 216
  and Western Europe, 95
Nazi-Soviet pact (1939), 7–9, 96
Near abroad
  and Andrei Kozyrev, 56, 60–63, 64–65,
    102–103
  and Boris Yeltsin, 54, 55, 56, 58, 61–67,
    103
  and bureaucratic conflict, 60–63
  and Commonwealth of Independent
    States (CIS), 53–57, 67(n1)
  defined, 53
  and economics, 54, 55, 66–67
  and military, 54–55, 56, 57–60, 61, 62,
    63–64, 66, 67, 68(n10)
  and Ministry of Foreign Affairs (MFA),
    60–63, 64–65, 67
  and nuclear weapons, 54–55, 57, 63–64,
    68(n10)
  and Russian citizenship, 54, 58–60,
    69(n14)
  Russian relations with, 63–67
  and Western Europe, 102–103
  See also Commonwealth of
    Independent States (CIS); *specific
    countries*
Nechayev, Andrei, 236
Nehru, Jawaharlal, 233
NEP. *See* New Economic Policy
New Economic Policy (NEP), 5
New Zealand, 138
Nguyen Co Thach, 203
Nguyen Manh Cam, 203, 204, 205–206,
  209, 211, 217, 219
Nguyen Van Linh, 203

Nicaragua, 12, 249
Niger, 290. *See also* Africa
Nigeria, 289. *See also* Africa
Nikolaenko, Valery, 292
Nikolayeva, Elina, 232
Nkrumah, Kwame, 284
Nogee, Joseph L., 7
Nong Duc Manh, 205
Non-Proliferation Treaty (NPT), 55, 64,
  80, 169, 188, 195–196, 229, 240–241
North Atlantic Cooperation Council
  (NACC), 82–83, 100–101
North Atlantic Treaty Organization
  (NATO), 41
  and Central/Eastern Europe, 78–80,
    82–83
  and Czechoslovakia, 82, 100–101
  establishment of, 11
  and Germany, 11, 79–80, 103
  and Hungary, 82, 100–101
  and Partnership for Peace (PFP), 32, 43,
    101–102
  and Poland, 82, 100–101
  and Russia, 82–83, 100–103
  and Slovakia, 82, 100–101
  and Western Europe, 100–103
North Korea
  and China, 167, 173
  and economics, 181–182, 184–185, 196–
    198
  and Japan, 138, 152
  and military, 181–182, 184, 186, 188,
    193–198
  and natural resources, 182, 194
  and nuclear weapons, 182, 184, 185,
    188, 193, 195–196
  recent developments of, 193–196
  and Soviet August coup, 185–187
  Treaty of Friendship, Cooperation and
    Mutual Assistance (1961), 187–189,
    194–195
  See also Korea
NPT. *See* Non-Proliferation Treaty
Nuclear Weapon Free Zone (NWFZ), 182,
  185, 196, 229, 240
Nuclear weapons
  and arms race, 10
  and China, 172, 174
  and India, 229, 233, 240

and Intermediate Nuclear Forces
(INF), 13
and Non-Proliferation Treaty (NPT),
55, 64, 80, 169, 188, 195–196, 229,
240–241
and North Korea, 182, 184, 185, 188,
193, 195–196
and Russia's near abroad, 54–55, 57,
63–64, 68(n10)
and Ukraine, 54–55, 57, 63–64, 68(n10),
118–119
See also Military
NWFZ. *See* Nuclear Weapon Free Zone

OAS. *See* Organization of American
States
Oil industry. *See* Natural resources
Olivier, Gerrit, 297
Oman, 274, 275. *See also* Central Asia/
Middle East
Organization of American States (OAS),
256–257
Ostpolitik (Brandt), 12, 95, 100

Pacific Islands, 138
Pakistan, 235, 240
Palestine Liberation Organization (PLO),
279–280
Pankin, Boris, 251, 258
Panov, Alexander, 196
Park Chul-un, 183
Partnership and Cooperation Agreement,
104–105
Partnership for Peace (PFP), 32, 43, 83
and Western Europe, 101–102
Pawar, Sharad, 236–238
Pentagonale (Central European
Initiative), 83–84
People's Republic of China (PRC), 159–
161. *See also* China
Perestroika, 18, 95, 113, 160–161, 249
Perry, William, 121
Peru, 248. *See also* Latin America
Petrov, Yury, 28–29, 192
PFP. *See* Partnership for Peace
Phan Van Khai, 218
Piliatskin, Boris, 293
Pipes, Richard, 3

Pladkov, Mikhail, 193
PLO. *See* Palestine Liberation
Organization
Poland, 76, 79, 80
economics of, 81, 104
and European Union (EU), 83
and geopolitics, 86
and Nazi-Soviet pact (1939), 8–9
and North Atlantic Treaty
Organization (NATO), 82, 100–101
and Solidarity, 73
and Soviet control, 10–11
and Soviet withdrawal, 72–74, 75, 96
and Visegrad group, 81, 83, 100–101,
102
See also Central/Eastern Europe
Popov, Yuri, 296–297
Posuvalyuk, Viktor, 289
Pozdnyakov, Elgiz, 126
PRC. *See* People's Republic of China
Presidency, 25, 26–32
Presidential Council, 31–32
Pressler, Larry, 235
Primakov, Yevgeni, 75, 82, 171, 183
Principe, 290. *See also* Africa

Qatar, 274. *See also* Central Asia/Middle
East
Qian Qichen, 162–163, 169–170

Rabbani, Burhanuddin, 271–272
Radio Irina (Voice of Freedom), 205, 209
Rahr, Alexander, 130
Rakowski, Mieczyslaw, 73
Rao, Narasimha, 231, 233, 241
Reagan, Ronald, 13, 95, 118, 285
Realism
and Cold War, 9, 12–13
and communist collapse, 1, 15, 18
and international politics, 2–3, 6, 14, 41
and Vladimir Lenin, 5
Riurikov, Dmitry, 29–30
Rodionov, I., 123
Rogachev, Igor, 187–188
Rogov, Sergei, 129–130
Roh Tae-woo, 182, 185–186, 189
Romania, 76
and Moldova, 86–87
See also Central/Eastern Europe

Rosenau, James N., 117
RPF. *See* Russian Pacific Fleet
Rubinstein, Alvin Z., 8, 15, 96
Ruhe, Volker, 100
Rumyantsev, Oleg, 61, 63
Russian Pacific Fleet (RPF), 145–147
Russian Revolution (1917)
   and class/national interests, 6–7
   and international politics, 3–4, 159
   and Soviet state consolidation, 4–6
Russo-Japanese Treaty (1855) (1875), 142
Russo-Japanese War (1904–1905), 142
Rutskoi, Alexander, 31, 37, 61, 85, 87, 107,
   122, 252

SACP. *See* South African Communist
   Party
Sakhalin Island, 141. *See also* Kurile
   Islands
Sakharov, Andrei, 264
Sakwa, Richard, 100
SALT. *See* Strategic Arms Limitation
   Talks
Samsonov, Vladimir, 174
Samsung, 190–191
San Francisco Peace Treaty, 142
Santer, Jacques, 105
Sao-Tome, 290. *See also* Africa
Sato, Eisaku, 143
Saudi Arabia, 274. *See also* Central Asia/
   Middle East
Security Council, 27–31, 42, 129
   and Interdepartmental Foreign Policy
    Commission (IFPC), 28, 30–31, 33, 44,
    45
   and Russia's near abroad, 61, 64
Senegal, 289. *See also* Africa
Serbia, 87–88, 120–121. *See also* Central/
   Eastern Europe
Servakov, 186
Shakhrai, Sergei, 121
Shaposhnikov, Yevgeny, 30, 140
Shatalin, Stanislav, 116
Shelov-Kovedyaev, 29, 34
Shevardnadze, Eduard, 64, 75, 79, 80, 113,
   122, 137, 183, 249, 250, 286, 287
Shikotan Island. *See* Kurile Islands
Shokhin, Alexander, 35, 104, 170, 174,

215, 241–242, 263
Shumeiko, Vladimir, 230, 254–255
Siberia, 144–145, 159, 175
Sierra Leone, 290. *See also* Africa
SIGINT. *See* Signals Intelligence
Signals Intelligence (SIGINT), 212
Simon, Jeffrey, 106
Singapore, 136
Skokov, Yury, 28–30, 129
Slovakia
   and North Atlantic Treaty
    Organization (NATO), 82, 100–101
   and Visegrad group, 81, 83, 100–101,
    102
   See also Central/Eastern Europe
Snegur, Mircea, 86
Sobchak, Anatoly, 162
Sokolov, Oleg, 193
Solidarity, 73
Somalia, 285, 287, 290, 291, 294–295. *See
   also* Africa
South Africa, 286, 287, 288, 291, 292–294,
   297, 298
   and apartheid, 293–294
   and China, 167
   and Convention for a Democratic
    South Africa (CODESA), 293
   See also Africa
South African Communist Party (SACP),
   291, 293–294
South Korea
   and China, 167, 177
   and economics, 182–185, 189–193, 196–
    198
   and Japan, 136, 138, 147–148
   1988–1991, 182–184
   recent developments of, 190–193
   and Soviet August coup (1991), 185–
    186
   See also Korea
South West African People's
   Organization (SWAPO), 286
Soviet policy (1917–1991)
   and class/national interests, 6–7
   and Cold War, 9, 18–19
   defining, 2–3
   and detente, 11–13, 17–18
   and domestic politics, 14–19
   and Germany, 7–9, 11

and Great War/Russian Revolution, 3–4

and ideology, 15–17, 18–19

and international politics, 3–14

and leadership, 16–17

and national security, 10–14

and policy-making, 23–26, 44

Russia's role in, 1–2

and state consolidation, 4–6

and Western influence, 17–18

Spain, 107

Spanier, John, 12

Spratly Islands, 211–212

Stalin, Joseph

and China, 159–160

and Eastern Europe, 10–11, 75–76, 77, 94

and Korea, 183, 198

and Kurile Islands, 137

and Nazi-Soviet pact (1939), 7–9

and Soviet ideology, 15–17

Stankevich, Sergei, 61, 251–252, 268

START. *See* Strategic Arms Reduction Talks

Star Wars (Strategic Defense Initiative), 13

Stepansin, S. V., 205

Stoessinger, John G., 8

Stoiber, Edmund, 97

Strategic Arms Limitation Talks (SALT), 125–126

Strategic Arms Reduction Talks (START), 64, 112, 120, 125–126

Strategic Defense Initiative (Star Wars), 13

"Strategy for Russia" (Council on Foreign and Defense Policy), 45

Supreme Soviet. *See* Legislature

Surkov, Alexei, 258

SVR. *See* Foreign Intelligence Service (Russian)

SWAPO. *See* South West African People's Organization

Syria, 276, 278–279. *See also* Central Asia/Middle East

Taiwan, 164, 176–177

Tajikistan, 53–54, 172, 235, 270–271, 281. *See also* Commonwealth of

Independent States (CIS); Near abroad

Thai Fung Ne, 215

Thatcher, Margaret, 75, 95

Tiananmen Square, 74, 160, 161, 165

Togo, 290. *See also* Africa

Tran Duc Luong, 205, 217

Treaty of Friendship, Cooperation and Mutual Assistance (1961) (North Korea), 187–189, 194–195

Treaty of Friendship and Cooperation (1989) (Cuba), 250, 258

Treaty of Friendship and Cooperation (1994) (Spain), 107

Treaty of Friendship and Cooperation (1993) (India), 239–241

Treaty of Friendship and Cooperation (1978) (Vietnam), 201–202, 206, 219

Treaty of Peace, Friendship and Cooperation (1971) (India), 239

Trotsky, Leon, 4, 17

Truman, Harry, 10

Tsutomu Hata, 196

Turkey, 235, 280–281

Turkmenistan, 53. *See also* Commonwealth of Independent States (CIS); Near abroad

UAE. *See* United Arab Emirates

Ukraine

and Black Sea Fleet, 40, 42, 56–57, 63–64, 67

and China, 167

and geopolitics, 80–81

and military, 54–55, 57, 59–60, 63–64, 66, 68(n10), 118–119, 237

and nuclear weapons, 54–55, 57, 63–64, 68(n10), 118–119

and Russian citizens, 58, 59

and Russian relations, 53–54, 55, 56, 63, 67(n1)

and Vietnam, 204, 205–206

See also Commonwealth of Independent States (CIS); Near abroad

UN. *See* United Nations

UNITA. *See* National Union for the Total Independence of Angola

United Arab Emirates (UAE), 274–276.
    See also Central Asia/Middle East
United Nations (UN)
    and Central/Eastern Europe, 87
    Human Rights Commission, 256–257,
        258
    and Korea, 184, 196
    and Russia's near abroad, 65
    Security Council, 13, 277–278, 291, 295
United States
    and Africa, 284, 286, 287, 291, 294–295
    and Andrei Kozyrev, 116, 118, 120,
        121–122, 123, 124, 126–127, 128–130
    and arms trade, 121–122
    and Boris Yeltsin, 113, 114–115, 116,
        117–120, 121, 124–128, 131
    and Bosnia, 119, 120–121
    and capitalism, 3–4, 15–17, 112–113
    and Central Asia/Middle East, 269,
        274, 277–281
    and Central/Eastern Europe, 77, 80,
        81, 83
    and China, 11, 12, 166, 168–169, 172,
        177–178
    and Cold War, 1–2, 9, 18–19, 111–112,
        115–116, 117–119
    and Cuba, 250–251, 259, 263–264
    and detente, 11–13, 17–18, 95
    and economics, 3, 112–117
    and India, 226–227, 234–235, 238, 241–
        242
    influence on Soviet ideology, 17–18
    and Iraq sanctions, 122–123
    and Japan, 136–137, 143, 146–147, 148–
        149, 150–151
    and Korea, 182, 196
    and Latin America, 247–248, 249–251,
        259, 263–264
    and Marxism-Leninism, 113, 125
    and Mikhail Gorbachev, 113, 122, 125
    and military strategy, 117–120
    and nuclear arms race, 10
    and Russian domestic politics, 124–132
    and Russian interest conflicts, 120–123
    and Russia's near abroad, 65–66
    and Strategic Arms Reduction Talks
        (START), 125–126
    and Strategic Defense Initiative (Star
        Wars), 13

    and Vietnam, 205, 220
    and Western Europe economics, 95–96
Uruguay, 248, 249. *See also* Latin America
Ushakov, Yury, 102
Uzbekistan, 53, 191, 205–206, 235, 271–
    272. *See also* Commonwealth of
    Independent States (CIS); Near
    abroad

Vanous, J., 76
Velayati, Ali Akbar, 273
Vietnam
    and Andrei Kozyrev, 206, 208–209, 212
    and Asia-Pacific Region (APR), 208–
        209
    and Boris Yeltsin, 204–205, 206
    and Cam Ranh Bay, 202, 207–213
    and China, 167, 201–202, 208, 210, 211–
        212, 219–220
    Commission for Trade, Economic,
        Scientific and Technological
        Cooperation, 217–218
    and Communist Party of the Soviet
        Union (CPSU), 203
    and economics, 202, 205–208, 213–219
    and late-Soviet politics, 202–203
    and Mikhail Gorbachev, 201–203
    and military, 202, 207–213
    and natural resources, 216
    and political relations, 201–207
    and post-Soviet politics, 203–207
    and Soviet ideology, 16
    Treaty of Friendship and Cooperation
        (1978), 201–202, 206, 219
    and Ukraine, 204, 205–206
    and United States, 205, 220
Vietsovpetro, 216
Visegrad group, 81, 83, 100–101, 102
Voice of Freedom (Radio Irina), 205, 209
Volsky, Alexander, 166–167
Vorontsov, Yuly, 32, 122
Vo Van Kiet, 206–207, 211, 212, 216, 217,
    219

Walesa, Lech, 82, 259
Waltz, Kenneth, 6–7, 11–12
Warsaw Pact, 71, 73, 75–77, 78, 79, 82, 83,
    100–101
Warsaw Treaty Organization, 11

Warszawski, Dawid, 146
Watanabe, Michio, 148, 151
Western Europe
  and Andrei Kozyrev, 99, 101–103
  and Boris Yeltsin, 96–97, 99, 101, 103, 107
  and Commonwealth of Independent States (CIS), 102–103
  and East-West Germany detente, 95–96
  and economics, 93, 94–97, 103–107, 115
  and European Bank for Reconstruction and Development (EBRD), 105–106
  and European Union (EU), 93, 103–107
  and German reunification, 75, 80, 93, 96–97
  and Germany's importance, 93–99, 103–104, 106–107
  and Mikhail Gorbachev, 94–96, 103
  and military, 93, 94–95, 96–97, 98, 99–103
  and natural resources, 95
  and North Atlantic Treaty Organization (NATO), 100–103
  and Partnership for Peace (PNP), 101–102
  and Russia's near abroad, 102–103
  and United States, 95–96
West European Union (WEU), 83–84, 102
West Germany
  and East-West detente, 95–96
  and reunification, 75, 80, 93, 96–97
  See also Germany; Western Europe
WEU. *See* West European Union
World War I, 3–4
Worner, Manfred, 101

Yakovlev, Alexander, 139, 183
Yarov, Yury, 206, 215, 218

Yazov, Yury, 206, 211
Yeltsin, Boris, 27–34, 36, 37–41, 43
  and Africa, 288–291, 293–294, 295–296
  and Central Asia/Middle East, 268–269, 277–279, 280–282
  and Central/Eastern Europe, 71, 78, 82, 84, 85, 86–88
  and China, 161, 164–166, 169–171, 172, 174, 175, 177
  and India, 225–226, 228, 229–230, 231, 232–233, 234, 239–240, 241–242
  and Japan, 138–140, 141, 144, 145, 148–152
  and Korea, 185–186, 188–190, 192–193, 195–196
  and Latin America, 255, 257, 261, 262–263
  and Russia's near abroad, 54, 55, 56, 58, 61–67, 103
  and United States, 113, 114–115, 116, 117–120, 121, 124–128, 131
  and Vietnam, 204–205, 206
  and Western Europe, 96–97, 99, 101, 103, 107
Yermakov, Alexei, 261
Yugoslavia, 40, 41, 42, 76, 87–88
  and nationalism, 81
  See also Central/Eastern Europe
Yushenkov, Sergei, 258

Zagorsky, Andrei, 104
Zhirinovsky, Vladimir, 37, 139, 277
  and Liberal Democratic Party of Russia (LDPR), 38, 84–85, 99
  and Russian nationalism, 71–72, 84, 289
Zimbabwe, 289, 290. *See also* Africa
Zyukov, Gennady, 260–261